STREAMS
of
CONFUSION

STREAMS
of
CONFUSION

Thirteen Great Ideas That Are
Contaminating Our Thought and Culture

BRAD SCOTT

CROSSWAY BOOKS • WHEATON, ILLINOIS
A DIVISION OF GOOD NEWS PUBLISHERS

Cover design: Cindy Kiple

Cover photo: Pal Hermansen / Tony Stone Images

First printing, 1999

Printed in the United States of America

Library of Congress Cataloging-in-Publication Data
Scott, Brad, 1949–
    Streams of confusion : thirteen great ideas that are contaminating
our thought and culture / Brad Scott.
        p.   cm.
    Includes bibliographical references and index.
    ISBN 1-58134-059-1 (pbk. : alk. paper)
    1. Apologetics. 2. Philosophy, Modern. I. Title.
BT1200.S36 1999
239—dc21
                                          99-11105
                                            CIP

15	14	13	12	11	10	09	08	07	06	05	04	03	02	01	00	99
15	14	13	12	11	10	9	8	7	6	5	4	3	2	1		

*To my wife Salli,
and my daughter Melanie,
for continually buoying my spirits*

*To my dad, Robert E. Scott,
for infusing me with the courage and
determination to boldly speak the truth*

*To my mom, Irene Scott,
for instilling in me the sensitivity and
courtesy to do so respectfully*

CONTENTS

	Preface	9
Chapter 1:	The "Hydroelectric" Power of Unquestioned Assumptions	17

First Stage in the Slide Toward Relativism

Chapter 2:	"Man Makes Right, Not God"	35
Chapter 3:	"Every Man Possesses an Innate Moral Sense"	53
Chapter 4:	"Man Is Good by Nature but Corrupted by Society"	69
Chapter 5:	"Happiness Is the Measure and Goal of a Good Life"	85

Second Stage in the Slide Toward Relativism

Chapter 6:	"Man, Too, Is an Animal"	103
Chapter 7:	"Material and Economic Causes Alone Produce Social Change"	121
Chapter 8:	"Only Slaves and Fools Restrain Their Wills and Desires"	137

Third Stage in the Slide Toward Relativism

Chapter 9:	"There Is No God, Only Unconscious, Mechanistic Causation"	159
Chapter 10:	"Christianity Is Primitive, and Even Christ Is Flawed"	175

Fourth Stage in the Slide Toward Relativism

Chapter 11:	"Life Is Meaningless"	195
Chapter 12:	"Free Will Is an Illusion"	211
Chapter 13:	"Everything Is Relative"	229

Fifth Stage in the Slide Toward Relativism

Chapter 14:	"All We Need Is Love"	249
Chapter 15:	A Defense of Christian Absolutism	267
	Appendix	288
	Notes	293
	Index	314

PREFACE

Where is the philosopher who would not deceive the whole human race, without hesitation, for the sake of his own glory?

—Rousseau,
Émile, "The Creed of a Savoyard Priest"

"'I want you to . . . picture the enlightenment or ignorance of our human condition somewhat as follows,'" says Socrates in Book VII of Plato's *Republic*. Thus begins one of the most famous illustrations in Western civilization—the allegory of the cave.

Socrates, as many readers may recall, goes on to describe a subterranean cave, with a long entrance as wide as the cave itself, in which men have been shackled since birth in such a way that they can only gaze straight ahead at a cave wall. Behind and above them burns a fire. Between the fire and the shackled men, and also above them, runs a road, in front of which is a screen. Day and night people appear above the screen, projected on the cave wall opposite the prisoners, displaying the objects of life and commerce. Sometimes the people behind the prisoners talk; sometimes they don't. Because the prisoners perceive only the shadows of the persons and of the actions on the wall before them, the shadows are their only reality.

Now that I have re-exposed you to the sooty air of Plato's cave, allow me to modernize the classical imagery. With the help of Plato, I intend to shed light on the genesis of this book.

An Updated Allegory

Imagine, instead of captives in a cave, prisoners in a modern surround-sound movie theater located in the middle of a Hollywood studio. Like Plato's cave-prisoners, all these people have been similarly shackled since infancy, unable to stand or look to the left or right. All that these twentieth-century prisoners know appears on the screen before them. Whether over many years they have witnessed *Sands of Iwo Jima*, *Ben Hur*, *The Time Machine*, *Inherit the Wind*, *The Manchurian Candidate*, *Cleopatra*, *Blow-Up*, *Portnoy's Complaint*, *Star Wars*, *Cliffhanger*, *Natural Born Killers*, *Pulp Fiction*, or *The Birdcage*, it's all the same. Their sense of reality has been conditioned and determined by what they have viewed.

Now, as in Plato's allegory of the cave, suppose someone unchains one prisoner and ushers him out into a brightly-lit lobby—or, better yet, outside onto the studio lot. Suddenly the released man beholds studio sets and street-clothed actors, at the same time finding himself in the midst of three-dimensional persons, objects, and actions as a golf cart whisks past him and a harried prop man jostles him on his way by. Naturally, we can imagine some of the liberated prisoner's experiences—the shooting pain of the light on his tender eyes, his terror and bewilderment, his disorientation as he is compelled to leave the darkness and enter the light.

Now put yourself in the place of this liberated captive, with the shackle marks still raw on your neck, wrists, and ankles. What changes are you experiencing as you discover that *at least* half of what you had always taken for granted as real is fictional—indeed, in many cases false? Since your miraculous escape from captivity, your perceptions have no doubt been undergoing drastic changes. Yet, of course, for your perceptions to be changing, your thoughts have to be changing too. What bewilderment you must feel! By the light of the blazing orb above, as you rub your eyes and stumble forth, you are not only seeing but thinking differently. What is this newly forming awareness—half perception, half thought—like?

As you stroll and gaze about the lots and sets, "familiar" objects, persons, and events appear curiously different. A woman who was a few weeks ago a glamorous queen steps out of a trailer looking thirty years older than she had looked on the screen. An alpine cliff to which some hero had clung for life a few days ago is now just a prop pushed off in a corner. Now, too, just as some of what used to appear normal appears abnormal, some of what used to appear benign now appears malignant. As you behold in real life the real actors who had peopled the screen, a formerly much-celebrated philanthropist, now standing off to the side flirting and diddling with two nubile pages, is obviously a philanderer of the worst kind. A formerly much-maligned bigot, now standing at the entrance of the theater pleading for the release of the other prisoners, is obviously a herald of freedom and equality. Who can now gauge your sense of disorientation and measure your nausea?

Even more to the point, let's say you do now grasp, for the first time in your life, that you are perceiving clearly and correctly. Before, you had been partly thinking and partly dreaming. Before, you had lived with gaps in your awareness and fuzzy patches in your head, but now, after your sudden liberation into the light, your awareness is whole and unbroken. Everything, revealed in a radiant new light, sparkles like a cache of gems and, more importantly, lies open before you like an illuminated text.

CONSEQUENT REACTIONS AND REFORMATIONS

No doubt, over time you pass through other unforeseeable experiences. At first you are overwhelmed by vexing questions. "Why," you wonder, "was I never before allowed to see as I do now? What am I to do with this magnificent new freedom and awareness? How shall I now live?" Then, as you adjust to your "new reality," you also begin to appreciate its salutary effects on your mind and life. You find that you are less troubled by confusion and doubt, worries and fears. Now, for the first time, you begin to grasp formerly vague, elusive concepts—for example, *free will* and *liberty*. Overwhelmed by gratitude, you then perhaps realize that you have for some reason been given a gift of which you are wholly unworthy. All you did was passively allow someone to lead you into the light, whereupon you discovered a more vivid, more meaningful world. "Why should I, of all people," you finally ask, "be so fortunate as to experience this sudden enlightenment, this evident change of perspective, heart, and mind?"

Soon, however, during this reformation of your sight and thought, two further insights strike you as significant, whirling your mind around as with the might of waters. These stem, you realize, from the fact that your newly reformed, newly liberated mind still retains within it the memories of your former unliberated mind. Thus you are able to apprehend simultaneously what you had experienced and thought before and what you experience and think now. This condition places you in an enviable position. Because you possess an uncanny objectivity and unbroken awareness, you can conclude, quite rightly, that thinking is *sometimes* but not *always* an unreliable tool; for when you knew no better, you thought erroneously about many things without realizing it, but you also thought correctly about some things without realizing it. As a prisoner you had comprehended human and causal relations to some degree. You can also conclude, again quite rightly, that thinking is only a reliable tool within certain limits, based on the original, prolonged conditioning and training of each subject's mind. After all, what you have really overcome since your awakening has been your previous conditioning, your bondage to a certain location and the limitations it imposed on your consciousness. These insights, you now realize, mark the beginning of your philosophical conversion and a missionary vocation.

Only now are you prepared to contemplate, with considerateness and compassion, the manacled inhabitants of your old world, your former companions. You feel distressed as you realize that those captives are, as you had once been, misperceiving and thereby suffering. They are perceiving only two-dimensional figures and lives; they are being force-fed stylized facsimiles and half-truths. Feeling the burden of your new knowledge, you find yourself prepared to embark not only on a quest to understand the causes of their bondage and misery but on a mission to liberate them. You know how clear perception and knowledge— indeed, how rich life itself—can be after a prisoner has been liberated from falsehood and fiction, illusion and delusion.

PRESENT APPLICATION

At a stage in my life, I too underwent a similar—though much slower, less dramatic—metamorphosis (punctuated by many ups and downs along the way). Until the age of twenty-eight, I had been an eager proselyte of my liberal professors and a sanctimonious acolyte of my pampered generation, bearing, I thought, the light of progress into the darkness of mindless tradition. *Of course* everything was relative, I thought. As a practitioner of Eastern religion also, I believed that "all truth is relative" and yet that "all truth leads to the same goal: Self-Realization or God-Consciousness." I also readily accepted the idea that feeling—intuition borne of personal experience or "soul" knowledge—was a reliable guide in any quest for truth or wisdom. Most of all, I believed that the shadowy figures of the great writers of the past three to four centuries had been the greatest benefactors of humankind—from Hobbes to Rousseau, Emerson to Thoreau, Darwin to Freud, Dewey to Huxley, Russell to Sartre, and so on. They were the unquestionable, unrivaled geniuses who alone could envision and engineer our social and evolutionary progress as a species. All the great philosophers and literary figures, my professors assured me, were trustworthy guides; so I imbibed the saccharine words of these geniuses as I would the elixir of life.

My transformation from conceited relativist to mortified absolutist began in graduate school while I was working on a doctoral degree in English. I encountered one professor, Dr. John O. Hayden, who challenged all my previous presuppositions with one assertion: Absolutes *must* exist, even if we can't always know or say what they are. Piqued by his challenge, I became feverishly preoccupied with the debate—dead already in the 1970s in academe—between relativism and absolutism. I began my search by reading books, dusty from long neglect, critical of Romanticism and transcendentalism, encountering such writers as James Russell Lowell, Irving Babbitt, and Yvor Winters along the way. Soon I encountered another sober-minded professor, Dr. James Murphy, who taught Augustine's *On Christian Doctrine* seriously and respectfully, not flippantly as many professors might have done. Then I encountered C. S. Lewis's *The Abolition of Man*. I won't relate any further autobiographical details. Suffice it to say, a new question soon began to plague me. What if most of what the "great modern thinkers"—and as a consequence most of what my liberal professors—had taught and said about morality and truth was wrong? What if all the while the great thinkers had had ulterior motives of their own? What if they too, like others, had most craved not truth above all else but fame, power, and prestige?

I began, in short, to entertain the possibility that modern man's faith in the progress of this age is misplaced. For me, this radical skepticism led to an unexpected result—my conversion to Christianity. This awakening, this change of heart and mind, this *metanoia*, marked the beginning of an even longer quest. For the next eighteen years I continued to undergo further challenges and changes—both as a Christian, naturally, and as a thinker—as I followed a new method of study. I began to reevaluate many of the great modern authors in light of my burgeoning Christian awareness of God, nature, and man. Soon, in fact, I found myself trying to unlearn by choice the learning that I had received by compulsion as an undergraduate and graduate student. The more I unlearned, the more I began to perceive the dire consequences that certain "great ideas" were having on modern society. Even as I honestly strove to avoid the oversimplification that comes from an outraged heart, I couldn't avoid the conclusion so well put by Mortimer Adler in the "Prologue" of his book *Ten Philosophical Mistakes* (1985):

> Those serious consequences not only pervade contemporary philosophical thought, but also manifest themselves in popular misconceptions [and misperceptions] widely prevalent today. They all tend in the same direction. They affect our understanding of ourselves, our lives, our institutions, and our experience. They mislead our action as well as becloud our thought.

Armed with this insight—and stung by the anguish it evoked in me as I contemplated the history of Western thought over the past few hundred years—this book, *Streams of Confusion*, was born. It became my way of trying to reexamine the record and humbly ask, "What if most of our modern philosophical and literary authorities aren't heroes but villains, not benefactors of humanity but destroyers of civilization?" Maybe, just maybe, the writings of the real heroes are languishing somewhere on musty bookshelves or, worse, providing landfill for a parking lot in London, Paris, or Bonn.

Quite naturally, I couldn't resist beginning this preface with a reference to the allegory of the cave. For years the allegory has been poised—complete with flickering lights and flitting shadows—at the fringes of my mind as I have thought about the distinctions between truth and falsehood, knowledge and ignorance, perception and misperception. In the chapters that follow I hope you will recognize why I not only borrowed the allegory of the cave but also took liberties in the way I employed it. Like the prisoners in the Socratic dialogue, I was indeed awakened from ignorance. Yet upon awakening, neither was I blinded by a common metaphysical light, nor was I ushered into an upper world of Platonic ideas. Instead, upon my release from bondage I encountered the Light of the World. Now, like the blind man in John 9:25, I can only declare, "One thing I do know. I was blind but now I see!" It is not due to the glory of men—any philosopher or professor—but to the glory of Christ that the world is different for me today.

I can only pray that this book may, in a similar way, bestow Light on all who read it and on those whose lives it touches.

THE "HYDROELECTRIC" POWER OF UNQUESTIONED ASSUMPTIONS

The human capacity for self-deception is as boundless as it is fathom-less. There are so many spurious routes our minds and hearts can take. Our unexamined thoughts can digress, take a brash detour, and rush eagerly down a new primrose path. If our wills concur, we embark on a new journey of hope or excitement, curiosity or intrigue.

Then, in light of our "new knowledge," we can explain our lives and our loves with an enviable simplicity. A new universe of choices, personalities, and identities yawns open before us, larger than life, and we step through a bright panorama of possibilities, unaware of—or dis-inclined to consider—the long-range consequences of our choices and actions on ourselves and others. Given the right set of circumstances and influences, any one of us, we come to realize, can be propelled in a new, and often dangerous, direction by the power of the ideas we accept or reject.

THE CONFLUENCE OF MODERN IDEAS

Daily, scores of people are making long-term, life-changing decisions. Daily, in fact, we confront innumerable cases of this or that type of con-version—in the way people think and act, perceive the world, or live their lives. People today, it seems, adopt or discard opinions and lifestyles as readily as they change long-distance carriers. Preferring the modern and novel to the tried and true, they grasp at the many ideas that converge on them, unconcerned about the sources or merits of the ideas. Especially if the ideas are intriguing, exciting, or liberating, people eagerly embrace them. Faced with such a smorgasbord of ideas, they can select those that suit their tastes and provide them, if necessary, with convenient rationalizations for their behavior. To understand this wholly modern, often incomprehensible tendency and process, let's consider a few representative examples drawn from everyday life.

Case 1. Jim Thompson, a young man of nineteen from a good Christian home, returns to a state university one fall as a sophomore. As he starts taking advanced courses in the social and natural sciences, he finds that his faith is beginning to fail him. He learns that the universe is a closed system and that life on earth has evolved by randomness and chance. Out of a chemically-based, prebiotic soup, life somehow sprang, multiplied, slithered along the bottoms of still-warm pools for aeons, and then dragged itself onto the shore, where, again over aeons, it split, amoeba-like, into a myriad of forms. The capacities of the mind, he learns, are genetically determined; beliefs and actions are environmentally dictated and controlled. All cultures and values are relative and equal. The Judeo-Christian faith is just *one* culturally conditioned belief system, now in its death throes, along with the puritanical, patriarchal forces that spawned it. He is further taught that homosexuality is a valid lifestyle and that the only salvation for America is a Socialist-minded pluralism, one that creates "a level playing field" for all cultural expressions.

By year's end, Jim writes to his parents, telling them that he is abandoning his faith—like the lifestyle of his parents, it's "anachronistic"—and he is moving in with his girlfriend. By spring break (no longer called Easter break), when Jim visits his parents for two days but refuses to attend Easter services, he has become fully converted to his new way of thinking. He is sporting an earring, deferring to his mauve-haired, nose-ringed girlfriend, and pontificating about gay rights, women's rights, and everyone's rights to do as he or she pleases and to experience happiness. He expects his parents to accept him the way he is, but he lets them know, in no uncertain terms, that they aren't all right the way they are. After reasoning and remonstrating with Jim, all that Mr. and Mrs. Thompson can do is pray for him.

Case 2. Always a positive thinker, Weldon Tester swore to himself at age twenty-one, with his Bachelor of Science in business management in hand, that he would be a millionaire by forty. At forty-one he is indeed a millionaire. Recently his ad agency won a prestigious award for a successful ad campaign that has earned his company not only kudos but contracts. His biggest new client to date, Surprise Jeans for Teens, is now asking him to develop a series of ads directed toward girls between the ages of twelve and sixteen using soft-porn imagery and themes. The CEO of the company wants to out-titillate even Calvin Klein. "The sexier the ads," she says, "the better."

For a short while Weldon hesitates to accept the project, troubled by the fact that his own daughter will be twelve in two years. But he quickly reasons that advertising merely holds a mirror up to society. It reflects culture; it doesn't create it. Besides, every parent is responsible for inculcating his or her "private values" into his or her own children, for creating the best environment in which to rear them. Advertising is a neutral medium whose sole purpose is to "grow" businesses. If people don't like a product or its ads, they don't have to buy it. They can show their disapproval with their pocketbooks. That's why we call it a "free marketplace." The bottom line in business is profits, not ethics. Finally, he reasons, "I have to look out first for myself and my family in this dog-eat-dog world." In the end Weldon accepts the contract with Surprise Jeans for Teens because he believes that values are mostly personal and relative anyway, not universal or absolute. "Hey," says Weldon to a friend, "I'm not my brother's keeper."

Case 3. Shirley Kirkland, a twenty-eight-year-old mother of two children, finished college seven years ago and married shortly afterwards. Since then she has achieved modest success as a human resources manager in a major electronics company while her husband, who has just finished law school and passed the bar, has joined a successful local law firm. Unfortunately, Shirley feels empty and dissatisfied. She feels that she needs to take some time to find herself.

She attends several meetings on codependency and dysfunctional families but soon feels that she isn't getting to the root of her problems. Then one day she picks up a local New Age journal from the grocery store and reads about a "master" teacher who will be lecturing on "the evolution of consciousness in the new millennium" at the local Evolving Consciousness Bookstore. His ad explains that advanced souls are feeling restless and discontent, while "baby souls" are slumbering in ignorance. His teachings are intended to help the advanced evolve in consciousness and prepare for the New Age. Shirley attends the lecture, gets swept up into the "master's" organization (The Divine Love League), and soon feels that, to be true to herself, she will have to leave her husband. Besides, she has met Larry, another advanced, evolving soul, and they feel they are soul mates, karmically connected from a past life. Because from a past-life reading she learns that her two children were formerly her parents who sold her to Gypsies when she was a small child, she knows that they will be simply reaping their own karma as her marriage breaks up. As for her husband, he was never part of her "group soul" anyway. Now she knows that she is free to evolve guiltlessly.

Examples of this kind abound today. Each of us can probably tell similar stories—about others, maybe about ourselves. At one time some of us thought we might find happiness through worldly success, peace through drugs, or wisdom through cults. True believers all, we proceeded with conviction for months or years at a time. Then just when all seemed good, it turned bad. Right became wrong. Up became down. We were jolted awake by our own private subterranean psychic earthquake, and a volcanic eruption of pain and confusion ensued. Unfortunately, we may learn too late that many of these routes our minds and hearts can take lead to a living "hell," a grief and guilt that we may have expected from the start but could not resist—or may not have expected and could not forestall. Our desires make us slaves, our minds fools. As Shakespeare so poignantly put it in "Sonnet 129" when speaking of the consequences of succumbing to unbridled lust:

> *All this world well knows; yet none knows well*
> *To shun the heaven that leads men to this hell.*

Often we well know, but not well enough, to exercise the virtues of thoughtfulness and prudence in the face of our painful doubts and inordinate desires.

Of course, it's not only individuals who are prone to self-delusion. Driven by groupthink, whole nations and groups can give way to apparent lunacy. The French and Russians had their bloody revolutions, the Nazis their barbarous Third Reich. America has its fads—its legions of youths in baggy pants; its obsessions with gangsters, pop stars, and sports figures; its penchant for changing presidents every four years based on nothing more than a promise of *change*. A man may yell, "I'm the new Son of God come to save the world!" and followers flock to him as eagerly as glassy-eyed hippies once flocked to Woodstock. Like lemmings leaping off cliffs, so many teens today follow their idols—pop "artists," movie stars, and rebellious peers—to almost certain destruction. Statistics show that many youths are already on a Bataan-like march to death. A survey cited in the *New York Times* in December 1994 reveals that marijuana use is on the rise among teens again. *The Statistical Abstract of the United States* for 1996 reveals that between 1983 and 1993 the violent crime rate among juveniles more than doubled (from 55 to 122 per 1,000). Between 1968 and 1993, even while the abortion rates were climbing and remaining high, birth rates among unmarried fifteen- to nineteen-year-olds more than doubled (from 158 to 357 per 1,000).[1]

And as McDowell and Hostetler so effectively illustrate in *Right from Wrong*, even evangelical Christian teenagers aren't exempt. McDowell's research reveals that in a three-month period 36 percent of those he surveyed had cheated on an exam, 66 percent had lied to parents or some other adult authority figure, 18 percent of the fifteen- to sixteen-year-olds and 27 percent of the seventeen- to eighteen-year-olds had engaged in premarital intercourse, and 70 percent of evangelical Christian teens felt that "what is right for one person in a given situation might not be right for another person who encounters that same situation."[2]

Ideas are powerful. Unchallenged, certain ideas can be dangerous, individually and collectively. Once a series of social or cultural effects, like the raging waters of a river, begins to roll, it becomes difficult to understand, much less control. For millions, one worldview, often consisting of several streams of thought, can become the *only* view that makes sense. Short of embracing a conspiracy theory, how then can we understand the chaos of values and the clash of worldviews around us? How can we cope with the confusion of tongues that marks modern lifestyles and discussions?

IDEOLOGICAL HEADWATERS

Surprisingly, without being simplistic, we *can* simplify the modern confusion of tongues a great deal. If we look carefully enough at the apparently chaotic modern scene, we can begin to observe currents and eddies of thought forming a single river of material effects. All of the technological and social "progress" that we see around us reveals certain patterns. All progress of condition, we soon begin to discover, simply mirrors the progress of a handful of great ideas.

The most prominent views that swirl around us today may actually be traced back to a dozen or so mega-ideas—persuasive, potent presuppositions. And these mega-ideas, in turn, may be traced back to a few dozen great thinkers who have lived and written within the past 350 years. Many people may recognize some of these influences. From Rousseau we have derived the ideas of "the social contract" and "the noble savage." Darwin introduced, though not for the first time in history, the idea of natural evolution. Nietzsche originated the term "God is dead." Other influences may be less apparent. John Stuart Mill (1806-1873), for example, introduced the modern idea that in matters concerning an individual only, the individual should remain the absolute sovereign of himself. And Aldous Huxley (1894-1963) helped usher in the drug craze of the sixties by experimenting with LSD in the 1950s and heralding psychedelic drugs as the new path to enlightenment in such books as *The Doors of Perception* (1954) and *The Island* (1962).

A number of great thinkers of the past and recent present, actually fewer than one might think, have thus had a tremendous impact on modern culture. What they have created has touched others. What they have written has influenced multitudes of disciples and average citizens alike, for good or ill. So much were they admired as beacons of truth in their respective ages that many of their contemporaries embraced their ideas uncritically. Rousseau, declaring that man is a "noble savage" corrupted not by his nature but by his society, effectively dislodged the notion of original sin from the frontal lobes of Western thinkers. The literary genius Byron created—and himself played—the Byronic hero, and generations of scholars have referred to him as a "type." Indeed, his type appears today as the Errol Flynns, James Deans, Mick Jaggers, Jim Morrisons, and Kurt Cobains among us. Nietzsche in *Thus Spoke Zarathustra* bade the supermen to leave the marketplace and embrace their impulses for good *and* evil. And one of his chief admirers, Adolf Hitler, aroused the German elite in the 1930s and whipped the German rabble into a frenzy that swept like a cyclone across Europe.

Thus when a gifted mind influences others, the process is as inevitable as the results are predictable. The process of influence that was at work in the seventeenth century is the same today. Prophet-like, the great thinker begins to write and speak. Whether authoritatively or tentatively, it doesn't matter. Mystic-like, he somehow echoes, or divines, the emerging desires and fears of his generation; he is able to address people's deepest concerns and most vexing questions. At first a few colleagues and disciples flock to his side. As his ideas gather momentum, others begin to concur with his assessments, perhaps after some initial resistance, until lesser luminaries, writers and teachers, begin to see as he sees and march to the beat of his drum. The word begins to spread in classrooms and journals, in tracts and newspapers, in the boardroom and bedroom as the new followers carry the ideas into the various areas of life.

In today's world, the advocates of the mega-ideas may be educators, psychologists, and media personnel—the moguls, producers, directors, writers, and "personalities." And with today's airwaves and cyberspace, old and new mega-ideas can rapidly spread, extending the influence of any great thinker, past or present; we in turn can more readily perceive the influence that any mega-idea is having on society. Kept clean and simple in design for mass consumption, the mega-ideas in time become orthodoxy. In our time, especially, the new orthodoxy (what many call *political correctness*) can then develop unchallenged—and reign supreme—within the universities, colleges, and schools, as Allen Bloom clearly demonstrated in *The Closing of the American Mind* or as Dinesh D'Souza explained in *An Illiberal Education*. Fashionably cynical and rebellious, many of the professors of the new orthodoxy ridicule the tradition upon which they feed, destroying it in the process, as Alvin Kernan so prophetically argued in his best-selling *The Death of Literature*. As those waters of the intellect sweep down the mountainsides, gaining momentum as they gather strength, just so are people moved.

Like rivulets streaming down mountainsides, then, the ideas of the great thinkers, who were indeed geniuses in their own right, begin to spread and widen in the same way that springs become waterfalls and waterfalls rivers. And down the ideas stream, starting as trickles but merging and forming a mighty river, drowning out nearby sounds with its roar, blinding with its reflected glitter all who stare directly into it. Most of us hear only the murmuring of lesser voices, those several removes from the alpine headwaters. What did Fritz Pearls or Abraham Maslow say? What did A. S. Neill or Jonathan Kozol say? What did Roseanne or Oprah say? Whether we like to or not, we are all reading and listening all the time, aren't we? As we do so, the torrents wash over us.

And there you have it: *Trickle-Down Ideonomics*.

By the time the mega-ideas of the great thinkers have reached the valley, where the Jim Thompsons, Weldon Testers, and Shirley Kirklands live, however, they have become murky water supplies. When forced to make a choice or face a crisis, most people, in the absence of a strong moral frame of reference, have little else to rely on for solace and wisdom. So they resort to the standard clichés, the diluted renderings of some great thinker's original philosophy. They say, "I've gotta be me." Or "If it feels good, do it." Or "I can do my own thing as long as I don't hurt anyone." Or "My life is meaningless." And in the background, far out of sight, are the shadowy figures of Rousseau, Hume, Mill, Sartre, and two dozen others whose ideas have shaped the fate of future generations. When someone like our New Age convert Shirley declares, "My only duty is to myself," she probably has no idea that a character in a late nineteenth-century play, *A Doll's House* by Henrik Ibsen, said the same thing in similar circumstances, or that Ralph Waldo Emerson paved the way for such a view in early nineteenth-century America, himself only echoing the European Romantics of an earlier generation. Tragically, the insight that fuels her new outlook and lifestyle more than likely isn't even her own.

AN AGE-OLD PROGRESSION OF ERROR

These mega-ideas, then, have trickled down from on high—through great minds—to the great moving mass of mankind, for whom they are now unexamined, generalized truths—or life-shaping presuppositions. Yet, unbeknownst to many, the ideas that have taken root in their minds are often falsehoods wrapped in apparent truths. Like viruses, the ideas carry not anodynes but diseases to which we are all susceptible—materialism, hedonism, rationalism, moral relativism, New Age subjectivism, and so on. In our day the result has been a fusion of a materialistic moral relativism and a humanistic exaltation of self.

Yet this slide toward chaos and immorality isn't a new phenomenon, nor is my recognition of the process original. I have discovered nothing new under the sun. Long ago the apostle Paul outlined in Romans 1:18-32 the timeless process for us. Although the existence of God is always evident in his creation, humans choose to ignore him and instead glorify themselves, thus rendering their thoughts futile and darkening their hearts. In this way they exchange the truth of God for a lie and worship and serve created things. As a result, God gives them over to sexual impurity and shameful lusts; and they engage in indecent, even perverted acts with one another—fornication, adultery, homosexuality. Because they have abandoned the knowledge of God, God gives them over to a depraved mind, "to do what ought not to be done" (verse 28). Filled with wickedness—greed, envy, deceit, malice, arrogance, disrespect—they invent new ways of doing evil. Worst of all, although they know that God punishes such evil with death, "they not only continue to do these very things but also approve of those who practice them" (verse 32). Evil, as much as misery, loves company, and so the evildoers spread their lies abroad. Soon falsehood is accepted as truth; rebelliousness, the fashion; self-indulgence, the norm; and self, the new deity.

Now, I'm not suggesting that most people today are hopelessly deluded. They aren't. They are just unaware of, or indifferent to, the process of trickle-down ideonomics (or perhaps they believe they are immune to it). Whatever the case, they aren't critical enough. Many are non-Christians; some are Christians. They are swept along by the currents of the age, clinging to whatever they can for safety and security, embracing and relishing the moment, not realizing that they may be drawing nearer and nearer to destruction—and encouraging others to do the same. By degrees they may compromise with the New Age and its "new" ways, enamored by its "toys" and technologies, deceived by the siren song of their own reflected images. All the while Western culture appears to be sliding down several slippery slopes toward eventual corruption and chaos. At the end of such a course, Christianity tells us, are judgment and death: "for those who are self-seeking and who reject the truth and follow evil, there will be wrath and anger" (Rom. 2:8).

A BRIDGE OVER TROUBLED WATERS

Therefore, to make informed and wise decisions today, people need to hear the other side of the story about the progress of the mega-ideas in the modern Western world—the progress behind the Progress. When they can stand back and critically study the mega-ideas, all of which most people will recognize, and reassess the work of the great thinkers, many of whom they may not recognize, they will be prepared to take a fresh look at the current condition of our culture. Pricked in conscience, perhaps they will seek to reform themselves, their families, and their society. By whatever rightful means possible, perhaps they will try to take the high moral ground and still the now-surging waters of moral and spiritual confusion. Then perhaps the catastrophe may yet be averted.

This book, then, seeks to tell the other side of the story and to urge people to think critically. There could be any number of starting points for a story of this kind—from the fall of Adam to the fall of Rome. But this study, being more modest in scope, begins in 1651 with the publication of a single book—Thomas Hobbes's *Leviathan*, a book that in its day rocked and shocked the Western world. That date, to be sure, is in some respects arbitrary. The first signs of modernism[3] began to appear, albeit modestly and gradually, about two centuries earlier in the writings of Erasmus, Machiavelli, Francis Bacon, Spinoza, and certain Jesuits (of the kind referred to in Pascal's *The Provincial Letters*) who rationalized and relativized the truth as it suited their purposes. Nevertheless, it was the writers of the Enlightenment—Hobbes, Locke, Hume, Voltaire, d'Holbach, and others—who brought to fruition any seeds planted by Renaissance writers. Therefore, I would mark the advent of the modern era with what I will call the Great Intellectual Shift, which occurred between 1651 and 1850.[4] With the publication of *Leviathan*, the old humanism became materialism; soon afterwards, materialism became subjectivism; then subjectivism became Romanticism—all within the space of about one century. Thereafter, the process that this book outlines—the slide toward relativism—became inevitable and calculable.

In the next thirteen chapters, I shall trace our current descent into relativism and pluralistic confusion and expose its hydra-headed source—the great thinkers themselves. As I do so, I shall also question and challenge their by-now virtually unquestionable mega-ideas, the mighty presuppositions, that have filtered down to us from their book-lined studies and garrets. The reader shall then see these mega-ideas for what they really are— not so much evolutionary insights poured down upon us from on high, but substantial threats to the sanity and safety of the human race. Just what are these mega-ideas? I intend to examine just thirteen of the most potent ones and then to demonstrate how they directly affect us today.

1. Man makes right, not God. The lawgiver alone determines what the civil as well as moral laws are to be.

2. Every man possesses an innate moral sense. All he must do is trust his feelings, especially as they relate to pleasure and pain, to know what is right and wrong.

3. Man is good by nature, born good but corrupted by society—by its systems, institutions, and conventions.

4. Happiness is the measure and goal of a good life. An individual may do whatever he feels is right for himself, as long as he doesn't hurt anyone.

5. Man too is an animal. Only the fit and sexually attractive survive.

6. Material and economic causes alone produce social change. Existence precedes essence. To reform society, its institutions and values, is to reform man.

7. Only slaves and fools restrain their wills and desires. All real men must be rebels and experimentalists.

8. There is no God, only unconscious, mechanistic causation at work in human psychology and society. Through science alone can man overcome his age-old infantile superstitions.

9. Not only is Christianity a primitive, superstitious, untenable religion, but Christ is a flawed "savior" who bears much of the responsibility for the ignorance and suffering of humankind before the rise of science.

10. Life is meaningless apart from man's self-initiated, self-assertive acts. A person creates his reality by acting heroically. A man is what he wills himself to be.

11. The nature of man is determined by his environment or predetermined by his genes or both. Individual responsibility and free will are illusions.

12. All is relative—all values, morals, standards, beliefs, etc. Truth itself is relative.

13. In a pluralistic, relativistic world, universal, unifying, nonjudgmental acceptance and love alone can reconcile our differences and bring us peace.

Arranged roughly chronologically according to their appearance in the popular mind, these thirteen commonly held mega-ideas reveal a progression of thought to which social "advancements" in the last three centuries bear witness. They also reveal another curiosity of the modern mind: contradictory premises, regarded to be true in themselves, can coexist simultaneously in the same mind (as in the case of numbers 10 and 11). Today many people suffer from a curious double-mindedness, a kind of schizophrenia of the conscience, as they try to live in the modern world, sometimes believing and accepting the mega-ideas, at other times doubting and barely tolerating them. When the thirteen presuppositions are examined and dissected, a reader can't help but see not only their inherent contradictions but also their dangerous implications.

For too long the intellects of men and women in the West have been held captive by the self-centered, centripetal forces of sectarianism and relativism. The thirteen mega-ideas listed above—and the distortions that attend them—have thus prevented modern people from taking the gospel message seriously and freely examining its claims for themselves. In the schools and media, Christianity's mistakes have been exaggerated, and its contributions minimized, if not virtually denied. The facts of history have been filtered and slanted. In fact, in many circles so-called experts have already proclaimed the death of the Christian worldview. How can people accept the free gift of the Gospel if they are ignorant of its true content? The message of Christianity can't be understood, much less embraced, until the intellect is set free.

A CULTURE ADRIFT IN A CRIPPLED SHIP

Although the thirteen mega-ideas discussed in this book have greatly changed Western civilization, they have not yet run it aground. As a culture, we can still find our bearings if we begin to practice discernment—

to critically distance ourselves from the mega-ideas, perceive their inherent flaws, and break their stranglehold on the modern Western mind.

True, we have every cause to be alarmed by our present circumstances. In a modern society forever courting novelty and sensual stimulation, victims of one kind or another abound. Poverty grates on the poor more than ever before because more than ever before material wealth and abundance dictate the measure of a man or woman. Because life apart from sensory enjoyment seems meaningless, despair and ennui haunt multitudes of young people in the same way that lions haunt the dreams of Serengeti plainsmen. Many wander from one high to another or seek an end to their confusion and enervation in suicide.[5] And, most unbearable of all, fear and loneliness paralyze many of our children. Many live in terror because of the violence, imagined or real, that daily touches their lives. And more and more of them are being forced by divorce to grow up without the direct and continuous care of one parent. The crisis of our age, as many of us have come to realize, is indeed a crisis of values. What and whom shall we value? And how shall we value them? More importantly, what price are we willing to pay to preserve and protect the values we cherish?

If the crisis is one of values, it's also a crisis of the mind and soul, perhaps more so than ever before. Generations ago the sources of our malaise were as much natural and economic as they were moral and spiritual. But modern science, with its attendant technology, has seen to it that the natural and economic affect us in the West much less, affording us a greater degree of physical comfort, security, and freedom than we have ever known. Naturally, we are still tempted to behave badly. We just fear less the consequences of our lapses; we feel more comfortable about, and secure in, our "personal choices" and "lifestyles." If we are prone to impatience, our insurance will reimburse us for the damage we do to our homes or cars. If we are prone to egotism, a new speedboat or big-screen TV will assuage our wounded egos or compensate for our dissatisfaction at work. And if we are prone to self-indulgence, the doctor will patch us up after we have clogged our lungs with tar or contracted an STD.

But these new assurances and options also have a darker side. In many respects they are, as Wordsworth once put it, "sordid boons." We now place our priorities, more than ever before, on our personal satisfactions and subjective moods of ease or *dis*-ease. Consequently, whenever we feel bored or ill at ease, we rush to "find" ourselves rather than devoting ourselves to some meaningful goal or worthy cause. Meanwhile, we find ourselves, instead, not only drifting from one emotional—or "spiritual"—high to another but also falling ill, becoming feverish, driven into delirium by a thirst that relativistic beliefs and materialistic preoccupations can never quench.

Yet it's precisely, and paradoxically, in this condition of the mind and spirit that we can find both opportunity and hope. For it's by the renewal of our minds and hearts that we can indeed effect our release, individually and collectively, from false ideas. By critically evaluating the mega-ideas and thus throwing open the windows of our minds, we will certainly gain refreshing new insights into ourselves and our culture. We will also learn several important lessons that may help us recover from our delirium and chart a new, more sensible course for future generations. All of this bondage to certain mega-ideas, to thoughts that aren't really our own, may in fact begin to outrage us, inspiring us with the twofold conviction that we *must* do something and that we *can* do something. Shall we, it's fair to ask, continue to let fifty, 500, or even 5,000 modern thinkers dictate how we should think and act?

With this book, I'm trying to do just that: to inspire readers to *re*form themselves and their culture. I'm urging them to challenge the assumptions that shape today's society and thus to become free men and women—equipped if they are Christians to separate the wheat from the chaff and so live a life more dedicated to Christ; equipped if they are non-Christians to understand better the culture in which they live, clarify their values, and perhaps even reconsider the claims that the Gospel of Christ makes upon every human soul. Non-Christian readers, I maintain, owe themselves the opportunity to hear the other side of the story before they say yea or nay to the insistent, oh-so-persuasive voices of this age.

A NAVIGATIONAL MAP OF THE BOOK

In closing, then, let me summarize my argument, restating it as unambiguously as I can. In the West during the past three to four centuries, a relatively small group of great thinkers has been capturing, stage by stage, the minds and imaginations of the educated and uneducated in society. These thinkers have advanced conclusions that have filtered down to us wherever we live, whatever we do. Over time these dozen or so ideas have taken on the status of unquestioned, and virtually unquestionable, *a priori* assumptions. Yet because today these mega-ideas are greatly, and often adversely, influencing current thought, values, and behavior, we owe it to ourselves to try to understand them in their original contexts, as well as in their present manifestations. We need not only to examine these mega-ideas closely and critically, but also to challenge them openly, exposing their harmful influences in our lives and the lives of others. Once we can reject as absurd the conclusions to which the initial mistaken mega-ideas have led, we will find ourselves in a position to reject the mega-ideas themselves as equally absurd. "That is the way a *reductio ad absurdum* argument is supposed to work," says Mortimer Adler. "When we are shown that we have been led to an absurd conclusion by logically following out the implications of an initial premise, we are expected to respond by rejecting that premise as itself absurd."[6] Thus armed and outraged, perhaps many more people today, despite the persuasive appeal of these ideas, may be prepared to understand why Christ still offers, as always, the only sane and salutary answer to all our deepest, most perplexing questions. The gospel message still remains timeless and universal. There is still indeed a rational basis for Christianity—what C. S. Lewis called a "permanent Christianity"—the absolute standards and truths of which are as relevant today as they were 400—or 2,000—years ago. The business of this book, then, will be "to present that which is timeless (the same yesterday, today, and tomorrow) in the particular language of our own age."[7]

Even if Christianity be a "delusion," as so many of its detractors claim—and, of course, I'm sure it's *not*—it's a "delusion" that can do a person good only and no harm, at least if it's faithfully and fully practiced. Like G. K. Chesterton, I too can't understand why so many people are today disillusioned with Christianity. "After all," as he put it, "nobody has ever tried it." Those very people who so readily and roundly dismiss Christianity are often the same people who have never really given it a fair hearing, let alone given it a chance to work miracles in their hearts and lives. Were they to allow the living Christ to save them by grace through faith, many would, I believe, realize that they were really free for the first time in their lives from self-delusion and its multitude of woes. Having known the truth, they would find that the truth had set them free.

FIRST STAGE

IN THE SLIDE TOWARD RELATIVISM

From 1651 to 1859,

Western man declared his autonomy,

emancipating himself from tradition and revelation,

the objective authority of God.

2

"MAN MAKES RIGHT, NOT GOD"

Between 1651 and 1700 European thinkers wrote over 109 books, articles, and tracts denouncing Thomas Hobbes's *Leviathan* and declaring the author to be the enemy of all right-thinking people.[1] So adverse was the reaction to this book, written by the sixty-three-year-old tutor, scholar, and bachelor, that in the wake of its publication in France in 1651 he was forced to flee to England for refuge. In France, among fellow expatriates, he had angered not only the royalist English refugees but the royalist Anglican divines, who feared that the Catholic authorities would retaliate against *them*. Soon afterward in England, he had to declare his submission to the Council of State before he could slink safely into retirement.

Even years later the furor hadn't entirely subsided. In 1666 Parliament threatened to take action against the book, and Hobbes was thereafter denied permission to publish any works on ethical matters.[2] In short, "When . . . [Hobbes] published the *Leviathan*," says Bertrand Russell, "it pleased no one."[3]

What had Hobbes written in *Leviathan* that could have aroused such controversy and outrage in seventeenth-century Christendom? In his book he seems to profess faith in Christ by repeatedly referring to "our Saviour" or "our blessed Saviour." He refers in a section entitled "Of Religion" (Part I, Chapter XII) to God's revelation of religion and law, sounding very much like a theist and supernaturalist:

But where God himself by supernatural revelation planted religion, there he also made to himself a peculiar kingdom, and gave laws, not only of behaviours towards himself, but also towards one another; and thereby in the kingdom of God, the policy and laws civil are a part of religion; and therefore the distinction of temporal and spiritual domination hath there no place.[4]

Parts III and IV of his book are entitled "Of a Christian Commonwealth" and "Of the Kingdom of Darkness." In Part III he takes Scripture seriously enough as an authority to cite and interpret numerous passages to prove that his philosophical conclusions are correct. In Part IV he decries pagan superstitions, "Vain Philosophy," and "Fabulous Traditions." At first glance, then, the book appears to be written by a Christian. Could his contemporaries have misunderstood him?

No. Hobbes definitely launched culture in a new and dangerous direction, for like the several writers whom he influenced over the next century and a half, he turned his sights toward materialism as his new polestar in matters of politics and philosophy. Although Hobbes didn't directly deny the existence of God or the authority of Christ, some writers in the eighteenth century, notably the French *philosophes* (Voltaire, Helvetius, d'Holbach, Diderot), and other writers in the nineteenth century did. War cries issued from many quarters, some resulting in revolutions, political and Romantic, others in spiritual turmoils and revivals. During this time the Inquisition expired, America and France sought political reforms and freedoms, and John Wesley introduced Methodism. Gradually a Great Intellectual Shift began to occur in the way men perceived themselves, their universe, and their deity.

Yet Thomas Hobbes was only the first in a long, albeit crooked, line of great thinkers who effected this shift in thinking. From 1651 to about 1850, great Western minds expended much of their energy in declaring their autonomy, emancipating themselves from tradition, and denying the role of revelation in human affairs. Hobbes's role was critical to this shift. Like a latter-day Democritus (ca. 420 B.C.), Hobbes reawakened materialism after centuries of slumber and advanced, perhaps unwittingly, the notion that not only civil but moral laws are man-made, not God-given. Only a sovereign ruler, he says, can dictate right and wrong. For the governed, whether these laws agree with God's laws is irrelevant.

Historically, *Leviathan* signaled the end of Scholasticism and thus also the end of the preeminence of theology in Europe. Afterward, only scientific rationalism was to be revered.

THE GREAT "MORTAL GOD"

From Medieval times philosophers like Augustine and Aquinas, in the tradition of the apostle Paul, had believed that God's natural laws mirrored, as through a glass darkly, God's divine laws. Natural laws (God's created order) allowed natural man (God's highest creation) to grasp part of the truth that divine law as revealed in Scripture brought to fullness. What the intellect couldn't fully grasp, divine revelation completed. No serious thinker, then, thought that natural law was superior to the authority of divine revelation. True, the great theologians held that the truths of natural law and the truths of Scripture were complementary, but they also presupposed that divine law—spiritual and moral—was pre-eminent and natural law subordinate, a mere reflection of the divine. Of course, this subordination of natural law to divine law also meant that reason was always inferior to faith, because the human mind, the seat of reason, was a *natural* instrument. In this way, for centuries, the claims of divine revelation always superseded the claims of natural reason.

But Thomas Hobbes, even though he didn't deny a correlation between divine law and natural law, undermined the traditional view by advancing four main theories in his controversial book *Leviathan*. If we examine his words within the context of his whole argument, it doesn't take us long to identify the gist of his ideas or the nature of his defection from the ranks of traditional theologians and philosophers. It was Hobbes who first turned the old tradition upside-down.

Matter and Sense Explain Everything

To Hobbes, not only the natural but also "the spiritual" could be explained mechanistically, by means of material processes. Like all empiricists, Hobbes found in sense experiences all the answers he needed. Indeed, at the beginning of his first chapter he tells us, "The original of [all our thoughts] is that which we call *sense*, (for there is no conception in a man's mind which hath not at first, totally or by parts, been begotten upon the organs of sense). The rest are derived from that original." Sense experience, therefore, creates thought. And sense experience coupled with motion, Hobbes tells us, makes automata of us all: "engines that move themselves by springs and wheels as doth a watch. . . ."[5] The motion itself is derived from the Artificer, a clockwork God reminiscent of the God of the Deists, who later appear in the eighteenth century.

To establish the strict material nature of all causes and effects, Hobbes debunks early in his treatise the rational claims of traditional theology and metaphysics about the nature of reality: "[I]f a man should talk to me of . . . *immaterial substances*; or of a *free subject*; a *free will*; or any *free* but free from being hindered by opposition; I should not say he were in an error, but that his words were without meaning; that is to say, absurd." It's simply meaningless palaver, then, when anyone attempts to discuss "immaterial substances" or "free will." Such abstractions can't be empirically verified. When one has rock-solid reality before him, it's a waste of time for him to speculate about matters that lie beyond his sense perceptions. In fact, it's absurd to make such self-contradictory statements. How can a substance, something material, possibly be immaterial?

In this passage Hobbes also gives us a hint of his determinism. He describes free will in mechanistic terms. To be free is to be free "from being hindered by opposition." In other words, if a man is strolling down an aisle and an opposing barrier striding his way—say, a bully—steps aside and lets him pass, the man is "free." When Hobbes asserts that "reason is the *pace*; increase of science, the *way*; and the benefit of mankind, the *end*,"[6] he is thundering a modern cry: mankind can only discover truth and promote human welfare by means of empirical, pragmatic science.

Many of his other conclusions represent equally intense assaults on traditional theology and metaphysics, from Plato and Aristotle to Luther and Calvin. Only a strict materialist like Hobbes could write such an absolute statement as "[D]esire and love are the same thing. . . ."[7] To say that desire and love are the same thing is to deny once again that there is a supernatural or spiritual realm. If love is merely tied to sensations and passions, then it must cease to have any meaningful transcendent dimension. It can neither broaden us into a deeper sense of our shared humanity, nor can it lift our minds into a contemplation of our "Artificer." If love, like desire, becomes a matter of mechanical attraction and repulsion, mere material processes, then it also ceases to have any ability to ennoble the lover and the beloved. If all is matter, how then can anything really matter?

Hobbes reveals the crudeness of his materialism even more clearly when he boldly claims: "[T]here is no . . . *finis ultimus* (utmost aim) nor *summum bonum* (greatest good) as is spoken of in the books of the old moral philosophers." If love is merely an impulse of attraction and humans have no unchanging hierarchy of aims and goods for which they can strive, then they must be motivated and actuated by things other than the spiritual and transcendent. Once again, for Hobbes, the causes are material and natural. Man is simply motivated by the desires for pleasure and power. To man in the state of nature, "private appetite is the measure of good and evil. . . ."[8]

Hobbes adds a few final nails to the coffin of theology when he asserts that religion arises from human impulse, another strictly material cause. "Seeing there are no signs nor fruit of religion but in man only," says he, "there is no cause to doubt but that the seed of religion is also only in man. . . ."[9] He goes on to maintain that the need for religion arises from a fear of the future. Supposedly he was speaking only of natural as opposed to revealed religion, but the implications of his view can't be mistaken. Bertrand Russell, writing two centuries later, acknowledges as much in one of his asides: "The rash reader may apply the same argument to the Christian religion, but Hobbes is much too cautious to do so himself."[10] By the twentieth century writers like Freud and Russell were in fact applying this same argument to Christianity.

Self-Preservation Is the Basis of Law

According to Hobbes the natural condition of the automaton called man is "a condition of war." The right of nature, *jus naturale*, is that each man shall "use his own power as he will himself for the preservation of his own nature." Left to himself, he will make use of his reason to preserve "his life against his enemies," thinking he "has a right to every thing, even to one another's body." Because such a condition of war can't reasonably endure for long if men want to preserve their lives, it follows that they should mutually transfer this right of self-preservation to some person or group of persons. Such a renunciation or transfer, says Hobbes, leads to a contract, the basis of government, and thus promotes peace. So "The final cause, end, or design of men (who naturally love liberty, and dominion over others) . . . is the foresight of their own preservation. . . ."[11]

Except under compulsion and by force, men won't obey such "laws of nature as *justice, equity, modesty, mercy,* and, in sum, *doing to others as we would be done to*. . . ." These laws are contrary to our nature, which is to preserve ourselves and to indulge our passions, which "carry us to partiality, pride, revenge, and the like." Therefore, "covenants, without the sword, are but words and of no strength to secure a man at all."[12] Men will naturally resort to barbarism and cruelty in the absence of external restraint. According to Hobbes, men could never govern themselves, for each, seeking to preserve himself, would always compete and contend with others.

True and False Are Merely Attributes of Speech

Indirectly Hobbes promoted, for the first time in modern Western history, the theory of relativism. True, at times in his treatise, especially in Part IV, he does quote and interpret Scripture, apparently taking its authority seriously. But he has ulterior motives for doing so, made clear by his use of Scripture within the context of his arguments and overall design. He uses passages as proof-texts, first, to prove that a sovereign ruler or ruling body must have religious authority and, second, to deny to the Roman Catholic Church, or any church for that matter, any claim to secular authority.

Despite his use of the Word, he basically has a disdain and distrust for words as instruments of truth. Man's appetites and desires for pleasure and power are such that he simply designates as good or evil that which he loves or hates. "But whatsoever is the object of any man's appetite or desire," asserts Hobbes, "that is it which he for his part calleth *good*; and the object of his hate and aversion, *evil*. . . . For these words . . . are ever used with relation to the person that useth them: there being nothing simply and absolutely so; nor any common rule of good and evil to be taken from nature of the objects themselves. . . ."

Judgments as to good or bad, virtuous or vicious, right or wrong, would thus all seem to be fickle. "For true and false," says Hobbes, "are attributes of speech, not of things. And where speech is not, there is neither truth nor falsehood." Each sense-bound man is alternately attracted to or repulsed by objects that in themselves are neither good nor bad. Man designates things as good or evil according to his tastes. Therefore, where there is speech, or words, every human judgment must be relative, neither true nor false, but true or false only relatively—that is, to the person rendering the judgment. "Error there may be," Hobbes continues, "as when we expect that which shall not be, or suspect what has not been; but in neither case can a man be charged with untruth."[13] Apparently man is in no position to grasp anything like the truth and thus can't be "charged with untruth" either.

Hobbes even denies the possibility that collectively men can arrive at anything approaching the truth. The greatest philosophers can't transcend their sense-bound minds to perceive general moral truths. "For moral philosophy is nothing but the science of what is good and evil in the conversation and society of mankind. *Good* and *evil* are names that signify our appetites and aversions, which in different tempers, customs, and doctrines of men are different. . . ."[14] In such words we can see the beginning of cultural relativism, a movement that didn't arrive on the scene with any real force until the nineteenth and twentieth centuries. Cultural relativism holds that the designations of good and evil vary from culture to culture according to custom and preference more than anything else. It's the view that "*x* is right" in our culture because "we like *x*." Cultural relativists, like Hobbes, are also most often ethical relativists, holding that there are no moral absolutes. From the fact that cultures differ in their definitions of right and wrong, they arrive at the conclusion—by way of a *non sequitur*—that "there is no such property as rightness."[15]

Seen from Hobbes's perspective, man's condition appears hopeless. "No discourse whatsoever," he says, "can end in absolute knowledge of fact, past or to come."[16]

The Might of the Civil Sovereign Makes Right

In what, then, lies our hope? Not in the moral insights of philosophers and theologians. Any "common rule of good or evil" must come "from the person . . . whom men disagreeing shall by consent set up and make his sentence the rule thereof."[17] For Hobbes, this person is the sovereign, whose authority is absolute. In disputes, his might makes right—in matters civil as well as ecclesiastical.

To Hobbes, it follows that not only the authority of the king but also the obedience of his subjects must be absolute in every matter. "And because [the king] is a sovereign," argues Hobbes, "he requireth obedience to all his own . . . the civil laws; in which also are contained all the laws of nature . . . the laws of God: for besides the laws of nature, and the laws of the Church, which are part of the civil law (for the Church that can make laws is the Commonwealth), there be no other laws divine."[18] In the civil laws of the king are included all the laws of nature. Beyond the laws dictated by the king there is no law, not even a separate law of God to which men might turn for help, for the king alone can interpret the law of God for men. Because it's impossible for men, either subjectively or objectively, to arrive at anything resembling the truth, the sovereign must dictate and enforce the law.

Because of the relativity of human judgment, even when interpreting divine Scripture, people need a final arbiter to decide for them what is right. This job of interpreting the words and will of God must also fall to the king. "For the points of doctrine concerning the kingdom of God have so great influence on the kingdom of man as not to be determined but by them that under God have the sovereign power." Normally when we obey authority, says Hobbes, it's always only men whom we obey anyway: "So that it is evident that whatsoever we believe, upon no other reason than what is drawn from authority of men only, and their writings, whether they be sent from God or not, is faith in men only." All faith is faith in men only. That being the case, we might as well place all our faith in the authority of one man, the sovereign and "chief pastor,"[19] who can provide us with peace and safety. To him alone we should owe our allegiance.

So absolute and supreme must be the rule of the king that should he misinterpret, misuse, deny, even oppose the Christian faith, men must still obey him. "And when the civil sovereign is an infidel," declares Hobbes, "every one of his own subjects that resisteth him sinneth against the laws of God (for such are the laws of nature). . . ." So how is a believer to live under an unbelieving sovereign? How is he to deal with laws that contradict the articles and rules of his faith? He must remember that his faith "is internal and invisible. . . ."[20] If he must violate his conscience to obey the king, he incurs no sin, claims Hobbes. The sin, if any, belongs to the king. And what happens if the Christian decides out of conscience to disobey the king anyway? He must accept the legitimate authority of the king to punish him.

Thus it's a man—a king but still a man, not God—who makes right. In this sense civil as well as moral laws may be taken to be man-made. They are made by the sovereign leader, who is the soul of the Leviathan, namely, the Commonwealth, a great "mortal god" instituted by men who have "willingly" transferred their rights to another, one man (or body of men).

Unfortunately, Hobbes overlooked a major flaw in his political theory. His system of government couldn't bring anything like permanent peace if man by nature is prone to conflict and competition. For in a Hobbesian world, people would still remain in a perpetual state of war with one another—if not neighbor with neighbor, then country with country—because human likes and dislikes, as Hobbes claims, must always differ. With all the varied opinions and tastes, with man's desire for "liberty" and "dominion over others," not even a potentate of the first magnitude could keep the peace for long. At the least, as Bertrand Russell points out, "international anarchy" would remain and always pose a threat to the Hobbesian state. If there is any validity to the position of Hobbes, Russell continues, it must argue "in favour of international government."[21] Therefore, by implication, if one were to continue to take Hobbes seriously, he would eventually have to affirm the need for a "new world order" and a "one world" government. We can only hope that humankind will never be willing to allow one "mortal god" to rule the world.

INFLUENCE OF THE MEGA-IDEA

Throughout *Leviathan* Hobbes reveals himself to be mainly an empiricist, materialist, and determinist. Because Hobbes denies the existence of "immaterial substances" and a "free will"—or at least claims that it's absurd to speak of them—he also reveals himself to be in some sense a nominalist, one who believes that man is "equipped with sensitive faculties only" and therefore doesn't possess a distinct intellect with which to grasp kinds, classes, and other subtleties.[22] He assumes that the mind and everything about it, including any putative intellect, is the product of the senses. For Hobbes, existence (matter) seems to precede essence (intellect, soul), whereas the old philosophers and Christian theologians believed that essence precedes existence.

By means of such an error, one can easily infer, as modern thinkers have, that if the senses create the mind, the mind of man creates the idea of God and God's laws. We have seen in our time the materialism of Hobbes carried to its logical extreme. Positivists tell us that figurative, metaphysical, and theological statements are meaningless because meaningful statements must be sensuous descriptions or logical inferences verifiable by the senses. Asserting that humans have no free will, behaviorists tell us that we are conditioned to be what we are by our environments, and geneticists tell us that we are programmed to be what we are by our genes. Meanwhile, the existentialists, chiming in like a chorus, tell us that God doesn't exist and life is meaningless.

The nature of the Hobbesian view of man and society comes into clearer focus when we assess the impact it's still having on us today. The effects, combining with other effects since his time, are complex but distinguishable. Rational observers of culture should be able to see that Hobbes and his kind largely rule the day. Today man, not God, does make right. Broadly speaking, however, the man-centered materialism of Hobbes has led to three main consequences that affect our life and thought today.

The Exaltation of Scientific Rationalism

Of course, Hobbes wasn't the first to assert that sense experience alone could give us true knowledge. Francis Bacon in his first aphorism of his *Novum Organum* (1620) declares, "Man, being the servant and interpreter of nature, can do and understand so much and so much only as he has observed in fact or in thought of the course of nature: beyond this he neither knows anything nor can do anything."[23] A generation later it was Hobbes (and John Locke) who bore this idea into the social and political arenas. In turn, the idea was propelled further into the mainstream of Western culture by the innumerable discoveries in science within the short span of a few centuries. After Galileo came Newton, and after Newton came Linnaeus, Cuvier, Lyell, and countless others, many of whom weren't materialists but theists. As we will see later, it wasn't until Darwin's time that materialism overflowed its banks and washed into people's everyday lives. When Bacon asserted, "beyond this he neither knows anything nor can do anything" and Hobbes a generation later concurred, they dropped an ever-tightening noose around the necks of scientific thinkers and philosophers. By establishing sense experience as the boundary beyond which the mind can't pass, they devalued other methods of thought and fields of study, subordinating them to scientific inquiry and submitting them, in turn, to empirical investigation. They made scientific rationalism the litmus test for all knowledge. Compared to the truths of science, the truth claims of speculative philosophy, arts and letters, and theology seemed more and more unsubstantial and in fact meaningless.

Today we have seen the bias for scientific rationalism greatly affect many areas of modern academic and intellectual life. Because the scientific view predominates in the universities, scientific and technological research is more highly prized than more traditional areas of study. The grant money flows into science-oriented departments. And in just the last fifty years other fields, like psychology, sociology, and even business, have had to become more "scientific" to keep pace with the advancements of "true" science. Now when we think of a person who studies human society, we think of a social *scientist*. Professors of business are now also statisticians, quantitative analysts, and researchers who study and catalog organizational behavior. Meanwhile, humanities, arts, and philosophy departments have shrunk, as would-be careerists choose other majors.[24] English departments only thrive to the extent that they devote their resources to developing basic writing competencies in students and preparing them to enter the technological work force of the twenty-first century. The word is out. Students who want to survive in the modern economy are best advised to major in biology, computer science, or business. After all, what can a humanities major *do*?

Since the time of Hobbes, theology has been hit harder than any other traditional area of study. Viewed more and more as an arcane and wholly subjective discipline, it has been shunted off to the fringes of the culture. The "serious" theologians today have to be progressives, genuflecting before empirical science or withdrawing from the rational arena altogether into realms of mystery. Teilhard de Chardin (1881-1955), for example, is admired for having first fitted the theory of evolution into his unorthodox theology. Rudolf Bultmann (1884-1976) is applauded for his efforts to demythologize Scripture. And Karl Barth (1886-1968) is heralded as the father of modern Protestant theology for confirming that there is indeed a supernatural *kerygma* (proclamation) that pervades and transcends tradition and the flawed texts of Scripture, thus guaranteeing that the essential truths of Christianity remain intact.

Many of today's progressive theologians simply remind us that Hobbes and other materialists have been for centuries bullying the theologians into uncertainty and diffidence. As early as *Leviathan*, Hobbes first lays the ax to theological tradition by proclaiming that he won't ascribe to God any feelings—"repentance, anger, mercy," "hope, desire," or "rational appetite"—"unless metaphorically, meaning not the passion, but the effect. . . ." Therefore, he "will attribute to God nothing but what is warranted by natural reason. . . ."[25] It's no wonder that the traditional theologians—Augustine, Aquinas, Luther, and Calvin—have fallen out of favor today. In the world of Hobbes, everything is either sense or *non*-sense.

But the amount of faith that many modern people place in natural reason—and even scientific rationalism—is unwarranted. Materialists like Hobbes and his ideological successors held that only sense experiences comprise the mind and that philosophical and theological statements are meaningless.[26] They reached such conclusions based, in part, on the questionable assumptions that this *natural* reason alone is reliable and that observation of material causes and effects is sufficient for discovering truth—namely, all that we *need* to know. Yet if there is no truth beyond sense experience and all human judgments are relative, how can we even speak of "scientific truth"? To do science, we have to be convinced that certain principles of logic are true and that it's more ethical to report data and draw inferences correctly than to do otherwise. In this way, science, too, must operate on certain assumptions—epistemological and ethical—that have nothing to do with sense data.

A form of reasoning that debunks all other forms of reasoning refutes itself, for it must assume as true the same principles of logic by which others, philosophers and theologians, reach their conclusions.

"Natural reason" has brought us to the very limits of skepticism as it tells us that everything in the universe is governed by randomness and chance. For in doing so, it must deny that any meaning exists whatsoever. Citing one of the ironies of modern thought, William Barret, an American philosopher, has observed that "the offspring" (science) has denied "the parent" (the mind).[27] Seen in this light, natural reason is little more than a dog chasing its own tail, and our much-vaunted scientific progress is a fool's game.

The Rupture of the Sacred and the Secular

Naturally, as people gravitate toward a materialistic view of mind and society, they begin to relegate the sacred to the realm of the irrational, or merely subjective. The sensuous becomes the only realm in which reason can legitimately operate. Outside of sense experience all is incomprehensible and therefore irrelevant to "real life." By subordinating the divine to the human, Hobbes was the first major thinker to drive a wedge between the secular and the sacred. How could anyone, after Hobbes, ever again rely on religion when it no longer rested on fact but on faith? To Hobbes, remember, faith was something "internal and invisible," quite distinct from the world of sense experiences in which secular policies and practices are carried out.

Today we see signs of this rupture, it seems to me, in the continuing debate over the meaning of "the separation of church and state." Hobbes as much as Locke affected the way we view the relationship between church (in his view, the realm of speculation and dogma) and the state (in his view, the realm of the sensible and scientific). It was these men who fired the first shot in a culture war that today has as much to do with presuppositions as it does with the U.S. Constitution. Using the words of America's founders, each side today marshals evidence for its interpretation of the founders' original intent. As in a chess match, each side seems to checkmate the other with lists of quotations. Evangelicals point, for example, to Jefferson's evident theism: "Can the liberties of a nation be thought secure when we have removed their only firm basis, a conviction in the minds of people that these liberties are of the gift of God?"[28] Secularists counter by demonstrating Jefferson's anti-Christian bias: "And the day will come when the mystical generation of Jesus, by the supreme being as his father in the womb of a Virgin Mary, will be classed with the fable of the generation of Minerva in the brain of Jupiter. . . ." Secularists then cinch the matter, they think, with Jefferson's conclusion: "But we may hope that the dawn of reason and freedom of thought in the United States will do away [with] all these artificial scaffoldings."[29]

On one side are those who fear that Christianity will be driven altogether out of American life; on the other, those who fear that Christians will impose their faith on everyone else. Underlying the debate is a suspicion on each side about the motives of the other. We Christians, naturally, oppose the secularist agenda, but we must do so, we must realize, regardless of what the Constitution or the founding fathers say. The real culture war is being waged over presuppositions, beliefs, and worldviews that predate the founding of the United States.

We may also see evidence of this schism between the secular and sacred in the way many of us live today in the United States. On the one hand, we have our secular life, the pace of which is dictated more by our senses than our intellects. We root raucously for football teams, sashay around in designer clothes, view salacious movies and music videos, and as consumers purchase everything from Altimas to Zima. We place career before family, run up credit card debts, and as parents raise good little materialistic girls and boys. Thus we eagerly embrace the crude but robust materialism of the age. On the other hand, we devote little time or thought to the sacred. Even though 93 percent of us, according to Gallup, believe in God, only 34 percent of us read the Bible weekly, only 42 percent of us attend church services weekly, and only 17 percent of us attend an adult Sunday school weekly.[30] We have little time for reflection, much less for prolonged Bible study or prayer. We regard the sacred as something strictly personal and subjective, and we behave as though our real lives and all real truths are to be found in the secular—in our science and technology, in our entertainment and politics. The sacred can't pervade or undergird our lives if our priorities are material and personal. The sacred is at best just another diversion in our hectic lives.

But if we believe that God exists, we can't live a double-minded existence. Either we accept what the sacred says about God, man, and the world (the secular), or we accept what the secular says about the world, man, and God (the sacred). This issue is crucial for Christians because we are called to love God with all our hearts, minds, souls, and strength. As long as we try to have it both ways, trying to serve Mammon *and* God, the secular *and* the sacred, our faith must remain unstable. And if our faith is unstable, we must not expect to "receive anything from the Lord" (Jas. 1:7). To exist as believers, we must, explains James I. Packer in summarizing the thought of Kierkegaard, "take the risk of whole-hearted *practical* commitment to God in Christ" (italics mine).[31] In short, we must *practice* what we preach; we must *walk* our talk. As long as we Christians remain double-minded, the world may rightly accuse us of hypocrisy.

The Devaluation of Tradition and Revelation

Because the ever-changing scenery of the secular holds more allure for people, it being more "real" than the sacred, people today tend to most value all that is new, trendy, avant-garde. But our current bias in favor of "progress" arose over 300 years ago. The empiricism of Hobbes, Locke, Hume, and others, according to Mortimer Adler in his book *Ten Philosophical Mistakes*, represented the first radical departure from the traditional philosophical thought that had begun with Aristotle.[32] Their view that all knowledge, as well as mind, arises from sense experience was an error in thought on top of which later philosophers built numerous other errors. Thus the first act of the first modern thinker, Hobbes, was to declare his autonomy from philosophical and theological tradition. The first step toward modernism was an act of defiance. In this way Hobbes and his successors set a precedent that holds to this day. Today nearly every tradition, especially religious tradition, is suspect.

Indeed, rebellion is a settled habit of mind today, affecting all alike, like a reflex. If the words written centuries ago by "ignorant men" or "dead white European males" no longer impress intellectuals, then how shall the words of parents carry any weight with their children? If the intellectuals enamored by materialism and skepticism are winking over the theological musings of the ancients, then how shall the words of teachers carry any weight with their students? Children, to be true to the spirit of the age, must look at everything cockeyed—doubtfully as well as suspiciously. When each new recording artist, "personality," or famous athlete is just a little more unorthodox than the one before—and when he is praised and rewarded for his eccentricity—we must naturally expect that fashions in thought and lifestyle within the pop culture will change faster than footwear. Intellectuals don't want to be like their predecessors, children don't want to be like their parents, and no one wants to be "square." So people keep jettisoning the past as they strive for "progress." They thus prize, above all else, their private interpretations of life and adopt or discard each man-made value that appears on the ever-new horizon.

As rebellion has become reflexive and habitual, its effects—cynicism and incivility—have also become more widespread. Cynicism is a pose that people strike today. They sneer and snarl at the past, even with little knowledge of it, if any. If they think of Europe and America, they imagine plundering conquistadors, whip-wielding slave-traders, leering Victorians, and preying robber barons. If they think of Christianity, they imagine Inquisitors in long dark robes, witch-hunters in pilgrim's dress, and hypocritical preachers in big-finned Cadillacs. The more people caricature and stereotype tradition, unfortunately, the less respectful they become of people in the present. The revolt against the past thus also leads to revolting behavior. Young and old, unwilling to accept traditional standards, daily disregard the rights of others to courtesy, personal space, and safety. Drivers no longer yield as often the right of way; loiterers in aisles no longer step aside. People swear and even spit at others. Meanwhile, antiheroes like Howard Stern and Roseanne become national celebrities, flaunting their fame and fortune. Material rewards, as always, serve as the best reinforcement for behavior, right or wrong.

By now we should recognize what kind of world the materialism of Hobbes offers us. In a world governed by the desire for self-preservation and bounded by the knowledge of the senses, nothing noble or sublime can really exist. Everyone will always be courting their own comfort and pleasure, their own ends, while an elite few, by means of might and money, take it upon themselves to impose *their* man-made rules on the sense-distracted many. In such a world, as individuals realize the "truth" that morals are merely man-made, they will more and more lose faith in traditional morality and revealed religion (now already seen as just one of many "man-made devices" for controlling behavior). Every hero will be regarded as selfishly motivated, every saint as psychologically aberrant. Men and women shouldn't then be surprised by the moral chaos that ensues. After all, "The moral code," Will Durant sagely observes, "loses aura and force as its human origin is revealed, and as divine surveillance and sanctions are removed."[33]

Yet if God created the natural order, as Hobbes concedes by referring to him as the Artificer (and as 92 percent of Americans still believe today), we must grant two fundamental points about ourselves and God. First, we must believe that man's reason, as part of the natural order, was also created and actuated by God. Therefore, we mustn't permit natural reason to subvert or supplant the authority of God in matters of truth and morality. Natural reason must operate in subordination to the will of God. It is cosmic presumption of the first magnitude for the created to marginalize the Creator.

Second, because God exists, we must regard moral law, like all natural laws, to be the creation of God, not man. To believe otherwise is to hold a fragmented view of creation. God created *everything* within—and outside of—the purview of man. Man *generates* thoughts and emotions, but God *created* thought and emotion. Man feels moral sentiments or ponders moral principles, but God created morality, just as God created truth, scientific and spiritual. But because we are created, because our senses and minds can't fully comprehend God, we mustn't conclude that we have no access to his truth. Nor should we assume that our only access is subjective. A God of truth, goodness, and love, if real, wouldn't abandon us in a prisonhouse of base impulses and sensuous experiences. He wouldn't be true to his nature if he kept us hopelessly hobbled by our own "mind-forged manacles."

Although we can't deny the subjective dimension of our experiences, we can, orthodox Christianity maintains, nevertheless approach God's objective truth by means of his revelation of himself—in creation, Christ, and Holy Scripture. True, God is so great, as Anselm put it, that he is *that than which nothing greater can be conceived.* Yet God is also personal, capable of breaking into history and into our lives—or else we should be forever stranded and isolated, deluded and forlorn, no more than mere cogs in the impersonal machinery of creation. In return for our worship, God gives us a true identity in relationship with him, nature, and others, a small price to pay for submission.

Inadvertently, perhaps, Hobbes cracked open still another door. By subordinating God and grace to man and nature, he was able to make a case in *Leviathan* for preferring monarchy over democracy, for permitting one man, a monarch, to make right. But, relying on many of the same presuppositions, later thinkers, under the banners of liberty and individualism, could make an even more appealing case for exalting *each* man as his own authority. Each man, a virtual law unto himself, would then possess the authority to make right. Only a century after Hobbes, various revolutionaries and Romantics would be raising just such a hue and cry: Why should a king, or a religion for that matter, be any better equipped to define human rights and wrongs than any rational or sensitive man is?

First, however, a new thinker, David Hume, would have to come onto the scene to convince other thinkers that they should, first, doubt the veracity of even their own sense experiences and, second, regard all knowledge to be subjective. By means of this radical skepticism about knowledge, he would originate yet another mega-idea and propel modern thinkers even farther away from the truth that God makes right, not man, and that man must, first and foremost, understand the ways of God.

"Every Man Possesses an Innate Moral Sense"

In the Scottish National Gallery, Edinburgh, hangs a portrait of David Hume painted by Allan Ramsay. Most evident in the portrait is the magnificent corpulence of the man. Cutting quite a figure, he sports a red coat and vest, both trimmed with wide gold embroidery, with a lacy cuff half-concealing one pudgy hand. Above the white scarf tightly wrapped around his neck appears his fleshy baby face, double-chinned, with a faint but genial smirk on his fulsome lips and a steely indifference in his pale close-set eyes. Atop his head sits a powdered periwig, too flat and small in proportion to his broad girth. He looks like a well-fed man in his prime, confident of his abilities, satisfied in his wants, well-fitted for social life.

This figure is no doubt similar to the one that graced the salons of France in 1763, years after Hume had written his famous works—*A Treatise of Human Nature*, *An Enquiry Concerning Human Understanding*, and *Four Dissertations*. His earliest work, *A Treatise of Human Nature*, had predated the work of Voltaire, Diderot, and the anti-Christian *philosophes*, thus establishing him as one of the vanguard of the Enlightenment. In Paris, at age fifty-two, he was lionized by the Parisian literati, among whom he was especially beloved by the ladies. Once at a party, when a few *philosophes* were growing jealous of his fame, d'Alembert remarked of him, quoting the Fourth Gospel: "*Et verbum caro factum est*" ("and the word was made flesh"). At once a female admirer rejoined, "*Et verbum carum factum est*" ("and the word was made lovable"). Unappreciated in England and pursued in

Edinburgh by the Presbyterian divines who wanted to charge him with infidelity, Hume greatly enjoyed the attentions he received in France.[1]

Yet in Hume we find no frivolous fashion-setter or attention-seeker, but a genius of the first order. Thomas Hobbes, by comparison, was a crude and hasty reasoner. Commenting on the prose of Hobbes, Russell says, "He is impatient of subtleties. . . ." And, "he wields the battle-axe better than the rapier."[2] Hume, on the other hand, displays in his writing a subtlety and thoroughness that readily secured for him his reputation by the middle of his life. So admired was he in his day that he corresponded with Montesquieu and Voltaire, the latter of whom referred to Hume in later life as "my St. David." He also met Turgot, d'Holbach, and Diderot; befriended Rousseau and Adam Smith; and influenced Bentham, Gibbon, and Kant, the latter of whom declared that it was Hume who had awakened him from his "dogmatic slumbers."

In our time the reputation of Hume remains strong. Bertrand Russell, one of the great philosophers of the twentieth century, gives Hume high praise: "He developed to its logical conclusion the empirical philosophy of Locke and Berkeley. . . . To refute him has been, ever since he wrote, a favourite pastime among metaphysicians. For my part, I find none of their refutations convincing. . . ."[3] According to Will and Ariel Durant, David Hume "was in himself the Enlightenment for the British Isles; there, except in political vision, he was essentially all that a dozen *philosophes* were for France."[4] To this day his criticisms of the classical design argument for the existence of God are considered virtually unassailable. In this regard, according to many, he set Anselm (1033-1109), Aquinas (1225-1274), and William Paley (1743-1805) on their ears. So much is this opinion still common today that recently one modern Christian philosopher thought it necessary to devote four and a half pages of his considerable talent to refuting Hume's by now classic criticisms of the design argument.[5]

Overall, the philosophical thought of Hume is complex. Because he advanced a number of formidable ideas, we can't oversimplify his philosophy, rightly labeled as skepticism and subjectivism. Still, it's fair to say that he advanced one major error, one mega-idea, that has tended to survive in the popular mind well into this century. Perhaps without intending to, Hume gave birth to a simple but powerful modern idea— namely, that each human being possesses within him or her an innate, wholly trustworthy moral sense. To grasp this simple mega-idea, however, we will first have to examine in this chapter two complex lines of his thought that undergird the mega-idea under consideration.

By unleashing yet another mega-idea, David Hume unquestionably propelled Western culture toward a subjectivist and relativistic approach to morality and truth, thus turning people inward on themselves, away from traditional notions of the objectivity of morality and truth. Like the other mega-ideas in this section of the book, this one has contributed to the growing sense today that man is an autonomous agent, capable of emancipating himself from tradition and rejecting revelation, the objective Word of God, whenever it suits him.

THE SENSIBLE, SENSITIVE, SENSATE MAN

Like Hobbes, Hume was undoing, philosophically, nearly 2,000 years of tradition dating back to Aristotle and kept alive well into the Renaissance by Christian theologians. Man, whose intellect had always been deemed an instrument of God when trained by reason and reined in by Scripture, now was to become an instrument of habit, more driven by necessity than ennobled by liberty. In fact, man no longer possessed an intellect separate from the senses but only a mind comprised solely of impressions and associations of ideas engendered by sense experiences. With this background in mind, we need to grasp the breadth and depth of the Humean mega-idea that continues to influence modern thought today.

The Mind Is Merely a Heap of Sense Impressions

"Hume begins," claim the Durants, "by accepting as a starting point the empiricism of Locke: all ideas are ultimately derived from experience through impressions."[6] Any ideas we possess are simply representations, only relatively accurate, of more intense impressions left by the senses on the mind. Like Hobbes, Locke, and Berkeley, then, he asserts that "the mind, so far as it functions as a cognitive instrument, is entirely a sensitive faculty, without any trace of intellectuality about it."[7] Hume, in his youthful *Treatise* (1739-1740), makes this definition of the mind clear: "what we call a *mind*, is nothing but a heap or collection of different perceptions, united together by certain relations, and suppos'd, tho' falsely, to be endow'd with a perfect simplicity and identity."[8] Ideas are held together by a principle of association, but all ideas, no matter how abstract they may seem to be, he claims in his more mature *An Enquiry Concerning Human Understanding* (1748), are derived from sense experiences only. "[W]hen we analyze our thoughts or ideas, however compounded or sublime," says Hume, "we always find that they resolve themselves into such simple ideas as were copied from a precedent feeling [sense] or sentiment. Even those ideas, which, at first view, seem the most wide of this origin, are found upon a nearer scrutiny, to be derived from it."[9] Hume even says that our idea of God is limited by our sense experiences and the impressions they create in our minds, concluding "that every idea which we examine is copied from a similar impression."[10] Hence, to Hume there is nothing to the mind "additional to the mental states."[11] The senses and sentiments establish the limits of all our thinking.

Naturally it's hard to see how anything like free will can possibly exist if the mind is solely a sense-bound instrument in both its origin and function. In Part I, Section VII of *An Enquiry*, Hume limits liberty, that is, any putative free will, to necessity. When considering liberty, he insists, philosophers should aim their inquiry not at questions of the soul but should confine themselves to a simple question: "namely, the operations of body and of brute unintelligent matter; and try whether they can there form any idea of causation and necessity, except that of a constant conjunction of objects, and subsequent inference of the mind from one to another."[12]

If we confine ourselves to the narrow realm of science, claims Hume, we shall discover that this "fantastical desire of shewing liberty," at best a mere "hypothetical liberty," is based on our understandable but questionable motive to explain behavior. But really, "By liberty . . . we can only mean *a power of acting or not acting, according to the determinations of the will*," a will that is necessarily just a mere component of the sense-bound mind.[13] The Durants concur in concluding that this line of Hume's thinking leads to a denial of free will: "Freedom of will, in this dissolving view, is impossible: . . ; 'will' is merely an idea flowing into action."[14] Thus, when the young man David decides to remain single rather than marry the young maiden Agnes, his choice is based merely on the sum of his impressions and habits as they have fitted him for life.

Belief Is Never Rational

Bertrand Russell writes, "The most important part of the whole Treatise is the section called 'Of Knowledge and Probability.'"[15] In this section Hume goes to great lengths to demonstrate that every examination of causation results in uncertain knowledge. Carrying us to the outer limits of skepticism, Hume asserts, "There is no object, which implies the existence of any other if we consider these objects in themselves, and never look beyond the ideas which we form of them."[16] All we have in our own minds are the ideas—namely, the representations—of the objects we perceive. From the standpoint of pure experience, we can't be certain that one object causes another, even if we have witnessed it do so before. In our minds we can see the idea of the object and our past associations related to that object, but we can't see the power of causation in any objects outside our minds. We can only affirm causality when we observe, in this moment, one object directly acting upon another, as in the case of a struck billiard ball colliding with another and driving it into a corner pocket. After observing the causality of the moment, though, we can't affirm that any other billiard ball will ever be struck, collide with another, or enter a pocket, even with the memories of billiard play still fresh in our minds.

Hume continues this line of thinking in *An Enquiry*, carrying this point even farther: "This proposition, that causes and effects are discoverable, not by reason but by experience, will readily be admitted with regard to such objects, as we remember to have once been altogether unknown to us; since we must be conscious of the utter inability, which we then lay under, of foretelling what would arise from them."[17] In this way Hume denies the primacy of reason, or rationality, as an instrument for making sense of the world of causality. He is also insisting that we abandon all hope of ever inferring or predicting, in advance of an experience, causal regularity in nature, for every object, just like those once unknown to us, is in some sense ever new. The revolving earth has made the sun appear to rise in the east many, many times in the past; nevertheless, we can't be certain that sunrise will occur again tomorrow. After all, we haven't yet directly experienced—outside of our minds—tomorrow's possible, or *not* possible, sunrise. We can with certainty only seize the moment in which the experience occurs. Thus Hume transports us into a twilight zone of pure skepticism.

Indeed, to Hume, there is no such thing as rational belief. Where knowledge is concerned, Hume arrives in his youthful *Treatise* at a point of utter skepticism:

> Thus, all probable reasoning is nothing but a species of sensation. 'Tis not solely in poetry and music, we must follow our taste and sentiment, but likewise in philosophy. When I am convinc'd of any principle, 'tis only an idea, which strikes more strongly upon me. When I give the preference to one set of arguments above another, I do nothing but decide from my feeling concerning the superiority of their influence. Objects have no discoverable connexion together; nor is it from any other principle but custom operating upon the imagination, that we can draw any inference from the appearance of one to the existence of another.[18]

At best, because "all probable reasoning is nothing but a species of sensation," any belief is only based on a "feeling concerning the superiority" of some "influence" felt by a person. Only "custom operating upon the imagination" leads us to infer "from the appearance" of one object "to the existence of another." Yet if relationships in space and time are only inferred by means of the "imagination," then perhaps everything is illusory. In *An Enquiry*, Hume does take this next leap into skepticism: "if the external world be once called in question, we shall be at a loss to find arguments, by which we may prove the existence of that Being [the external world] or any of his attributes."[19] In this way, as Russell puts it, Hume "ended . . . with the conviction that belief is never rational since we know nothing."[20] Ironically, Hume began as an empiricist in the tradition of Bacon, Hobbes, Locke, and Berkeley, but in the end he refuted empiricism itself.

What, then, is left to us as a gauge of truth, especially moral truth, if belief is never rational? What might be the role of reason in any inquiry? Considering Hume's original empiricism, his belief that the scientific method reliably leads to truth, we must find his answer to be bewildering, especially if we would wish to cling to anything like scientific truth. Hume's response may be to some an overstatement,[21] but he says it anyway: "Reason is, and ought to be, the slave of passion."[22] We certainly can't overlook the consequences and implications of the view advanced by Hume in this statement. This view, in its own way, is consistent with Hume's overall epistemology and leads logically and inexorably to his next conclusion, our mega-idea.

Moral Feelings Are Innate and Reliable

Obviously, if the mind is merely a heap of sense impressions and belief is never grounded in reason (nor should it be), as Hume maintains, then we will have difficulty explaining the inducements and motivations for moral behavior within a civil society. To overcome this difficulty, Hume returns briefly to the empiricism of Hobbes but mainly foreshadows the hedonistic ethics of utilitarianism, a movement that didn't begin until a few decades later with Jeremy Bentham (1748-1832) and James Mill (1773-1836), the father of John Stuart Mill.

In Book III of *A Treatise*, entitled "Of Morals," Hume asserts that "Moral distinctions [are] not derived from reason" but from passion. Reason can't compel us to act or not act: "reason has no influence on any passions and actions. . . ." Reason is powerless before the mighty torrent of the passions. It's also an inadequate judge of what is right or wrong, true or false. Because "our passions, volitions, and actions, are not susceptible of any such agreement or disagreement," they can't possibly "be pronounced either true or false, and be either contrary or conformable to reason." Morality, then, "consists not in . . . any *matter of fact*, which can be discover'd by the understanding."[23] Hume thus holds that moral distinctions are subjective and emotional, not objective and rational. Echoing Hobbes and foreshadowing Bentham, Hume says that our feelings of approbation and blame, pleasure and pain dictate what is virtuous and what is vicious:

> . . . virtue is distinguished by the pleasure, and vice by the pain, that any action, sentiment or character gives us by the mere view and contemplation. This decision is very commodious; because

it reduces us to this simple question, Why any action or sentiment upon the general view or survey, gives a certain satisfaction
or uneasiness, in order to shew the origin of its moral rectitude
or depravity, without looking for any incomprehensible relations
and qualities, which never did exist in nature, nor even in our
imagination, by any clear and distinct conception.[24]

By the time he wrote *An Enquiry*, he was so certain that morality is subjective that he defended his view in the following way, unmistakably
demonstrating the faith that he placed in feelings:

The mind of man is so formed by nature that, upon the appearance of certain characters, dispositions and actions, it immediately feels the sentiment of approbation or blame; nor are there
any emotions more essential to its frame and constitution. The
characters which engage our approbation are chiefly such as contribute to the peace and security of human society; as the characters which excite blame are chiefly such as tend to public
detriment and disturbance. . . . [25]

Unlike Hobbes but like the utilitarians, however, Hume found the subjective moral sense to be reliable: the characters we praise chiefly "contribute to the peace and security of human society"; the characters we
blame "tend to public detriment and disturbance." Not only that, but
he found the moral sense to be a wholly sufficient guide. "Nothing can
. . . concern us more," says Hume, "than our own sentiment of pleasure
and uneasiness; and if these be favourable to virtue, and unfavourable
to vice, no more can be requisite to the regulation of our conduct and
behaviour."[26]

Underlying our feelings of approbation and disapprobation, then,
is a trustworthy natural sympathy, "the chief source of moral distinctions." Moreover, this natural mechanism of sympathy is innate: "a
sense of morals is a principle inherent in the soul, and one of the most
powerful that enters into the composition."[27] By our feelings of approbation or disapprobation, pleasure or displeasure, we can naturally
determine whether a character trait or action is virtuous or vicious. Thus
an innate moral sense serves as the basis of our moral judgments. Can

it err? Hume doesn't address this issue, nor does he link the moral sense to evolutionary development as Darwin was to do later. By Appendix II to the second *Enquiry*, he regards it to be not only an innate sense of sympathy in man but an original instinct of benevolence or humanity. In fact, this sense of "humanity" becomes "a special original instinct prompting [us], *ceteris paribus*, to prefer pleasure to pain, no matter whose."[28]

In sum, to Hume, say the Durants, "Our moral sense comes not from Heaven but from sympathy." The principle of sympathy—or inborn benevolence—"and not the voice of God (as Rousseau and Kant were to imagine) is the origin of conscience." Clinching the argument that Hume does indeed hold that each man possesses an innate, ever trustworthy moral sense, the Durants add, "This law of sympathy, of communal attraction is, says Hume, as universal and illuminating in the moral world as the law of gravitation in the material cosmos."[29]

THE INFLUENCE OF THE MEGA-IDEA

Ironically, this mega-idea, which has influenced us greatly today, was generated by a philosopher who, by his own admission, engaged in his skeptical philosophy mainly for the sake of his own amusement. It was simply an agreeable way for him to pass the time. Had he abandoned his musings, he said, "I *feel* I shou'd be a loser in point of pleasure; and this [pleasure] is the origin of my philosophy."[30] Hume as a true skeptic was also aware that he had to remain skeptical of his own skepticism and convictions because he knew that an "hour hence" the real world would mightily intrude—like indigestion after a meal of raw squid—upon the skeptic and the reader.[31] With this impracticality in mind, the Durants rightly conclude, "A skepticism that confessedly is abandoned in actual life must be wrong in theory, for practice is the final test of theory."[32]

Unquestionably, Western culture didn't feel the full impact of this mega-idea until the Romantic era burst onto the scene and a few subsequent mega-ideas pushed it into the modern mainstream. Nevertheless, in our time this mega-idea is as ubiquitous as graffiti, as intractable as the common cold. Today we are heirs, it seems to me, to three main consequences of Hume's general speculations as well as the mega-idea that each man possesses an innate moral sense, the sole test of which is inward and experiential.

A Radical Skepticism

If you have ever conversed with a youth who just completed a year of university training, you may have had your discussion interrupted abruptly when he asked, smirking, "Yes, but what is truth? What is reality?" When faced with such questions, we can hardly find a suitable response, for the skepticism of the inquirer is so entrenched as to be unsusceptible to appeals to common sense or objectivity. Today this skeptical stance is commonplace, not just among our youth and educators but also among the general population. After all, if I can trust my innate moral sense, why must I trust you or reason with you? "Hey, man, that's your reality. This is mine."

Throughout the twentieth century certain modern scientists have become skeptical of not only our but their knowledge of the world. In general, skepticism holds that what can't be proven by scientific reason shouldn't be believed; yet science today seems to challenge even empirical knowledge, as Hume did. Some modern atomists have argued that everything is made up of atoms, and so our perceptions of whole objects—for example, several paved lots full of pickups—are illusory.[33] Others, studying reason itself as an object, have arrived at an even more startling skepticism. Speaking of the type of scientist who engages in such study, C. S. Lewis explains: "his own reason appears to him as the epiphenomenon which accompanies chemical or electrical events in a cortex which is itself the by-product of a blind evolutionary process. His own logic, hitherto the king whom events in all possible worlds must obey, becomes merely subjective. There is no reason for supposing that it yields truth."[34] In our century, too, quantum physicists, inspired by the work of Werner Heisenberg, speak of an "uncertainty principle," which seems to portend a future for science in which no one will be certain that causality or regularity *really* occurs in the universe. Still more recently, some philosophers of science, notably Thomas Kuhn, have concluded that there is no "objective sense in which science is rational." According to J. P. Moreland, "Kuhn holds that there is no such thing as neutral facts or data. Observation is theory-laden; that is, our perception of the world is not a perception of a mind-independent 'given.' The 'world' we see is itself determined by our theories about the world." What is the radical skepticism that results from such a view? "Two different people with different paradigms or theories actually see different things."[35]

But full-blown skepticism of the kind advanced by Hume didn't appear in any widespread popular way until the 1960s. It does, after all, take a while for a mega-idea to trickle down to the bespectacled and sandaled youth. In that era skepticism became a virtue, a high-priestly vocation. Students were supposed to question everything. They were to challenge the values of their parents, the motivations of their leaders, the history and traditions of their country, the mores of society. "What is reality?" they asked, because presumably they wanted to be "real" themselves. Reality, they were told, wasn't what it seemed to be. It was; it wasn't. Mescaline and LSD, the Beatles with their dream of "strawberry fields forever," Jefferson Airplane with their command to "feed your head," and Jimi Hendrix with his challenge, "Are you experienced?"—all these influences beckoned the young to test the limits of litmus. They were to challenge everything, except of course their professors (unless they were challenging their professors to learn how to challenge other people's ideas better). And they were to question everything, except of course their own skepticism about reality, truth, and tradition.

Even worse, today this skepticism shows itself—Hobbes-like, as a distrust of truth claims and authority figures—among many of our young people. Students as young as nine and ten have little respect for their teachers. Teens frown at parents who counsel them, rolling their eyes as if to say, "Yeah, sure." Parents may love, reason, cajole, implore with all the fervor of a Mother Teresa, and yet the child, insensible to wisdom (because of course it's old-fashioned and uncool), will assume that any dispute over values involves a clash of realities—*mine* and *theirs*. And the defense for their skepticism is their untested, unsupported belief that they have an innate moral sense within them, a sure compass that will enable them to discern right from wrong without any reference to external authority—be it parental, institutional, or historical. If something pleases them, it must be right; if it displeases them, wrong. Truly, such skepticism is loony.

The Subordination of Faith to Reason

In declaring that reason ought to be the slave of passion, Hume was making a bold and dangerous claim. Nevertheless, he trusted reason—that is, *his* reason—just long enough also to take a parting shot at faith in several of his works. No wonder the atheistic *philosophes* of his day idolized him. And no wonder rationalistic subjectivists of one kind or another adore him today.

In particular, in *An Enquiry* Hume sets out to debunk miracles, just as he had done in *A Treatise*. By doing so successfully by means of reason, he fostered in Western thought an anti-supernatural bias. In launching his attack, he makes the by-now famous statement, "A wise man, therefore, proportions his belief to the evidence."[36] And then he sets about disproving, like a good naturalist, the reality of miracles: A miracle violates the laws of nature; the laws of nature can't be violated; hence miracles can't exist because we have never directly observed these laws violated. He concludes, hiding behind the words of a fictional friend, that religion should be left to the "vulgar and illiterate."[37] Even worse, he ends *An Enquiry* with an assertion dogmatic enough to shock a Salem witch-hunter:

> When we run over libraries, persuaded of these principles, what havoc must we make? If we take in our hand any volume; of divinity or school metaphysics, for instance; let us ask, *Does it contain any abstract reasoning concerning quantity or number?* No. *Does it contain any experimental reasoning concerning matter of fact and existence?* No. Commit it then to the flames: for it can contain nothing but sophistry and illusion.[38]

If Hume's hostility toward religion isn't evident in these words, then we only have to turn to his *Dialogues Concerning Natural Religion*, published after his death. In this book, through three characters, Demea (the orthodox Christian), Cleanthes (the Deist), and Philo (Hume, the skeptic), Hume makes it clear that he can respect Deism but he can't abide the orthodoxy of the unskeptical Christian, Demea, who departs, abashed and defeated, at the end of Part XI.[39]

If metaphysics, theology, and faith can't reside in the realm of reason, they must remain in the realm of passion or sentiment. But clearly this is no solution for theists who need reasons for their faith. If belief, as Hume maintains, is never grounded in reason, the believer can only take refuge in feeling, and feeling by itself, as anyone with an ounce of maturity knows, is an unreliable guide. Unfortunately, in this century Christians, it seems to me, have, like the surrounding culture, accepted the premise that belief is simply a matter of feeling. Thus many believers have been driven like sheep by the wrong masters into pietism or quietism, sometimes willingly withdrawing into a cozy safety, thereby abandoning the field of rational discourse in favor of the delights of subjectivity. Or they have become committed secularists who keep their theologizing to a minimum, in mixed company preferring to discuss even politics rather than religion. Faith, in Hume's world, after all, is irrational.

Sad to say, many Christians today have retreated from the battleground where ideas are debated because they fear either that reason might contaminate them or that they might fall before the sword of reason. Yet Christians must remember that their faith *is* rationally defensible. They must ever be ready to contend for the faith (Jude 3) and to give a reason for the hope that is in them (1 Pet. 3:15). Even Paul, in Acts 17:16-34, spoke boldly before the Athenian Areopagus, before the Epicureans and Stoics of his day, unafraid to engage in rational debate with them.

Professor Phillip E. Johnson of University of California Berkeley puts this modern prejudice against religious faith powerfully and succinctly: "One of the most important stereotypes in naturalistic thinking is that 'religion' is based on faith rather than reason, and that persons who believe in God are inherently unwilling to follow the truth wherever it may lead because that path leads to naturalism."[40] In short, intellectual theists just aren't as smart—or as well adjusted—as their agnostic and atheistic counterparts. Today thoughtful Christians must try to prove the world wrong.

Runaway Subjectivism

A subjectivism that holds that an internal moral sense is validated solely by feelings of pleasure and displeasure is committing at best a hedonistic error, at worst a solipsistic blunder of major proportions. The hedonistic error mistakes pleasure for the good and displeasure for the bad. This system works fine if I (and most others) find that charitable actions please and hateful actions displease. But what if John and Joan's pleasure is shooting up heroin? Or what if on a supposed scale of pleasures Dirk says that listening to Marilyn Manson is more pleasing and edifying than listening to Mozart whereas Deb claims that attending *Hamlet* is more pleasing and edifying than attending a hockey game? Or worse, what happens if the practice of abortion arouses my disapprobation but your approbation? How, then, can we say that there is any innate moral sense common to us all? The worst effect of this line of ethics is that it encourages solipsism, imprisoning every person inside his own subjectivity, his own sentiments, as he tries to decide right and wrong for himself—and others incidentally—on the basis of passion, since, of course, reason no longer has any claim to authority in matters of morality. A solipsist, believing that his own interior is all that exists, will in the end see everyone else as illusory objects or, worse, as means to his own ends. At this point morality must surely break down.

When my wayward impression is my truth and yours is yours, we have no real means of communicating. All we can really say, postmodern-style, is that you have your truth and lifestyle and I have mine. Or you feel one way, and I feel another. It's your opinion or my opinion. Then, to account for differences in personality, people can appeal to nonsensical clichés: "Perception is reality" or "Reality is what you make of it." Although I recognize why people resort to such clichés—and also acknowledge the grain of truth in them—I must still insist from a rational, not a subjectivistic, point of view that the statements are nonsensical. Clearly, reality is always reality, perception always perception. In the sentence "Perception is reality," the verb *is*, a linking verb, makes the subject and complement equal, as in "Robert is a grandfather." Logically speaking, I can't say that perception and reality, two different categories, are equal, no more than I can say, "Robert is the sky." Even metaphorically the statement doesn't work, for it's too vague to be meaningful.

Moreover, my perception doesn't constitute reality. Like a hippie under the influence of a hallucinogen or a patient in the throes of schizophrenia, I may simply be very wrong about reality. Nor can I claim that *my* perception constitutes *my* reality since I would be again grossly misusing the word *reality*. Reality doesn't exist simply in my head. Finally, I also err if I say, "Reality is what you make of it." As a limited, contingent being, I can't make reality whatever I *want* to make of it whenever I *want* to, as the generalization suggests. Within my life or psyche, I can change some things, but I can't change others. I can't, for example, at the age of forty-eight change myself into a lean, mean world-champion heavyweight boxer (especially since I'm a mild-mannered middleweight with a short reach and crooked spine who has never stepped into a ring to box). When we hear expressions like those analyzed above, we may grunt our assent, but we can't really pretend that communication is occurring.

In such a subjectivistic climate, we might expect an almost complete breakdown in rational discourse. We don't have to look far today to see that such is the case. People prefer tabloids to newspapers, tell-all talk shows to thoughtful commentaries. TV is rife with nonsensical, sensate-oriented dramas and sitcoms, in which nothing is really supposed to make sense, not even, in many cases, the plots. The sensible subjectivism of Hume and his ilk has led—whether or not he could foresee it (or cared to foresee it or not)—to a preference for passion and sentiment. Disinclined to examine our own motives, we wryly wink when the preacher, who appeals to objective standards of morality, is caught in adultery, but applaud when the TV diva, who appeals to subjective standards of morality, comes out of the closet to celebrate her lesbianism. It doesn't have to make sense, remember; it only has to feel good. If we are pleased, we give our approbation. Our approbation makes right.

"The growth of unreason throughout the nineteenth century and what has passed of the twentieth," declares Bertrand Russell, "is a natural sequel to Hume's destruction of empiricism" and his "rejection of the principle of induction."[41] For through the destruction of empiricism and induction—hence, rationality—a new religion of subjectivism has arisen. At the pinnacle of this new religion stands man, the great advocate of a liberalism that maximizes the freedom of the individual but minimizes his responsibility and accountability. According to Phillip E. Johnson, this "liberalism" derives from and "refers . . . to the secular legacy of philosophers such as Thomas Hobbes, John Locke, David Hume, Adam Smith and John Stuart Mill. Its essence lies in a respect for the autonomy of the individual."[42]

But we haven't yet covered even half the story of Western culture's slide toward relativism. Still, we are on our way to understanding how one mega-idea, the mega-idea of Hume, can open a Pandora's box of even more dire cultural effects. The plot is about to thicken. For "The cleverest reasoner in the Age of Reason [Hume] not only impeached the causal principle of reason, he opened a door to the Romantic reaction that would depose reason and make feeling its god."[43]

"Man Is Good by Nature but Corrupted by Society"

Jean-Jacques Rousseau, in his *Confessions*, owned that he had exposed his buttocks in alleys as a teenager to female passersby, had stolen a ribbon once and incriminated an innocent maid, had engaged in a *ménage à trois* with one Madame de Warens, and had dispatched all five of his illegitimate offspring to orphanages as soon as they were born. Publicly he began to reveal such details of his life in 1762, at the age of fifty, while reading his manuscript in the salons of Paris. His foes, fearing his attacks on them, quickly acted to have the government squelch his public readings. They were successful in silencing him at a time when he was trying not only to confess his transgressions but also to vindicate himself before his enemies, real and imagined.

One writer, however, has been less kind in his assessment of Rousseau's motives in writing the *Confessions* (and perhaps more to the point with regard to the mega-idea we will be examining in this chapter): The confessions "were, in opposition to those of Augustine, intended to show that he was born good, that the body's desires are good, that there is no original sin."[1]

During his life and since his death, Rousseau has remained a controversial, influential figure. While living, he befriended, then either alienated or offended several of his contemporaries—Voltaire, Grimm, Diderot, various *philosophes*, even David Hume. As the noble "Citizen of Geneva," he gained the support of churchmen and noble patrons, then lost it just as quickly. He was admired everywhere for his talents, even if some suspected him of madness and hypocrisy. In later years he was hounded from country to country, living like an exile. After his death he became the hero of the French Revolution as from every quarter arose the cries, originally his cries, of liberty, equality, and fraternity. Since his death he has been affirmed to be the father of Romanticism,[2] and he has continued to influence modern generations with his ideas of the noble savage and the social contract, among others. Because of his warmth of heart and sincerity, he has remained much beloved in many circles.

And yet he remains also a powerful yet somehow fragile, pitiful genius whose mind rose to breathless elysian heights but also plunged to profound depths of vanity and paranoia. When Rousseau visited England, Hume tried to help him secure the favor of others. After the two men had their falling out at the instigation of Rousseau—with the result being that Rousseau bitterly spurned one of his few true well-wishers—Hume wrote to a friend: "[Rousseau] is like a man who were stript not only of his clothes but of his skin, and turned out in that situation to combat with the rude and boisterous elements, such as perpetually disturb this lower world."[3] The charismatic Rousseau, though in many ways as lovable as an eccentric uncle, remains an enigmatic figure.

The Noble, Perfectible Savage

Although the influence of Rousseau has been oversimplified at times, it's safe to say that he launched a mega-idea that has had sweeping effects on culture down to our day. More than Hobbes or Hume, Rousseau made a virtue of the autonomy of man and the sacredness of man's subjectivity. Since his time, Goethe, Schiller, Byron, Emerson, and many other Romantics, including the iconoclasts and individualists of our day, have found fuel for their beliefs in the wood crib of Rousseau's writings. What views could he have propounded that have been so influential in the world of thought and the realm of culture? To answer this question, we will consider two main lines of his thought: first, the view that institutions corrupt and debase human character and morals; and second, the view that man is naturally good, especially in the condition of nature before human society—property, competition, and institutions—arose.

Institutions Deform and Corrupt

Because Rousseau maintained his beliefs pretty consistently throughout his life, we can concentrate on just a couple of his works to grasp the gist of his thought about society. In his *Discourse on the Origin and Basis of Inequality Among Men* (1754), Rousseau makes it clear that he is convinced that all institutions, civil and religious, corrupt men, although he does grant a special place to early forms of paternal authority. "As for paternal authority," he says, "which some writers see as the origin of absolute government and all society, it is enough to point out . . . that nothing is farther removed from the ferocious spirit of despotism than the gentleness of that authority."⁴ Especially in light of modern feminist doctrine, this claim of the darling of liberals seems particularly controversial, but clearly he believed that forms of paternalistic authority as found in family structure are mostly benign and antedate the corruption that he so deplored.

In Part I Rousseau sets out to refute the views of his predecessors, notably the premise of Hobbes that men are driven solely by a need for self-preservation. Rousseau, unlike Hobbes, denies that the natural condition of men is a state of war that only the creation of a civil society can quell, if and when they willingly surrender their individual rights to a sovereign. On the contrary, Rousseau holds that man is motivated by a natural sense of compassion that "contributes to the preservation of the whole species." He holds, moreover, that "inequality is scarcely felt in the state of nature." Civil society itself is the problem. It developed by various "accidents that . . . improved human reason while deteriorating the species, made man malicious [in some translations, *wicked*] while making him sociable and, from that remote beginning, brought him and the world to the point where we see them now."⁵ And this "point where we see them now" is a state of corruption reached by a number of marked stages.

In Part II Rousseau traces the stages of this corruption. Like an early anthropologist, he details the original state of primitive man, his development of language, and at last his organization into communities. In this latter stage the problem began. As humans banded together, they began to make invidious comparisons between different men and women. Opposition arose as people began to evaluate one another. "Jealousy was born with love; discord triumphed, and the gentlest of passions received sacrifices of human blood." The "great revolution," however, came with metallurgy and agriculture. Soon more evil followed: "The division of land necessarily followed from its cultivation, and once property had been recognized it gave rise to the first rules of justice . . ." in order to resolve the attendant conflicts that arose between man and man. Worse still, inequalities developed as some who were stronger worked harder and acquired more—all of which inequalities were exacerbated by "inequalities of exchange, and differences among men, developed by differences in circumstances," which began to influence the fate of individuals.[6]

Once civilization reached this level of conflicted complexity, says Rousseau, it's easy to imagine the rest. Clearly, "the successive inventions of the arts, the progress of language, the testing and employment of talents, the inequality of fortunes, the use or abuse of wealth" were the causal links that continued to promote the corruption. In summarizing the course of this descent from primitive innocence, Rousseau declares with some fervor: "Such was, or probably was, the origin of society and laws, which gave new fetters to the weak and new strength to the rich, permanently destroyed natural freedom, established the law of property and inequality forever, turned adroit usurpation into an irrevocable right, and for the advantage of a few ambitious men, subjected all others to unending work, servitude, and poverty."[7] And according to the reasoning of Rousseau—much to the chagrin of his Enlightenment friends—all civilized learning, as represented by the sciences and the arts, has also played a significant part in promoting inequality and corrupting morals since primitive times.

If we look beyond Rousseau's *Discourse on Inequality Among Men*, we will find that he found the same tendency toward corruption in the institutions of religion, specifically Christianity. In *Émile* (1762), sounding like Hobbes despite himself, Rousseau characterizes his mistrust of metaphysics in his section on the Savoyard Vicar: "General and abstract ideas are the soul of men's greatest errors; the jargon of metaphysics has never led to the discovery of a single truth, and it has filled philosophy with absurdities. . . ." Surely we can sympathize with his assessment up to this point, for any metaphysics divorced from the lives of men must be useless. However, Rousseau's indictment extends farther. He casts doubt on several articles of the Christian faith. He denies the existence of an Evil One: "Man, look no farther for the author of evil: that author is you." He questions the existence of hell. He challenges the existence of miracles on very much the same grounds as did Hume.[8]

So to what *does* he subscribe as an authority in matters of faith? To natural religion and to the feelings. All he needs is natural religion. He trusts himself, finding the principles of truth "in the depths of my heart, indelibly written there by nature. I have only to consult myself about what I want to do: What I feel to be right is right, what I feel to be wrong is wrong. Conscience is the best of all casuists. . . ." If only men had always held to this view of religion, listening "only to what God says in their hearts," says Rousseau through the Savoyard Vicar, "there would always have been only one religion on earth." It's not good to let "a few strange and doubtful customs . . . destroy the general agreement of all peoples. . . ." The Vicar, in the end, touts universalism, the truth of all religions, and adopts an "involuntary" attitude of skepticism toward Christianity, for the "Gospel," says he, "is full of incredible things, *contrary to reason*, which no sensible man can comprehend or accept" (italics mine).[9]

But wait a minute! I thought Rousseau told us that we were to trust feelings, not reason. Rousseau may be trying to have it both ways here, at least for the sake of maintaining his anti-institutional bias. Nevertheless, he is introducing a novelty into the history of theological discourse and exposition. According to Russell, with this novelty, in fact, Rousseau may well have invented modern liberal theology: "Modern Protestants who urge us to believe in God, for the most part, despise the old 'proofs,' and base their faith upon some aspect of human nature—emotions of awe or mystery, the sense of right and wrong, the feeling of aspiration, and so on. This way of defending religious belief was invented by Rousseau."[10] In this way, Rousseau so effectively discounted human faith in not only civil but also religious institutions—and after all, the church of Christ is an institution—that as humans looking for truth we have only one recourse left to us. We must adopt his major premise, his mega-idea, about the nature of man.

Man Is Naturally Good

In this simple "truth," for Rousseau, lies the salvation of our souls and even our corrupted civilization.[11] For anyone who would doubt that

Rousseau ever thus exalted human nature and denigrated civilization, we can consider his own most unequivocal words in this regard. They can leave little doubt as to his opinion:

> I think I have shown that man is naturally good. What then can have depraved him to such an extent, except the changes that have happened in his constitutions, the advances he has made, and the knowledge he has acquired? We may admire human society as much as we please; it will none the less be true that it necessarily leads men to hate each other in proportion as their interests clash, and to do one another apparent services, while they are really doing every imaginable mischief.[12]

Thus, we are born good. But then what depraves us? Civilization and society—our constitutions, advances, and acquired knowledge. The more we have concourse with one another, the more we clash; the more we clash, the more we practice to deceive.

Throughout the *Discourse on the Inequality Among Men*, especially in Part I, we encounter ample evidence of Rousseau's admiration for primitive man and his antipathy toward tradition. Here we encounter the cornerstones of Rousseau's thought as they affect us today: the nobility of the "primitive" man, the perfectibility of human nature, and the reliability of the heart in its natural state. From the beginning of his discourse, he makes it clear, too, that he knows what religion commands and what the Bible teaches about "the state of nature immediately after the Creation" as it relates to the inequality of man. Nevertheless, he purposely distances himself from traditional theology by saying that he intends to "form conjectures, based solely on the nature of man and the creatures around him," speaking in terms "applicable to all nations. . . ." He intends to give us the true history, he says, not the one written "in books by your fellow men, who are liars," but the one written "in Nature, who never lies." Later, in this same vein, Rousseau concludes *The Discourse* by saying that he elaborated his system "solely by the light of reason, independently of sacred dogmas that give sovereign authority the sanction of divine right."[13] In this way, in *The Discourse* Rousseau willfully emancipated himself from Christian tradition.

Man in his original state, a noble-savage state far out of time and mind, lived his days in tranquil innocence, claims Rousseau. "His placid soul [was] wholly absorbed in the feeling of his present existence, with no idea of the future. . . ." He was possessed of "pure emotion" and "natural compassion." Such "savages are not evil precisely because they do not know what it is to be good; for they are prevented from doing evil not by the development of understanding or the restraints of law, but by the quiescence of their passions and their ignorance of vice. . . ." Thus, naturally "Savage man is steeped in peace and freedom. . . ." So the original state of man is good and noble. And "it is only the spirit of society, and the inequality that society engenders, which thus change and debase our natural inclinations."[14]

Man, however, is perfectible too. Along with an innate sense of compassion, man possesses, unlike animals, "the capacity for self-improvement."[15] Without this capacity man would be no better than a brute, and yet this capacity, this "almost unlimited faculty," says Rousseau, "is the source of all man's misfortunes" because it draws him out of his primitive state. It "gives rise to his knowledge and errors, his vices and virtues, and eventually makes him a tyrant over himself and nature."[16] Ironically, then, that which makes us human leads also to our corruption.

Still, if his other books, *The Social Contract or Principles of Political Right* and *Émile*, have any merit, that must surely consist in trying to show us how we can perfect our political system, in the former case, and our education system, in the latter. Clearly, although Rousseau saw perfectibility as an operative principle in the debasement of men, he didn't see it as a trait that humans should abandon. Instead, they should, he believed, embrace it in the true sense: to achieve equality, fraternity, liberty. The process, however, does seem to be double-pronged. "Man," says one scholar, "because he possesses the faculty of self-improvement, is capable of perfecting his nature and likewise is distinct from animals in having what is, in effect, the same capacity to make retrograde steps. . . ."[17]

Through the words of the Savoyard Vicar, we have seen that Rousseau, like Hume, believed that man, because he possesses an innate, trustworthy moral sense, can trust his heart. On this score not much more needs to be said, except to demonstrate that Rousseau expressed again and again the same faith in feeling in his more philosophical *Discourse on Inequality Among Men*. Passion, he says, again like Hume, is the best teacher: "human intelligence owes much to the passions. . . . It is by their activity that our reason is improved. . . ." Natural man can trust, because of his placid soul, his first humane impulse: "lacking wisdom and reason, he always thoughtlessly obeys his first humane impulse." In him, compassion, as we have seen, is the "natural feeling which, by moderating the activity of each individual's self-love, contributes to the preservation of the whole species." To behave compassionately, natural man need only abandon himself to his peaceful, gentle nature. "The fact is," declares Rousseau, "that nothing is gentler than man in his original state; placed by nature at an equal distance from the stupidity of brutes and the pernicious understanding of man in the civil state, and limited by both instinct and reason to warding off dangers that threaten him, he is restrained by natural compassion from harming others needlessly."[18] Ah, if only we could return to such an innocent, original state or, better, wholly trust our deepest sentiments! Rousseau knew that we could never return to that original state, but he did believe, as the Savoyard Vicar declared, and as countless Romantics believed after him, that man could hearken to his gentler, inner voice and live a wiser, more genuine life.

THE INFLUENCE OF THE MEGA-IDEA

In general Rousseau, echoing the emphasis on sentiment and sensibility that was already developing as a reaction to the Enlightenment in his day, simply played midwife to the birth of Romanticism. It was the Germans who had truly sired it. Rousseau simply ushered it, with a certain panache, into the world in France and carried it, in a neatly swaddled little bundle, to the British Isles. Since his day Rousseau has had far-reaching effects on literature, morality, and culture in general, all of which stem from the mega-idea he introduced—that man is by nature good. Specifically, in our modern context, we can attribute to his handiwork, it seems to me, three main phenomena that still exist today: our slavish acceptance of the cult of personality, our unquestioned exaltation of private intuition, and our dismissal of the concept of original sin.

The Origin of the Cult of Personality

To understand the cult of personality, we can begin more easily from our end of the telescope. Today a "personality," as William Zinsser suggests by way of a humorous definition in *On Writing Well*, is one of "that vast swarm of people who are famous for being famous—and possibly nothing else." But we can perhaps be more precise than Zinsser by thinking of most of these "personalities" as being unique in some regard and usually admired for their uniqueness, as well as for their "magic" and "magnetism," as much as for any "talent" they may or may not possess. Once a person acquires the status of a "personality," of course, the person also acquires, in some measure, a certain claim to stature, to authority and expertise, in matters often unrelated to his uniqueness or talent. In modern times, from Oliver Stone to Barbra Streisand, from Elvis to Elton John, from Muhammad Ali to Dennis Rodman, from Whoopi Goldberg to Ellen Degeneres, personalities are looked to for direction. Around many of them grows a cult of fawning fans eagerly awaiting their next outlandish act or pontificated opinion. Modern men and women have become charisma junkies. And the media—from tabloids to talk shows—feed them as casually as old men scatter seeds before pigeons in Central Park.

This cult of personality, this tendency to regard a single individual to be invested with more than reasonable authority and stature, began, I believe, when Rousseau announced in the *Confessions* his bold plan to hold himself up as an exemplar:

> I am forming an enterprise *which has had no example*, and whose execution *will have no imitator*. I wish to show my fellow men *a man in all the truth of nature; and this man shall be myself.*
>
> *Myself alone.* I know my heart, and I am acquainted with men. *I am not made like any one of those who exist.* If I am not better, *at least I am different.* If nature has done well or ill in *breaking the mold in which I was cast*, this is something of which *no one can judge except after having read me.* (italics mine)[19]

In making this declaration, Rousseau inaugurated the Romantic trend to exalt any individual as a worthy study in himself, even the quite ordinary "unique" individual. Just look at the presumption in his language. He knows that he is unique, and that fact in itself is a virtue. To him "no example" and "no imitator" need exist. He alone is a sufficient study because he knows himself to be unlike "any one of those who exist" and because in him, one man, all the truth of nature resides. It's merely sufficient, too, that he is "different." Of course, also, nature broke the mold in which he was cast. But of course we readers shouldn't judge, "except after having read" him. He demands that we accept him on his own terms. What must we fear? After all, we will find that Rousseau, no matter what his "sins" may have been, is essentially good. He writes his life large for us so that we, in some measure, can feel good about ourselves, no matter what our foibles or trespasses may be (and most of the time his confessions will be comforting for us because our sins appear on such a far smaller scale).

This cult of personality continued to develop with the English Romantics. It was poets like Shelley, and most especially Byron, who perfected the art of projecting their personalities onto the world, perceiving in the uniqueness of their strong passions a virtue worthy of garnering a following. Lord Byron never concealed his infatuation with his half sister (consult his exquisite poem "When We Two Parted") and openly carried on amours with married women across Europe. He became a rebel not just because he flouted traditional morality, but because he *had* to be rebellious if he were to be true to his heart. Even his ending was Romantic and has ensured the survival of his cult-like status to this day. After mounting a horse to fight on behalf of Greek independence, he fell suddenly off his saddle, dead, his brain in the final stages of syphilitic disintegration. Later, creative types like Thoreau and Poe, Oscar Wilde and Van Gogh, F. Scott Fitzgerald and Virginia Woolf, Ernest Hemingway and Andy Warhol managed to carry on this tradition.[20] They struck their own poses, Madonna-like, thus ensuring that they would be remembered throughout history as much for their eccentricities as their expressions of "art."

Today the cult of personality thrives unabated (and unabashed), with newer and wilder forms ever ready to replace earlier, more sedate forms. Any rebellion grounded in the sincerity of the heart remains fashionable. Today, however, the cult figure doesn't have to be a literary or artistic genius. Anyone about whom others feel sentimental or passionate qualifies. When an overnight success like Rosie O'Donnell weeps adoringly as Barbra Streisand appears on her talk show, she is disingenuously ensuring her own immortality as much as Streisand's.

Obviously, such cult figures must assent to the cult that builds around them; yet when they do, the rest of us, ironically, regard such self-congratulation and self-promotion as a virtue, not a vice. Our slavish attachment to the cult of personality is so unreasonable and involuntary today, in fact, that when a princess with questionable morals dies one week and a saint dies the next—a saint who had died daily in the service of the poor for years—we weep more passionately over the death of the princess. After all, it's the heart that matters: The one who was most unique and inexplicable, most open to question and "sincere," commands much more of our adoration and respect.

Rousseau-like—or Byron-like, Thoreau-like, Marilyn Monroe-like, or Madonna-like—the princess was true to herself, even in defiance of tradition, thus proving once again that people are basically good by nature, especially if she performed one or two acts of charity that may have cost her nothing. Meanwhile, when the bodies of the princess and the saint were prepared for burial, who recalled Jesus' insight in Luke 21:1-4. "As he looked up, Jesus saw the rich putting their gifts into the temple treasury. He also saw a poor widow put in two very small copper coins. 'I tell you the truth,' he said, 'this poor widow has put in more than all the others. All these people gave their gifts out of their wealth; but she out of her poverty put in all she had to live on.'" The adherent of the cult of personality is incapable of appreciating, let alone making, such distinctions. In adoring the unique, he finds innumerable rationalizations for his own uniqueness.

The Exaltation of Private Intuition

Another curious manifestation of Rousseau's mega-idea is that we have come to trust private intuition more than objective truth, especially as it comes to us through our "grasp" of the "truths" of nature. Individual intuition has become a surer instrument of truth than the mind because the heart is in a better position, being pure and good, to read the book of nature. "'The God I worship,' declares the Savoyard Vicar, 'is not a God of shadows secreted in books. . . .'" His truth is accessible to all men through many forms. "The God of revelations speaks in too many tongues," says Robert Wokler in summarizing this thought of Rousseau.[21] By the time Ralph Waldo Emerson was writing of the value of intuition in his essay *Self-Reliance* (1840), such sentiments had become regarded as utterly reliable. Emerson pushed the creed of Rousseau's Savoyard Vicar nearly to its limit: "Trust thyself: every heart vibrates to that iron string," says he. "Nothing is at last sacred," he continues, "but the integrity of your own mind." According to Emerson, "the only right is what is after my constitution; the only wrong what is against it."[22] Later, in writing two poems, "Brahma" and "Maia," Emerson concurred with Rousseau—and modern New Agers—that the revelations of God are spoken through many tongues.

But this exaltation of intuition simply corresponds with the Romantic era's exaltation of feeling. And feeling by itself, no matter how private or intense it may be, proves nothing. If intuition, essentially feeling, becomes a criterion by which we judge truth, then truth must change according to the subjective whims of each person, and certainly revelation becomes in such cases entirely a private matter. What your heart says may well contradict what my heart says. It's simply an unwarranted assumption, touted by Rousseau and his intellectual heirs, that conscience can function as an infallible guide or that nature has written its universal truths upon the heart. Believing and not believing, according to Rousseau, rely entirely on the individual, on whose heart natural religion has writ its truths. "This form of argument," says Bertrand Russell, "has the drawback of being private; the fact that Rousseau cannot help believing something affords no ground for another person to believe the same thing." Speaking as an atheist but almost echoing the concern of any modern evangelical Christian, Russell argues quite rightly that "The rejection of reason in favour of the heart was not, to my mind, an advance."[23]

With the aid of Rousseau and his heirs, we have thus seen the rise in our era of natural religion, aka New Age belief, ranging from the reawakening of pagan rites to the enshrining of Eastern mysticism as a legitimate field of inquiry on an equal footing with Christianity. I already mentioned Emerson's contribution, but others contributed to the current climate in America as well: Thoreau, Whitman, Madame Blavatsky and Annie Besant (the founders of Theosophy), the Unitarians, the Rosicrucians, Gerard Manley Hall, the Unity School of Religion, Religious Scientists, and others. Intuitionalism has provided fertile soil for all sorts of modern phenomena, including spiritism, psychic research, near-death experiences, and various obsession with altered-states aware-ness. After all, who can challenge these "manifestations"? They are sub-jective. They are grounded in the private experiences of millions of Americans and Europeans who are convinced that the sacred resides within them, ready to be accessed through their intuitions and attune-ment with nature. To such, the heart doesn't lie, and nature, as inter-preted by a good heart, doesn't lie.

"But," as Russell puts it, "the new theology of the heart dispenses with argument; it cannot be refuted because it does not profess to prove its points." It only allows us "to indulge in pleasant dreams." It's indeed ironic that an atheist of Russell's stature should conclude, "if I had to choose between Thomas Aquinas and Rousseau, I should unhesitatingly choose the Saint."[24]

The Demise of the Concept of Original Sin

The most serious consequence, by far, of the mega-idea unleashed on culture by Rousseau is its annihilation of the concept of original sin. If people are good by nature, original sin can't exist. Doubtless, Rousseau realized that he was debunking the concept. One need only recall the the-ology of the Savoyard Vicar. Russell asserts, in fact, that Rousseau's mega-idea is "the antithesis of the doctrine of original sin and salvation throughout the Church."[25] The Durants, themselves avowed agnostics, concur: "Rousseau rejected the doctrine of original sin and the redemp-tive role of the death of Christ."[26] Rousseau believed, moreover, that "the harsh doctrine of original sin" was the invention of Augustine and the theologians.[27] It's no wonder that six years after the publication of *Émile*, with its section on the Savoyard Vicar, Jonathan Edwards, the American Puritan, made a noble effort to salvage the concept in his last work, *The Great Christian Doctrine of Original Sin Defended* (January 1768). Although *Émile* had been condemned, banned, and burned in France, Edwards was too late. *Émile* had done its job effectively.

So effectively had it done so that today no one but a fundamental-ist or evangelical speaks seriously of original sin. As any apologist or evangelist knows, a Christian earnest about spreading the Gospel had best avoid the term. Consider the connotation it has acquired since Rousseau's day. It suggests that we aren't good in any respect but are

each *all bad*. Of course, original sin doesn't mean that we are always as
bad in our thoughts and deeds as we can possibly be, just that our whole
being in every part has been affected by sin. But once people believe that
people are *naturally good*, they can only assume that if Christians say
man is born with original sin, those Christians mean that man is *naturally or exclusively bad*. The classical notion of original sin merely
declares that just as Adam contained within him, because of his free will,
the capacity to disobey God (as of course he eventually did), so do we.
We carry this propensity within us as part of our human nature. A more
modern definition runs this way: This predisposition toward sin, which
doesn't detract "from individual responsibility," does "highlight the
inbuilt factors within environment and heredity which push us towards
disobedience, and it corresponds to observable facts about universal
human nature."[28]

The doctrine of original sin, thus viewed, is realistic and reasonable.
We are often predisposed toward disobedience or "lawlessness" (1 John
3:4). What theist can deny that we have all sinned and fallen short of
the glory of God (Rom. 3:23)? It's the mega-idea of Rousseau—that men
are naturally good—that is unrealistic and unreasonable.

In modern culture today the implications of the demise of the concept of original sin are all too apparent—and sad. As people trust their
gentler, inner voices and hearken to the natural goodness within them,
they can readily free themselves from traditional guilt, it is said. If I'm
okay engaging in premarital sex, then you're okay being a homosexual.
If I'm okay smoking pot, then you're okay ogling pornography. If I'm
okay cheating on my taxes, then you're okay cheating on your wife. As
long as we are all sincere about our choices, needs, and lifestyles, what
else matters? We only have to impose limitations on what we say or do
so that we don't violate anyone else's freedom to trust his heart and act
sincerely. Any belief in original sin, on the other hand, may raise that
ugly specter of guilt that we long ago overcame in our progressive march
toward moral freedom and enlightenment. So naturally it's better to side
with the angels, the modern voices of scientism and pop psychology,
than with the demons, those benighted Christians who still take seriously the words of ignorant men written long ago. Besides, without original sin, with only goodness naturally reigning in the hearts of men and
women, there to be tapped like a pitchy syrup from a New England

maple tree, modern man has no need for salvation. From what does he need to be saved? Now he can save himself just by hearkening to the dictates of his naturally good heart, Rousseau-style, his ears attuned to the whispered words of nature proffered like leaves on the wind as they drift past him like so many pieces of ancient parchment, full of symbolic import, and perhaps Druidic lore.

But when original sin has dissolved into the river of the new mega-idea, what can replace it if man is to have some inducement toward morality or some way to direct his benevolence toward social ends? Our next writers, the utilitarians, offer us a mega-idea that can, they promise, provide us with a "hedonistic calculus" guaranteed to overcome the philosophical excesses inherent in the mega-ideas of the writers who maintained that man, not God, makes law, that each man possesses an innate moral sense, and that every man is born good. The utilitarians try to bring reason back into the picture, along with a good healthy dose of pragmatism and empiricism, to establish a basis for moral consensus. But they fail. They introduce a mega-idea that only *seems to* provide a corrective to the runaway tendency toward subjectivism.

Perhaps they could foresee, as Russell brutally points out, that the logic of Rousseau carried, *reductio ad absurdum*, to its outer limits leads to social horror and disorder. Writing during World War II, Russell declared, "At the present time, Hitler is an outcome of Rousseau." If Rousseau, gentle soul that he was, could be raised before us by some modern witch of Endor or Mephistopheles, I'm sure he wouldn't appreciate Russell's comparison. Then again, after the death of Rousseau, it *was* the bloody Robespierre who seemed to love him best.

"HAPPINESS IS THE MEASURE AND GOAL OF A GOOD LIFE"

Of the early and most prominent utilitarians, Jeremy Bentham (1748-1832) and James Mill (1773-1836), Bertrand Russell writes, "Both believed in the omnipotence of education."[1] And with the calculation of a sober pedagogue and ideologue, James Mill imposed this belief on his son John Stuart Mill (1806-1873), by far the greatest and most influential of the utilitarians. By age three the young Mill began his study of Greek and mathematics. By eight he had read the whole of Herodotus and six dialogues of Plato. Before twelve he had studied the Greek and Latin poets. By thirteen he had mastered such subjects as political economy and logic, ingesting Aristotle whole in the process. By the junior Mill's own admission, his education had catapulted him "a quarter century ahead of his contemporaries."[2] Even more impressively, John Stuart Mill managed to raise the cause of utilitarianism, an icy philosophy in the hands of Bentham and his father, "from calculus to humanity."[3] In the presence of J. S. Mill, a reader can't help sensing the scope and genius of the man as he writes in a genteel and judicious style, soberly anticipates and refutes objections, and carefully marshals examples to support his utilitarianist philosophy.

So in philosophical terms, what exactly were J. S. Mill and his predecessors advocating? What was this newfangled utilitarianism? Utilitarianism, according to *The Dictionary of Cultural Literacy*, is "A system of ETHICS according to which the rightness or wrongness of an action should be judged by its consequences. The goal of utilitarian ethics is to promote the GREATEST HAPPINESS OF THE GREATEST

NUMBER."[4] As a school of thought, it began as early as the late seventeenth century with Joseph Priestley, John Gay, and Jeremy Bentham; gained ascendancy in the nineteenth century in the work of John Stuart Mill; and re-arose later in the pragmatism of such men as William James, the brother of Henry James, and John Dewey.[5] The aim of the utilitarians "was to test all institutions, government or church or the law, in light of human reason and common sense in order to determine whether such institutions were useful—that is, whether they contributed to the greatest happiness of the greatest numbers of men." To the logical minds of such men as Bentham:

> Man's traditional customs, the very past itself, were of little interest . . . ; everything had to be tested afresh in terms of the Utilitarian formula. Such a test, if applied to a long-established institution like the Church of England, or to religious belief in general, could have, and did have, disruptive effects. Was religious belief useful for the needs of a reasonable man? To the Benthamites the answer was evident: religious belief was merely an outmoded superstition.[6]

In this way the utilitarians set out, perhaps without a conscious design to do so, to complete the work originally begun by Hobbes and Hume. They sought to devise a perfectly rational human ethics that could effectively grant man the autonomy he deserved and liberate him from the unenlightened authority of his past, particularly from Christian tradition. They offered just one more emancipation proclamation that would grant man the sacred sovereignty over himself that he so desired.

A Morality with No Need of God

Wouldn't it be wonderful to find a wholly human morality that would help humans split the horns of every ethical dilemma and provide them with a *certain* way to create legislation that would result in the good of most in any nation? Many philosophers have sought such a principle. Kant, for example, tried to find a universally applicable principle with his categorical imperative: namely, that each would act in such a way that the rule on which he acted would be capable of being adopted by all rational humans. But as J. S. Mill aptly observes, the categorical imperative is a failure: "But when [Kant] begins to deduce from this precept any of the actual duties of morality, he fails . . . to show that there would be any contradiction, any logical (not to say physical) impossibility, in the adoption by all rational beings of the most outrageously immoral rules of conduct." Then Mill concludes, "All he shows is that the *consequences* of their universal adoption would be such as no one would choose to incur."[7]

In other words, all that Kant could offer was a subjectivistic ethic. Perhaps a Kantian might find it ethical to smoke opium daily as a way to enhance his creativity and sensitivity. But what would induce others not to adopt the same conduct if they could rationalize the behavior in the same way? Discussing the damaging consequences of the universal adoption of such conduct, claims Mill, simply doesn't go far enough in resolving the ethical problem. Mill wants proof—which to him of course only utilitarianism can provide—that it would be impossible for a rational person, whether he be tempted to do so or not, to choose "immoral rules of conduct."

Mill and the utilitarians were confident of their success in creating a wholly rational ethics. Their ethics is based on two premises, one of which is grounded in an empirical observation of human behavior, the other of which is the result of the universalization or generalization of that empirical observation. From these premises arises a third, brought to perfection by J. S. Mill in his essay *On Liberty*, in which he argues that the happiness of the individual, properly conceived, contributes to the general happiness. When an individual pursues his own interests, as long as he doesn't hurt anyone else in the process, he is contributing to the "greatest happiness of the greatest number of people."

Pleasure and Pain Explain Virtue and Vice

We can find incipient signs of this view in the works of the empiricists. It was certainly seminal in Locke and explicitly stated as we have seen in Hume. Hume, remember, declared in "Of Morals" that "Nothing can . . . concern us more than our own sentiment of pleasure and uneasiness; and if these be favourable to virtue, and unfavourable to vice, no more can be requisite to the regulation of our . . . behaviour."[8] Other names may be added to the list of those who promoted this line of thought: Francis Hutcheson (1694-1746), who may have been the first to use the idea of the greatest-happiness principle; David Hartley (1705-1757), who introduced the term "association of ideas"; Helvétius (1715-1771), who was one of the French *philosophes*; and Joseph Priestley (1733-1804), to whom Bentham attributes the theory of "utilitarianism."[9] Among the most noteworthy of those who began the school of utilitarianism was John Gay (1669-1745), not to be confused with the poet of the same name (sixteen years his junior).

In "Dissertation Concerning the Fundamental Principle of Virtue or Morality" (1731), John Gay sets the stage for later utilitarians. He argues that our approval of morality is grounded in our own happiness or, when we can't perceive this end, in an association of ideas that "may properly enough be called habits." Pleasure and pain, because they impel the individual to select one and avoid the other, are adequate indicators of virtue and vice, says Gay. For the individual, they represent the principle of all action. "And therefore, as pleasure and pain are not indifferent to him, nor out of his power, he pursues the former and avoids the latter." He does concede that an act is meritorious "Whenever . . . the particular end of any action is the happiness of another." However, Gay is more concerned to prove, as he says in his closing paragraph, that it's "necessary in order to solve the principal actions of human life to suppose a moral." Yet differing from Hume, he denies "that this moral sense" is "innate or implanted in us." Strictly speaking, our moral principles "are acquired either from our own observation or the imitation of others."[10] In short, moral principles are learned.

The Greatest-Happiness Principle Is the Basis of Morality

Jeremy Bentham echoes Gay's viewpoint numerous times in "The Introduction to the Principles of Morals and Legislation" (1789), but carries his observations of behavior farther to prove that the pleasure and pain of the individual point to a grander principle that may be applied to society and government. He says in Chapter 1, "Nature has placed mankind under the governance of two sovereign masters, *pain* and *pleasure*." But they "point out what we ought to do, as well as . . . determine what we shall do,"[11] not only for our own good but for the good of the many. Because Bentham was the head of the "Philosophical Radicals," the Benthamites, who disseminated the utilitarianist philosophy and advocated many social reforms as well, we must consider his thought in some detail before proceeding. Only then can we appreciate the contributions of that latter-day utilitarianist, John Stuart Mill, the real genius of the movement.

The greatest-happiness view, as conceived by Bentham, was based on a deterministic view of human psychology. According to Russell, "To Bentham, determinism in psychology was important, because he wished to establish a code of laws—and, more generally, a social system—which would automatically make men virtuous. His second principle, that of the greatest happiness, became necessary . . . to define 'virtue.'"[12] As Bentham says, we are under the governance of pleasure and pain, and yet he sees no conflict between the interests of the individual and the interests of the community when the principle of utility is properly understood. We must concentrate on the consequences of actions. "What happiness consists of we have already seen: enjoyment of pleasures, security from pains."[13] At the same time, in seeking my happiness—the increase of pleasure, the avoidance of pain—I'm furthering the happiness of others too. Unfortunately, for utilitarianism to work legislatively, a person must believe, naively it seems to me, that a legislator can be fully committed to this ethical system privately and publicly. "A man may be said to be a partisan of the principle of utility," says Bentham of the committed follower, "when the approbation or disapprobation he annexes to any action, or to any measure, is determined by and proportioned to the tendency which he conceives it to have to augment or to diminish the happiness of the community; or in other words, to its conformity or unconformity to the laws or dictates of utility."[14]

Can a legislator really be trusted to look out for the interests of the many as well as his own? Is there really any axiomatic principle that would guarantee such a correspondence between his personal happiness (grounded in *his* pleasure and pain) and his concern for the common weal? To be sure, asserts Russell, "Bentham's adoption of the principle of 'the greatest happiness of greatest number' was no doubt due to democratic feeling, but it involved opposition to the doctrine of the rights of man, which he bluntly characterized as 'nonsense.'"[15] Of course, a doctrine of the rights of man *would* be nonsense to a determinist, one who sees everything in mechanistic terms.

The doctrine of the rights of man, moreover, would be nonsense to one who finds no absolute ground of right and wrong beyond utility. In a quest for a perfect "natural ethic,"[16] Bentham discounts theology and Scripture as offering any help in deciding matters of right and wrong. Sounding like Hobbes, he claims that men's interpretations of sacred writings simply differ too much for those writings to be of any real use. When theologians speak, "It is plain, therefore that . . . no light can ever be thrown upon the standard of right and wrong, by anything that can be said upon the question, what is God's will."[17]

Nevertheless, Bentham implies that adherence to his principle of utility is more likely to result in conformity to the will of God. He provides no adequate answer for how that can possibly be so, unless we search for the answer in his determinist premise and assume that pleasure and pain alone may adequately instruct and guide us. If such is the case, however, belief in God is unnecessary, and God himself is redundant. By Bentham's own admission, "The principle of utility requires nor admits of any other regulator than itself."[18] And that's that.

John Stuart Mill didn't really overcome all the deficiencies of utilitarianism, but he did lend it more respectability at a time when people had become suspicious of emotional excess ("enthusiasm") in the wake of Romanticism, and religious dogma in the wake of Darwinism. In *Utilitarianism* (1863), Mill adheres mainly to the Benthamite line. By way of definition he states, "The creed which accepts as the foundation of morals *utility*, or the *greatest happiness principle*, holds that actions are right in proportion as they tend to promote happiness, wrong as they tend to produce the reverse. . . . By 'happiness' is intended pleasure, and the absence of pain; by 'unhappiness,' pain, and the privation of pleasure." To clarify this basic description, he does offer some refinements, not found in Bentham, as he distinguishes, like a true follower of Epicurus, between levels of pleasure. There are higher kinds of pleasures—of the imagination, intellect, moral sentiments—that "are more desirable and more valuable than others." And this ranking must be so if individuals are to become ennobled and thus ennoble others, promoting the general good: "if it may possibly be doubted whether a noble character is always the happier for its nobleness, there can be no doubt that it makes other people happier, and that the world in general is immensely a gainer by it."[19]

In the main, Mill was offering an ethic that satisfied his contemporaries because it didn't require adherence to traditional doctrine of any kind, though it did maintain that morality exists. It held to one ultimate standard: "that standard is not the agent's own greatest happiness, but the greatest amount of happiness altogether." Mill is even bold enough to declare that because God desires the happiness of his creatures any revelation of God on the topic of morals "must fulfill the requirements of utility in a supreme degree." Nevertheless, like Bentham, he does see utility as an ultimate and sufficient test, "from whence it necessarily follows that it must be the criterion of morality. . . ."[20] Again, if such is true, who needs theology or even God? Utilitarianism, argues Mill, is a wholly adequate ethical system.

Individual Liberty Promotes the Happiness of the Greatest Number

This idea, brought to its full by J. S. Mill, is much beloved by progressives and libertarians today. Although a progressive himself, Mill was nevertheless motivated in writing *On Liberty* (1859) as much by a fear of a tyrannical majority (or what he called "collective mediocrity") as he was by a love of democratic liberty. Although for many reasons the essay is complex—and at times leaves many questions unanswered—Mill asserts that his view of liberty is based on a simple principle. "That principle is," asserts Mill, "that the sole end for which mankind are warranted, individually or collectively, in interfering with the liberty of action of any of their number, is self-protection. That the only purpose for which power can be rightfully exercised over any member of a civilized community, against his will, is to prevent harm to others. His own good, either physical or moral, is not a sufficient warrant."

Throughout his essay, Mill tries to qualify this seemingly egalitarian principle in numerous ways, but it still amounts to the same thing, a view that we hear expressed all too often today: *Do your own thing as long as you don't hurt anyone.* "The only part of the conduct of anyone," Mill continues, "for which he is amenable to society, is that which concerns others." Of course, what this concern might be, case by case, despite Mill's intricate examples, remains vague. No matter how we cut it, Mill is implying that each individual is the complete ruler of himself. "In the part which merely concerns himself, his independence is, of right, absolute. Over himself, over his own body and mind, the individual is sovereign."[21] In the last three decades how many times have we heard the cry "It's my body!" issue forth from the lips of people who were just doing their own thing.

True to utilitarianism, Mill believes that such liberty—namely, diversity of opinion and practice—will advance both individual and collective happiness in society. "It is not," says Mill, "by wearing down into uniformity all that is individual in themselves, but by cultivating it, and calling it forth, within the limits imposed by the rights and interests of others, that human beings become a noble and beautiful object of contemplation. . . ." In this way humans can make "the race infinitely better [and] worth belonging to. In proportion to the development of his individuality, each person becomes more valuable to himself, and is therefore capable of being more valuable to others." Thus to cultivate individuality is to cultivate humanity: "it is only the cultivation of individuality which produces, or can produce, well-developed human beings. . . ." Mill perceives this "spirit of liberty, or that of progress or improvement" as being the "progressive principle" behind all human advancement.[22]

As Mill makes clear later in *Utilitarianism*, he believes that his principle is entirely sufficient as a basis for ethics, so much so that he suggests that, at best, Christianity has only a minimal role to play in the process of advancement. "I think," he says in *On Liberty*, ". . . it a great error to persist in attempting to find in the Christian doctrine that complete rule for our guidance which its author intended it to sanction and enforce, but only partially to provide." Mill's presumption about the Author's "intention" notwithstanding, he asserts in the same vein that we must look beyond "exclusively Christian sources" of ethics "to produce *the moral regeneration of mankind* . . ." (italics mine).[23] Already in Mill, who had worked for many years for the East India Company, we can see the first glimmers of the idea of the global village about which we hear so much today.

THE INFLUENCE OF THE MEGA-IDEA

This mega-idea, since its inception, has kept men confident in their own powers to create and apply a "logical" man-made code of morality. The confidence with which this position has been argued to the present day is staggering. Many liberal theologians across the country still regard the greatest-happiness principle as an adequate measure in matters of morality, even though the principle conceals a serious unresolvable philosophical error, contradicts the Christian (and even commonsense) view of individual responsibility, and promotes a dangerous worldview in which all ethical decisions must inevitably fall to some elite group of taste and right makers. In no way can happiness serve as the measure and goal, much less guarantor, of a good life. Happiness, as a condition as full of pleasure and as free of pain as possible, must forever remain an elusive, subjective state to which none of us can say we have an absolute right. Saying that we have a right to such happiness is foolish and absurd.[24]

The Misapplication of a Hedonistic Calculus

As we have seen, in the crudest versions of hedonism, this view confuses contentment, temporary satisfaction, with happiness and identifies the good with the pleasurable. Mortimer Adler offers a devastating refutation of utilitarian logic in chapter 5 of *Ten Philosophical Mistakes*. Even conceding that Mill, like Epicurus, "distinguishes between pleasures that are more or less desirable," namely, that the pleasure of reading Ecclesiastes is greater than the pleasure of raiding the cookie jar, he still claims that the hedonistic formulation results in a major problem. Says Adler, "it does not solve the problem of moral values; whether they are objective and universal, or subjective and relative."[25] Bertrand Russell offers an even more devastating criticism in a lucid paraphrase of Mill from *Utilitarianism*. Pointing to Mill's circular logic, Russell claims that Mill is simply saying, "Pleasure is the only thing desired; therefore pleasure is the only thing desirable."[26] This logic does, to be sure, seem flawed by circularity. Thus, continues Russell, if "'desirable' is a word presupposing an ethical theory," then we certainly can't "infer what is desirable from what is desired."[27] Happiness, conceived in this way, must forever remain subjective. It can't really tell us what we "ought" to do.

But we must remember that the utilitarians advance another side to their theory of ethics—namely, that in striving for my pleasure, I would be striving for the happiness of others also, recognizing that it would be in my best interests to do so. And if I look out for them, they will look out for me, and we shall all be happy. If behavior *x* works, if it promotes my happiness and the happiness of others, then it's good. To make the system work, utilitarians have often resorted to a hedonistic calculus. By this method, when considering an ethical issue, they make columns for each choice, breaking these columns further into pleasure- or pain-inducing categories. Then as they analyze the issue and seek a solution, they add and subtract the pleasures and pains until one side of the equation outweighs the other. The best choice would be the one that would result in the greatest happiness for the greatest number of people.

But who can avoid stumbling into pitfalls with this hedonistic calculus? If I set out to compute a hedonistic calculus with a committee of well-intentioned peers, for example, what guarantee do I have that we can transcend groupthink (or wishful thinking)? And on any controversial issue, how can I be sure that we really have the foresight to perceive the immediate and remote impact of our decision on society, namely, *most* people? Consider abortion. I dare say that if pushed against a utilitarian wall, quite as many informed people today, faced with the same body of complete evidence, will decry the practice as a blight on society as will herald it as a benevolent resolution to the problem of unwanted children. What other issues are really capable of being solved on purely utilitarian grounds? Are practicing homosexuals harming others besides themselves? Supposedly, 70 percent of Americans oppose same-sex marriages. But will the 30 percent step forward to explain, by means of a hedonistic calculus, that the majority is wrong? By doing so, wouldn't the minority be forcing unhappiness on the majority, assuming that both groups had whisked out their calculators and performed their hedonistic calculus?

To be reasonable, were we to consider some social good, it would really only be *after the fact* that we could say that one ethical course was better than another for most people concerned. But even then utility would fail us because most results, in terms of individual perceptions of happiness and contentment, are mixed. Were the Reagan years, on balance, good or bad for most people in America? Has affirmative action, on balance, been good or bad for most in America in contributing to the common weal or in promoting life, liberty, and the pursuit of happiness? It depends on whom you ask. Again, looked at in this way, happiness, as a condition as full of pleasure and as free of pain as possible, must remain forever subjective—and relative too.

If utilitarianism is too sophisticated and contradictory for even the most devoted utilitarians, what then can remain of it in our modern culture except a crude form of utilitarian hedonism? We see its fruits, I believe, in the unchecked consumerism of today. Inasmuch as I am devoted to capitalism, my good is your good—or so I think. Nevertheless, the fulfillment of my pleasures becomes my happiness, so long as on balance my pleasures outweigh my pains—or so I think. So if I keep raising capital, as well as disposable income, so that I can satisfy my sensuous, material desires for luxury cars, big-screen TVs, new furniture, and so on, I can keep up with—or exceed as in the cases of Donald Trump and Bill Gates—the satisfaction of the other happy people around me. And of course if I have trouble keeping up, trouble responding to the lures of the ads that bombard me daily, then I can always resort to the use of my credit cards or a home-improvement or debt-consolidation loan. In this way, we believe we are contributing to the greatest happiness of the greatest number of people. We spend. They spend. Everyone goes home happy, right?

The Rationalization of One's "Own" Anything

Because utilitarianism must of necessity degenerate into crude hedonism, we find ourselves confronted as a society today by all sorts of people who insist that they be allowed to do their own thing as long as they don't hurt anyone. Unconsciously paraphrasing Mill's *On Liberty*, they assert that they have the liberty to engage in premarital sex, smoke marijuana, or adopt a homosexual lifestyle as they see fit, autonomous individuals all, because no one else is "harmed" by their behavior. Unfortunately, what we begin to witness—from kindergartners to senior citizens—is a smugness about being free to do one's "own thing." "Hey," runs the argument, "my own thing isn't hurting anyone!" Perhaps some even assume that pursuing their own good is advancing the good of all. But how can they be certain? They can't.

Most hedonists, in fact, especially those who have cynically concluded that utilitarianism doesn't work, don't care about any benefit or harm to others. If they did, they would adopt a more objective view of their own behavior (the behavior they exemplify before or recommend to others)—disregarding their immediate gratification and considering the impact of their behavior on others, including future generations. Then they would have to ask hard questions. Will currently promiscuous youths who later marry find themselves so jaded by sex that they will fail to experience the beauty of sexual union with their spouses, thus preventing them from fully trusting another and achieving true intimacy? Could this possibly diminished capacity to love lead to higher divorce rates? Wouldn't the future children of such marriages then be the real victims of the earlier ill-considered premarital sex? When the children of such unions reach *their* adult years, how will *they* view relationships? When *they* attain to positions of authority in education or the media, how will *they* portray relationships? Will they, too, merely transform *Peyton Place* into *Melrose Place*, smirking all the way to the bank? We could ask similar hard questions of marijuana smokers, homosexuals, pornographers, careerists, and countless others. But we can be fairly certain of the common hedonistic reply: "None of that matters as long as *I* am happy."

Naturally, when pleasure is seen as an end in itself, whether or not it conduces to anyone's good beyond oneself, no one will argue, with any conviction, that there is a hierarchy of pleasures that can guide us in our choices. True, borrowing unconsciously from the cultural coinage of Christianity, many will say that it's better to love than hate, better to give than receive. But when it comes to the specific decisions, they will slip into a benumbing way of thinking. "Isn't it more loving to accept premarital sex than to condemn it?" they will blandly argue, able to apply the general principles but without any critical sense of distinctions about love and permissiveness, mercy and justice. Because the utilitarian ethic is hedonistic and thus ultimately subjective, it can never rest on an incontrovertible hierarchy of pleasures and serve as a guarantor of the greatest happiness of the greatest number of people. Or can it? Under one condition, yes, the ethic can work.

The Silent, Deadly Advancement of the Elite

Suppose we could establish a hierarchy of legitimate pleasures capable of securing the good life for the individual and most others based on reason alone, without the need for the constraining force of religion. What would the underlying criteria be by which we could determine where any pleasure might fall on the hierarchical scale? Clearly, finding a criterion of judgment could be a problem. Who shall decide on this criterion? Who shall say, after all, that listening to a CD of Mozart or Bach is more ennobling—and more conducive to the good of the many—than listening to a CD of Courtney Love or Billy Ray Cyrus? Believe it or not, John Stuart Mill had an answer—and it was a chilling one.

For utilitarian ethics to work socially, we must presume the existence of a benevolent elite who will dictate taste—enlightened Epicurean-style. Even though utilitarians will permit, by the Millean principles expressed in *On Liberty* and *Utilitarianism,* maximum freedom of choice to the individual, they will naturally have to determine the standards by which pleasure can be measured as good or bad. Says Mill, these arbiters—legislators, if you will—will necessarily have to be the ones who are in the best possible position to make that choice: "the test of quality, and the rule for measuring it against quantity, being the *preference felt by those who in their opportunities of experience, to which must be added their habits of self-consciousness and self-observation, are best furnished with the means of comparison*" (italics mine).[28] Perhaps Mill was referring to Oxford and Cambridge graduates only or to the progressive wing of Parliament. Later, it's true, Mill appeals to the "conscientious feelings of mankind" as the sanction of a standard.[29] Nevertheless, we mustn't mistake his real bias. In *On Liberty* Mill makes it clear that he isn't elevating the judgments of the hoi polloi. While on one page he insists on the importance of genius, on the next page he decries "collective mediocrity," which he had lamented as the ascendant power among mankind. He complains, moreover, of "the present low state of the human mind."[30] Undoubtedly, utilitarianism—or any hierarchical hedonism—can only work when an elite establishes and enforces its own standards by propaganda and education. The utilitarian types will of course need various apparatuses for such social control.

We don't have to look far for proof that the utilitarian ethic is still much favored today among progressives. Many groups of elitists are today trying to weasel their way into pop culture and to undo tradition. In recent history, one enduring group of elitists who is trying to tell us what is good for us is the feminists. Despite recent scientific studies that prove that the brains of men and women are wired differently, making many of their needs, wants, and communication styles *naturally* different,[31] utility-driven feminists keep insisting that men and women are the same and should be performing the same types of work in all cases, including fighting alongside men in foxholes or supervising male inmates in maximum-security prisons.

Other groups abound as well—environmentalists, multiculturalists, homosexuals, evolutionary biologists, computer techies, postmodernistic academicians, and so on. Each vies for control—sometimes singularly, more often collectively—recognizing that a progressive utilitarian ethic must ultimately be based on the premise that might makes right. Or, better, they realize that those who control the means of propaganda control the minds of the many and can urge their particular brand of "happiness" on the majority in the "global village."

Perhaps the chief culprit in the utilitarian power struggle is the Hollywood media. From ABC to MTV to TNT, the media have our eyes and ears—and hence our brains. Listening to them, we would have to conclude that they are the modern dictators of morality, aided and abetted naturally by all the above-mentioned progressive groups, from whom they derive their moral clout. Propaganda-style, ABC producers even ran an ad on the back page of *TV Guide* (August 9-15, 1997), distancing themselves from the "elitists" (ironically, those who criticize TV) with the most loaded language they could muster and then declaring sanctimoniously, "TV is good." "TV," ABC declared, "binds us together." If the ad were tongue-in-cheek, it's hard to find the tongue or the cheek in this rousing last sentence: "Let us climb the highest figurative mountaintop and proclaim, with all the vigor and shrillness that made Roseanne a household name, that TV is good."

TV moguls want to beget culture, not just reflect it. They *want* to create household names, and they *want* to reengineer our sense of values. Even as I write, the show *Ellen* is pushing us to the next level of acceptance of lesbianism by introducing Ellen's first "encounter" with a woman on the air. Other shows depict gay characters in a favorable light, with the number of such characters out of proportion with their presence in the society at large. Who can overlook the apparent agenda in this instance, promoted by TV and its progressive backers, to normalize gay relationships and convince us eventually to support legislation that would render same-sex marriages legal? Despite the folksy protestations of ABC, the media moguls, who amass money, design and disseminate messages, and wield uncanny power, comprise a large segment of today's elite. It's disingenuous for them to pretend otherwise.

Christopher Lasch in his last book, *The Revolt of the Elites and the Betrayal of Democracy,* argues that the elites are withdrawing into a little world of their own, where they can feel safe and superior. Have we therefore nothing to fear from this new breed? Indeed we do. They consist of all those corporate managers and all those professionals, he tells us, who create and control information. In revolt against "Middle America," they are restless, migratory, and cosmopolitan. Even worse, says Lasch:

> They have mounted a crusade to sanitize American society: to create a "smoke-free environment," to censor everything from pornography to "hate speech," and at the same time, incongruously, to extend the range of personal choice in matters where most people feel the need of solid moral guidelines. When confronted with resistance . . . they betray the venomous hatred that lies not far beneath the smiling face of upper-middle-class benevolence. Opposition makes humanitarians forget the liberal virtues they claim to uphold. They become petulant, self-righteous, intolerant. In the heat of political controversy, they find it impossible to conceal their contempt for those who stubbornly refuse to see the light. . . .

A couple of lines later Lasch makes the attitude of the new breed of elites toward the rest of us—"the masses"—unmistakably clear: Everyone who represents any cause—for example, the restoration of traditional family values—that impedes their progressive agenda they regard "with mingled scorn and contempt."[32] The new elitists may well win the day not because they have right but because they have might, along with a good deal of money, on their side.

Clearly, our current state of moral affairs proves that utilitarianism is untenable. As the elitists know too well, pleasure and happiness are subjective and relative, no matter how many genteel, well-intentioned John Stuart Mills may arise to argue that the hierarchy of pleasures that promotes general happiness is self-evident to people of culture and experience. Not only elitists but cynics, realists, and even evangelical Christians know better. Self-interest, even when bedecked in the Victorian garb of utilitarianism, can never be "enlightened," only benighted. Where subjectivity rules, there can be no such thing as "enlightened self-interest."

So where do we go from here? Once man has become autonomous, what comes next? Tradition, we are now told, is inferior to progress; faith and revelation, to reason; reason, to private intuition. In only two centuries we can witness the birth of a new myth. It's the myth of the "the new man," who has ascended the throne once occupied by God, Scripture, and sacred tradition. In the newly forming modern societies governed by the social contract, mankind, so runs the argument, has achieved the freedom for which he has longed since the dawn of time. He has reclaimed his birthright: "His freedom in the mythical state of nature was complete autonomy. He was a law unto himself."[33] Now, according to writers from Hobbes through Mill, man has regained his autonomy, within the limits of good taste and government, of course.

But up until the time of Mill, man was still man, a human still a human, a little above the animals, a little below the angels. As we observe our culture enter its second stage of decline on the way to relativism, we will find that man's assumption about his humanness, his claim to a unique status in creation, must soon disintegrate also. Publishing *The Origin of Species* in 1859, the same year in which Mill published *On Liberty*, Darwin rocked the world, changing it forever with a new presupposition: man is just a highly evolved animal.

SECOND STAGE
IN THE SLIDE TOWARD RELATIVISM

———

From 1859 to 1900, man declared himself

to be an evolving, progressing animal, possessing unlimited

potential. From then on, existence was presumed

to precede essence, and naturalism began to reign supreme

among the leading intellectuals.

———

6

"MAN, TOO, IS AN ANIMAL"

Bertrand Russell's assessment of Charles Darwin, written a half century ago, now seems obvious, if not trite: "What Galileo and Newton were to the seventeenth century Darwin was to the nineteenth."[1] Darwin was the same for the twentieth century. Today nearly every schoolkid knows that Darwin is the father of evolutionary theory. Many people don't realize, however, that the thought of Darwin had plenty of precursors—from Anaximander (610-570 B.C.) and Democritus (460-370? B.C.) to the French biologist Jean-Baptiste Lamarck (1744-1829) and Darwin's own grandfather Erasmus Darwin (1731-1802), who wrote his books *Zoonomia* and *The Temple of Nature* from an evolutionary perspective. One modern science writer even includes David Hume in the list of influences.[2] Darwin admits, moreover, in his "Introduction" to *The Origin of Species* (1859) that he derived his theory of natural selection or "the survival of the fittest" from the population studies of Thomas Malthus (1766-1834).[3] Modest man that Darwin was, he in fact carefully gives credit where credit is due by referring to many of his influential scientific colleagues in "An Historical Sketch" at the beginning of *The Origin*.

Many people don't realize, either, that Darwin wasn't as confident of his theory as the quotation by Russell, if taken at face value, might suggest. A scan of the table of contents of *The Origin* will reveal how sensitive Darwin was to legitimate objections to his theory. He concedes a number of times to the inadequacy of the fossil record in offering convincing support of his theory. He does so in Chapter VI, "Difficulties of the Theory," Chapter X, "On the Imperfection of the Geological Record," and Chapter XV, "Recapitulation and Conclusion." In the end he could answer such "questions and objections only on the supposition that the geological record is far more imperfect than most geologists believe,"[4] yet wouldn't concede that the imperfect record seriously damaged his theory. He was hopeful that future investigation would reveal the thousands of missing links that were necessary to prove his theory. Even in *The Descent of Man* (1872), in which he declares that the progenitors of man are apes, he refers in his "General Summary and Conclusions" to the speculative nature of much of his thought in the book: "Many of the views which have been advanced are highly speculative, and some no doubt will prove erroneous. . . ."[5]

At home his confidence may have also been undermined somewhat by his wife, who once appealed in a letter to him to understand her religious faith and to appreciate why she might have some difficulties with his theories. Darwin, revealing his sensitivity toward her misgivings, wrote simply at the bottom of her letter: "When I am dead, know that many times I have kissed and cried over this."[6] Surely, the theologically trained Darwin recognized the implications of his theories for believers.[7]

Perhaps in part for this reason, the frail, retiring Darwin took twenty-three years to publish *The Origin* after the return of the *Beagle* from the Galapagos Islands and another twelve years to publish his *Descent of Man* after the publication of *The Origin*. From the start, too, Darwin needed help in spreading his word. He needed his intellectual "bulldogs"—Thomas H. Huxley, the Englishman, and Ernst Haeckel, the German, and also Herbert Spencer, the great Victorian social scientist—to carry his theory out into the world where it could be declared not theory but fact. It wasn't Charles Darwin but T. H. Huxley, the grandfather of Julian and Aldous Huxley, who defeated Bishop Wilberforce in the famous public debate held before the British Association of Oxford in 1860. Since then, the many supporters of Darwinism have continued to grow among the outspoken segments of the population—from the ACLU in the famous Scopes Trial of 1925[8]; Francis Crick, who with James Watson co-discovered the double helix of DNA; the late Carl Sagan, who spoke as authoritatively about evolution as he did about astronomy; and more recently, Richard Dawkins, the formidable evolutionist and zoologist of Oxford, who has written the influential books *The Blind Watchmaker* and *The Selfish Gene.* Fortunately, evolutionary theory has had its formidable skeptics and critics too. During the time of Darwin there were Louis Agassiz, professor of zoology at Harvard, and Richard Owen, the first director of the Natural History Museum of London. And many continental scientists, of whom in America we hear little, have always had serious doubts about the theory.[9] Recently several scholars of the first rank, including Phillip E. Johnson, Alan Hayward, Del Ratzsch, and Michael J. Behe, have been offering thoughtful challenges to evolutionary theory on several fronts—from the paucity of proof in the fossil record to the mathematical improbability that life originated by chance to the new discoveries about the material irreducibility of DNA and RNA information.[10] The theory of evolution is even starting to come under fire publicly, as a debate on William F. Buckley's *Firing Line,* which aired late in 1997, proved. If Phillip E. Johnson, professor of law at University of California Berkeley, is right, just as the great "scientific" thinkers Marx and Freud have fallen from their high stations during our lifetimes, so will Darwin. "I am convinced that Darwin is next. . . . His fall," says Johnson hopefully, "will be by far the mightiest of the three."[11]

Any public challenges to macroevolution, or Darwin's "general theory" of evolution, must certainly be welcomed by reasonable skeptics. But the real crisis, as I have been arguing in this book, really involves values. The theory of macroevolution has contributed greatly to the modern slide toward relativism, leading modern men and women—as well as children and teenagers—to conclude that *all* change—material or moral—is "evolution," and all evolution is progress. Without realizing it, people unquestioningly accept Darwin's faith: "as natural selection works solely by and for the good of each being, all corporeal and mental endowments will tend to progress towards perfection."[12] Before we can understand the harmful effect that Darwinism has had on culture and ethics, however, we need to review a few of the basics of Darwin's theories as they appear in both *The Origin of Species* and *The Descent of Man.* This new stage in the decline of modern morals, in our study of the history of ideas, can't be understood apart from the implications of Darwin's naturalistic, empirical, utilitarian, materialistic science.

THE HIGHEST-ORDER ANIMAL

The first five chapters of *The Origin* shouldn't arouse controversy. Based on studies of animal husbandry, plant hybridism, and life on the Galapagos Islands, Darwin "merely proposes that new races and species arise in nature by the agency of natural selection."[13] Such a proposal is truly modest because we can observe that change occurs in nature. We can understand how over time various factors, inclining species toward competition with other species or the environment, can make finch beaks longer or shorter, moth wings gray or white, or human skin black, brown, yellow, or beige. We can understand how over time woolly mammoths might become elephants; big saber-toothed cats, Bengal tigers. Many refer to this part of Darwin's theory as "special evolution" or microevolution. A reasonable person is likely to accept the preponderance of evidence for this part of the theory.

The theory creates controversy among critics, many of whom are simply labeled "creationists," when it sets out to generalize from the modest "special theory" to the bold "general theory" or macroevolution. The general theory, says Michael Denton, is more extreme: "It makes the claim that the 'special theory' applies universally; and hence that the appearance of all the manifold diversity of life on Earth can be explained by a simple extrapolation of the processes which bring about relatively trivial changes such as those seen on the Galapagos Islands." When people think of evolution, it's this aspect of it, according to Denton, of which they think.[14] They also think of this aspect when they accept the conclusions of science about the origin and development of life on earth—and most especially the origin and development of man.

Therefore, we need to understand the main outlines of Darwin's thought as they relate to his specific conclusions, however tentative they were at the time, and our interpretation of them today. We must understand the origins of the dogma of Darwinism—or "the fact of evolution"—and begin to skeptically regard some of its claims.

Favorable Variation and Natural Selection Explain Evolution

In Darwin's system, variation—in the sense of individual differences within species—precedes natural selection. In *The Origin* Darwin

explains, "Some have . . . imagined that natural selection induces vari-
ability, whereas it implies only the preservation of such variations as
arise and are beneficial to the being under its conditions of life."
Variation in nature isn't "due to chance," says Darwin (unlike many of
his modern-day followers), but is related to numerous factors: "vari-
ability is generally related to the conditions of life to which each species
has been exposed during several successive generations." These changes
can affect the whole organism or just parts of it. Always one must consider the "nature of the organism" and "the nature of the conditions."
Darwin, cautious as he was, however, was reluctant to leave change to
conditions alone: "we may safely conclude that the innumerable complex co-adaptations of structure, which we see throughout nature
between various organic beings, cannot be attributed simply to such
action." Despite much complex analysis of examples, he concludes that
"Our ignorance of the laws of variation is profound." Nevertheless, he
asserts that "we have reason to believe that it is the steady accumula-
tion of beneficial differences which has given rise to all the more important modifications of structure. . . ." Making what appears to be an
aesthetic judgment, he even claims that many modifications add to "the
beautiful and harmonious diversity of nature."[15]

Natural selection, driven by competition among and within popu-
lations, determines who lives and who dies—or which variations persist
and which disappear—based on which modifications are advantageous
for survival. This process Darwin calls "the struggle for existence" or
"the survival of the fittest." Natural selection, says Darwin, applies to
groups; sexual selection applies to individuals, resulting in greater offspring for the desirable—namely, the most vigorous and best
adapted—males. The variations that favor preservation are always the
best. They incline toward improvement. According to Darwin:

> But if variations useful to any organic being ever do occur,
> assuredly individuals thus characterised will have the best chance
> of being preserved in the struggle of life; and from the strong
> principle of inheritance, these will tend to produce offspring sim-
> ilarly characterised. This principle of preservation, or the survival
> of the fittest, I have called Natural Selection. It leads to the
> improvement of each creature in relation to its organic and inor-

ganic conditions of life, and . . . in most cases, to what must be regarded as an advance in organisation.[16]

Darwin goes on to say on the same page that "the more diversified the descendants become, the better will be their chance of success in the battle of life." Despite the apparent struggle of life that prevails, he reminds us later that natural selection, as it relates to the formation of structures and organs within individuals, "acts solely by and for the good of each."[17] In sum, we learn from Darwin that the best signs of survival point in the direction of increasing diversity, adaptability, utility, and complexity within organisms.

Darwin's logic, however, isn't impeccable. He lays the groundwork for his theory—which is driven by favorable variation and natural selection—by using a false analogy. He likens natural selection to artificial selection in animal husbandry. He tries to mask his false analogy by claiming that man only "unintentionally exposes organic beings to new conditions of life."[18] Using the word "unintentionally," he tries to blot from the mind of the reader any notions of intelligent design that might in fact also apply to the origin and development of species in the natural world. But clearly animal husbandry and plant hybridism *are* guided by the hand of an intelligent designer—man. Darwin's closed naturalistic system would surely have suffered a crushing blow had he conceded that a supernatural Designer exists. For if such design were present, then the fingerprints of the Creator might still be found within creation, as Romans 1 so beautifully argues.

Fortunately, today the design argument is making a comeback as a number of scientists, as I mentioned earlier, are making discoveries in molecular biology at the biochemical level about the vast differences between matter and information and are reconsidering the laws of probability as they relate to variation and natural selection.[19]

All Life Has Evolved by Slow Descent over Aeons

Another key component of Darwinism is the conclusion that species evolve by means of *slow* "descent by modification," according to the principles of variation and natural selection. Darwin is so confident of the process that he waxes eloquent in Chapter IV of *The Origin*: "Slow

though the process of selection may be . . . I can see no limit to the amount
of change, to the beauty and complexity of the coadaptations between
all organic beings, one with another and with their physical conditions
of life, which may have been effected in the long course of time through
nature's *power of selection, that is by the survival of the fittest"* (italics
mine).[20] Notice how Darwin carefully qualifies his use of the word
"power," lest we conclude that he is being anything other than naturalistic and materialistic in his explanations. Darwin's theory, then, rests on
the "fact" that mutations take place slowly by means of the "power of
selection." Nature can't, he agrees with the ancients, proceed by leaps:
Natura non facit saltum. Darwin's theory won't allow for saltations: "for
natural selection acts only by taking advantage of slight successive variations; she [nature] can never take a great and sudden leap, but must
advance by short and sure, though slow steps."[21] We can only imagine
the gleam in the modest Darwin's eyes when he contemplated "the beauty
and complexity" of such mutations over the long reaches of time.

Despite Darwin's satisfaction with his theory of descent, T. H.
Huxley warned him that his "dogmatic gradualism" could lead his theory into trouble.[22] How would it stand, even as Darwin concedes in *The
Origin*, if sufficient transitional forms weren't eventually found? By
Darwin's own admission, the fossil record was incomplete and imperfect in his time. Although he does try to rationalize the incomplete record
of his day in a number of ways, he does make two honest admissions—
in the hopes, naturally, that the fossil record would one day be complete.
First, he acknowledges that the paucity of geological evidence is "the
most obvious and serious objection" against his theory,[23] admitting that
the absence of his intermediate—"missing"—links from the record
raises serious "questions and objections." Yet, he says, he must proceed
on "the supposition that the geological record is far more perfect than
most geologists believe."[24]

Second, he concedes that the Cambrian explosion (500,000,000
years ago) poses serious problems for his theory. "If numerous species,"
he says, "belonging to the same genera or families, have really started
into life at once, *the fact would be fatal* to the theory of evolution
through natural selection" (italics mine).[25] To ward off this fatal blow,
he again appeals to the imperfection of the geological record and then
on the next page resorts to speculation, indeed to circular reasoning:

"Consequently, if the theory be true, it is indisputable that before the lowest Cambrian stratum was deposited, long periods elapsed, as long as, or probably far longer than, the whole interval from the Cambrian age to the present day; and that during these vast periods the world swarmed with living creatures."[26] On Darwin's big "if," it would seem, much of modern evolutionary theory rests. The theory simply *has* to be correct, maintains Darwin. Who among us, then, dares dispute it?

Unfortunately, the inadequate fossil record and the Cambrian explosion continue to frustrate the claims of Darwinism. Too many gaps still exist, just as they did in Darwin's day.[27] Paleontological and geological records may have been incomplete in Darwin's day, but they are much more complete today. We may well have already unearthed what amounts to nearly 90 percent of the existing record. "Of the 329 living families of terrestrial vertebrates 261 or 79.1 percent have been found as fossils and, when birds (which are poorly fossilized) are excluded, the percentage rises to 87.8 percent. . . ."[28] So where are all the intermediate forms that Darwin predicted would be found?

Naturally, the gaps that persist today have led some thoughtful scientists to counter objections to macroevolution by maintaining that saltation does occur—or to search for other trends in the fossil record. Most prominent among the paleontologists are Niles Eldridge and Stephen Jay Gould, who have posited the theory of "punctuated equilibrium" to explain the sudden origination of new species and their failure to modify thereafter. In brief, they maintain that sometimes the evolutionary process drags for long periods and then unexpectedly makes leaps forward, thus explaining why there are few convincing intermediate forms between, say, reptiles and birds. But most evolutionists of note reject the Eldridge-Gould hypothesis, still clinging to Darwin's gradualism.

Man Has Descended from a Common Ancestor, Probably Arboreal

Having laid the groundwork in *The Origin*, Darwin can now arrive at his most morally disastrous conclusion: man, too, is an animal. In the last chapter of *The Descent of Man*, Darwin claims, "The main conclusion here arrived at . . . is that man is descended from some less highly organised form. The grounds upon which this conclusion rests will never be shaken, for the close similarity between man and the lower animals" is based on "facts which cannot be disputed." More specifically, "We thus learn that man is descended from a hairy, tailed quadruped, probably arboreal in its habits, and an inhabitant of the old world." Only savages, the usually modest Darwin asserts dogmatically, can "any longer believe that man is the work of a separate act of creation."[29]

Does Darwin ascribe even humbler origins to humans? Despite some of the qualifications he offers in both *The Origin* and *The Descent of Man*, he certainly does. If man is an animal, he too must have evolved from some less highly evolved form than even apes. "Analogy," he says in *The Origin*, "would lead me one step farther, namely, to the belief that all animals and plants are descended from some one prototype." They derive from a "common origin," or they "descended from some one primordial form."[30] Man isn't just an animal, a mammal, but in some strange way a mollusk, insect, and amoeba. After all, "Man still bears in his bodily frame the indelible stamp of his lowly origin."[31] But then analogies rarely prove anything with certainty.

Once man is regarded as an evolving animal, becoming more variegated and complex as he adapts to his environment, what changes in thought might be effected in the minds and behavior of people reared on such a presupposition? "Man is an animal," you may say. So what?

The Influence of the Mega-Idea

How a "theory" can alter moral perceptions and beliefs is no more clearly shown than by the theory of evolution. Based on naturalistic and empiricist, even materialistic, presuppositions dating back to the seventeenth century, the theory of evolution has been used as a battering ram in the continuing assault on Christianity in particular and theism in general. Some of the passionate advocacy of the theory may be chalked up, I believe, to bad motives—and an antipathy toward religion and supernatural revelation. Of course, the tyranny of the Roman Catholic Church, squabbles among Protestant sects, and outbreaks of violence among Roman Catholic and Protestant countries (for example, the bloody Thirty Years' War, which ended in 1648) didn't help Christianity retain the loyalty of many great thinkers. But once the critiques of the Faith were unleashed, the critics quickly set out to ravage all the supernatural claims of Christianity. This continuing feeding frenzy among intellectuals has led as much as anything else to the current prominence of Darwinism. So let's look briefly at what Darwinism itself has not so innocently unleashed in our time, and the ideologies, practices, and prejudices it has spawned.

Social Darwinism

The term *social Darwinism* is often used as a rallying reproach of the radical left against rapacious capitalism, but I'm not using the term in that sense at all. The origin of the social Darwinist view is often unfairly attributed to Herbert Spencer who, like many other Victorians, believed in the limitless possibilities of progress. True, Spencer did believe in the necessity of competition among men in furthering the evolution of society as an organism. Yet he wasn't, as Denton puts it, "the only intellectual at the time to draw an analogy between the competitive spirit of the free market economy as the driving force behind social and economic progress and Darwin's concept of natural selection as the driving force behind evolution."[32] In short, social Darwinism, whoever its proponents may be, is the view that the principle of natural selection, the survival of the fittest, does—and indeed *should*—apply to organisms socially and economically, just as it does biologically. The fitter *animals* are always better fitted for the struggle for existence. The circular logic of social Darwinism is obvious: only the fit humans succeed in the marketplace or society; and thus those humans who do succeed must obviously be the fit ones.

The rationalizations that may follow from this logic are always contemptible. In late-nineteenth-century America and England, the most industrialized of nations, it meant that certain captains of industry, owners of sweatshops, and privileged landowners could explain why they occupied the top rungs of society. They were fitter than the poor. Today the rationalizations of social Darwinism still persist, it seems to me. If we adopt the media's view of society, for example, the upper-middle and upper classes are the fittest. Urging us to aspire to those levels, ads and other pop cultural forms continually impress us with the manifold toys and joys of the rich and famous. Meanwhile, the average man can gauge his success as a "competitor" if he can afford to drive a new sports utility van, live in the 'burbs, and send his 2.3 kids to a private school. The

sexually attractive and fit thrive in the movie, sports, and music indus-
tries, setting standards that the rest of us can never meet and establishing a pace that can only lead to coronaries for most of us.

Thus a new message is beginning to emerge as technology advances:
"Can you keep up?" Alvin Toffler presents this message in his book
Powershift, in which he implies that the possessors of information of the
future who can move the fastest will carry the banner of evolution for
the species: "Primitive organisms have slow neural systems. The more
evolved human nervous system processes signals faster. The same is true
of primitive and advanced economies. Historically, power has shifted
from the slow to the fast—whether we speak of species or nations."[33]
Only the genetically fittest—the fastest, most complex—will succeed and
possess the power and means to survive.

Will Durant in *The Pleasures of Philosophy* points out that T. H.
Huxley was horrified when he considered where the theory of evolution
might lead socially, but Durant then quickly points out that he doesn't
think Darwin had such a callous view in mind. Durant contends that
Darwin believed that evolving man, man in his higher state, is governed
by social instincts and sentiments of sympathy.[34] True, Darwin does discuss the development of moral qualities, the conscience, along utilitarian lines in *The Descent of Man*. But the idea that these qualities could
arise from natural selection, as Darwin claims, is based more on faith
than science. Like Bentham and Mill, Darwin claims that "the greatest
happiness principle indirectly serves as a nearly safe standard of right
and wrong."[35] Like Hume, Darwin finds in man an innate sympathy. In
short, in terms of moral philosophy Darwin simply falls back on the
work of his predecessors without fully considering the implications of
the ruthless competition that underlies the process of evolution. In fearing the implications of a ready social acceptance of Darwinism, T. H.
Huxley proved himself to be the sager philosopher.

Always an astute analyst, Bertrand Russell also understood the theory well: "Darwinism was an application to the whole of animal and
vegetable life of Malthus's theory of population, which was an integral
part of the politics and economics of the Benthamites—a global free
competition, in which victory went to the animals that most resembled
the capitalists." Russell adds, perhaps sarcastically, "Darwin's 'Survival
of the Fittest' led, when thoroughly assimilated, to something more like

Nietzsche's philosophy than like Bentham's."[36] At the end of *The Descent of Man*, Darwin confirms the observations of Russell: "Man, like every other animal, has no doubt advanced to his present high condition through a struggle for existence consequent on his rapid multiplication; and if he is to advance still higher, it is to be feared that he must remain subject to a severe struggle." Darwin says that he approves of this competition, lest man "sink into indolence, and the more gifted men would not be more successful in the battle of life than the less gifted." Indeed, declares Darwin, "There should be open competition for all men. . . ."[37] If competition is so fierce, one might reasonably ask, why would some vague sense of "sympathy" induce a man to consider the welfare of the greatest number above his own?

We also find a couple of other conclusions in Darwin that might embarrass his modern followers. My purpose in introducing these conclusions into the record on Darwin is to rattle the faith of those who have been taught to see in all of Darwin's theorizing a kind of inevitability and infallibility, as though the man were scientist par excellence. First, in *The Descent of Man*, Darwin defies the truisms of feminism. The word *man* carries added sexist significance since Darwin concludes that "Man is more courageous, pugnacious and energetic than woman, and has a more inventive genius." Man's intellect is superior to woman's, he tells us: "The chief distinction in the intellectual powers of the two sexes is shewn by man's attaining to a higher eminence, in whatever he takes up, than can a woman. . . ." Man, then, is the better, fitter competitor socially.

Second, Darwin suggests at the end of *The Descent of Man* that his theory not only argues for the importance of universal education but also perhaps for a consideration of eugenics. He shrinks from advocating eugenics, but he does advise that "Both sexes ought to refrain from marriage if they are in any marked degree inferior in body or mind . . .," and "all ought to refrain from marriage who cannot avoid abject poverty for their children." Darwin admits that "if the prudent avoid marriage, whilst the reckless marry the *inferior* members [this will] tend to supplant the *better* members of society" (italics mine).[38] But who are these "better" members? Clearly, the fit, the rich, the intelligent competitors. Surely, if Darwin missed the mark in some matters, then he may have missed the mark in others.

If readers are unconvinced about the persistence of social

Darwinism, I will relate a brief personal story. Not long ago in a college class, one of my brightest students, a science major, argued for the legalization of drugs on the basis of a frank social Darwinism. To my horror, he explained it to me in private in this callow, callous way: "If we keep supplying drugs to the poor and 'stupid' people who want them, then they will all kill themselves off over time. We will thus end up with a more highly evolved society, full of smarter, fitter people."

Legal Positivism

Hobbes, as we have already found, claimed that man, not God, makes law. Darwin certainly agreed with this view—man responds to the "approbation and disapprobation of his fellows."[39] But Darwin made law strictly a naturalistic phenomenon. In time the stronger animals win. They make the laws. This ethical consciousness, according to Harold O. J. Brown, is the one by which we abide today: "we believe that men and women can make laws and that the concept of an unjust law is a contradiction in terms" because it is man-made law, not "divine command" that sets the boundaries of justice. No longer, says Brown, do we appeal to a "Law above the laws." Today it's the written laws that create the justice. And these are based on "several varieties of sensate ethics, including utilitarianism and hedonism as well as varieties and modifications of these systems."[40] In Darwinist terms, law justifies itself as the will of the fittest—namely, those in power. It's not just men who make the law but *certain* men—for example, the king or body of rulers advocated by Thomas Hobbes.

Notice, too, how much of the law today hinges not just on precedent (common law and tradition) but on legal language and technicalities. Who among us would dare to enter the deep waters of legalese and complicated judicial procedure? Few of us, for example, can appreciate the rights of a child molester who hasn't been "properly mirandized" or of a drug dealer whose stash was uncovered without a "properly served warrant." Few of us would think it prudent to draft a child custody and support agreement, according to what is right and fair under God, apart from attorneys and a court system. Legal mumbo jumbo and bureaucracy make slaves of us all. It may be for this reason that majoring in law is one path to social mastery and empowerment today.

Also, today the Supreme Court is necessarily, in light of legal positivism, invested with far more authority and respect, as a body of persons, than ever before. It can dispense not just law but morality. The recently overturned Amendment 2 voted into law by the citizens of Colorado may serve as an excellent case in point. Coloradans had simply voted that no special rights or privileges be granted to homosexuals by any legislative bodies in the state. The amendment didn't deny any civil or legal rights to homosexuals. Nevertheless, led by six members, the Supreme Court struck down Amendment 2, calling it unconstitutional. Says law professor Phillip E. Johnson of University of California Berkeley, they managed "to find in the Constitution a principle that laws based on 'animosity' toward homosexuality are unconstitutional."[41] The crisis in law thus becomes one of authority and power in almost every case. As Brown puts it:

> The simplest and most straightforward expressions of the will of the people, given for example in popular referendum, can immediately be overthrown by state or federal judges allegedly on the basis of the Constitution. In fact, the Constitution means only what the judges want it to mean at any moment, neither more nor less. Popularly voted constitutional amendments can speedily be declared "unconstitutional" by unelected judges.[42]

When no law exists above man to guide and govern him, appealing to his heart, mind, and conscience, then surely the might and money—or the fitness—of the lawmakers must make right. When we cease to bow before God, we then naturally bow before Mammon.

The Debasement of Man

Most frighteningly, a man who is nothing more than an animal has nothing beyond himself, his pleasures and satisfactions, for which to strive. The art and literature of the past century certainly testifies to man's increasing preoccupation with himself as a dwarfed, sense-bound creature. Consider literature since Darwin's day, and certainly since Freud's day, by which time most writers had shed the last vestiges of Victorian fussiness. By the late nineteenth century French writers like Zola,

Flaubert, and Baudelaire began to reveal the darker side of the human social animal. He was a fraud and hypocrite. "Adulteries without love, sins without punishment or redemption," says Allan Bloom, "became the authentic themes of their art."[43] Although an American like Kate Chopin explored at the turn of the century the sexual liberation of a woman in *The Awakening*, British writers of the early decades of the twentieth century really set the pace in redefining our heroes and heroines downward. During this time, James Joyce wrote *Ulysses*, and D. H. Lawrence *Lady Chatterley's Lover*. The American writers came later: Hemingway with his decadent characters in *The Sun Also Rises* and Henry Miller with his amoral hero in *The Tropic of Cancer*. Even in serious studies of language today, in the field of linguistics, no one questions the new orthodoxy about the diminished nature and stature of man. We are, linguists tell us, simply "languagized animals," with, according to Noam Chomsky, a genetic propensity toward the development of language. We are chattering animals in Reeboks.

A loss of sexual morality also seems to play a large part in the debasement of man. According to Arnold Toynbee, such a loss is particularly lamentable because "Sexual license is an expression of a loss of faith and hope in mankind's future."[44] Consider the damage alone that the famous Dr. Alfred C. Kinsey has done to modern sexual morés. "Annals of Sexology: DR. YES," an article published in the Summer 1997 issue of *The New Yorker*, tells the sordid story of a book that overreached its legitimate influence. In the late 1940s, for example, *Life* magazine likened the impact of *Sexual Behavior in the Human Male* (1948) to Darwin's *The Origin of Species*. With the gift of hindsight, *The New Yorker* article points to the flaws in Kinsey's research methodology, "which virtually guaranteed that he would find what he was looking for." It exposes the flawed statistics that have shaped American social thought and policy for nearly fifty years (e.g., that at the time 10 percent of American males were homosexual, that 85 percent had engaged in premarital sex, and that between 30 percent and 45 percent had taken part in extramarital affairs).

The article also details the many sexual perversions in which Kinsey himself engaged and the many sexual obsessions to which he was enslaved. The writer, James H. Jones, asserts that Kinsey "was, in reality, a covert crusader who was determined to use science to free

American society from what he saw as the crippling legacy of Victorian repression." Yet he postured before the public as a benign, detached scientist. "His approach," says Jones, "to what he liked to call 'the human animal' was . . . 'agnostic.'"[45] Kinsey had a hidden agenda, revealed to us in the 1960s, at last fulfilled by the late 1990s.

When a human becomes an animal, he must lose confidence in himself. He will then need to have his self-esteem boosted and his psyche therapeutically adjusted so he can cope with his diminished stature. He will just have to accept his insatiable need for sex and his endless capacity for violence. He is an animal. If his fetuses, mere animal tissue in utero, can't be guaranteed the good life before birth—if the parents are too poor or ignorant—abortion becomes a legitimate option in the struggle for existence. Animals, moreover, must have rights too, for they have the same claim to the space on this planet as man. People who think otherwise, according to the philosopher Peter Singer, are "speciesists." Humans have no special rights. "Animal liberationists do not separate out the Human animal," says one animal rights activist, "so there is no rational basis for saying that a human being has special rights. A rat is a pig is a dog is a boy. They're all mammals."[46] In Oregon, owls displace farmers. In California, hawks prevent a dam from being built that might protect the lives and property of a million people, and snail darters hold up the development of a marshland. And in the slums of Los Angeles or New York, what, asks Peter Singer, "are we to do about *genuine conflicts of interest* like rats biting slum children?" (italics mine).

"I am not sure of the answer," Singer muses, "but the essential point is just that we *do* see this as a conflict of interests, that we recognize that rats have interests too."[47] Many of the present generation, fortunately, still do *not* see rats' "biting slum children" as representing a "genuine conflict of interest." However, if not checked, certain propagandists, hammering away at our children, may well convince them within the next few decades to become "vegans," abandon their speciesism, and embrace the "interests"—read "rights"—of rats.

What, then, is a human being? An animal, a replaceable creature, a zero. No wonder so many science fiction movies in the past fifty years have depicted frenzied birds pecking out the eyes of humans, scurrying insects overrunning towns and feasting on inhabitants, springing raptors outwitting and devouring humans, eerie-looking aliens conquering the planet without conscience or etiquette. We humans are losing ground. We are no longer reaching, with our art, literature, and culture, for heaven but are being dragged toward one of two earthly nightmares. In one, some of us are racing to keep pace with our technology, to maintain our competitive edge, while millions of competitors, haunting us day and night, rush to catch up with us and displace us if they can in the impersonal world of consumerism. Like the hunted, such among us can enjoy no rest.

In the other nightmare others of us, beleaguered and overwhelmed, are being driven back toward the irrational and subjective, toward a new tribalism or a nostalgic return to primitivism. In romanticized rainforests we can heal ourselves with tree moss and flee like the other prey from different kinds of predators who lie in wait for us there—New Age hucksters, hustlers, and false messiahs. When we view our current worldly plight in this way, perhaps the Bible's timeless characterization of our situation is more apt than ever before. As always, our fear—even if not properly understood—is entirely justifiable as we find ourselves ducking for cover. "Your enemy the devil," warned the apostle Peter, "prowls around like a roaring lion looking for someone to devour" (1 Pet. 5:8).

With such thoughts in mind, it's hard to accept the Darwinian—or evolutionary—faith that all evolution is progress toward perfection. But such has been the faith of many since the time of Darwin—from the researchers like Kinsey who wanted to liberate us from our sexual hangups to the teenagers of today who argue quite seriously that MTV, premarital sex, and rap music all represent quantum leaps forward in evolution and moral consciousness. From this point on in this book, the writers become ever more committed to all the implications of this new evolutionary view and agenda. As we move to Karl Marx, we will see how evolutionary theory began to spill over the banks of biology and add credibility to the growing belief that matter alone is real and that man, once he frees himself from the fetters of the past, has the unlimited potential to achieve a bold and bright future.

"Material and Economic Causes Alone Produce Social Change"

The Berlin Wall fell; the Soviet Union collapsed; Russian cosmonauts and American astronauts now cavort weightlessly in space together. These days all our communiqués seem to come from Russia with love. Recently, moreover, *The Black Book of Communism*, an 846-page scholarly tome and best seller in France, has further besmirched the reputation of communism. In it the authors blame communism for the deaths of from 85 to 100 million people globally. One of the authors, Stephane Courtois of the National Center for Scientific Research in Paris, a former Maoist and leftist himself, avers "that mass murder and terror were an inherent part of communism."[1] People, it would seem, are reveling in the fall of communism and the failure of the Bolshevik Revolution. Communism, one may conclude, is all but dead in the West. Certainly, then, the ideas of Karl Marx (1818-1883) can have little impact on Europeans, *much less* on Americans, as we teeter giddily on the cusp of the twenty-first century.

But in fact, the opposite is the case. Not only are Socialist and Communist movements still alive and well throughout the world, but the ideas of Karl Marx are more influential today than they were a century ago. Marx has had many interpreters, and from him have been borne many forms of socialism and communism. Just as we call to mind a Lenin, Stalin, or Mao Tse-Tung when we think of Marx, we must also call to mind kinder, gentler luminaries like George Lukács, Antonio Gramsci, or Herbert Marcuse. The vision and ideology of Karl Marx still inspire many people in the world today. Surprisingly, they also influence American social thought. Even the so-called man on the street is heir to at least one mega-idea of Marx. Because of it, he views history and even institutions in a way that isn't at all Communist but *materialistic*. Along with Thomas Hobbes and modern scientific positivists, Karl Marx has been most responsible for promulgating the modern materialistic view of society and social relations. Stated briefly, the idea holds that social progress (or social evolution) always stems from material causes alone. Like evolution, it's therefore natural, inevitable, and necessary.

To most Christians today—and to Christendom for 1,800 years—such materialism views reality upside-down. It holds, as materialism always does, that existence precedes essence. If such were true, then humans would be justified in facilitating the movement of history through revolution and societal manipulations—in short, through social engineering. From the vantage point of the materialist, changes in circumstances govern changes in human consciousness. Therefore, to reform society, its institutions and values, is to reform man, to make a new man, which people like Marx still want to do in our day. History will result in progress, they believe, but humans can cooperate with evolution by accelerating the changes in their institutions, especially through education and political action (aka consciousness-raising).

Christians, on the other hand, believe that essence precedes existence. A man must have a changed heart, which produces beneficial results in his "consciousness," before he can create lasting beneficial changes in his social order. Reformed hearts, minds truly recast in the image of Christ, result in improved circumstances and institutions in which compassion, social justice, and morality may then predominate and benefit one and all.

Marx was no respecter of Christianity or religion. He consciously set out to debunk the claims of the Faith, which he saw as an impediment to progress. It was he who said, "Religion is the sigh of the oppressed creature, the heart of a heartless world, and the soul of soulless conditions. It is the opium of the people." And then he unabashedly added, "The abolition of religion as the illusory happiness of the people is the demand for their real happiness." As far as Marx was concerned, "once the other-world of truth has vanished," the world of faith, then he and his kind would be able "to establish the truth of this world," the truth of materialism.[2] Therefore, his materialistic mega-idea, no matter how elegantly it may be adorned or sincerely applied by its modern proponents, must be viewed as antithetical to the values and vision of Christianity.

HEGEL ON HIS HEAD

Through the writings of Hegel (1770-1831), Marx became one of the followers of Hegel. He joined the "Hegelian left," consisting of materialists, like himself and Feuerbach, and German Higher Critics, like David Strauss and Bruno Bauer. Say the Durants of this group, "the 'Left' expanded in attacks upon religious and political orthodoxy."[3] Like Hegel and the Hegelians, Marx believed in the dialectical nature of history. Simply put, this dialectical movement is based on a threefold view of actions and ideas in historical contexts: first comes thesis, then antithesis, then finally synthesis. Despotic monarchy (thesis), for example, bred its opposite, scores of oppressed people who struggled for freedom (antithesis). The clash of these two elements of the dialectic then led to democratic reform (synthesis). So in effect, A and not-A clash until B results; then B and not-B will clash until C results; and so on. Thus may be represented Hegel's dialectical movement of history as it ascends toward its great consummation—the full realization of Reason or the unfoldment of the Absolute. Hegel's view was undergirded by a *dialectical idealism*. For him, as for classical philosophers, ideas existed first: essence preceded existence.

Marx, however, by his own admission, "turned Hegel on his head." Marx, striking out in an opposite direction from Hegel, advocated a *dialectical materialism*, he informs us in the second "Preface" to *Capital*. "With me . . .," says Marx, "the ideal is nothing else than the material world reflected by the human mind, and translated into forms of thought."[4] He later adds, "The religious world is but the reflex of the real world."[5] Again, and perhaps more clearly, he says in the *Manifesto of the Communist Party* that man's consciousness "changes with every change in the conditions of his material existence, in his social relations and . . . social life."[6] In short, material conditions alone make us what we are: *existence* precedes essence. As James Q. Wilson puts it, "Marxism . . . is a relentlessly materialistic doctrine in which morality, religion, and philosophy have no independent meaning; they are, in Marx's words, 'phantoms formed in the human brain,' 'ideological reflexes,' 'sublimates of their material life-process.'"[7] This frankly materialistic view is marked by some distinct conclusions about human society and progress.

History Progresses by Means of Class Struggles

Because for Marx, "matter, not spirit, is the driving force" in history, explains Bertrand Russell, "the politics, religion, philosophy, and art of any epoch in human history are . . . an outcome of its methods of production, and, to a lesser extent, of distribution."[8] The means of production, according to Marx, are always in the hands of the ruling class. In feudal society, the nobility controlled it; later the Guild masters controlled it, having wrested it from the nobility; in modern industrial society, the bourgeoisie capitalists, having wrested it from the old Guilds, control it. In this way one economic class rises to power, creates its opposite, and then is supplanted by it. According to Marx, "The history of all hitherto existing society is the history of class struggles."[9] And so history progresses.

In the industrial era, the bourgeoisie capitalists, owing to their total control of production, create a vast oppressed, discontented proletariat, the working class of wage-earners. In *Capital*, Marx stresses, sometimes with great fervency, that this class is reduced, like slaves, to a mere subsistence livelihood by the cold calculations of a capitalism that purposely creates surplus value for the bourgeoisie, the owners and employers: "Capital cares nothing for the length of life of labour power. All that concerns it is simply and solely the maximum of labour power that can be rendered fluent in a working day. It attains this end by shortening the extent of the labourer's life, as a greedy farmer snatches increased produce from the soil by robbing it of its fertility."[10] Having been uprooted from their farms and former trades, they reside in the cities where they become cheap labor, exploited by their oppressors, the capitalists. As they grow in numbers, they begin to oppose their masters, the ruling class, while the ruling class promotes its values in order to preserve the *ancien regime*—all its institutions, including Christianity, and its culture, including its most cherished values. Thus is borne the dialectical struggle of modern times.

Writing of his own era, Marx observes, "Along with the constantly diminishing number of the magnates of capital, who usurp and monopolize all advantages of this process of transformation, grows the mass of misery, oppression, slavery, degradation, exploitation. . . ."

Nevertheless, declares Marx, "with this . . . grows the revolt of the working class, a class always increasing in numbers, and disciplined, united, organized by the very mechanism of the process of capitalist production itself." With such conditions prevailing in industrial Europe of the nineteenth century, something had to snap. Revealing an indebtedness to Hegel, Marx predicts the "evolutionary" outcome of the struggle: "But capitalist production begets, with the inexorability of a law of nature, its own negation. It is the negation of negation."[11] Marx believed he had discovered a law of nature that complemented the laws of evolution. Thus, it's no wonder that he originally had thought of dedicating *Capital* (1867) to the father of evolution, Charles Darwin.

In *Manifesto of the Communist Party*, first written by Marx and his lifelong collaborator Friedrich Engels in 1848, Marx reveals his intentions and sympathies even more fully in the now-famous lines: "[The Communists] openly declare that their ends can be attained only by the forcible overthrow of all existing social conditions. Let the ruling classes tremble at a Communist revolution. The proletarians have nothing to lose but their chains. They have a world to win." Clearly, Marx wanted to stand poised at the vanguard of historical progress. Clearly, he believed that violence, perpetrated by vast armies of workers, was necessary for the new order to arrive. "Workingmen of all countries, unite!" he and Engels cry at the end of the *Manifesto*.[12] As revolutionary Communists have always noted, "You have to break a few eggs to make an omelet."

Progress Favors Socialism and a Classless Society

In the "Preface" to the 1888 edition of the *Manifesto*, Engels informs the reader that the proletariat can't attain its emancipation from the bourgeoisie without, "once and for all, emancipating society at large from all exploitation, oppression, class distinctions and class struggles."[13] With an almost megalomaniacal zeal, he is bold enough also to declare a few lines later that this proposition is "destined to do for history what Darwin's theory has done for biology. . . ." For Engels and Marx, then, the necessary outcome of the evolutionary struggle is socialism, or communism—the abolition of property and class. Where class exists as fostered by the bourgeoisie, no other bond remains between humans "than naked self-interest, than callous 'cash payment.'" "Free" competition and trade have brought into the world nothing but "shameless, direct, brutal exploitation." Even worse, "The bourgeoisie has torn away from the family its sentimental veil, and has reduced the family relation to a mere money relation."[14] Therefore, the new synthesis—borne of the economic, class-driven dialectic—will be a classless society, one in which everyone is "leveled" so that oppression can cease to exist forever.

Such conclusions, however, seem based more on faith than reason. Why should socialism be any better, any more compassionate and just, than capitalism? How can a society ever be classless, free of "class antagonisms," when humans always differ in their abilities and energies? And would such a classless state be good for all—or just, as systems were in the past, only for a few? Some 150 years after the publication of the *Manifesto* and a decade after the disintegration of the Eastern bloc, we can confidently answer some of these questions. We can readily see the naiveté in the vision of Marx. In hindsight we can also see that Marx wasn't even a true Hegelian in his application of the dialectic. As the Durants accurately observe, "Karl Marx . . . thought that capitalism contained the seeds of socialism; that the rival forms of economic organization must clash in a war to the death; and that socialism would prevail. A more consistent Hegelian would have predicted a union of both, as in Western Europe today."[15]

Why couldn't Marx foresee this inevitable synthesis about which the Durants speak? Obviously, like most other human beings, he had an agenda, one based more on his faith in materialism than in his rational commitment to Hegelianism. We all want to see oppression and misery end, but Marx, having rejected faith in God, foresaw social upheaval and revolution as the only solutions to injustice. If "the ruling ideas of each age have ever been the ideas of its ruling class,"[16] then the ruling class must somehow be violently overthrown.

To Alter Man's Institutions Is to Reform Man

To understand the social agenda of Karl Marx, one must not only remember his advocacy of materialism but also understand the contempt he felt toward the bourgeoisie (the middle class) and Christianity. In the *Manifesto* he approvingly claims that "Christian ideas succumbed in the 18th century to rationalist ideas." He attributes "the ideas of religious liberty and freedom of conscience merely . . . to the sway of free competition within the domain of knowledge." He anticipates bourgeois objections to communism and then dismisses them disdainfully a few lines later: "But let us have done with the bourgeois objections. . . ." These "bourgeois objections," among others, insist that "Communism abolishes eternal truths," "religion," and "all morality, instead of constituting them on a new basis. . . ." In an impatient answer to the objections, Marx appeals, almost superciliously, to historical relativism: "What does this accusation reduce itself to? The history of all past society has consisted in the development of class antagonism . . . that assumed different forms at different epochs."[17] In short, his "ignorant" critics are too myopic to even see that they are operating within their own class-dictated prejudices and presuppositions. The bourgeoisie, he assumes, just don't get it.

And because they don't—and *can't*—get it, Marx advocates altering the institutions and thought forms of man, not merely through revolution but through propaganda. Marx and Engels created the International Society in the 1840s for just this purpose, not just to rouse the workers but to transform culture. Karl Marx, as late as 1879, only a few years before his death, admits in an interview with the *Chicago Tribune* (January 5, 1879) that his goal had always been "the emancipation of the human race" and "a higher social condition." To this end, he advocates state education. And he claims that "as socialism grows, religion will disappear. Its disappearance," he says, "must be done by social development, in which education must play a part." As early as 1843 in a letter written to his friend Ruge, he was advancing a similar tactic. He wanted to establish the new world order through a critique of the old, using current theory and knowledge as tools. He didn't favor "hoisting a dogmatic banner," but he did subscribe to "the ruthless criticism of the existing order. . . ." He wanted to awaken people to their "real" plight. "The reform of consciousness consists *entirely,*" he argues, "in making the world aware of its own consciousness, in arousing it from its dream of itself. . . ." Indeed, the journal published by Marx and Engels at that time was to have as its credo "the self-clarification (critical philosophy) of the struggles and wishes of the age."[18]

Seen in this light, Marx was the first advocate of consciousness-raising, in the modern sense. Today Americans ruthlessly criticize themselves, and Western culture ruthlessly criticizes itself, but both steer clear of criticizing others who are "different." After all, if historical relativism is true, we can't be certain that one set of cultural values is better or truer than another. If we made such an assumption, remember, we would be "bourgeois."

INFLUENCE OF THE MEGA-IDEA

Effects, as we are more and more seeing, crisscross, conjoin, and merge. Because the mega-ideas often stream one into another, they can produce similar, or at least tangentially related, consequences. As I mentioned in Chapter 1, in fact, lines of development, the brooks, descend from on high and branch—and sometimes branch again—as they roll toward the mighty river of ethical relativism. Distinct effects stem from each mega-idea, and yet it's easy for the reader, deja-vu style, to get the impression that we have seen this effect before, only in a different form and context. The effects continue to rise like a tide, mounting up, rolling forward, but they continually fulfill one purpose in our examination—to reveal the modern slide toward relativism. They appear eerily familiar, not always because they overlap, but because they form the tides and eddies of our own everyday lives. Such may be said of the consequences that follow from the Marxian mega-idea that all social change stems from material causes alone. Ever since the propaganda of Marx and other philosophical radicals found its way into our cultural lives, it has produced certain distinguishable, all-too-familiar effects.

A Blanket Contempt for Middle-Class Values

With the advent of the radical 1960s and in the wake of McCarthyism, an equivocation in a precise socioeconomic term occurred, it seems to me. It was inaugurated by a newly initiated generation of baby boomers who had been taught to admire revolutionary causes and despise traditional values—for example, the sexual "hang-ups" that writers like the Communist Herbert Marcuse found so deleterious to social progress. It was probably also aided by Karl Marx himself, who used his terms loosely at times as well. The term *bourgeoisie*, which referred to a minority of rulers and owners of the means of production in Marx's *Capital*, became simply "the middle class." Obviously, most of the people whom we designate today as the middle class don't own the means of production and don't manipulate the proletariat, the ever oppressed underclass. The middle class includes government workers, teachers, truck drivers, and even steelworkers, whose unions have improved their lots in life. Today *middle class* is as much a lifestyle as a mind-set. Nevertheless, the term *middle class*, also *bourgeoisie*, in the 1960s soon began to carry its own onus, especially for those college students who had been reared in middle-class homes and suburbs. The guilt of the "ruling class" was collectivized. Everyone who possessed—and everything that embodied—bourgeois, or middle-class, values became suspect.

To this day, sometimes ferociously, the assault on "middle-class" values continues unabated as a politically correct cause in academe.[19] A person is "middle class" in this pejorative sense whether he is economically comfortable or just plain culturally and morally conservative. Anyone who possesses a strong work ethic, cherishes traditional family values, and sticks to commonsense principles of right and wrong is suspect. In academe he is the one whose values are ridiculed as traditional, xenophobic, jingoistic, sexist, homophobic, and racist. And if he is a conservative Christian, he is not *only* a middle-class oppressor but a lower life form, a prescientific throwback to the "Dark Ages." All textbooks are aimed at educating this low-browed fellow to make him more socially aware, more global and tolerant in his outlook.

In my field, for example, *every* freshman literature text has been revised by academic publishers to include literature written by formerly "disenfranchised" groups, groups that didn't fit into the formerly "homogenous" middle-class worldview, groups with different values. Sadly, many classics are jettisoned to make room for "culturally diverse" works, often without regard to literary value. Even some "global" literature of debatable quality is included to broaden the horizons of the narrow-minded. But of course the goal of the social engineers isn't the formation of aesthetic judgment but the reformation of middle-class consciousness on a new basis.

Likewise, in the media, especially in the TV programs and movies produced in Hollywood, the same reflexive assault occurs. In fact, *middle-class* has already been redefined. On TV the assistant mayor in *Spin City* hops from bed to bed without a single middle-class qualm but remains thoroughly and perfectly middle-class in materialistic terms. The main character in *Ellen* was quintessentially middle-class too, with her heterosexual friends, spiffy apartment, and job at the bookstore cum coffee house, even when agonizing over going to bed with a new lesbian lover. Many other TV characters, curiously most often through humor, serve also as critiques of the traditional middle class with its antiquated sexual morés and codes of honor—the pals on *Seinfeld, Drew Carey,* or *Caroline in the City,* for example. Humor may simply be the most disarming, most effective form of propaganda. But serious dramas (*New York Undercover, Melrose Place*) and talk shows (*Jenny Jones, Jerry Springer, RuPaul*) also play their part in this assault. Through their topics and guests, they document the disintegration of the middle-class family, proffering meaningless palaver about "tolerance" as the only alternative. Meanwhile, the USA Network does its part, guaranteeing in a *TV Guide* ad "to break at least 20 percent more commandments than any other line-up" (February 1-7, 1997).

Far more effective in destroying and redefining middle-class values, however, have been the movies in recent years. Of course, there are many egregious examples: *The Piano, Pulp Fiction, Natural Born Killers, The Birdcage,* and so on. But there are more subtle ones too. Consider the much-touted movie *The English Patient.* Wide-eyed students, thinking it a literature lover's dream come true, urged me to watch it. When I did, I did enjoy the exotic settings captured by the exquisite cinematography, the elegance of the diction, and the reach of the saga-like plot. But I was depressed rather than uplifted by the film. The plot pivots not upon an idealistic romance but a sordid affair. Two spoiled rich people deceive a decent chap of a husband. Then when through a kind of poetic comeuppance the hero and heroine meet horrible fates, one a lonely death, the other painful convalescence, we are supposed to view them as tragic figures.

Yet there was nothing sublime or noble about their deeds or lives. They defied middle-class—in their case upper-middle-class—morés and then acted out a maudlin tragedy when they should have fallen instead on their knees in repentance, not for having lost each other, but for having lost their honor and humanity. For "love," the main character betrayed his friends and his country. Such is the romanticism of a Rousseau. Such also is the hedonism of humans who accept their place as animals within a meaningless universe, in which self-defined "love" alone becomes meaningful. As in many modern movies, the theme developed in *The English Patient* celebrates the loosening rather than the strengthening of traditional social relationships.

Thanks to the sensuous cornucopia served up by Hollywood—on TV, in movies, even through popular music—Americans are quietly enjoying their bread and circuses, quite possibly while others are doing the serious thinking and long-range social planning for them. In part, such contempt for middle-class values is a Marxist holdover, based on a disdain for the *ancien regime*, the Judeo-Christian heritage from which Western culture sprang, and on a misplaced faith in the miracle-working power of social change. All change isn't progress, and much of it isn't good.

A Continual Demand for Consciousness-Raising

From every quarter, it seems, we are being urged to change, to grow, to raise our consciousnesses. The dream of the classless—multicultural, pluralistic, nonsexist—society is still alive and well in Western culture, perhaps more so than it was during the time of Karl Marx. Some groups want equality of result as well as equality of opportunity. Most others with this dream want to smash the old barriers that have traditionally defined cultural, sexual, and moral distinctions. Two modern movements that have played major roles in this effort have been feminism and multiculturalism. In the tactics they employ, both, I believe, draw heavily on the materialistic presupposition that if people can only be changed from the outside, by being reeducated or reprogrammed, then society will change for the better. Thus we can be pushed more certainly and rapidly toward that next evolutionary leap forward—a classless, genderless society.

Feminism has been attempting to make the dream a reality for decades. The modern feminist movement began honorably and modestly as an attempt to make society guarantee women an equal opportunity in the workplace—to receive "equal pay for equal work" and to work in the careers of their choice. Nevertheless, from the beginning there was a radical element to the movement as many young college women of the 1960s scrubbed off their makeup and burned their bras, and as the militant voices of women like Gloria Steinem and Betty Friedan reverberated over microphones across the college campuses of our nation.

Soon enough, many of the educated, young, radical women received tenured professorships and continued to further the feminist agenda.

They pushed for abortion rights and the Equal Rights Amendment. They established Women's Studies programs on campuses to set the historical record straight about women's contributions in various fields, to liberate ignorant women from their false identities, and to censure men for their insensitivity and bigotry. By the 1980s dead white European males (DWEMs)—the great classical, Christian, European, and American male leaders and thinkers from the past—had become the enemy. Meanwhile, many sensitive, guilt-ridden young males capitulated to the new feminist vision. At one University of California campus where I taught in the mid-1980s, I heard many men making solemn pledges to the movement by openly proclaiming to each other, "Yes, I'm fully committed to feminism" or, more strangely, "I'm a feminist too."

The feminists, now largely victorious, have set up their small but powerful empires in many areas of our culture. Joining ranks, they have formed cadres, legions, and well-poised phalanxes of politically savvy true believers. In my field, for example, the feminists have long been an imposing presence. Ten years ago in one English department of a major university where I worked, feminists and their sympathizers had, as one full professor complained to me, "taken over" the political reins of the department. Today, alongside other schools of literary theory—formalist, deconstructionist, psychoanalytical—there is also feminist literary criticism. In a typical college textbook used in lower-division introductory literature courses and read by impressionable freshmen, the authors define and explain feminist criticism in this way:

> Feminist critics hold that literature is merely one of many expressions of a patriarchal society whose purpose is to keep women subordinate to men. Thus literature . . . helps to condition women to accept as normal a society that directs them to become nurses rather than doctors, secretaries rather than attorneys or corporate executives, sex symbols rather than thinkers. . . . Beyond this general critique of patriarchy, feminists differ in their detailed analyses. Some have reexamined history to show that a literary canon created by males has slighted and ignored female authors. Others . . . have come up with fresh readings that challenge conventional interpretations, focusing on how women are empowered *in* literary texts or *through writing* literary texts. Some, believing that

language itself allows men to impose their power, use literary analyses to expose the gender bias of language.[20]

Despite the seemingly neutral wording in this passage, the usual feminist crotchets and shibboleths appear. *Patriarchy*, which has conditioned women to accept their inferior status in society, is evil because it allowed men to subordinate—read "dominate"—women. Feminist critics have had to reexamine—read "reinterpret" or "rewrite"—history to give "slighted and ignored female authors" their due. Therefore, radical feminists are now engaged in a righteous power struggle as they seek to empower women and disempower men. They want to raise—that is, change—our consciousnesses and level the playing field. They want G.I. Jane to be as much a reality as Dr. Quinn, Medicine Woman.

Multiculturalism, a more recent phenomenon, has been gaining ground within the past decade or two. On the surface "multiculturalism" sounds benign. Most "cultures" want to live together and get along. Moreover, multiculturalism, along with its allied concepts of diversity and pluralism, is simply descriptive of an indisputable reality in America, as Harold O. J. Brown concedes in *The Sensate Culture*. Our country does, in fact, consist of many peoples, many races and ethnicities. But of course such has always been the case—hence, our motto *e pluribus unum* ("out of many one"). On the other hand, multiculturalism is also prescriptive and proactive. It has its several proponents, usually among the elite, who celebrate the differences among us and politicize them, insisting that we view European culture as chauvinistic and oppressive, and traditional American culture as dogmatic and exclusionary.[21]

Academic multiculturalists, states Gene Edward Veith, Jr., dean of the School of Arts and Sciences and associate professor of English at Concordia University-Wisconsin, "indict Western civilization for its assertion of absolutes and universal principles, which have allegedly resulted in racism, imperialism, sexism, homophobia, and the whole litany of post-Marxist evils. Today," continues Veith, "universities and . . . public schools, the media, and policy makers at almost every level— are dismantling the concept of a unitary American culture in an attempt to establish a 'multicultural' state."[22]

In effect, multiculturalism divides or "tribalizes" people and "balkanizes" the country. It insists, post-Marxist style, that every expression of culture is equal and all truths relative, depending on whose culture or historical epoch is being discussed. It insists that the study of other cultures be given equal time in our American schools. In this way multiculturalism, whether by means of education or politics, becomes "a pattern to be imposed on a society by persuasion, pressure, and for some, even by force. Such is the dictate of the movement known as political correctness: that pluralism, multiculturalism, and diversity be praised, encouraged, and if necessary imposed on Western culture."[23] Thus committed multiculturalists seek to reengineer society along their new lines.

In reality, though, the movement masks an underlying politics of suspicion and mistrust. Like feminism, it proceeds from the position that the majority culture—Western culture or the middle class, if you will—has always been hostile toward the interests of minorities. Driven by ulterior motives, like the villainous bourgeoisie of Marx, the mainstream culture always, deep down, wants to oppress the minorities, disregard their interests, and suppress their voices. In the end the various minorities, however, can't trust each other either as they jockey for recognition and political clout. "In practice," claims Christopher Lasch, "diversity turns out to legitimize a new dogmatism, in which rival minorities take shelter behind a set of beliefs impervious to rational discussion." Such "physical segregation" of these homogenous groups, says Lasch, "has its counterpart in the balkanization of opinion."[24] In this way, not just country but community begins to disintegrate, and so does rational discourse.

The social engineers, whether feminists or multiculturalists, seem to believe that if they can reeducate people and manipulate our institutions, society will "evolve." We will arrive at the classless society of the future, where antagonisms of every kind will no longer exist, because the restrictive, repressive dogmas of Western culture will have been overthrown. Change language, feminists and multiculturalists say, and you will revolutionize perceptions. Change institutions, they say, and you will revolutionize relationships. Change perceptions and relationships, and a liberated humanity will arise, free at last of the *ancien regime*. By means of this agenda, violent revolution will prove unnecessary, and everyone, now raised high on the tiptoes of consciousness, will live happily ever after. But clearly, because of the confusion of tongues that may result from this de-genderized, de-culturized "revolution," life in such a world may not be fit for anyone to live.

A Predilection for Synthesis

So what, then, is the best way to effect such changes and silence dissent? Through an education that stresses synthesis—sometimes called "consensus"—rather than rational discourse. Traditionally, based on Judeo-Christian and Greco-Roman presuppositions, Western thinkers accepted that truth and falsehood exist. They employed rational analysis and discourse rigorously to pursue the truth. In *On Sophistical Refutations*, Aristotle acknowledges that arguments are often "dialectical": people "reason from premisses generally accepted, to the contradictory of a given thesis."[25] Still, in thought and word, Aristotle held, truth exists. "As there are in the mind thoughts . . . which must be either true or false, so it is in speech."[26]

Francis Schaeffer put the same thought beautifully and simply in *The God Who Is There*. Until very recently, people took antithesis seriously, for it pervaded their thought: "They took it for granted that if anything was true, the opposite was false. In morality, if one thing was right, its opposite was wrong. The little formula, 'A is A' and 'If you have A it is not non-A,' is the first move in classical thought."[27]

Today, however, we have abandoned the classical—but not the Hegelian-Marxist—dialectical method. We seek agreement, consensus, win-win solutions—in short, *synthesis*. The method that we now teach our children and promote throughout society is simple really. Conflict, it holds, is healthy and necessary, but resolution and harmony are better. By discussing our differences, "dialoguing," seeking to resolve either-or dilemmas, we arrive at a consensus, at new "higher" solutions to old problems. And these new solutions, in some Hegelian, Marxian, Darwinian way, are supposed to represent advances. Gradually, as a society, proponents of this approach believe, we are learning to accept and respect our differences so that we can better cooperate and live in harmony. But just as Marx couldn't foresee the future, neither can these people. This new agenda itself may well lead to fragmentation, not synthesis, to conflict, not harmony.

If applied in the realms of ethics and faith, this method is a prescription for disaster. Where ethical choices are concerned, many issues have and will always have two sides; but we won't be certain what these issues are if progressives keep preaching synthesis. Issues like drug addiction, homosexuality, adultery, and even, for example, the practice of female circumcision among our new Middle-Eastern citizenry don't

lend themselves to "synthetic" solutions. Either x is right or it's wrong.
Common sense—indeed our Judeo-Christian heritage—tells us that
child pornography is wrong. It tells us too that genocide is wrong. Where
is the synthesis to be found in such cases? When something is clearly
wrong, there is no room for "values clarification." The solution is to
choose the right course and reject the wrong. Where faith is concerned,
the same dialectic, either x or *not x*, must remain. Any attempt at synthesis leads to inconsistency and irrationalism.

Christianity is particularly susceptible in this regard, for it's grounded
in the most basic of antitheses. As Schaeffer puts it, "We must not forget
that historic Christianity stands on a basis of antithesis. Without it, historic Christianity is meaningless. The basic antithesis is that God objectively exists in contrast (in antithesis) to His not existing." When it comes
to believing in God or not, where is the possibility for synthesis? The position a person takes makes all the difference in the world, says Schaeffer:
Which of these two is the reality alters "everything in the area of knowledge and morals and in the whole of life."[28] Seen in this light, synthesis
is rarely, if ever, an effective solution to serious dilemmas.

Up to this point in the book, most thinkers have in one way or
another been rationalists, and their mega-ideas have presupposed the
existence of order in the universe. They believed that by means of reason, either scientific or philosophical, they could discover the truth. Even
the unorthodox Marx was essentially a rationalist. Says Allan Bloom,
summarizing the thought of Marx in his *Closing of the American Mind*,
"although men, according to him, are in the grip of the historical process, that process itself is rational and has as its end the rational freedom
of man." In the writings of Marx, then, "Man remains, somehow, the
rational animal."[29] However, with the next writer, Friedrich Wilhelm
Nietzsche (1844-1900), and his mega-idea, reason and restraint are
thrown to the wind. The irrational is embraced.

Glimmers of rationalism appear over the next century. But somehow once Nietzsche emancipated his *Übermenschen*, his supermen, and
declared that "God is dead," nothing could ever be quite the same again.
The days of rationalistic vigor and optimism were soon to come to a
tumultuous end. Alas, the "innocent" eras of the *philosophes*,
Romantics, utilitarians, and dialectical materialists would soon begin to
fade out of memory.

"Only Slaves and Fools Restrain Their Wills and Desires"

In 1933, just thirty-three years after the death of Friedrich Nietzsche, Adolf Hitler visited the Nietzsche Archive in Weimar at the request of Nietzsche's sister, Elisabeth. While he was there, she presented him with her brother's walking stick and an anti-Semitic pamphlet by Bernhard Förster. Even faced with such a fact, apologists for Nietzsche claim that he wasn't anti-Semitic himself, even if his sister was, and they insist that Hitler's admiration for Nietzsche was misplaced. Hitler misunderstood the great philosopher of ethics and advocate of the aristocratic will-to-power. According to admirers, the prolific Nietzsche, who went insane in 1889 and died of syphilitic complications in 1900, was a far more sophisticated, complicated thinker than most simplistic critics can grasp. As one young woman, a fresh graduate of the University of California Berkeley, explained to me recently, almost chidingly, "Nietzsche has been misunderstood and misinterpreted. He was really a mystic."

Despite such caveats, Nietzsche does leave behind enough fascistic footprints in his works to allow someone like Hitler to glimpse a trail leading, albeit crookedly, to something akin to Nazism. In *On the Genealogy of Morals*, for example, Nietzsche does speak of the Aryan race as the original "race of conquerors and *masters*," and he does decry the "blood-poisoning" that has resulted from the mixing of the races. At fault are the Jews and Jesus of Nazareth, who overturned the morality of the "masters" and allowed the morality of the "slaves" (the "herd") to prevail. Nietzsche's assault seems all the more racist when he declares, "It has been the Jews who have, with terrifying consistency, dared to undertake the reversal of the aristocratic value equation . . . and have held on to it tenaciously by the teeth of the most unfathomable hatred (the hatred of the powerless)." When Nietzsche dreamed that another Napoleon would arise in history,[1] what else was a misguided zealot like Adolf Hitler to think of the destiny of Germany and the role of the "hateful," "powerless" Jews? Hitler and his National Socialists not only studied Nietzsche but expropriated his theories, catapulting them, *reductio ad absurdum*, to their "logical" extreme.

Nevertheless, we must concede that Nietzsche was a brilliant and complex figure. He did pass through his share of *Sturm und Drang* (storm and stress) on his way to formulating his philosophy. He started as a good Lutheran boy, lost his faith, earned a doctorate in philology, trotted after Wagner for a while like a lost puppy, slipped into a depressive nihilism, and reemerged as a heroic atheist with a new vision of history and a new psychology of man. He regarded his philosophy to be comprehensive, courageous, optimistic, and life-affirming, even though he often bitterly and contemptuously criticized Judeo-Christian tradition and rationalistic science. To Nietzsche, their ethics and rationalism were products of a sickly slave, or herd, mentality that had resulted historically in mediocrity, conformity, and near cultural death.

Opposed to this mentality, according to him, was the vibrant nature of the aristocracy, whose morality was grounded in a healthy will-to-power that produced geniuses and resulted in social progress. The will liberates, he was fond of saying as he tried to convey his message to generations of readers whom he knew would largely remain deaf to his pleas. One can't pass over his voluminous work without experiencing some awe at the genius of the man. His place in the study of the history of ideas is secure. "Nietzsche," as Allan Bloom says, "opened up the great terrain explored by modern artists, psychologists and anthropologists, searching for refreshment for our exhausted culture in the depths of the darkest unconscious. . . ."[2]

For this reason also, however, Nietzsche is one of the most dangerous thinkers of modern times. "He went," as Bloom says, "to the end of the road with Rousseau, and beyond."[3] He introduced us to the idea of the creative supermen, who operate best beyond good and evil, and he extolled such men, these "sovereign individuals," as the real masters and benefactors of humanity.[4] What youthful reader, eager for fresh truth and creative vitality, disenchanted with his station in life and want of recognition, wouldn't be tempted to embrace this viewpoint? How could he deny himself identification with the supermen? Thus Nietzsche opened the door to something more than the study of the "darkest unconscious." Over the past hundred years, he also placed before readers, especially the "creative" ones, a temptation to overarching pride and egocentrism. In carrying this new subjectivistic individualism to its extreme, Nietzsche set the stage for a new human identity founded on excessive self-esteem and self-interest, with experience, often for its own sake, being the new test of truth, and with evil becoming quite as necessary to the development of man as good. After Nietzsche, restraint and prudence became vices; spontaneity and impulsiveness, virtues.

THE NOONTIDE OF THE BLOND BEAST

Nietzsche asserted that the salvation of man would be found not in religion or tradition, those products of the slave mentality, but in the rebirth and ascendancy of the supermen, the noble races. Although the noble leave the term *barbarian* in their wake as they conquer, they are nevertheless to be preferred, tyrants though they may sometimes be, over the tame and "irremediably mediocre" men. "One may have every right to remain fearful and suspicious of the blond beast beneath all noble races," concedes Nietzsche, "but who would not a hundred times prefer fear accompanied by the possibility of admiration [for the supermen] to *freedom* from fear accompanied by the disgusting sight of the failed, atrophied, and poisoned?"[5] The question, of course, is directed toward men *like* Nietzsche, who feel contempt for the "slave morality" of the common man. For contempt, superciliousness, is precisely the appeal of Nietzsche for many elitist, creative thinkers. And yet historically the blond beasts who rampage about, wielding their axes and swords, cleaving skulls, don't hail from intellectual circles but from brutish clans. Or they are comprised of highly disciplined legions of mercenary soldiers, as was the case during the Roman Empire, sent or led out by an iron-willed leader bent on conquest and booty.

But of course the modern followers of Nietzsche don't want to face these implications, the chief of which is brutally ironic: they would likely be among the first to fall before the broad sword of the blond beasts. People don't face such obvious implications when they receive a philosophy piecemeal or, worse, when they don't understand the underlying presuppositions upon which a philosophy rests. Therefore, before we can understand the full implications of Nietzscheanism, we must understand the main lines of his thought that run like the strands of a steel cable through all his clever insights and catchy aphorisms, making one thought quite as dreadful as the next.

Der Gott Ist Todt

First, we must understand that Nietzsche was an atheist (not a mystic). In *Thus Spoke Zarathustra* (1883-1884), he states outright in several places that God is dead. In Part I, at the end of chapter 2, Zarathustra is amazed that the hermit to whom he has just spoken hasn't yet discovered the truth that Zarathustra has discovered: "'Could it be possible! This old saint has not yet heard in his forest that God is dead!'"[6] In Part II, Zarathustra declares that "God is a supposition." In fact, he says, "*if* there were gods, how could I endure not to be a god! *Therefore* there are no gods."[7] Given Nietzsche's line of thought, if there are no gods, then there is no one God either. Later in Book III, speaking to the supermen, the "Higher Men," Zarathustra declares of God, "But now this God has died!" Other characters, moreover, refer to him as "the Godless Zarathustra," and he approvingly accepts the appellation: "Yes! I am Zarathustra the Godless!"[8]

Likewise, eminent scholars acknowledge that Nietzsche was an atheist. As early as the *Gay Science* (1882), explains the Nietzschean scholar R. J. Hollingdale, Nietzsche held that God is dead and the world is "meaningless and chaotic."[9] Both Bertrand Russell and Will Durant acknowledge Nietzsche's atheism. Russell says that "Nietzsche is not interested in the metaphysical truth of . . . any religion; being convinced that no religion is really true. . . ."[10] Durant refers to the "hilarious atheism" of Nietzsche in *Thus Spoke Zarathustra*.[11] Even admirers of Nietzsche admit that he was an atheist. Says Allan Bloom, almost admiringly, "[He] replaces easygoing or self-satisfied atheism with agonized atheism. . . ."[12] Agonized or not, Nietzsche regarded any belief in God as a great impediment to human enlightenment. For "the awakened, the enlightened man says: I am body entirely and nothing beside. . . ."[13]

Nietzsche also attacked religion of any kind, but most especially Christianity. He speaks unfavorably of Judaism: "with the Jews *the slave revolt on morals* begins." It was the "hateful" Jews who triumphed over the superior morality, "all the *nobler* ideals," of the aristocracy.[14] He also casts Buddhism in a dim light, for in it he saw nihilism and the utterly worthless morality of compassion.[15] But he positively inveighs against Christianity and Jesus Christ. When criticizing Wagner in *On the Genealogy of Morals*, he refers to Wagner's "return to the sickly ideals of Christianity. . . ."[16] Given time, Christianity, he was sure, would destroy itself.[17] *In Thus Spoke Zarathustra*, the narrator speaks of the "false values and false scriptures" of Christianity. In its churches, he claims, is a "counterfeit light."[18]

But Nietzsche reserves some of his harshest denunciations for Jesus Christ. The "new love" of Christ sprang from hate, he claims.[19] "Truly," he blusters, "there have been greater men and higher-born ones than those whom the people call Redeemer."[20] In Part IV of *Thus Spake Zarathustra*, however, the narrator carries the insult about as far as he can as he bids the supermen to rise and reject the values of Christ: "It may have been good for that preacher of the petty people to bear and suffer the sin of man. I, however, rejoice in great sin as my consolation."[21] No one can mistake the contempt and condemnation here: Jesus is "that preacher of the petty people." Therefore, in some sense, Jesus too is petty, not of a noble caste, not in any sense a superman.[22]

In this way, Nietzsche opposed any form of transcendentalism, metaphysics, or supernaturalism. As far as he was concerned, there are no absolute truths or codes of ethics handed down to man, intuitively or concretely. Repeatedly Zarathustra bids men to smash their tablets of laws as they embrace the creative power that arises from the historically inevitable atheistic catharsis. "Absolute, honest atheism," one of the last phases of the development of the old ideal, "is the outcome of a two-thousand-year training in truthfulness, which finally forbids itself *the lie of belief in God*."[23] In reality, Nietzsche wished that men would concur with his view of history and welcome the will-to-power resident within the supermen, the only leaders worthy of obedience and reverence.

Traditional Morality Is Based on Resentment

Marx contended that he could explain history in terms of a dialectical movement of class and economic conflicts. Over time the conflicts would be marked by progress toward some higher end. Nietzsche, by contrast, contended that he could explain history in terms of the incessant conflict between just two groups: the aristocracy (the few supermen) and the "slaves" (the mass of common men). For Nietzsche, however, the struggle wasn't really progressive (except that he longed for the "noble" to arise again) but cyclical or, better, repetitive. He believed in something he called "eternal recurrence," a view not at all like reincarnation. For Nietzsche, everything occurred again and again in history exactly the same: "I shall return eternally to this *identical and self-same life*," says Zarathustra (italics mine), "in the greatest and the smallest," to once more "teach eternal recurrence" and to "tell man of the Superman once more."[24] At least a couple of critics have noted that Nietzsche's preoccupàtion with this idea alone, quite apart from his syphilitic condition, could have driven him mad.

The process of the conflict between the aristocrats and slaves is straightforward. The groups represent two distinct ethical views: "a *Herren-moral* and a *Heerden-moral*—a morality of masters and a morality of the herd."[25] The aristocracy consists of the courageous and sometimes cruel predators whose goal is power and conquest. Nietzsche says, "There is no mistaking the predator beneath the surface of all these noble races, the magnificent blond beast roaming lecherously in search of booty and victory; the energy of this hidden core needs to be discharged from time to time, the animal must emerge again.. . . ."[26] These blond beasts conquer, then create their own rules of order and morality. From their will-to-power alone can genius arise and culture flourish. By contrast, the slaves, the herd, are motivated by resentment ("*ressentiment*," says Nietzsche, using the French word). Resenting their masters, they, who also, like all humans, are driven by the will-to-power, respond slavishly by creating "nothingness" since they aren't powerful enough to overthrow, at least not at first, their masters. Out of revenge they rebel by developing their small virtues of sacrificing and doing without, of preferring good over evil, restraint over impulse, compassion over cruelty, moderation over excess. Quite detestably, according to Nietzsche, they preach conformity and strive for equality among men. In the end, aided by their priests, they adopt a life-denying ascetic ideal: a "hatred of the human, and even more of the animal, of the material," a "fear of happiness and beauty," and "an aversion to life," as Nietzsche conceives of it.[27]

Summarizing the conflict between the groups, Douglas Smith says, "So the central opposition between aristocratic and slave moralities is accompanied throughout by the opposition between their respective informing principles of an active and healthy will to power, forever seeking to increase its power in physical terms, and a reactive and sickly *ressentiment*, desperately seeking to preserve, through devious intellectual means whatever power it has attained to."[28] These contemptible slaves who restrain their desires and impulses, who deny or warp their will-to-power, are fools and weaklings, to be sure, but they do form a mob-like majority. Eventually, therefore, the slaves do wrest control from the aristocracy wherever they grow in numbers, as readily in Japan or China as in Europe or the Middle East. In Europe these "weak men" who also "want to be strong" determine that "at some time their 'kingdom' should also come—they call it simply 'the Kingdom of God.'"[29]

With such a view of conflict and history, Nietzsche, like Marx, was one of the first true ethical and cultural relativists. Wherever the masters exist, they establish by force of will their own codes and culture. In response, wherever the slaves exist, they first resentfully react by accepting the codes of conduct of their conquerors and then later by elaborating their own. As the aristocracy and slaves clash, so goes the theory, cultures do what they do, and various ethics are necessarily born. Says Smith, "Nietzsche's interest in ethics is an anthropological one, and terms such as 'morality' and 'morals' are used more or less neutrally to designate relative sets of values and beliefs, rather than absolute moral truths."[30] Thus God can die because he is, after all, merely a "supposition" of the slaves and their priest class, and one supposition may easily replace another as the various clashes occur and advance over time. It's the Superman, the creator, "who *creates* a goal for mankind and gives the earth its meaning and its future; he it is who *creates* the quality of good and evil things."[31] No one else can do this. As Zarathustra exclaims, "Unchanging good and evil does not exist!"[32]

Now the Superman Must Arise and Rule

As a self-proclaimed spokesman for the master race, Nietzsche advanced a drastic solution to what he viewed to be the problem of the age. Having concluded that "decadence" is to be found "not in deviation from respectable social convention but in conformity to it,"[33] Nietzsche concluded that it was time for the supermen, a new species of superior men, to regain control of history and culture. Society and culture, the run of common men, have only been a means to an end: "the ripest fruit on their tree the sovereign individual, the individual who resembles no one but himself, who has once again broken away from the morality of custom, the autonomous supramoral individual . . . the man with his own independent, enduring will. . . ."[34] These creative geniuses and tyrant-artists, these blond beasts driven by the will-to-power, must behave outrageously, even cruelly to usher in the new age. Man must die so that the superman can be born, for "man is something that must be overcome."[35]

The supermen must arise and destroy the rule and the law of the rabble. As "higher men" they must not only release themselves from the strictures of the past but destroy the culture of the slaves. They must despise the current masters, the inferior men, the petty people of the marketplace who say "We are all equal" and who "preach submission and acquiescence and prudence and diligence and consideration and the long *et cetera* of petty virtues." The "higher men" must overcome the rabble. Proud of their role, impervious before opposition, they must smash the law tablets of the small people, "the good and the just." "Whom do [the slaves] hate most? Him who smashes their tables of values, the breaker, the lawbreaker—but he is the creator." Rising to a frenzied pitch, Zarathustra in Part III urges his followers to even shatter the good people along with their law tables: "*Shatter, shatter the good and just!*"[36] Thus the supermen transform culture through what Russell calls "aristocratic anarchism."[37] Says Zarathustra, "I tell you: one must have chaos in one, to give birth to a dancing star." Much later, he adds, "He who has to be a creator always has to destroy."[38]

In their contempt for the small men, the supermen must live dangerously and experimentally, embracing even evil, mercilessly establishing their rule. To achieve this new goal, such spirits must be especially tough. They must be "strengthened through wars and victories," driven by "a need for conquest, adventure, danger, pain. . . ." The goal itself requires "a kind of sublime wickedness, a last, self-assured intellectual malice. . . ."[39] "War and courage," Zarathustra tells his disciples, "has done more great things than charity." To be great, then, the superior men must live dangerously: "The devotion of the greatest is to encounter risk and danger and place dice for death." They must, moreover, be experimentalists, a band of "many experimenters," unleashing their potential for great evil and good, without guilt. They must excel in great wickedness. "For evil," declares Zarathustra, "is man's best strength. 'Man must grow better and more evil'—thus do *I* teach. The most evil is necessary for the Superman's best." Written on the new tablets of the supermen must be a new law: "*Do not spare your neighbor!*" Then they will not only rule as gods but will replace God: "Once you said 'God' when you gazed upon distant seas, but now I have taught you to say 'Superman.'"[40]

Inevitably, the superior men must also usher in a new type of philosopher. The old ones, says Nietzsche in *Beyond Good and Evil*, thought they could uncover the Truth, but they were wrong. "They all pose as if they had discovered and reached their real opinions through . . . cold, pure, divinely unconcerned dialectic . . . while at bottom it is an assumption, a hunch . . . —most often a desire of the heart that has been filtered and made abstract—that they defend with reasons they have sought after the fact."[41] The coming philosophers will instead be relativists. They will be offended "if their truth is supposed to be a truth for every man—which has so far been the secret wish and hidden meaning of all dogmatic aspirations." Their judgment will simply be *their* judgment. And they will regard as self-contradictory the term *common good*. For "whatever can be common always has little value. In the end . . . great things remain for the great, abysses for the profound, nuances and shudders for the refined, and, in brief, all that is rare for the rare."[42]

Curiously, Nietzsche, who set out to revolutionize culture, didn't seem to regard his teachings in this same light—as merely relative. For if all truth is relative, then all claims to truth, including Nietzsche's, are self-refuting. Even if a relativist were to advance 1,000 truths, his number of truths would still remain 0, because relativism, in effect, always multiplies truth by 0. "To declare," argues Smith, "that all truths are nothing more than interested and partial perspectives on events which are neutral in themselves assumes that the theory of perspectivism itself is true." In short, Nietzsche's perspective of history as comprised of merely relative perspectives on truth "leaves itself open to dismissal as merely another groundless perspective."[43]

INFLUENCE OF THE MEGA-IDEA

Readers with common sense can readily see that the theories and conclusions of Nietzsche are extreme and outrageous. Undeniably, in his
writings, as Durant puts it, "he takes . . . a sophomore's delight in shocking."[44] Using today's slang, we might even be tempted to call him, even
before the advent of radio, the first "shock jock." Nevertheless, ever
since his death Nietzsche has been taken more and more seriously as a
thinker of the first magnitude because many of his conclusions accord
with modern insights, of one persuasion or another. So sure of his
insights was he, says Durant, that he believed that, like him, "Men who
could think clearly soon [would perceive] what the profoundest minds
of every age had known." Then Durant summarizes Nietzsche's insights
in this way: "that in this battle we call life, what we need is not goodness but strength, not humility but pride, not altruism but resolute intelligence; that equality and democracy are against the grain of selection
and survival; that not masses but geniuses are the goal of evolution; that
not 'justice' but power is the arbiter of all differences and all destinies."[45]
Carrying forth implications found in the theories of Hobbes, Malthus,
Schopenhauer, Darwin, Marx, Spencer, and others, Nietzsche contributed greatly to the rising tide of modern secular thought. He especially helped foster the modern notion that genius must be unfettered
and spontaneous—even to the point of irreverence.

As we have been doing, we won't concern ourselves with the why
but with the what in relation to the mega-idea of Nietzsche. What has
been the impact on modern society of the idea that the true creative
giants don't restrain their will-to-power and their desires but instead live
dangerously and flout contemptuously all traditional moral codes?
Through the analysis that follows, the answer to the question "Why are
people so easily influenced by Nietzsche?" will become obvious.

The Release of the Will-to-Power

Living dangerously and spontaneously, experimenting with drugs or
lifestyles, thumbing one's nose at traditional morality, releasing the
"blond beast"—these have become the popular pastimes and postures
of the last few generations. If wisdom and strength—popularity and

coolness—become equated with spontaneity and impulsivity, while restraint and prudence become vices, then each individual, in the name of his own willful genius, can rationalize almost any "original" decision or action. In effect, each person, a law unto himself, is set free to rationalize, "I'm different from the crowd; therefore I'm superior to the crowd." And many people are doing so today. In the 1960s youths grew their hair long, experimented with drugs, and moved in with girlfriends or boyfriends, much to the chagrin and shock of their parents. But the parental chagrin and shock lent, to the minds of the young, further credibility to their actions, justifying the creation of a new morality of "superior" genius and insight.

In recent years, youths have been perpetuating the same trend. They dye their hair purple, sport nose or navel rings, guiltlessly toy with bisexuality, and attend raves, where exotic drugs are dispensed like Pez. In this way a virtue continues to be made of nonconformity and rebellion. As long as the young feel jazzed, they continue to revel in the ever restless, never satiated will-to-power.

Ironically, of course, this release of dark primordial force—of the repressed id and submerged creative "blond beast"—hasn't resulted in the emergence of any supermen or superwomen, except in fictional portrayals. According to Bloom, the Nietzschean dream hasn't been realized in the least: "Now all has been explored; light has been cast everywhere; the unconscious has been made conscious, the repressed expressed. And what have we found? Not creative devils, but show business glitz. Mick Jagger tarting it up on the stage is all that we brought back from the voyage to the underworld."[46] Fortunately, Bloom didn't live long enough to see Marilyn Manson, Courtney Love, or the Spice Girls tarting it up on the stage. Yet Bloom's words remain as true today as they were in 1988. There is no refreshment, says Bloom, in this "gutter phenomenon."

Even adults, however, are enamored by the "virtues" of impulsivity and power, especially by the promises of excitement and self-fulfillment. Certainly anyone can attest to the popularity of such sports as skydiving or bungee jumping, motocross racing or snowboarding. Excitement produces a high of sorts as people leave the world of the staid and stodgy and push themselves "to the limits." Not long before this writing, Princess Diana died in a car wreck with her playboy lover while his driver was incautiously trying to outrun the paparazzi. Then John Denver died in the crash of his "experimental" airplane. Later one of the young Kennedys and Sonny Bono, in separate incidents, died while skiing. Many like to "live on the edge" and "go for the gusto," at least on weekends. Just as people seek adrenalin and endorphin rushes, they also seek self-empowerment and self-improvement of an egocentric type. In the worlds of self-help gurus like Anthony Robbins and channelers like Nick Bunick, megalomania is no longer regarded as an illness, except in textbooks that employ the term in a technical sense. Such teachers disseminate—or channel from angels—a new and positive wisdom aimed at helping others release the power and potential that already resides within them. Individuals, they teach, are supposed to love themselves unconditionally, uncritically, and focus on the goals that will fulfill them personally. Some of them even press their followers to transcend, in Nietzschean fashion, good and evil. For example, Frederick Lenz in his best-selling *Snowboarding to Nirvana* (1997), in the style of Carlos Castaneda, preaches "tantric sex" and the illusoriness of life, including the self. The main character engages in casual sex with Danish and German women during his travels without a twinge of guilt.[47] Empowered, superior people, remember, don't feel guilt.

But clearly if such attitudes become widespread, they can lead to moral chaos and error. Each person can then justify his own choices simply because they make him feel empowered. And then what spews up from the depths of the culture? Klansmen and Nazis. Drug lords and gangbangers. Child molesters and WICCAN priestesses. Rebellion and nonconformity always satisfy and amplify the will-to-power, justifying the actions of their adherents through subjective empowerment. Forbidden fruit, as they say, always tastes sweeter. But true wisdom, as Christianity teaches, is to be found through restraint, discipline, and morality as these are made possible through faith in Jesus Christ. Because we Christians *believe* that Jesus is who he claims to be, he grants us life—eternal and abundant life: "I am come that they might have life, and that they might have it more abundantly" (John 10:10, KJV). At that time, he gives us the power—the power on which we depend—to help us live restrained, disciplined, moral lives—in short, lives pleasing to God. God alone empowers. "The Spirit gives life" (John 6:63).

In one sense, therefore, Nietzsche had it right: there is a will-to-power. But he also had it wrong: it's a Will-to-Power. We aren't to find life—refreshment and creativity—through our own finite will-to-power but through our reliance on God's infinite Will-to-Power. As humans we are weak, yet "by God's power" we live through Christ who enables us to serve others (2 Cor. 13:4), and his "power is made perfect in weakness" (2 Cor. 12:9). He is powerful enough to complete the work that he begins in us (Phil. 1:4-6). For this reason Christians, no matter what their circumstances, have cause to rejoice: "Now to him who is able to do immeasurably more than all we ask or imagine, according to his power that is at work within us, to him be glory in the church and in Christ Jesus throughout all generations, for ever and ever! Amen" (Eph. 3:20-21).

The Modern Mania for Novelty

We can readily observe that the desire for novelty is closely allied to the will-to-power. Indeed, it's the fruit of the tree. When the actions, attitudes, practices, and beliefs of people cease to "empower" them, as surely these novelties will, where then do people turn? Naturally, to *newer* actions, attitudes, practices, and beliefs. Over time any self-asserted form of the will-to-power must disintegrate according to the laws of entropy, growing stale by degrees, producing languor and ennui. Soon enough, the *newer* expressions become merely akin to the passé expressions from which people had fled. The unconventional becomes conventional, the new old. Then with ears, fingers, and feet all atingle, people must fly off again, seeking some new thrill—a *still newer* habit, hobby, lifestyle, sexual orientation, self-help technique, or educational method.

This quest for novelty has become a settled trend in our culture. As early as 1941, writes Harold O. J. Brown, the sociologist "Sorokin spoke of the 'feverish tempo of . . . accelerated change that excludes a creation of lasting values: yesterday's values are obsolete today; and today's values will be obsolete tomorrow.'" Referring as much to today as to yesterday, Brown goes on to ask, "How can anything lasting be created in this maelstrom of constant change? The whole culture is in constant turmoil." Even "religions and philosophies come and go almost as rapidly as office buildings and factories."[48] Today, it seems, we can count on finding more change in our society than in our pockets.

Once again in the generational gyrations of the youth culture, especially, we see this trend. Consider the history of pop music. In the 1950s Elvis could hardly swivel his hips on stage or TV without arousing the ire of parents. But people adapted, and Elvis became an icon. In the 1960s John Lennon raised a heated debate when he blurted out that the Beatles were bigger than Jesus Christ (and parents hadn't even had time to get used to their haircuts yet!). At about the same time, on stage Mick Jagger was perfecting his erotic maneuvers, and the Who were smashing guitars and amplifiers. But parents began to accept the long hair and spontaneous lifestyles of their kids, and they all settled down once again to uneventful Thanksgiving dinners. Then onstage in the 1970s and 1980s Alice Cooper and David Bowie practiced cross-dressing and wearing makeup while KISS engaged in erotic tongue-flicking and Madonna practiced stripteasing. Again people adjusted, enjoying or tolerating these "artists" while they cavorted in the novel realms of yuppiedom. By the 1980s and 1990s, onstage or in music videos, zombie-like bands like Mega-Death, Nirvana, and Nine Inch Nails began to celebrate nihilism and hedonism, even devil worship, while the rappers jumped into the fray with their in-your-face railing and finger-pointing. Rhymes or no rhymes, the rappers weren't trying to inspire us, like poets of old, to noble deeds.

As always, people have adjusted; indeed, they expect more and more novelty and kinkiness from their entertainers. Meanwhile, Elvis is the king, the Beatles and Rolling Stones are classic rockers, and Madonna and Ice-T get starring roles in movies and TV shows. People not only revel in the novel but reward it, the more outrageous the better. Thus we get a Dennis Rodman. Is he athlete or entertainer? If he is hero or role model, it's only for those who succumb to the mania for novelty.

But again the mania for novelty isn't restricted to the young. Businesses and educational institutions are always ripe for novel ideas and methods, tested or untested. Experimentation itself, remember, is a value, the tried and true suspect. In one way or other, the will-to-power always finds its consummation in the novel—for instance, in employee empowerment or workplace diversity seminars. Let's consider, however, a crude example. We may perhaps best witness the quest for novelty in the explosion of pornography and the general celebration of the bizarre during the past five decades. Adults have been purchasing pornography publicly and openly since the early days of *Playboy*. Yet *Playboy*, compared to latecomers *Oui* and *Hustler*, seems tame. And now with the availability of pornography on cable and the Internet—from "free pics" to CD-ROMs to chat-room sex for straights, gays, lesbians, and bisexuals—hard-core sex is spreading from a few rags and downtown shops to cyberspace. With each new encroachment people's shame diminishes. The abnormal seems normal. People are selling themselves as objects to make a buck, and others are regarding them, quite casually, as objects. "Hi! Call Brittany for hot phone sex" runs an ad; and soon, as more and more of such ads appear, few scarcely bat an eye. Instead, people tune in to Jerry Springer to hear Brittany's story, a tale of triumph, not woe.

Once again we may find ourselves at the bookshelf, thumbing through the works of Nietzsche. In pornography, as many will acknowledge, we find a contempt for women. Nietzsche, with his will-to-power, fed this contempt, for to him, women were inferior. In *Thus Spoke Zarathustra*, he expresses the *Playboy* philosophy perfectly: "The true man wants two things: danger and play. For that reason he wants woman. . . ." Or again, "Man should be trained for war and woman for the recreation of the warrior. . . ." Woman, he says later, is to be a "plaything." Nietzsche may even appeal to the philosophy of *Hustler* readers and even seedier aficionados of pornography. After all, it was he who said, "Are you visiting women? Do not forget your whip!"[49] [Of course, I'm having some fun here at Nietzsche's expense], but the point remains valid. In the world of today, because of the continual quest for novelty, including sensual novelty, people may well be transforming themselves into a species of perverts, becoming a culture of prostitutes and johns. Christopher Lasch, in fact, sees the prostitute as a kind of symbol of our modern culture:

> The fact that she lives in a milieu of interpersonal relationships does not make her a conformist or an "other-directed" type. She remains a loner, dependent on others only as a hawk depends on chickens. She exploits the ethic of pleasure that has replaced the ethic of achievement, but her career more than any other reminds us that contemporary hedonism, of which she is the supreme

symbol, originates not in the pursuit of pleasure but in a war of all against all, in which even the most intimate encounters become a form of mutual exploitation.[50]

Nietzsche's will-to-power, his encouragement of conflict and war, his desire to destroy morality—all these motives are too clearly seen in modern culture. The obsession with novelty is numbing us as a culture to the misery of others and killing our moral sense. Isn't the death of the moral sense precisely what Nietzsche sought as a way to make way for his superior men, his *Übermenshen*?

The result is all too clear. We are not only becoming, as Pitrim Sorokin and Harold O. J. Brown have insisted, a degenerating sensate culture but, as Christopher Lasch has insisted, a culture of narcissism, in which I love myself so dearly that I can't possibly make any commitments to you. Besides, why should I? If my power exceeds yours, I may well be one of the *Übermenschen*. (On the other hand, as Neil Postman has put it, we may well all be just "amusing ourselves to death.")

A Contempt for Christianity

Finally, Nietzsche more than any other thinker of his time or since has made it possible for Christianity to fall into disrepute. To be sure, the *philosophes* lambasted the church, T. H. Huxley outwitted Bishop Wilberforce, and Marx coolly referred to religion as the opiate of the masses. Moreover, soon enough we shall see how Sigmund Freud, Bertrand Russell, and others joined the assault against Christianity. Nietzsche, however, brought to the fore two devastating critiques of Christianity that have fostered a contempt for the Faith. First, with his cultural relativism and his view that Christianity was born, reactively and hatefully, from an ignoble slave mentality, he cast suspicion on the high purposes and value of Christianity. The slaves, after all, are small, weak, hypocritical, and inferior. Blocking the way of the aristocracy, they teach sacrifice, compassion, equality, and justice, all of which Nietzsche hated. Second, by attacking Jesus Christ personally, not just questioning the historicity of the accounts about him as the Higher Critics had done, he opened the door to a kind of sacrilege that can know no bounds or end. Having trickled down to the average person of today, these two critiques have bred cynicism and suspicion with regard to Christianity.

At the sophisticated level, we are heirs today of a "hermeneutics of suspicion" that began with Nietzsche but became associated by the 1960s with Freud and Marx as well. By means of cultural relativism, many people regard with suspicion the values and truth of writers of previous generations. Especially in academe, readers approach classic texts with "a style of interpretation which uncovers latent meanings through a suspicious reading of an untrustworthy surface (for Nietzsche, this took the form of the discovery of the operation of will to power in supposedly disinterested values . . .)."[51] In the grip of deconstructionism, developed by Jacques Derrida, academically trained readers look not for objective but hidden meaning in texts, thus deconstructing them. "The hermeneutics of suspicion," says Veith, "sees every text as a political creation, usually designed to function as propaganda for the status quo."[52] Great works of literature, including the Bible, are especially suspect, as they mask the ulterior motives of the original writers—the bigoted, small-minded oppressors. Hence the critics, with their axes to grind, divide into small militias—Marxist, feminist, multiculturalist—trying to raze the traditional canon of Western literature and the values espoused by it.

Because Christians are the most traditional group—and therefore the most likely to have "ulterior" motives—suspicion falls more squarely and fully on them than on others. Again, at the cultural level we witness many legal and social attacks on the Christian faith. We needn't recount them at this point. The evidence is ample. Phillip E. Johnson in *Reason in the Balance* refers at length and in detail to the "marginalization" of Christians today. And so does Gene Edward Veith, Jr., who aptly summarizes the crisis in this way: "Christianity has been excommunicated from the culture at large—systematically excluded from the schools, the intellectual establishment, and the media."[53] Other Christians, such as Dr. James Dobson and Chuck Colson, have also spoken or written eloquently of this marginalization. The real victims of this suspicion, however, are individual believers who, thanks to Nietzsche, are viewed as having ulterior, less-than-worthy motives. A few believers, the uncharitable and ill-tempered ones, may justify this suspicion, but most don't. Many liberal Christians, for example, simply keep their mouths shut about their faith and speak in conciliatory tones about "ecumenism." Who can suspect *them?* Conservative Christians, there-fore, bear the brunt of the attack, becoming the real foils in the effort to debunk Christianity. Characterized as straw men, they are lampooned for their traditional morality and willingness to obey Scripture (which, of course, as a document, is terribly suspect).

Unfortunately, the average nonbeliever imbibes uncritically this cynicism, suspicion, and skepticism about the motives of Christians, and so won't listen when the Christian attempts to share his faith. The words the Christian speaks, like those of any text, are open to multiple inter-pretations. No objective meaning remains. Objectivity is impossible. Dogma becomes anathema. Thus the real enemies of culture and moral-ity—the Rousseaus, Marxes, and Nietzsches—are ignored, and Christians are made the scapegoats amid a generation of people who, without knowing why, simply know that they know better than "to fall for the Christian message." Because of the influence of Nietzsche, who, ironically, despised the common man (and most especially woman), many common men and women unconsciously echo today the preju-dices of Nietzsche when faced with even the most sincere of Christian witnesses.

But the work of Christians in the world today may very well be to overcome the prejudices of such nonbelievers by presenting and exem-plifying the *genuine* Faith. "Whenever men say they are looking for greater reality," argues Francis Schaeffer, "we must show them at once the reality of *true* Christianity. This is real because it is concerned with the God who is there and who has spoken to us about Himself, not just the use of the symbol *god* or *christ* which sounds spiritual but is not."[54] The will-to-power, with all its dark predatory motives and super-abundance of creative energy, can't stand up to scrutiny when it's care-fully examined. Anyone can know the philosophy of Nietzsche by its fruits. Likewise, anyone should be able to gauge the value of our faith in Jesus Christ by our fruits. What good is our faith without any sign in our lives of the power thereof? With such in mind, the clarion call that needs to issue from every church may simply be this: "Come to us, all you who labor and are heavy-laden, and we will show you our Savior by the power of our love!"

Allan Bloom, as we discovered earlier, claimed that Nietzsche had opened the door to the dark unconscious so that we could glimpse its awesome contents and exult in the ubiquitous will-to-power behind all our passions and ratiocinations. If it was Nietzsche who opened this door, then it was the next writer, Freud, who strode over the threshold and entered the forbidden, mysterious mansion of the underworld, at once setting about cataloguing the furniture and redecorating the interior. With Freud—and the psychoanalytical, scientifically minded school that originated with him—a new dominant group of thinkers clambered onto the stage of history. A smug cadre of atheists and agnostics, these thinkers continued the work of dismantling tradition begun by their intellectual forebears. Of course man is an animal. Of course neither God nor absolute morals exist. Of course man is repressing some of his best impulses along with some of his worst impulses. Aided by the new savior, science, these thinkers believed they could eliminate misery from the world and raise mankind to a new as-yet-unimagined pinnacle of achievement and progress.

Third Stage

in the Slide Toward Relativism

———

From 1900 to 1947, man decided that he didn't need

the "dead" God of his fathers any longer, for now

he had science and the greatest-happiness principle

to guide him toward a more enlightened future

for humankind. Sense-bound reason

was now cut loose from God.

———

"THERE IS NO GOD, ONLY UNCONSCIOUS, MECHANISTIC CAUSATION"

After the publication of *The Interpretation of Dreams* in 1900, the year that Nietzsche died, Sigmund Freud rose gradually from relative obscurity to international prominence as a psychoanalyst. Since then, through scores of direct and indirect affiliations, Freud has influenced many major figures in many fields of study. In his own field, he had his first students—Carl Jung, Otto Rank, Alfred Adler, Anna Freud—and his later followers—Melanie Klein, Donald W. Winnicott, Karen Horney, Jacques Lacan. In the social sciences, he influenced Ruth Benedict, Herbert Marcuse, and Michel Foucault. In the literary world, he sparked the imaginations of Thomas Mann, James Joyce, D. H. Lawrence, Graham Greene, and countless others. Freud, during his life, even carried on a correspondence with Albert Einstein, initiated by the younger Einstein apparently, over the causes of war. Both, it turned out, were pacifists.

Today we continue to experience the powerful effect of Freud on modern culture. The most obvious evidence appears in the everyday terms that nearly everyone uses. Although Nietzsche first introduced the term *id* and C. G. Carus the term *unconscious*, Freud not only expropriated these two terms but also popularized many others: *ego, superego, complex, libido, erogenous zones, narcissism, neurosis, anxiety, hysteria, obsession, compulsion, repression, oral fixation, anal retentiveness, wishful thinking, sublimation, death wish, dream analy-*

sis, consciousness, and so on. Today we are concerned about the status of health of our egos. We know what a healthy libido is, and we know that repression is bad. And every high schooler knows what a phallic symbol is. We grow alarmed when we feel that we are becoming anxious or, worse, neurotic, because we don't want to develop complexes or obsessions—although we already suspect that we have too many. Ironically, the word *anxious* is so common today that it's even being used in place of *eager,* as in "Fred, I'm anxious to see your new car."

Although this vocabulary has been infiltrating Western culture for a long time, it only began to have a real impact in America from the 1940s on. According to Allan Bloom, who attended the University of Chicago in the mid-1940s, "the fling with Freud" in academe began "during the forties and fifties."[1] This fling was still in full swing within academe in the 1960s and 1970s, even in fields as seemingly far-flung from psychology as English. At my alma mater, a professor of medieval literature practiced psychoanalytic literary criticism on Chaucer's *The Canterbury Tales,* finding at every turn of the page fresh evidences of phallic symbols and Oedipus complexes.

Without a doubt, then, Freud has been an influential thinker. In his own time, we know, he also was charismatic and dynamic, indefatigable as a researcher, writer, and speaker. But he was also equally capable of pettiness, vanity, and neurosis. He eventually alienated most of his students, who worked devotedly with him for a time and then later broke from him for various reasons—some theoretical, some personal. An excerpt from a letter written to Freud by Carl Jung may provide us with some insight into the character of Freud and the reasons for the defections of his disciples. Trying to be honest, Jung explains some of his frustrations as he writes to Freud just before their inevitable break:

> May I say a few words in earnest? I admit the ambivalence of my feelings towards you, but am inclined to take an honest . . . view of the situation. If you doubt my word, so much the worse for you. I would, however, point out that your technique of treating your pupils like patients is a *blunder.* In that way you produce either slavish sons or impudent puppies. . . . I am objective enough to see through your little trick. You go about sniffing out all the symptomatic actions in your vicinity, thus reducing every-

one to the level of sons and daughters who blushingly admit the existence of their faults. Meanwhile you remain on top as the father, sitting pretty. For sheer obsequiousness nobody dares to pluck the prophet by the beard and inquire for once what you would say to a patient with a tendency to analyze the analyst instead of himself.[2]

Obviously, working with Freud was a pretty intense experience. To enter his inner circle was to be *treated*—and even controlled—by him. He had an agenda, a mission, a scientific vocation, and he was loath to let anything or anyone get in his way. The man who untangled complexes was apparently pretty complex himself.

The influence of Freud, despite its pervasiveness, however, has been unhealthy for modern culture. By invading the psychological realm with the new scientism, Freud not only opened before us the phantom world of the dark, powerful unconscious but also helped frame the materialistic, mechanistic, deterministic worldview of the twentieth century. He supported the naturalistic view that we live in a closed system in which only that which can be sensed and measured can be classified as knowledge. He maintained that there is no God and that all religious faith is illusion and superstition, born of the dark primitive fears and urges of the irrational unconscious. He held that science alone can provide us with true knowledge.

THE WEIRD NEW "SCIENCE" OF THE UNCONSCIOUS

Freud expressed his commitment to science many times, although he wasn't really all that scientific himself when pushed hard enough. In his writings he frequently admitted that many of his insights were mere speculations, and thus open to revision. True, such admissions make him sound all the more empirical and flexible, but they can also represent defensive tactics. In his correspondence with Einstein, for example, he reveals a certain defensiveness and antirationalism as he comments on his controversial "death instinct": "It may perhaps seem to you as though our theories are a kind of mythology and, in the present case, not even an agreeable one. But does not every science come in the end to a kind of mythology like this? Cannot the same be said of your own physics?"[3] If Einstein's physics were mythology, then much of modern science would cease to exist as science. Surely Freud, who believed that only science could save humanity, wasn't really being serious. Or was he? Only an examination and estimation of his major theories can help us decide to what extent Freud himself contributed to our scientific, as well as practical, understanding of human nature.

Unconscious Factors Determine Human Personality

Freud was a psychological determinist. He believed that each person is programmed by unconscious factors to think and behave as he does. In *The Origin and Development of Psycho-Analysis* (1910), Freud says that "the psycho-analyst is distinguished by an especially strong belief in the *determination* of the psychic life. For him there is in the expressions of the psyche . . . nothing arbitrary and lawless . . ." (italics mine).[4] A few pages later he admits that some might find it difficult to accept his theories on intellectual grounds because they "are not accustomed to reckon with *a strict determination of mental life*, which holds *without exception* . . ." (italics mine).[5] Some might argue that it's foolhardy to claim that any aspect of the mental life "holds without exception," but not so Freud. Apparently he thought he could shush his detractors by claiming that they just weren't "accustomed to reckon with" the fact that *every* expression of the psyche is determined by some law.

Making this determinism more explicit, Freud asserts in *Civilization and Its Discontents* (1929) that the purpose and object of life for the human animal is pleasure or happiness, as dictated by the pleasure-principle: "As we see, it is simply the pleasure-principle which draws up the programme of life's purpose. This principle dominates the operation of the mental apparatus from the very beginning; there can be no doubt about its efficiency. . . ."[6] Freud has no doubt about this. The purpose of life, he informs us, is strictly drawn up, or determined, by the pleasure-principle. That "principle" creates the "programme" of life and dominates the efficient "operation of the mental apparatus." From the beginning, then, humans are machines, mere apparatuses, with nothing "arbitrary" or "lawless" about their development. That being the case, we needn't expect to find in human nature anything resembling free will.

In first fleshing out his theory of the unconscious as the primary repository of unseen, repressed factors, Freud carefully detailed the role of childhood and early adolescence in the development of psychopathology. Anxiety, for example, he saw as originating in the trauma of the birth experience.[7] Even more significant to him were the sexual experiences of children—early sensations, autoerotic stimulation, and awareness of the opposite sex. When stifled by overscrupulous adult society, these early experiences result, Freud held, in the repression of wish-fulfillments and in sexual pathogenic complexes. In turn, these repressed complexes result in mental illnesses—that is, in later consciously expressed symptoms of hysteria, neurosis, depression, and so on.

Because Freud studied mostly extreme pathological cases from his own era and culture, he thereby inferred hastily, it seems to me, a universal and uniform causal relationship between sexual repression and mental disease. He then could assert that most mental diseases are traceable to the early sexual life of the child: "psycho-analytic investigations trace back the symptoms of disease with surprising regularity to impressions from the sexual life," thus revealing "that the pathogenic wishes are of the nature of erotic impulse-components." This conclusion could then lead him, in circular fashion, to a principal Freudian tenet: "to disturbances of the erotic sphere must be ascribed the greatest significance among the aetiological factors of disease" in both sexes.[8] He was thus affirming nothing more than that the effect proves the cause and the cause proves the effect.

Based on this work, Freud elaborated a theory of psychological development that he then generalized to fit everyone, "healthy" as well as "unhealthy" individuals. Undeterred as always, he contrived his by-now famous Oedipus complex to explain the relationships among the key components within his framework: the conscious and unconscious; the id, ego, and superego. He made this theoretical complex central to his analyses in such works as *Civilization and Its Discontents* and *New Introductory Lectures on Psycho-Analysis* (especially when he launched his assaults on theism). But he most clearly and carefully describes the Oedipus complex, it seems to me, in *The Ego and the Id* (1923). Put simply, Freud claims that a child, wishing to possess sexually the parent of the opposite sex, comes to hate the parent of the same sex as a rival. In this way, "the triangular character of the Oedipus situation" then causes complications for the child and "gives rise to the Oedipus complex."

Out of guilt, the child, who doesn't want to hate one parent, allows the rejected parent to form the character—or play the role—of his superego, that part of his mind that tells him what he ought and ought not to do, his conscience. This process also modifies the ego, attenuating it or strengthening it. Says Freud, "The super-ego retains the character of the father, while the more intense the Oedipus complex was and the more rapidly it succumbed to repression . . . the more exacting later on is the domination of the super-ego over the ego—in the form of conscience or perhaps of an unconscious guilt."[9] From below the ego, the id, along with the libido, may still rear its satyr-like head, but the superego will strive to keep it in check, aided by unconscious repression (the process that keeps memories buried) and the reality principle (the sense of limitations imposed on the ego by the world). And so the machine of the psyche will run—kuh-chunk, kuh-chunk—towards a conflicted state of either *relative* integration or *relative* neurosis.

Through painstaking observation of this machinery, Freud confidently tells us in *The Origin and Development of Psycho-Analysis*, the therapist may thus learn everything about the psychic life of a patient. The savvy therapist finds meaning in the minutiae of dreams, significance in every trifling, bungling act—forgetfulness, clumsiness, slips of the tongue or pen. He regards every detail to be a symptom that directs him to the "discovery of the hidden complexes of the psychic life."[10] Thus as he comes to understand the programmed operations of the human machine, he also comes to understand the programmed operations of its inner parts. When seen in this light, the psychotherapist seems more like a mechanic than a counselor.

Civilization Evolves by Means of the Life- and Death-Instincts

After World War I Freud began to extend his theories beyond his clinical discoveries and circle of colleagues by setting out to explain the development of culture. Like Hobbes, Rousseau, Darwin, Marx, and others, he offered his own theory as to the evolution of civilization. Like Hobbes, he maintained in *Civilization and Its Discontents* that man is driven by the desire for self-preservation, even though "The natural instinct of aggressiveness in man, the hostility of each one against all and of all against each one, opposes this program of civilization." Like

Rousseau, he was even willing to explore the idea that "our so-called civilization itself is to blame for a great part of our misery, and we should be much happier if we were to give it up and go back to primitive conditions."

Like Darwin, he believed that "the evolution of civilization may be simply described as the struggle of the human species for existence." Like Darwin also, he held a debased view of man. After all, at one point Freud declares, "Man, too, is an animal"—adding his own little twist in the next breath—"with an unmistakable bisexual disposition." Saying that each human "represents a fusion of two symmetrical halves," Freud goes on to speculate that possibly "each half was originally hermaphroditic."[11] Such speculation about human nature must strike almost anyone as unaccountably crude and bizarre.

Freud regarded aggression to be not only innate in the human species but also, if given enough leash, necessary to the survival and health of the human species. Man and civilization have always evolved and still evolve because two principles constantly war: the life-instinct (*Eros*) and the death-instinct (*Thanatos*). "I know," claims Freud, "that we have always had before our eyes manifestations of the destruction instinct fused with erotism, directed outwards and inwards in sadism and masochism. . . ." But because of the superego in the form of conscience, because of guilt, "the *dread of losing love*," we curb our aggressive tendencies and renounce our need for instinctual gratification. Unfortunately, "the price of progress in civilization is paid in forfeiting happiness through the heightening of the sense of guilt."[12] Such guilt, the repressive force that inhibits aggression, he felt, has gone too far at our stage in human evolution. It leads to mental illness and makes life too hard for people.[13] The demands of the sadistic superego are too harsh. It seriously disables the sexual life of civilized man.[14] It can even motivate one to turn to crime.[15]

"Consequently," says Freud, "in our therapy we often find ourselves obliged to do battle with the super-ego and work to moderate its demands."[16] One even senses that Freud might have applauded the sexual revolution of the 1960s when he says, "A certain part of the suppressed libidinous excitation has a right to direct satisfaction and ought to find it in life. The claims of our civilization make life too hard for the greater part of humanity, and so further the aversion to reality and the origin of neuroses. . . ." Then he concludes, "We ought not to go so far as to fully neglect the original animal part of our nature. . . ."[17] What a curious overstatement! Who but religious celibates have ever "fully" neglected the original animal, or sexual, part of their natures?

Ultimately, for Freud, science offered the best hope of salvation for future generations. Psychology, he says in *New Introductory Lectures*, is proud to identify itself with the scientific *Weltanschauung* (world-view).[18] Moreover, he says, "Our best hope for the future is that the intellect—the scientific spirit, reason—should in time establish a dictatorship over the mind."[19] Science is the best way to promote "the good of all." Indeed, through the assistance of science, now man "has nearly become a god himself."[20] Obviously Freud pushes his faith in naturalistic science about as far as it can go. He reveals himself to be a card-carrying materialist.

Belief in God Is an Illusion

In the materialistic, unconscious-driven system of Freud, it follows, then, that religion, faith in God, must be infantile and regressive. Indeed, in *Future of an Illusion*, Freud does indeed brush aside religion as an illusion. In *Civilization and Its Discontents* Freud dismisses belief in God almost self-righteously, so sure is he that such belief is grounded in early childhood dependence on the father or in early man's dependence on patriarchal family groups. The poor "ordinary man," says he, can't imagine Providence in any form other than that of "a greatly exalted father." Freud's scientific humanism forbids him from showing anything but pity for the benighted believers who hold to Christianity or any other faith. "The whole thing is so patently infantile, so incongruous with reality," he laments, "that to one whose attitude to humanity is friendly it is painful to think that the great majority of mortals will never be able to rise above this view of life." Ultimately, he concludes, belief in God is really unhealthy because it represents "mass-delusion" and "mental infantilism."[21] In his view, only those who would stand in the way of progress would revert to the Faith of their fathers. "Really," one can imagine Freud sputtering and fuming, "shouldn't we outgrow all that absurdity and nonsense?"

Despite his critique of theism, however, Freud didn't seem capable of questioning his own motives or perceiving the fallacies in his own "scientific" logic. If everyone is deterministically driven by complex, often elusive unconscious forces, then Freud too was driven by the same. If repression or resistance keeps people from fully grasping the contents of their unconscious, then Freud too couldn't fully grasp his hidden motives or fathom his dark depths. If everyone is driven by sexual motives and wishes to kill his father, the "father figure," then perhaps Freud hadn't yet stopped hating his own very real authoritarian father. Perhaps Freud's dismissive critique of theism merely represented his own infantile wish to kill, once and for all, his own overscrupulous father-formed superego, his sense of "ought," "guilt," and external authority. Freud is therefore in no position to set up his conclusions as truth since they, like everyone else's, are equally grounded in ulterior, deterministically-driven unconscious motives.

If we accept the Freudian worldview, argues C. S. Lewis, then either all thoughts or only some thoughts must be "psychologically tainted at the source." If all thoughts are tainted, then Freudianism is quite as tainted as Christianity or any other system of thought. If only some thoughts are tainted, we must determine "which are tainted and which are not." In either case, the man who cries "tainted!" lands in a pretty pickle. As Lewis puts it:

> It is the same with all thinking and all systems of thought. If you try to find out which are tainted by speculating about the wishes of the thinkers, you are merely making a fool of yourself. You must first find out on purely logical grounds which of them do, in fact, break down as arguments. Afterwards, if you like, go on and discover the psychological causes of the error.
>
> In other words, you must show *that* a man is wrong before you start explaining *why* he is wrong.[22]

Here, then, we encounter the grievous, egregious error in approach and logic to which Freud succumbed. He argued *that* theism—that is, Christianity—is wrong without proving *why* it's wrong. The best that he could do was to say that its demands are too hard (for example, the command to love one's neighbor as oneself).[23] And such an accusation isn't a rational argument but rather a personal judgment rooted in his assumption that all thought is tainted by ulterior erotic, aggressive motives. Alas, out of the heart the mouth speaketh!

INFLUENCE OF THE MEGA-IDEA

In early 1998 O. J. Simpson hypothesized on CNN that *if* he had killed Nicole Simpson, such a homicidal act would only prove that he had loved her greatly. To anyone with common sense, this logic sounds twisted, but it's perfectly Freudian, perhaps showing that Simpson himself had been undergoing psychotherapy at the time. For Freud speaks of just such a paradox in "The Ego and the Id": "Now, clinical observation shows not only that love is with unexpected regularity accompanied by hate (ambivalence) . . . but also that in many circumstances hate changes into love and love into hate."[24] Was O. J. trying to tell us that the violence of the deed, being a clear manifestation of hatred, might only reflect—in reverse, so to speak—an equally intense love? If he wasn't confessing to the deed, then why, Freudian-style, was he rationalizing the violence?

As the great thinkers, as well as their mega-ideas, become more contemporary, it's easier to see their influence, as the example of O. J. Simpson illustrates. They transform our language; we adopt theirs. But let's consider some perhaps not-so-obvious effects that Freud's mechanistic, atheistic view of human psychology and personality is still having on us today as a society. When properly understood, the legacy of Freud may seem stranger than science fiction.

Introspection to the Extreme

For many people today, because of the psychoanalytical approach of Freud—and, to a lesser extent, the subjectivism of Hume and the Romanticism of Rousseau—the inner world of the mind and emotions is more real and present than it needs to be. Since Freud's day, this inner-directedness has led many to undertake, like hunters on safari, dangerous, unhealthy journeys into the uncharted regions of the self. Indeed, many are addicted to introspection-by-reflex. They find themselves marking their moods as often as a malaria patient checks his temperature. The Socratic "Know thyself" becomes "Heal thyself" as they seek to understand the dark mysteries of their unconscious, or subconscious, minds. Anxiously, young and old ask, "What am I feeling now? Why am I feeling that way? Do I feel good or bad? Why do I keep thinking such and such a thought? What's wrong with me? Am I paranoid? Do I have ADD or ADHD?" Having heard so often of *abnormal* psychology, they ask, "Am I normal?" At the very least, like cardiac patients fretfully checking their pulses, they worry about their self-esteem and wait for self-actualization, turning to books and experts for advice. In fact, they have already learned, as many of my students now write, that everyone must "love one's *self*" (the word *oneself* having dropped from their vocabulary).

Commenting on these trends, Allan Bloom says, "Once Americans had become convinced that there is indeed a basement to which psychiatrists have the key their orientation became that of the self, the mysterious, free, unlimited center of our being."[25] Is it therefore any wonder, as many culture observers agree, that people are today becoming more egocentric and narcissistic than ever before?

Modern culture, to be sure, encourages this preoccupation with one's private inner self. Starting as early as the 1940s and 1950s, everyone began to brood. Several major actors brooded in their movie roles: Orson Welles in *Citizen Kane,* James Dean in *East of Eden* and *Rebel Without a Cause*; Marlon Brando in *A Street Car Named Desire* and *On the Waterfront*; and Richard Burton in *Look Back in Anger.* The Beat poets brooded. Rod Serling brooded. Everyone also began to search their psyches for the sources of their angst. Saul Bellow exposed deep-seated conflicts between father and son in *Seize the Day.* Philip Roth explored the neurotic roots of onanism in *Portnoy's Complaint.* Many writers have resorted to the use of "stream of consciousness," which resembles Freudian "free association," to capture the inner worlds and motives of their characters. The Beatles ran to the Maharishi to learn how to pacify their inner worlds, and Woody Allen has produced a spate of films that chronicle, albeit humorously, the conflicts of the inner-directed man preoccupied with sex (*Eros*, the life-instinct) and death (*Thanatos*, the death-instinct). Today, in fashion ads and music videos, we see hollowed-out men and women, too jaded or bored to brood, looking like burned-out junkies. This anguished introspection has become the cliché of our times. Who isn't anxious, eccentric, or bored? Meanwhile, psychologists and psychiatrists thrive, as statistics reveal that mental illness in American society is continually increasing and, Proteus-like, ever changing.

But the fact is, although the Socratic dictum "know thyself" has a time-honored history, we needn't carry its counsel to Freudian extremes, constantly and desperately striving to save ourselves from inner conflicts and "complexes." We often "find ourselves" more fully, in fact, through outer- and other-directedness. We are more likely to test our mettle, to identify our strengths and weaknesses, when we invest ourselves in healthy relationships and goal-driven activities than when we constantly and morbidly analyze our moods. When we engage others—to console, help, teach, mentor, and so on—we are more likely to discover the hope and poise, the trust and esteem, that we can't find in ourselves by all our introspective forays into the unconscious. Better than being *just* other-directed is also being, first and foremost, *Other*-directed. A love of God draws us out of the charnel houses of ourselves, uplifts us, and empowers us. Such is the Christian perspective, no more beautifully put than by Jesus Christ himself: "For whoever wants to save his life will lose it, but whoever loses his life for me will find it" (Matt. 16:25). Healthy self-examination and self-criticism are good, but only if they incline us toward greater dedication to worthy goals and greater commitment to a love of others and, most especially, of God, the almighty Other, through whom alone we find self-knowledge and power for living.

A Treatable Illness for Everyone

Freud, as we know, primarily studied mentally ill people. So for him and his disciples, treatment or therapy became the hallmark of their approach. In society today, individually and collectively, we see what Philip Rieff referred to in 1966, in his book of the same title, as "the triumph of the therapeutic." Christopher Lasch, in *The Revolt of the Elites and the Betrayal of Democracy*, agrees that the outcome of Freudian psychoanalysis has been a "therapeutic view of the world." As the practice of psychoanalysis began to spread, "Sickness and health replaced guilt, sin, and atonement as the dominant concerns guiding those who struggled to make sense of the buried life of the mind."

In time this practice led to a "suspension of moral judgment" among the practitioners and a "permissive atmosphere" within psychoanalytic sessions.[26] Spilling out into society, this therapeutic attitude and approach has provided an escape hatch for just about everyone who suffers from some "deviancy." From laziness to violence, from teen rebellion to child molestation, everyone can find a ready excuse for his misconduct. Whether he needs legal representation or not, he *will* need therapy—and if he can't afford a counselor, one will be provided for him. And the whole society picks up the tab for scores of social programs aimed at *treating* people, whether by helping them to build their self-esteem or by providing them with mental health services until they can reclaim the children whom they have neglected or abused.

Therapy becomes everyone's responsibility, but only because, thanks to Freud and others, we are individually no longer really responsible for our own acts. Remember, in Freud's estimation, the tyrannical superego, fostered by the education of parents and society, can even compel people to commit crime. Who, then, can be held fully responsible for his actions, driven deterministically as he is by the dark forces of his mysterious unconscious, by sexual urges and aggressions? Should we then not weep for the Menendez brothers? Besides, think of the advantages for everyone: If I'm not to blame, you're not to blame. And, really, I'm okay and you're okay. In this way, more and more people can experiment with their ids and excuse themselves from their guilt, which is from the Freudian standpoint unhealthy anyway. Why shouldn't we, as they used to say in the 1960s, "let it all hang out"? Fortunately, for now, along with many Christians, many non-Christians in our post-Christian era still possess a Judeo-Christian "superego"—that is, they still believe in personal responsibility and accountability. Unfortunately, such people largely represent a generation, born during the Depression era, that is fast disappearing from the scene.

From the Christian point of view, if there is anything like a "superego"—namely, in traditional parlance, a *conscience*—it can be yielded wholeheartedly to God in Christ. The superego doesn't have to be a tyrant or taskmaster of the kind conceived by Freud. It doesn't have to place such impossible tasks before a man that he can only fail and succumb to his primordial passions or regress into infantile neuroses. The conscience touched by Christ carries no onus, for Jesus speaks encouragingly to us: "Come unto me, all ye that labor and are heavy laden, and I will give you rest. Take my yoke upon you, and learn of me; for I am meek and lowly in heart: and ye shall find rest unto your souls. For my yoke is easy, and my burden is light" (Matt. 11:28-30, KJV). We can surrender our "superego" to Jesus Christ, who then can transform it into a healthy guide, a wise counselor, a friend to the "ego," whose forgiveness extends into the darkest depths of the "id." This Lord can conquer "the death-instinct" with all its aggressiveness and replace it with an abundant *agape*-driven "life-instinct." More important, a *whole self*, now transparent before and beloved by God, can find peace and joy.

We don't have to surrender, then, to a Freudian reductionism, "according to which moral reasoning and motivation are merely the expression of hidden drives and reflexes, largely of a sexual nature."[27] As always, it's the Christian worldview that provides a radical, hopeful, and encouraging alternative to any of the world's mega-ideas.

Fashionable Disbelief

Freud smugly and superficially dismissed the validity of religion, not on rational but on personal psychological grounds. Unlike Marx and Nietzsche, he didn't need to resort to contempt, for Marx and Nietzsche had already done enough damage of that kind. Instead, a true secular humanist and enlightened scientist, Freud simply expressed his bewilderment at the fact that so many could still fall prey to the illusion of faith. He could afford to take a more subtle approach. In *The Future of an Illusion* and *Civilization and Its Discontents,* he makes his humanistic antipathy clear, as we have seen, but others in and out of his field have followed his lead. Today it's positively fashionable to ignore or dismiss the claims of orthodox Christianity.

Today it's indisputable that among those in academe, the urbane and sophisticated, religion is simply a prop—an opiate or repressive strategy—for the weak. Man's nature is no longer understood in Classical or Christian terms. Most of today's professors have been reared on Freud, whose "classical psychoanalytic theory is based quite explicitly on a specific, highly materialistic view of man's nature."[28] Others, the younger set, have adopted a postmodernistic stance, expropriating the language of Freud and his intellectual progeny but denying the veracity and validity of any single view of man except the one that regards man to be a dysfunctional but languagized animal. One of my colleagues not long ago, glancing at me during a meeting, declared earnestly, almost sadly, "Well, of course, we know today that

Christianity is a dying religion." To people like him, because truth has become relative in our new pluralistic, multicultural world, Christianity, like all the old schools of thought and forms of belief, will also soon be sinking into the La Brea tar pit of time. The death of Christianity is thus inevitable because it's an old prop. The truly heroic, intelligent professors and students look elsewhere for answers, leaving belief to the unfit (in Darwinist terms) and infantile (in Freudian terms).

Popular culture is rife with this prejudice as well. In a culture in which disbelief is fashionable, Christian music and literature is becoming ever more ghettoized. Christians own their own book and music retail stores, publishing houses, even TV and radio stations. With rare exceptions, Christian music doesn't air on secular radio stations. Most Hollywood producers steer clear of producing any movie or TV show that might reveal a Christian bias. When they do produce a TV show that doesn't caricature or lambaste Christians outright, they air one about angels that not only confutes Christian theology but also omits any mention of Jesus Christ, whose forgiveness is presumably being proffered to the wayward characters who receive the angelic ministrations. Or producers air a show about a comic Anglican priest who counsels others when he himself isn't confused about sex or upset about his stolen motorcycle, yet who never makes any references to Jesus Christ. Everyone likes to see a Christian's feathers ruffled today. It plays well in the media. And it promises endless amusement to people who have concluded that Christians themselves are walking textbook cases for Freudian psychoanalysis. Seen through the eyes of the pop culture, too many Christians are just clones of Dana Carvey's "church lady," ready to purse their lips at the latest lapse in social morality, prissily speculating as to its cause: "Could it be . . . Satan!?"

But who really wants the twisted human nature and clinically cold treatments bequeathed to us by Freud? The materialistic limitation he placed on knowledge makes man a mechanism driven by unconscious urges and disturbances, forever a neurotic victim in need of ongoing analysis and ego adjustment. Such materialistic determinism ignores the valid human hunger for the transcendent and supernatural, regarding it as merely superstition. To Freud, who clearly misunderstood Christ and the Gospel, faith in God is simply pathological—explainable in strictly materialistic (or naturalistic) terms. Yet Freud, who ascribed rationality only to that which is scientifically observable and measurable, clearly failed to examine, much less understand, his *own* psychoses and motivations. Freud and his school have left us, their modern heirs, with a dark and diminished view of humankind that has for countless people resulted in more bondage to despair than liberation from guilt. These people, seeking mental well-being in the prognostications and pronouncements of psychotherapy, have been wrecked on the shoals of the theories of a single man. Surely, even the most legalistic form of Christianity hasn't wreaked such havoc in the lives of so many modern people. Surely, then, genuine orthodox Christianity, grounded as it is in a loving relationship with a living Christ, is as worthy of consideration as the speculations of an effete Sigmund Freud.

Ironically, just as Freud and Einstein found common ground in pacifism, so did Freud and the chief proponent of our next major mega-idea, Bertrand Russell. Freud and Russell were also linked by other bonds. They both were atheists, and they both believed that science could save us, whereas Christianity had debilitated us. Russell, however, carries Freud's criticisms a step farther, as we shall see. As deeply humane as Russell was, he was bold enough to blame many of the ills of civilization on Jesus Christ, the most humane man in history. Furthermore, he also allied himself with Freud by advancing Freud's conclusions about the injurious effects of guilt, especially on the young, who were being taught by their uptight elders to avoid premarital sex. Long before the baby boomers ignited the sexual revolution of the 1960s, Russell had already hoisted its flag in 1936, three years before the death of Freud and thirty-one years before the Summer of Love.

10

"CHRISTIANITY IS PRIMITIVE, AND EVEN CHRIST IS FLAWED"

Bertrand Russell may well have been the longest-lived, most renowned atheist and pacifist in the history of the world. He died in 1970, just three months before his ninety-eighth birthday. During his near-century of life, he published about fifty-five books, most of which were popular rather than technical. In mathematics, logic, and epistemology, however, he is famous for his creation of Russell's Paradox (1901); his *Prinicipia Mathematica*, coauthored with A. N. Whitehead in three volumes (1910, 1912, 1913); his *Introduction to Mathematical Philosophy* (1919); and his philosophy of logical analysis. All of these accomplishments he achieved before the age of fifty. Upon the death of his brother in 1931, he assumed the family title, Lord Russell. A little later, in the 1930s, he won two prestigious awards—the London Mathematical Society De Morgan Medal and the Sylvester Medal of the Royal Society. And in 1950 he won the Nobel prize for Literature for his *History of Western Philosophy* (1945). Offering high praise, the historian Will Durant dubbed Russell the Pythagoras of the twentieth century.[1]

But Lord Russell wasn't merely a high-powered scholar. He was also a high-profiled social figure and political activist. During his life he married four times and also served two jail sentences for his pacifism, one near the end of World War I (1918) and one just before the escalation of the Vietnam War (1962). Although he taught at the University of Chicago, UCLA, and Harvard in the 1930s and 1940s, he was banned from teaching at City College of New York in 1940 because a court ruled that his immoral, atheistic character would have a pernicious effect on students.[2] In 1955 he published, with the permission of Albert Einstein, who died shortly before its publication, the *Russell-Einstein Manifesto*, a document that called on scientists of the USSR and USA to jointly oppose nuclear weaponry. In the 1950s he was a founding member of the Pugwash Conferences, which in 1995 won the Nobel peace prize for their efforts in minimizing the role played by nuclear weapons in the world. And he was the founding president of the Campaign for Nuclear Disarmament, the organization that invented the peace symbol that Vietnam protestors wore throughout the 1960s and that certain liberals still plaster on the back windshields of their beat-up VWs and Peugots, just to the right of their Greenpeace logos.

This sketchy summary gives only the slightest hint as to Russell's personality and influence. Yet it's evident that there were, as Will Durant puts it, two Russells: a pale pre-World War I mathematical logician of considerable genius and a robust post-World War I social critic and activist.[3] The same man who wrote about logic and set theory also delivered the now-famous lecture *Why I Am Not a Christian* (1927) and wrote *Has Man a Future?* (1961). The same man who introduced the axiom of reducibility also flirted for a time with communism. He even waffled at times on the question of whether he was an agnostic or atheist. As "a philosopher" speaking to a philosophical audience, he said, "I should say that I ought to describe myself as an Agnostic, because I do not think that there is a conclusive argument by which one can know that there is not a God." But "to the ordinary man in the street I think I ought to say that I am an Atheist, because when I say that I cannot prove that there is not a God, I ought to add equally that I cannot prove that there are not the Homeric gods."[4]

In fairness to Russell, he should be allowed to characterize himself and his life in his own words before we dissect his ideas. In "What I Have Lived For," the prologue to his autobiography published not long before his death, he explains:

> Love and knowledge, so far as they were possible, led upward. . . . But always pity brought me back to earth. Echoes of cries of pain reverberate in my heart. Children in famine, victims tortured by oppressors, helpless old people . . . and the whole world of loneliness, poverty, and pain make a mockery of

what human life should be. I long to alleviate this evil, but I cannot, and I too suffer.[5]

As this passage proves, Russell regarded himself to be a man of great compassion. And in a manner of speaking, he certainly was, even if the reader concludes with me that his social ideas were wrongheaded and dangerous. Obviously, the scope of Russell's influence was amazing as he effected changes in everything from set theory and logical positivism to social policies and sexual morés. But we will only concern ourselves with his popular works and opinions on social and political issues. Then we will be able to isolate Russell's particular influence as it relates to the thesis of this book. Put simply, the philosopher Bertrand Russell, as an atheist and staunch advocate of rationalism, made popular the idea that science alone, because of the technological progress and human good it brings, not Jesus Christ, can save and advance culture. In the writings of Russell, moreover, we find that not only is Christianity, as Freud told us, a primitive, superstitious, untenable religion, but Christ himself is a flawed "savior" who bears much of the responsibility for the ignorance and suffering of humankind before the advent of science. After Russell and others like him, neither individuals nor institutions were thought to need Christianity, even for pragmatic reasons.

THE NEW AND IMPROVED SECULARIST FUTURE

Bertrand Russell believed in freedom and happiness as supreme goods, deplored all dogmatic faiths (Christian, Hindu, Marxist, or otherwise), and held that education should strive only to develop in students a scientific habit of mind. "Whatever can be known, can be known by means of science," he asserts in "The Philosophy of Logical Analysis," although he adds in his typical flexible way, "but things which are legitimately matters of feeling lie outside its province."[6] He states, for example, "God and immortality, the central dogmas of the Christian religion, find no support in science." Nor do ethics. Therefore, because we are "the ultimate and irrefutable arbiters of value," because scientific but not ethical knowledge exists, we must rely on science to help us determine the ends we desire. We can't "decide what sort of conduct is right or wrong except by reference to its probable consequences. Given an end to be achieved, it is a question for science to discover how to achieve it. All moral rules must be tested by examining whether they tend to realize ends that we desire."[7] This curious combination of optimistic scientific rationalism and vague subjectivistic ethics led Russell to some unusual and radical—but recognizably modern—conclusions.

Only Rationalistic Humanism Can Save Us

Russell was convinced that science would soon yield all the answers about nature and man. "Physical science," he claims, "is thus approaching the stage when it will be complete. . . ." Indeed, already we know that "Mental phenomena seem to be bound up with material structure." Like many empiricists and scientists from Hobbes to Freud, he thus accepted the view that humans are mechanisms, mainly victims of biological factors. People with bad habits, he says, for this reason shouldn't be judged but repaired as we repair broken motorcars, and criminals should be treated as we treat someone with the plague. In this way, sounding a familiar modern note, he likens people with character flaws—say, addictions—to faulty machinery, and he likens antisocial behavior—say, violence—to disease. To Russell, science is unveiling such truths by slow degrees, forcing its way against the old dogmas and precepts, guiding us away from irrational moral judgments and toward rational nonjudgmental enlightenment. "In this world," says Russell, "we can now begin a little to understand things, and a little to master them by help of science. . . ." We no longer need to cravenly cower in fear and ignorance under the shadow of religion as we once did. "Science can teach us, and I think our own hearts can teach . . . to look to our own efforts here below to make this world a fit place to live in. . . ."[8]

Russell likewise believed that philosophy, once purged of all its unscientific accretions—metaphysics, ethics, and theology—could contribute greatly to human and social progress. In "The Philosophy of Logical Analysis," he speaks warmly of a "Modern analytical empiricism" that will have "the quality of science rather than of philosophy," that will be "able to tackle its problems one at a time, instead of having to invent at one stroke a block theory of the whole universe." Says Russell optimistically, "by these methods, many ancient problems are completely soluble." To be effective, such logical analysis must also be divorced from moral considerations that might suppress the truth. "[T]he true philosopher is prepared to examine *all* preconceptions. When any limits are placed, consciously or unconsciously, upon the pursuit of truth, philosophy becomes paralyzed by fear." We must acquire "the habit of basing our beliefs upon observations and inferences as impersonal, and as much divested of local and temperamental bias, as is possible for human beings." He was so confident of this habit of mind that he believed it could "be extended to the whole sphere of human activity, producing, wherever it exists, a lessening of fanaticism with an increasing capacity of sympathy and mutual understanding."[9]

Russell didn't seem to recognize, however, how crippling his rationalistic approach could be to free thought and meaningful action. For surely, in preferring empirical explanations and rejecting traditional philosophical categories, Russell was himself shutting a door to free inquiry. He was declaring, in effect, "Thou shalt not study theology or metaphysics." In doing so, he was establishing a new dogma—one that was not only avowedly materialistic and deterministic but also overly skeptical and punctilious. In the end, an ever flexible, objective philosopher of the Russellian kind may find that, once freed of fear-borne dogmas, he is paralyzed by a new kind of fear. Falling prey to skepticism, he may come to doubt his own tainted motives and inadequate powers of observation. Writing for the Hearst newspapers on July 20, 1932, Russell clearly perceived the danger of habitual skepticism and uncertainty. Ironically, however, he couldn't perceive how his philosophy of logical analysis was contributing to the problem. In his editorial "On Modern Uncertainty," he says fretfully and impatiently of his generation of diffident intellectuals, "This state of affairs, if it continues, must plunge the world more and more deeply into misfortune. The scepticism of the intelligent is the cause of their impotence. . . ."

Can we have any doubt today that rationalistic humanism, with its excessive faith in science, has in fact rendered much of the intellectual world impotent and effete in social and moral matters? Modern rationalism—naturalistic and relativistic—has already rendered many intellectuals morally catatonic. Wandering the halls of academe, they can envision in horrific detail the extinction of the African rhino or a hole in the ozone while stepping absentmindedly over the morally fallen bodies of the young that lie gored and scorched at their feet. Possessing no "block theory of the whole universe," a practitioner of logical analysis can't see the rainforest for the trees.

All Religion Is Borne of Fear

To Russell, the single most powerful impediment to progress was religion, particularly Christianity. Like writers from Lucretius (96?-55? B.C.) to Freud, he held that belief in the gods or God stems from a cringing and simpering fear. Religion, he believed, has done inestimable harm because of its opposition to truth throughout history. Russell often repeats this theme in his writing. He decries Old Testament massacres, the Crusades, the Inquisition, the tyranny of the church in matters of sex and marriage.[10] People, he asserts, accept religion not on rational but "on emotional grounds." Thus because religion is based "primarily and mainly upon fear," it has led deplorably to multifarious fanaticisms and abuses of power. "Fear," after all, "is the parent of cruelty, and therefore it is no wonder if cruelty and religion have gone hand in hand." Even later in life he continued to cling to this view. In his "Preface" to the 1957 edition of *Why I Am Not a Christian*, he says that some have rumored that he has slackened in his opposition to religious orthodoxy. The rumor, he says, is baseless: "I am as firmly convinced that religions do harm as I am that they are untrue."[11]

To Russell, then, it followed that all the traditional arguments—or "proofs"—for the existence of God were invalid and untrue. In *Why I Am Not a Christian*, Russell attacks each of the traditional arguments, according to his own ranking from the strongest to the weakest: the first-cause argument, the natural-law argument, the design argument, and the moral argument. But by covering them all in only eight pages, he doesn't really do justice to any of them. Just consider this fact: In over 250 pages of *Summa Theologica*, Thomas Aquinas, just one classical theologian, dealt with twenty-six questions (each broken down into several propositions) on the topic of God alone, his existence and nature. Russell's treatment of the first-cause argument is almost juvenile: "If everything must have a cause, then God must have a cause."[12] But even Aristotle, not to speak of Aquinas, had long ago answered this question by defining God as the Uncaused Cause.

Similarly, when dismissing the design argument, Russell oversimplifies it, almost facetiously, by pointing to evil in the world: "Do you think that, if you were granted omnipotence and omniscience and millions of years in which to perfect your world, you could produce nothing better than the Ku Klux Klan or the Fascists?"[13] Wouldn't it be fair in such a case to accuse Russell of pandering to emotion just as he accuses theists of basing their faith on emotion? Later, in a BBC debate with F. C. Copleston in 1948, Russell restates his opposition to the "proofs" of God's existence. He refuses to accept the classical terms "necessary" and "sufficient" in reference to the being of God. As for the moral argument—far from accepting that good and bad are only meaningful in relation to a Supreme Being—he reduces questions of good and bad to a trivial perceptual analogy: "I don't have any justification [for distinguishing between good and bad] any more than I have when I distinguish between blue and yellow." When pushed, he says— sounding a little like Hume and J. S. Mill—that morality boils down to feeling, but not simple feeling "but rather a feeling as to the effects" of certain actions.[14]

Despite Russell's radical criticisms of religion, he isn't able to provide anything like an impeccable logical refutation of the foundational belief in Deity. In fact, in the end he seems to take refuge not in rationalism but in subjectivism. As I suggested of Freud earlier, perhaps Russell's critique of religion was also born out of an unconscious motivation—in Russell's case, a fear of its call and demands. How else can we explain his lapses into sarcasm and invective when he writes of Christianity? When he dissected Christianity, did he ever consider dissecting his own outrage and indignation? For surely there has been just as much cruelty in the world without the presence of religious influence as with it. Surely, case by case, nation by nation, people have divided and fought throughout history more over trifling desires than over differing dogmas.

Even Jesus Christ Was Seriously Flawed

Russell ventured farther than any writer before him in his irreligiosity. Breaking new ground, he assailed the character of Jesus Christ, not on general historical grounds as Nietzsche had done, but on specific personal grounds within the framework of rational discourse. In *Why I Am Not a Christian*, it's true that he first concedes that he finds aspects of Christ's moral character admirable. But then he quickly adds, "historically it is quite doubtful whether Christ ever existed at all. . . ." Still, he says that he will concern himself "with Christ as he appears in the Gospels."[15] Then he takes off the gloves as he argues that Christ and his church have retarded progress.

He levels two main criticisms at Jesus, then concludes that Jesus has been responsible for much of the suffering in the world since his time. First, Jesus wasn't omniscient. Says Russell, Jesus clearly believed according to the Gospel record that he would return soon: "[Christ] certainly thought that His second coming would occur in clouds of glory before the death of all the people who were living at the time." After referring to several proof-texts, Russell concludes that "He was not so wise as some other people have been, and He was certainly not superlatively wise." Second, he argues that Jesus Christ wasn't profoundly humane. Christ's belief in hell, claims Russell, was as a moral defect: "I do not myself feel that any person who is really profoundly humane can believe in everlasting punishment."

Russell goes on to refer to Christ's "vindictive fury" against his opponents, comparing it unfavorably with the attitude of Socrates toward his persecutors. He thinks that Christ really missed the mark when he declared, "Ye . . . generation of vipers, how can ye escape the damnation of hell?" (Matt. 23:33, KJV). With urbane restraint, Russell remarks of this verse, "It is not really to my mind quite the best tone. . . ." To Russell, a person with proper kindness wouldn't have unleashed such terrors into the world. He regards Christ's belief in hell to be a "doctrine that put cruelty into the world and gave the world generations of cruel torture . . ." and concludes that "the Christ of the Gospels . . . would certainly have to be considered partly responsible for that." After complaining that Christ was perversely mean to the Gadarene swine he sent headlong into the sea and to the fig tree he blighted, Russell concludes his criticisms by maintaining that in wisdom and virtue Christ doesn't even measure up to Buddha or Socrates.[16]

Of course, Russell also includes the church, all Christian churches, in his indictment. Resorting to sweeping generalizations, something a savvy logician should know better than to do, he declares that "*every* moral progress that there has been in the world, has been *consistently* opposed by [all] the organized *churches* of the world" (italics mine). He labels the church "an opponent of progress and improvement" because it insists that people follow what *it* calls morality and thereby inflicts "undeserved and unnecessary" misery on people. The church "has chosen to label as morality a certain narrow set of rules of conduct which have nothing to do with human happiness," which for Russell is the *sine qua non* of life. It was unjust of him to assert that the churches hold that morality has nothing to do with human happiness.[17] Quite the opposite is the case. Christians believe that a faith in God that bears fruit in obedience to God is the only sure way to happiness in the present or the future: "Blessed is every one that feareth the LORD; that walketh in his ways. For thou shalt eat the labor of thine hands: happy shalt thou be, and it shall be well with thee" (Ps. 128:1-2, KJV). After setting the example of service and sacrifice by washing the disciples' feet, Jesus said, "If ye know these things, happy are ye if ye do them" (John 13:17, KJV). Such obedience to Christ leads to a peace that passes understanding—and that peace is happiness.

Russell purposefully set out to demolish—and abolish—religion, regarding it as both untrue and harmful. Of course, thinkers from Hume through Freud had already laid the groundwork for the dismantling of Christianity within Western culture. Russell joined them by asserting that science is based on reason, Christianity on fear. Science, he held, will help man overcome the old reactionary superstitions. In this way Russell simply flip-flopped traditional perceptions of science and religion, in effect placing a halo over the head of scientific rationalism and horns on the head of religion, then left the rest of the work of reforming our social institutions and culture up to us. As Russell put it, "universal happiness can be secured," but only if we "slay the dragon that guards the door, and this dragon is religion."[18]

THE INFLUENCE OF THE MEGA-IDEA

Russell's influence, as we have seen, wasn't so much as a philosopher but as a popular writer. In a way Russell thus represents a new trend in the twentieth century. The genius who would influence culture must step out of his ivory tower, or off his fancy estate, if he would effect change in the world. Marx realized this fact, and so did Freud, and both wanted to change culture. Hobbes, Hume, Rousseau, Mill, Darwin, and Nietzsche could prefer the private over the public life and still influence others. Perhaps they were less keen on effecting changes in culture, although that seems unlikely given the ubiquitous desire for renown. Rather, all they lacked was the wholly modern sensibility that the world is a stage. As communication and cultural uniformity make the world seem smaller, the possibilities for renown and influence increase exponentially. Such an insight may well have occurred to Bertrand Russell, a man who operated popularly on the world stage, albeit urbanely and modestly. For Russell's influence today seems pervasive and permanent, reaching from the lowliest inner-city ghettoes to the highest reaches of government.

Everyone's New "Right" to Sexual Happiness

Russell placed a high premium on the possession of happiness for everyone. To Russell, happiness is such a fundamental human right that anything, as he sees it, that stands in the way of securing it must be opposed. Such an obstacle is religion, and so also is traditional morality, especially as it applies to relations between the sexes. "Moral rules," says Russell, "ought not to be such as to make instinctive happiness impossible. Yet that is an effect of strict monogamy in a community where the numbers of the two sexes are very unequal."[19] Thus monogamy is better breached than observed if unhappiness might result for one or more parties.

Russell was convinced that "Very few men or women who have had a conventional upbringing have learnt to feel decently about sex and marriage." This indecent attitude, fostered by Christianity, has led to deceitfulness and great unhappiness. It "has made marriage unsatisfying both to men and to women, and the lack of instinctive satisfaction has turned to cruelty masquerading as morality."[20] Because conventional moral teaching is thus causing the young to cruelly suffer, he therefore seeks a compromise in "Our Sexual Ethics" (1936) between "complete promiscuity and lifelong monogamy." He boldly recommends for the young premarital sex, birth control, and cohabitation between boys and girls of the "same class." Considerable freedom should be granted to young unmarried people "as long as children are avoided." To the married, he offers no-fault divorce: "divorce should be possible without blame to either party."[21]

Anyone should hear the war whoop of the sexual revolution in this seemingly modest counsel of Russell. Sex before marriage, birth control, cohabitation, no-fault divorce—this is *our* brave new world. Behind his words, written more than sixty years ago, anyone should also be able to hear the cries of single mothers and fathers, the wails of discarded children, the disillusioned sighs of the young when they contemplate marriage. In our time the sexual revolution is over: the revolutionaries won. We have been liberated. Now we are free to experience the highest rates of divorce, single parenthood, child poverty, and venereal disease that we have known during this whole enlightened century.[22] Now we can accept as commonplace, as our movies and TV shows illustrate, as our coeducational dorms prove, that we have shed the hang-ups of our uptight Christian forebears who disapproved of premarital sex and cohabitation.

Where is the resulting increase in happiness that Russell and kindred reformers promised us? Over "sex," characters get into cat fights on soaps; people go to blows on tell-all talk shows. Prostitutes still walk the streets. Jealous lovers still murder each other. Singles, having no paucity of partners from whom to choose, still lie at home weeping and pining for true love. In ninety-seven years of life, Russell himself was married four times and had numerous affairs. There needn't be a correlation, other than coincidental, between these salacious biographical details and Russell's advocacy of sexual liberation, but the circumstantial evidence for ascribing ulterior motives to him is strong enough to make us pause. Why did Rousseau want us to live freely and naturally? Why did Marx or Nietzsche want to overturn the cultural systems of their day? Why did Freud and Russell want us to liberate our libidos? When I attended college in the 1960s and 1970s, the strongest, most outspoken proponents of sexual liberation were always young men. Even at nineteen I knew why.

In "We Have No 'Right to Happiness,'" C. S. Lewis aptly refutes the illogic of the Bertrand Russells. First, he points out that we have no more "right to happiness" than we have to being six feet tall or being a millionaire's son. As he says, "we depend for a very great deal of our happiness or misery on circumstances outside all human control." Then he goes on to suggest that what many progressives mean by happiness is the right to pursue sexual happiness. The Freuds and Russells say, "Let's get rid of all this prudery. It's damaging people and deforming relationships." To Lewis, such progressives are attempting to treat sex "as no other impulse in our nature has ever been treated by civilized people." Unlike other impulses, it shouldn't have to be bridled. What's the result, according to Lewis? In the name of this overarching passion, "every unkindness and breach of faith seems to be condoned provided that the object aimed at is 'four bare legs in a bed.'" In allowing this impulse to "supersede all the ordinary rules of behaviour," we are setting a dangerous precedent and establishing a "fatal principle" when it comes to seeking individual happiness. In the future we may well find ourselves, says Lewis, writing in 1963, advancing "toward a state of society in which not only each man but every impulse in each man claims *carte blanche.*"[23]

When observed in this light, Russell's ethics turn out in the end to be subjectivistic. Russell concedes as much when he says in his debate with F. C. Copleston, "It is not direct feeling about the act by which I should judge, but rather a feeling as to the effects."[24] Despite the utilitarian escape hatch that Russell bores for himself, he is still saying that he bases moral decisions on "a feeling." In his essay C. S. Lewis was hoping that we would see the dangers of such subjectivistic ethics.

In sexual matters, however, I suspect that people have more often applied the advice of Russell than heeded the alarms of Lewis. Russell promised that "universal happiness" was possible and "that, in a community where men live [prompted by love, guided by knowledge], more desires will be satisfied. . . ."[25] How many, in the absence of a strong faith, can resist such an appeal? Humans have always craved universal happiness and the fulfillment of more desires.

The Vogue of Liberalism

To be a liberal is to be an agnostic. To be a liberal is to be hot, hip, cool—fashionably current, progressive, knowledgeable—like Bertrand Russell. To be a liberal is also to be an activist for the "right causes." After all, too much skepticism, as Russell warned in "On Modern Uncertainty," can make intellectuals so impotent that they yield the political and social field to those "who are too stupid to know when their opinions are absurd," thus allowing the world to be "ruled by fools." For this reason perhaps, Russell himself became a social activist. Through his adherence to pacifism, advocacy of sexual freedom, and opposition to the Vietnam War, Russell helped set trends for modern liberals. Curiously, however, Russell's liberalism turns out to be just as dogmatic as any Christian orthodoxy. Russell, in his "Liberal Decalogue," tells liberals, "Have no respect for the authority of others, for there are always contrary authorities to be found," and "Do not fear to be eccentric in opinion, for every opinion now accepted was once eccentric."[26] Elsewhere, when Russell calls for toleration and cooperation, we can be certain that he isn't asking that these virtues be extended toward Christian believers.

In the media today, we observe all too clearly the liberal bias that Russell and his heirs passed on to us. Whether in dramatic portrayals or in news stories, depictions of Christians are negative; they are often represented as dogmatic fanatics who oppose "sex" and "happiness." By contrast, liberals—even the agnostics and atheists—are portrayed as tolerant and compassionate. There is ample proof of this bias in the media. In the mid-1980s Lichter and Rothman in their book *The Media Elite* startled many Americans with their research. They concluded that the media elites hold views that differ strikingly from mainstream America. Whereas 54 percent were willing to say they held views "left of center," only 19 percent characterized themselves as conservative. Whereas only 47 percent of the elite thought adultery morally wrong, 85 percent of Americans believed it morally wrong. And 86 percent of the media professionals admitted that they rarely if ever attended church services.[27]

The Media Research Center (MRC) of Alexandria, Virginia, has arrived at similar conclusions as revealed in its book *And That's the Way It Isn't*. Through extensive studies, surveys, and analyses, the MRC has concluded that Americans are being given a liberally slanted view of their country, in part because the media elite, says Steven Allen, "have little contact with conservatives and make little effort to understand the conservative viewpoint." Following Russell's lead, they don't have to and they don't want to. It's no wonder, then, that the MRC found that "conservatives were far more likely than liberals to be painted as ideologues and extremists." Even that media sage Walter Cronkite has admitted to the liberal bias: "I think most newspapermen by definition have to be liberal. If they're not, by my definition of it, then they can hardly be good newspapermen."[28]

In academe, whose graduates assume positions of leadership in the media, the liberal bias is stifling. The pacifism, toleration, and agnosticism of Bertrand Russell have assumed the high moral ground on most university campuses. Most professors are liberal and proud of it. In fact, many are looking forward to a new world order in academe, even the more moderate liberals like Louis Henry Gates of Duke University, formerly of Cornell. In an interview with Dinesh D'Souza for his book *Illiberal Education*, "Gates identified what he called 'a rainbow coalition of blacks, leftists, feminists, deconstructionists, and Marxists' who had now infiltrated academia and were 'ready to take control.'" It was only a matter of time before the old guard would retire and the new guard would reign. "'Then, of course,'" said Gates, "'the universities will become more liberal politically.'"[29]

If one reads books by Dinesh D'Souza, Allan Bloom, Alvin Kiernan, and William J. Bennett on the status of modern education, it's hard to see how our institutions could become any more liberal than they already are. Of course, eighteen-year-olds fresh out of high school are easy prey for proselytizing liberal professors. And many of them eagerly get involved in the efforts to further the "cause of social justice" on their campuses. In defense of political correctness, they will join such organizations as the Union of Democratic Intellectuals and the Center for Campus Organizing, which has published its own book for unmasking and combating conservatives on campus, entitled *Uncovering the Right on Campus: A Guide to Resisting Conservative Attacks on Equality and Social Justice*.[30] When these activists who have tilted at "right-wing conspiracies" apply for positions in the media—or in other academic institutions—they will possess sterling credentials, references, and résumés.

Having myself crossed over from the left to the right, I can testify to the tyranny of liberalism in academe and society. Liberals have contempt for conservatives, regarding them as less intelligent. If one evinces even the slightest trace of conservatism, doors will slam up and down the corridors of a campus, for students and scholars. Faced with such insurmountable professional and peer pressure, how can the young resist succumbing to the wiles of the left on university campuses? Liberal academicians don't respond any more gracefully to criticism from the Americans who deplore such trends. Such Americans just don't understand the complexities of academia, said one UCLA professor at a scholarly conference. "It's like trying to reduce a Henry James novel to a tele-gram." Or they are just stupid, claimed a University of California Berkeley professor; they are people "who don't know the difference between Plato and NATO."[31] Meanwhile, liberalism remains in vogue, as tyrannical as any dead white European male despot of the Middle Ages or Renaissance ever was.

The Demotion of Jesus Christ

Before Bertrand Russell was critiquing Jesus Christ, others had already been disassembling the cross of the Savior of the world. Among scholars, David Strauss (1808-1874) and Ernest Renan (1823-1892) had written their humanizing, demythologizing accounts of Jesus, calling much his-torical detail into question. Among occultists in the nineteenth century, Levi Dowling wrote *The Aquarian Gospel of Jesus Christ*, a channeled retelling of the life of Jesus in which he is made out to be an Essene and Gnostic who believed in reincarnation. At about the same time that Russell was writing, the Theosophists were having their crack at revi-sionism also. Madam Blavatsky wrote *The Secret Doctrine* in 1925, and Yogi Ramacharaka (an American) published his *Mystic Christianity or the Inner Teachings of the Master* in 1935. Already a few East-Indian yogis had left their marks as well, Swami Vivekananda as early as 1893 and Swami Yogananda as early as 1925, neither of whom hesitated to reinterpret Jesus Christ in light of their own spiritual heritage. Presumptuous, spurious accounts and reinterpretations were cropping up everywhere.

An intellectual of tremendous caliber, Bertrand Russell facilitated this revisionism in a distinctive way. By finding fault with the character of Jesus Christ, Russell helped to demote him within Western culture. Jesus was just a man, wise but not superlatively wise, certainly no wiser than Socrates or Buddha. Through reason and science, man is now in a position to decide what is best for himself and his future. Cut loose from tradition, he no longer needs to rely on deities in the sky or a "God-man" who possessed only a few relevant answers to life's problems and who in fact may have done just as much harm as good to the cause of human progress.

The new secular, agnostic culture that was arising in the wake of rationalism and scientism left a void into which anyone with a soapbox and a novel message could step. Now demoted, Jesus was on an equal footing with other wise men. First, the wise men being introduced to us were the lightbearers from other traditions—Zen Buddhism, Tibetan Buddhism, Hinduism. Then came the self-proclaimed wise men to fill the void—the Rudolf Steiners, G. I. Gurdjieffs, L. Ron Hubbards, Stephen Gaskells, Carlos Castanedas, and Frederick Lenzes. Most recently, a new phenom has appeared on the horizon, Nick Bunick, who claims to be the reincarnation of the apostle Paul.[32] Notice the proliferation of new gurus and paths in the past thirty years alone, a veritable smorgasbord of choices, among which Jesus Christ becomes lost. Now that Christ has been demoted, he has therefore also been marginalized. The secular and agnostic biases can flourish alongside the New Age revisions of spirituality, united by a single cause—to render the historical Jesus Christ and orthodox Christianity innocuous, and as invisible as possible. Agnostic and atheistic secularists and New Agers alike don't even want the image of Santa Claus to remain on a courthouse lawn, much less the image of Jesus Christ in a public park.

Neither New Age subjectivism nor scientific rationalism can replace Christianity as a repository of truth. New Age "truths" and "paths" lack anything like a firm foundation and more often than not bristle with self-contradictions.[33] Moreover, the truth of science itself is often subject to reexamination and revision and, by Russell's own admission, can offer us no answers in the area of morals: "There remains . . . a vast field, traditionally included in philosophy, where scientific methods are inadequate. This field includes questions of value. . . ."[34] In Russell's world, as hard as we strive for happiness, we are only left with "feelings" in regard to the consequences of actions and with scientific improvements in our comfort and security. Even with our toaster ovens and TVs, our vaccines and computers, we are only left with a fuzzy optimism about the benefits of scientific progress and a blind faith in the revelations of human reason. With "love and knowledge," we will work it out, says Russell. If we genuinely pity others who suffer, we will build a better world. In the end, Russell's message is naive at best, disingenuous at worst.

Despite what Russell and others say, all attempts at social and scientific progress are vain and empty without faith in God as Creator and in Christ as Redeemer, Lord, and Guide. Without faith, people must invariably fall back on themselves, becoming egocentric and ultimately despondent as they realize that where human needs are concerned, atheism and scientism are as cold, hard, and inhospitable as icebergs bobbing in the sea. Without faith, people must also individually conclude that they are laws unto themselves, responsible only for themselves (and their own) when push comes to shove, as it literally does, in the narrow straits of life.

History supports this insight, as we will see soon enough. For according to our next mega-idea, advanced by modern existentialists like Jean-Paul Sartre, modern man is already irremediably trapped within his own subjectivity, stranded on the pitching sea of a godless, meaningless universe. And in response, man can only feel anxious and forlorn as he chooses to act by impulse in a world devoid of divine assistance and transcendent absolutes. Because of this loneliness and insignificance, man must suffer, no matter what kind of work, humane or otherwise, he undertakes. Neither a heroic atheism nor a noble scientism will provide him with satisfaction either. As Russell himself put it toward the end of his life, he had longed to alleviate the suffering in the world, but he couldn't, so he too had suffered. Apparently in the end the words that resonated for Russell weren't those of Jesus but of Buddha, the one he thought the more enlightened of the two: "All is suffering."

Where there is no God, there is no hope.

FOURTH STAGE
IN THE SLIDE TOWARD RELATIVISM

From 1947 to the present,

man has asserted that all truth and moral norms

are relative— indeed, meaningless—while

an elite few have taken advantage of the situation

to promote various progressive agendas.

Now intuition has been cut loose from God.

"LIFE IS
MEANINGLESS"

Significantly two French publications by Jean-Paul Sartre first appeared in English in 1947—*No Exit and the Flies* and *Existentialism*. The *Stranger* by Albert Camus had already appeared in an English translation the year before. Sartre's more philosophical treatise *Being and Nothingness*, written in 1943, wouldn't appear in English until 1956, and Martin Heidegger's celebrated treatise *Being and Time*, written in 1927, wouldn't appear in English until 1962. Thus, by the late 1940s many English-speaking readers were first introduced to existentialism solely through the popular works of Sartre and Camus. In Camus's *The Stranger* they read of the indifferent, atheistic Meursault, the antihero who finds it impossible to weep at the death of his mother, ends up murdering an Arab, and concludes that life is absurd. In Sartre's *The Flies*, they read of the unrepentant Orestes who asserts, "And there was nothing left in heaven, no right or wrong, nor anyone to give me orders." And in Sartre's gloomy *No Exit*, they first encountered the now-famous line "Hell is other people."

Even then, after reading the literary works and the book *Existentialism*, they didn't realize that the very term *existentialism* was new. As to the origin of the term, "Reports . . . differ, but it seems to have been coined towards the end of World War II by the French philosopher Gabriel Marcel as a label for the currently emerging ideas of Jean-Paul Sartre and [his life-long lover] Simone de Beauvoir." Apparently Sartre rejected the term at first but then soon embraced it, as early as the fall of 1945.[1] Until then no so-called "existentialist" treatises had used the term. Apparently this disagreement over the relevance and accuracy of the term continues to this day among scholars. Is there really a coherent philosophy of existentialism? Walter Kaufmann says there isn't. "Certainly, existentialism is not a school of thought nor reducible to any set of tenets. The three writers who appear invariably on every list of existentialists—Jaspers, Heidegger, Sartre—are not in agreement on essentials."[2] David E. Cooper of Durham University says there is. Although he doesn't minimize the differences between writers, he states that he can "demonstrate that there is a coherent, definable philosophy of existentialism. . . ." How does he begin to define the school? "It is generally agreed that if Heidegger and Sartre are not existentialists, then no one is. A natural policy, therefore, is to apply the name to these two, and then to others according to their kinship with them."[3]

And the kinship appears to be legion, although Sartre himself speaks of just two types—atheists and Christians. Among the atheists, says Sartre, were "Heidegger, and then the French existentialists and myself." Today, according to the University of Southern California library, we can add a couple of psychologists also—Abraham Maslow and Rollo May.[4] Modern historians of philosophy also add Nietzsche, Camus, and countless literary figures, including the postmodernists Jacques Derrida and Richard Rorty. Among the Christian existentialists, says Sartre, are "Karl Jaspers and Gabriel Marcel, both Catholic."[5] Modern historians of philosophy include Soren Kierkegaard and Dostoyevsky (pointing to the *Brothers Karamazov*, Part II, Book V, Chapter 5, "The Grand Inquisitor"). Still others add the names of Rudolf Bultmann, who had been a friend of Heidegger, and Paul Tillich. But these Christians hardly fit the profile of an orthodox believer. Kierkegaard, admits Cooper, "described his hero of authenticity, the 'knight of faith', as *'suspending the ethical'* . . ." (italics mine). Indeed, writing of all existentialists, he adds, "Generally, terms like 'ethical' and 'moral' are not ones to which existentialists are partial."[6]

To understand existentialism, its nature and impact on modern society, we will focus on Jean-Paul Sartre, using his essay "Existentialism and Humanism" (1947) to help us grasp the main tenets of the school. However, a few references to Heidegger and Camus along the way will prove useful too. Put simply, for now we can say that existentialists hold that life is meaningless apart from man's self-initiated, self-assertive acts.

Every person, each being, must come to accept that his condition is one of *Angst* (anxiety), forlornness, and despair. He is alone in the universe, without a God to give him hope or certitude—or a sense of *a priori* values. Nevertheless, a human being can create himself and his own meaning by thinking and acting heroically, because a man is only what he wills himself to be. A man's existence, his action, always precedes his essence.

HEROIC ATHEISM IN A MEANINGLESS WORLD

The philosophy of Heidegger and Sartre, in particular, we must acknowledge to be complex, just as most philosophies are complex, sometimes even tedious and obscure. Just consider some of the terms we have to stub our toes on when slogging through the works of Heidegger and Sartre. We must stumble over *Dasein* ("being" or "being there"), *Eigenlichkeit* ("authenticity"), *Angst* ("anxiety") and *Sorge* ("caring," "worrying") as they relate to the existence of a human "being" thrown into the world of *das man*, the world of "they," where temporality rules and one can lose authenticity and freedom if he misses *der augenblick*, the moment of vision.[7] Sartre seems less obscure than Heidegger but poses difficulties too, as he draws heavily on the philosophy of Heidegger. Like Heidegger, he vexes us with different types of being (*l'être*)—being-in-itself (*l'en-soi*) and being-for-itself (*le pour-soi*)—as well as with nothingness (*le néant*), all of which can produce vertigo in the ego (*l'ego*) of the reader.

In light of this complexity, David E. Cooper protests that the popularized version of Sartre's existentialism differs from his real philosophy. Most people, says Cooper, misunderstand existentialism because they rely too heavily on the hastily composed "Existentialism and Humanism," which Sartre later regretted publishing. "For there are passages here which do encourage the view that commitment and moral decision can only be irrational *actes gratuits*, or based upon nothing but inner conviction." In this essay, too, "there is much talk of abandonment and despair, but not set in the wider context of Sartre's philosophy which lends proper sense to such notions." Cooper further claims that Sartre and Simone de Beauvoir were both troubled by the popularization of existentialism in the late 1940s when it became in vogue "among black-clad youths prowling between the *Tabou* and the *Pergola*...."

These writers disliked "the chic appeal which feigned *ennui* and despair apparently had for young Parisians of the time." Cooper laments that few of these youths had read the 600 pages of *Being and Nothingness* and that their unconventionality "had less affinity with [Sartre and de Beauvoir] than with the 'hippies' of the 1960s or the 'punks' of the 1970s."[8] He could have easily extended the affinity to the Beats of the 1950s also. In fact, Maynard G. Krebs of the 1950s TV show *Dobie Gillis* was a parody of the by-then popular existentialists on the American scene.

But people and culture are most affected by what is received popularly, by what snippets and images, engendered by the writers themselves, trickle down to the average fellow waiting at a stoplight in his red Renault and black beret. For this reason we have no choice but to consider the most popular words and ideas of Sartre and his crew. We will thus best be served if we start with Sartre's own definition of atheistic existentialism:

> It states that if God does not exist, there is at least one being in whom existence precedes essence, a being who exists before he can be defined . . . and that this being is man, or, as Heidegger says, human reality. What is meant . . . by saying that existence precedes essence? It means that . . . man exists . . . appears on the scene, and, only afterwards, defines himself. If man . . . is indefinable, it is because at first he is nothing. Only afterward will he be something, and he himself will have made what he will be. Thus, there is no human nature, since there is not God to conceive it. Not only is man what he conceives himself to be, but he is also only what he wills himself to be after this thrust toward existence.[9]

In this passage we discover all the themes of existentialism, primarily the critical references to "being" derived from Heidegger's thought: "The essence of Dasein lies in its existence," and "Dasein is its possibility."[10] According to Michael Inwood, in this sense, "Dasein is not a definite actual thing, but the possibility of various ways of being."[11] Through existence alone—acts of will, choices—man, claims Sartre, creates himself and any putative essence to which he lays claim. After all, to Sartre, "there is no human nature," and there is no God, only man's being (*l'être* or *Dasein*); thus man has no essence—that is, no *a priori* soul. In the face of such nothingness, all acts of will require great courage since man as being has been merely "thrust toward existence" by his birth, which he obviously didn't choose. Still, insists Heidegger, man can triumph over his existence and destiny by making "the Resolute Decision."[12]

In this connection we must consider two more points. First, the existentialist believes that *Dasein* can fall prey to what Sartre calls "bad faith" and lose his authenticity. To possess "good faith," he must be sincere, honest with and true to himself, as he continues to create himself. Second, based on the continuous project of *being*, self-conceiving, and willing, Sartre says elsewhere, "it is impossible for man to transcend human subjectivity."[13] A man can only really act and speak for himself, since he knows only himself. In fairness to the existentialists, though, it should be acknowledged that they aren't solipsists. They do accept the existence of a world external to *Dasein*, what Heidegger referred to as *Welt* (the public world) and *Umwelt* (the private world), believing that "man essentially . . . is Being-in-the-world."[14] In fact, they acknowledge that circumstances can at times limit the choices of *Dasein*.

With this background, we are prepared to consider the three main influential themes that appear in Sartre's still very much anthologized "Existentialism and Humanism."[15]

Man Is Filled with Anguish

Heidegger used the word *Angst*, which Sartre translates as "anguish" and "anxiety." Others have used the term "dread." Man *is* anguish, says Sartre. "What that means is this: the man who involves himself and who realizes that he is not only the person he chooses to be, but also a lawmaker who is, at the same time, choosing all mankind as well as himself, can not help escape the feeling of his total and deep responsibility." A man makes his own choices, but he does so aware that he is also, in a sense, a role model. Therefore, he must accept the awesome responsibility of making choices, knowing that he is absolutely free. Here Sartre establishes a kind of subjectivistic ethics: an honest person should always ask himself, "Am I really the kind of man who has the right to act in such a way that humanity might guide itself by my actions?" Says Sartre, "if [one] does not say that to himself, he is masking his anguish."[16]

When faced with this anguish-ridden responsibility, a man mustn't take refuge in quietism but must act, finding his meaning along the way.

"All leaders know this anguish," says Sartre. Still, they act, envisioning a number of possibilities but not really knowing, not absolutely, which course is the right one. When they choose—actually invent—an action, "they realize that it has value only because it is chosen." And this realization and acceptance of their responsibility after the fact is also part of their anguish. Apparently, then, the questions a man asks before acting steel him for acting, making him consider others and take responsibility, but they don't provide him with certain guidance as to how to act. He has, to a large extent, to invent the values that determine his actions. As Sartre says later in the essay, "to say that we invent values means nothing else but this: life has no meaning *a priori*. Before you come alive, life is nothing, it's up to you to give it meaning, and value is nothing else but the meaning you choose."[17] All of this reliance on subjectivity, being-for-itself or being-in-itself, is the burden of anguish.

If humans can rely on no *a priori* sense of right and wrong, they will have to rely on feelings. When it comes to decisions, feelings of satisfaction can stem from devilish delusions as readily as from divine insights. Even if before acting humans rely on the question, "What if everyone acted that way?" they still can arrive at no definitively ethical decision. An individual may well want everyone else to be able to do as he does. "It would be fine with me," he might answer, "if everyone else smoked marijuana." Or he might respond, "I see no harm to society in kiddy porn." In such cases, however, he would only be answering the question in terms of his own biases and preferences, which most existentialists will readily acknowledge. For this reason Sartre can say that a person can give meaning to an action—or determine the value of an action—only after he has acted. All *Angst* does, then, is to "intimate to us our radical freedom and individuality."[18] It helps us gird up our loins to do, but it doesn't help us do "right."

Man Is Burdened with Forlornness

According to Sartre, the term *forlornness* was a favorite of Heidegger. It means "only that God does not exist and that we have to face all the consequences of [his nonexistence]." As a result, the existentialist, far from exulting in this knowledge, feels forlorn and distressed. With the loss of God "all possibility of finding values in a heaven of ideas disappears . . . ; there can no longer be an *a priori* Good, since there is no infinite and perfect consciousness to think it." Man is forlorn, says Sartre, quoting Dostoyevsky, because "If God didn't exist, everything would be possible." And for the existentialist, God *doesn't* exist. The existentialist is forlorn because he knows that "man is condemned to be free. Condemned, because he did not create himself, yet, in other respects is free; because, once thrown into the world, he is responsible for everything he does."[19] Sartre seems simply to be saying that we are bound to have to do our "own thing."

Because man will interpret any omen or sign that he might stumble over in his life to suit himself, he must ignore omens in making decisions. Instead, he must realize that he has "no support and no aid" and that he is therefore "condemned every moment to invent" himself. Sartre then cites the case of one of his students. Briefly put, during World War II the young man had to decide whether to serve his country and avenge his brother's death by joining the French Resistance against the Nazi occupation or to fulfill his mother's wishes and remain at home with her since she looked to him as her last remaining hope in life. The young man, coming to the sage Sartre, was graced with the following wholly existential advice: "You're free, choose, that is, invent." In other words, Sartre urged the young man to do what he would do, and having done what he decided to do, he would have done it. Then Sartre draws this conclusion: "No general ethics can show you what is to be done; there are no omens in the world."[20]

Won't such a forlorn subjectivism, once embraced, simply lead to irrational rebellion? Won't it just flush wild-eyed reformers of every stripe out of the woodwork? After all, now that we are free to choose, to invent, let us rebel and reform. In the face of an absurd world, claims Albert Camus, that is just what the authentic person will do. Asked in an interview if he thought the attitude of the rebel in the face of absurdity could be adopted by the majority or only a few, Camus called for the courage of rebellion from those who know the truth. "The men of our time, whom we encounter in the streets, show in their faces that they know. The only difference is that some . . . show more courage. Besides, we have no choice. It is either [rebellion] or nihilism."[21] As Sartre often did, Camus may have been speaking more as a Marxist at this point. Like Sartre, he was convinced, at least at this stage in his life, that man must revolutionize civilization "without the help either of the eternal or of rationalistic thought." Unaided, man's challenge was to create his own values and, especially in France and Europe in the mid-1940s, "create a new civilization or else perish." Heroic atheist that Camus was, he was willing to undergo the suffering involved in building a new civilization.[22]

Surely, we can already see that existentialism is a philosophy of despair, as the next section announces. What happiness has atheistic existentialism brought, with its uncertain subjectivistic free choices and rationalized irrational rebellion? Ironically, a thinker who is often linked with the existentialists, but in fact wasn't an existentialist by any means, provided us with a sounder psychology over 300 years ago. In a typically abbreviated way, Blaise Pascal reasons in *Pensées*, Section II:

> *First part*: Misery of man without God.
> *Second part*: Happiness of man with God.[23]

Without God, Pascal concludes, there can be no happiness. Happiness exists in and with God alone. When man is cut loose from God to depend on himself alone, he can only lose his way, not just spiritually but morally as well. Without God, there also can be no morality. When the only absolute truth for an existentialist is the Cartesian "I think; therefore, I exist,"[24] there can be no objective, absolute truth or morality by which we can make decisions. In Sartre's subjectivistic world of choice, the best one can hope for is "intersubjectivity" by means of which man can create "community."

Man Is Saddled with Despair

Sartre says *despair* has a simple meaning: "It means that we shall confine ourselves to reckoning only with what depends upon our will, or on the ensemble of probabilities which make our action possible."[25] Summarizing Heidegger's thought on this matter, Inwood says, "The date of my birth limits my position in time, and consequently the possible course of action open to me, in a way that the place of my birth does not limit my position in space."[26] In this way the existentialist tries to come to grips with his circumstances and seize the possibilities inherent in those circumstances. Armed with this understanding, "I should involve myself," says Sartre, "then act on the old saying, 'Nothing ventured, nothing gained.'" "Man," he declares, "is nothing else than his plan; he exists only to the extent that he fulfills himself; he is therefore nothing else than the ensemble of his acts, nothing else than his life." Thus, in the face of any circumstantial limitations, action and reality are all that count. "What we mean is that a man is nothing else than a series of undertakings, that he is the sum . . . of the relationships which make up these undertakings." In his own case Sartre says that he is going to do everything in his power to bring about socialism, for he is certain that there is no reality for him except in such action.[27]

In other words, the existentialist accepts his circumstantial limitations but acts in the here and now anyway, without any expectations beyond the moment of possibilities. Says Sartre, "The moment the possibilities I am considering are not rigorously involved by my action, I ought to disengage myself from it, because no God, no scheme, can adapt the world and its possibilities to my will." For Sartre, this attitude means that he can't trust anyone or anything beyond the present probabilities, preferring to live for the choices of today than to die for the "possibilities" of tomorrow. Given that humans are free and that there is no constant human nature for him to rely on, Sartre says, "I can not count on men whom I do not know by relying on human goodness or man's concern for the good of society." A few lines later he states the point bluntly: "I've got to limit myself to what I see."[28] So this is the despair—being with others perhaps, but being alone with one's own limited choices, renouncing any hope beyond the present moment of possibilities.

What is left, according to Sartre, isn't pessimism, "but an optimistic toughness." He trusts that "there is a universality of man; but it is not given, it is perpetually being made." Choice in man remains absolute even if there is a "relativeness" to "each epoch" and "cultural ensemble." Moral choice he compares to making a work of art. Man, in choosing his own ethics, is making himself. In doing so, however, he is choosing freedom, accepting responsibility for himself, and creating his own meaning in the face of meaninglessness. In the end Sartre believes that his despair serves as an affirmation and that his detractors simply misunderstand the game plan. "Existentialism," he concludes, "is nothing else than an attempt to draw all the consequences of a coherent atheistic position." It isn't trying to plunge man into despair at all. It's "optimistic" because it's "a doctrine of action."[29]

INFLUENCE OF THE MEGA-IDEA

On the world stage, as Marxist activist, philosopher, playwright, and novelist, Sartre cut a ten-mile-wide swath as barren as the Sahara. Sartre struck a quirky pose, from his lifelong liaison with Simone de Beauvoir, whom he never married, to his refusal to accept, in typical existentialist fashion, the Nobel prize for literature in 1964 (a prize, by the way, that Camus readily accepted in 1957). Worse still, confronted by modern science and the modern condition, Sartre, along with other existentialists, promoted the profoundly disturbing conclusion that life is meaningless. As a result, many modern people, adults as well as teens, now view life with an excessive amount of anxiety, dread, and despair. Yet by Sartre's own admission, existentialism "is the least scandalous, the most austere of doctrines. It is intended strictly for specialists and philosophers."[30] If that is the case, why has existentialism overflowed the little lily ponds of the "specialists," scandalously inundating modern culture like a spring flood?

David E. Cooper complains that the emphasis on self-estrangement and inauthenticity in modern culture is a Californian, not existentialist, invention. When people respond to slogans that encourage them to shed their false self and discover their real self, they are responding to California gurus. These teachers, claims Cooper, have more in common with "café existentialists" than with Nietzsche, de Beauvoir, or Sartre.[31] Yet Cooper is blinded by bias. The "true" existentialists have left their fingerprints all over the crime scene of modern culture.

The Flight from the "Absurdity" of Life

First, many people today flee from commitment to others and reject the eternal verity of moral values because, like existentialists, they accept that life is absurd, that the "truths about the human condition [are] *Angst* and the anticipation of death."[32] Whether or not these people have read the *Myth of Sisyphus* by Camus, they have accepted quite unconsciously that reality is irrational "because it is 'chaotic' and shot through with antinomies and paradoxes." Everything, in other words, is fraught with ambiguity and contradiction. Or they may agree with Sartre that "man is a useless passion" (*une passion inutile*).[33] Or they may have read or viewed plays produced by the Theater of the Absurd, plays by Eugene

Ionesco and Samuel Beckett. Or finally they may have just watched modern movies like *Kalifornia*, *Reservoir Dogs*, or *Natural Born Killers* and felt the chill of absurdity bristle the hair on the backs of their necks.

This sense of the instability of reality has led more and more to widespread apathy and ennui—especially among the young, who have not yet experienced the "reality-therapy" afforded by work and family. "It was," after all, "central to The Existentialist's accounts of absurdity and freedom that the 'directives' by which people guide the large decisions in life cannot be given a final foundational justification." Existential freedom, in fact, requires a person to "distance" himself and perhaps "refuse" the beliefs and values that shape his "directives"—namely, the beliefs and values of his culture.[34] What do we see in the rebellion and experimentalism of youth, in their fashions and entertainment, but the expression of indifference toward traditional values? Why does a youth pierce nose, tongue, nipples, and belly button? Why are so few shocked or dismayed by a politician's entanglements with nubile interns? Because it's all meaningless and absurd anyway, they believe. It doesn't really matter in any large context. Indeed, it's really quite boring since everybody is doing the same kinds of things. So who cares? At the same time, what do we find in our uncritical embrace of technology, something to which Neil Postman refers in his book *Technopoly*, but a desperate flight from indifference? We believe in technology so rabidly because we must believe in something, even if it portends our doom as it isolates us more and more from one another.

Everything, say the young and restless at heart, is changing—or, more hopefully, "evolving"—anyway. The only real being is the self. "There is truth," says Heidegger, "only in so far as Dasein is and as long as Dasein is."[35] And yet "There is no truth in the sense of correspondence to the facts nor are there . . . any criteria for telling whether a view is true or not. The best one can do is to be 'primordial,' to go back as far as one can towards the source, disregarding the current wisdom of the *they*." When making decisions, people just won't find any objectively correct answers. Therefore, "The best one can do is to be resolute, to withdraw from the crowd, and to make one's decision in view of one's life as a whole."[36] If locked in this frame of mind, a person can rationalize almost any self-chosen behavior. And most of these behaviors, because humans are prone more to vice than virtue, to egocentrism than altruism, will be rooted in hedonistic preoccupations—from spraying graffiti on a neighbor's fence to cultivating marijuana in one's garage, from cutting others off on the freeway to get home in time for the first kickoff to spending exorbitant amounts of money on hot tubs, luxury cars, and Bahamian cruises. *Dasein*, like a voracious open mouth, must be satisfied, even if everything else is absurd.

But remember, Rousseau laid the axe to the root of the Christian notion of original sin long ago; and Bertrand Russell, also no doubt aided by many liberal theologians, cut the tongue out of the Christian message, weakening the witness of Christ, robbing Christianity of its moral and salvific force. Therefore, when sensible people wonder how they are going to stem the tide of moral chaos in society, even when they feel prepared to take up moral arms against the madness, they must calculate the damage that has already been inflicted on Christian culture. To start, they need only consider what weapons have already been pilfered from the trenches of their allies and stockpiled within the arsenals of their enemies.

The Quest for the "Authentic Self"

When it came to *being* or *being there*, the existentialists held that there was an authentic as opposed to inauthentic *Dasein* (Heidegger) and bad faith as opposed to good faith (Sartre). The inauthentic self is always caught in the "they." The self of bad faith is always insincere and dishonest with itself. The genuine self, standing alone in its *Angst* and courage, never pretends.

After all, the resolute, authentic *Dasein*, which races ahead to its death and assesses its possibilities in the visionary moment, "cannot simply follow what *they* say about right and wrong, nor can it appeal to any established moral code."[37] To be sunk in the chatter of the *they* is to remain in inauthenticity and bad faith. Naturally, then, one must revolt, in clichéd fashion, against what *they* say. The antithesis of inauthenticity and bad faith is sincerity, which presents itself not as a *state* but as a demand and ideal. "It is necessary," says Sartre, "that a man be *for himself* only what he *is*." This statement captures well the definition of being-in-itself and "the principle of identity."[38]

Now that the existentialists have offered us a formula for finding ourselves and for forging an identity, we can march forward into the brave new world of sincerity and freedom. As long as we are sincere, "honest" with ourselves and others, we can justify almost any decision as a search for authenticity and identity. We will remain true to ourselves and expect others to do the same. In this way, each of us, doing our own things, will be "okay." Having advanced beyond Nietzsche who celebrated the will-to-power, we will instead embrace a will-to-freedom. As long as we feel free, we will feel authentic, alive. In this way, choices may proliferate as rapidly as newly discovered desires. In this new world of sincerely made choices, acted out in freedom, we will of course have to stretch tolerance to its limit. For how can any one person really know if another is being authentic and sincere? He can't. Therefore, he will have to remain silent in the face of all manner of free expressions. Are teens making a ruckus in the supermarket? Is a fellow student cheating on an exam? Is a high-profile politician engaging in perverted, illicit sex acts? Because there are no objective morals, because we don't want to be labeled as *they*, because we don't want to impede anyone else's freedom of choice or expression, we had best remain silent. Besides, we can always find solace in the sincerity, honesty, and authenticity of our own freely chosen employments and enjoyments, shrugging our shoulders and saying, "Hey, live and let live."

But is this really the world we want? Most right-thinking people hate it, yet still they do nothing. Perhaps we have forgotten the old dictum, "Evil flourishes when good men do nothing." Or perhaps we have forgotten that we are indeed our brother's keeper. The modern quest for self and the modern insistence on toleration are leading to the privatization of people's personal lives and to the paralysis of their spiritual and moral organs of action. As a starting point, perhaps we Christians need to pray as David did: "I am your servant; give me discernment that I may understand your statutes" (Ps. 119:125). Then we will "be able to discern what is best and may be pure and blameless" (Phil. 1:10), prepared thereafter to speak and act appropriately—as Francis Schaeffer might have put it, lovingly confronting the world.

The "Comforting" Embrace of Depression

Depression, of course, isn't really comforting. But to what does all this authentic freedom lead? If we can't find comfort in our freedoms, then we shall find it in our disbelief and despair. If life is absurd, as the existentialists insist, then existentialism, as part of life, is absurd also. How can I know if Heidegger accurately measured my *Angst* or defined my *Dasein*? How can I know if Sartre, imprisoned for a while by the Nazis and traumatized by war, understood good faith and bad faith? Furthermore, existentialism can't offer value or satisfaction even in action since action too must be meaningless, no matter how I try to dress it up with meaning. The rationalization itself would seem to be an act of bad faith or dishonesty. The contradictions and ambiguities always remain, even if I am honest and sincere, even when I act against injustice.

In the essay "Bad Faith" Sartre himself admitted that the attainment of sincerity is impossible: "what can be the significance of the ideal of sincerity except as a task impossible to achieve, of which the very meaning is in contradiction with the structure of my consciousness." As soon as we posit our being, says Sartre, we surpass that being—reaching "not toward another being but toward emptiness, toward nothing."[39] Elsewhere, in "The Desire to be God," he says, "The only being which can be called free is the being which nihilates its being"—that is, renders itself meaningless.[40] Finally, in two plays, *Dirty Hands* (1949 in English) and *The Condemned of Altona* (1961 in English), Sartre deals with the problem of responsible political action and concludes both plays with the suicides of the main characters.[41] Where was Sartre leading us and leaving us?

And what are we to make of his formula, "Consciousness is a being, the nature of which is to be conscious of the nothingness of its being"?[42] Throughout existentialism we seem always to be left with the ultimate, though curious, choice between being (*l'être*) and nothingness (*le néant*). The only impact such a dichotomy can leave on many sensitive souls is to create in them an either/or dilemma. They must possess all or nothing— exhilarating fulfillment or depressing emptiness. There can be no middle way, no Aristotelian mean. Yet no matter how they choose, they will still remain, according to Sartre, anxious, forlorn, and hopeless, because such is the human condition. Is it any wonder, then, that many overwhelmed teens and adults today, faced with such a dilemma, feel alienated from friends and family—alone *and* lonely? In *Man's Search for Meaning* Viktor Frankl, who wasn't an existentialist, calls the state of meaninglessness in which many find themselves today the "existential vacuum." The symptoms of the vacuum he lists as boredom, aggression, distress (that is, anxiety), depression, and addiction.[43] These sound like treatable clinical ailments, as indeed they are, not the fruits of a liberating worldview.

Anyone who tries seriously to live existentialism—which of course was only intended for "specialists and philosophers"—will no doubt end up someday lying in a fetal position in the far corner of an inside bedroom closet.

The logical course for many who have been influenced by existentialism isn't heroic atheism or "optimistic toughness" but hopelessness. Since the popular advent of existentialism, we have seen enormous increases in the incidences of mental illness and suicide in our country. I'm mindful of the fact that I will be accused by some of resorting to an oversimplification or post hoc fallacy, but I would still insist there is a correlation between existentialism and all the identity crises in our society (just as surely there is a correlation between the other mega-ideas and mental *dis*-ease in our culture).

The numbers should speak for themselves. Youth suicide rates continue to increase. Since 1960, according to the National Mental Health Association, the suicide rate for young people ages fifteen to twenty-four has nearly tripled. Suicide, in fact, is the "eighth leading cause of death in the U.S. and the third leading cause of death among people aged 15 to 24."[44] Among males in this age group, according to the Department of Health and Human Services, the suicide rates have more than tripled since the 1950s, the era during which existentialism was introduced into the U.S. The current suicide rate for young males remains "twice as high" as the overall rate in the U.S.[45] Nevertheless, according to the Mayo Clinic, citing figures from the Centers for Disease Control, although "males are four times more likely to die from suicide than females," "females are far more likely to attempt suicide than males." Even more shockingly, suicide rates are increasing among children between the ages of five and fourteen, and suicide rates for children in the U.S. are "two times higher than in other industrialized nations."[46]

At the same time, mental illness in general seems nearly epidemic in the U.S. Consider these figures put out by the National Mental Health Association: 51 million Americans experience a mental disorder in a single year, with 7.7 to 12.8 million adolescents and children suffering from mental disorders, and with 9.1 million Americans overall suffering from major depression and 19.9 million Americans experiencing phobias. Naturally, the costs in dollars as well as human life are staggering. "Mental illnesses impose a multibillion dollar burden on the economy each year, the total in 1990 amounting to $147.8 billion." Ironically, "More than 31 percent of those costs ... are for anxiety disorder."[47] Apparently most people have failed the existentialist *Angst* test, finding their meaning at last in "nothingness" instead of "being." Surely, divorce, violence, and other factors have contributed to the current psychic disintegration in the U.S., but the existentialists and their kind, who produce philosophy, plays, poetry, and films, who lecture in the halls of academe, have to answer for the part they have played in the breakdown. Told long enough that everything is absurd or meaningless, what young man or woman wouldn't go insane?

Although the existentialist mega-idea appears in some ways to contradict those of, say, Russell and Darwin, it is compatible with modern belief. It agrees with science that the universe is a closed system. It also provides people with another atheistic alternative to theism in general and Christianity in particular. It allows a man to find his own meaning in his own self-assertive acts, whatever they may be, as long as he feels "alive" when he acts. This radical subjectivism can only injure, entrap, and delude people, however, because it leaves them anchorless and rudderless, without any faith in God or ultimate purpose in life other than, again, their own happiness or pleasure. Surely, the similar answers provided, at different times, by Hobbes, Hume, Rousseau, Mill, Darwin, and Russell have already proven untenable in this regard.

Curiously, in contrast, the existentialist mega-idea appears to contradict the mega-idea of the next group of thinkers, the environmental and genetic determinists. The existentialists held that man possesses free will. Indeed, Sartre expresses nothing but contempt for any form of determinism, whether environmental, biological, or psychological. "There's no such thing as a cowardly constitution." A coward makes himself a coward, just as a hero makes himself a hero.[48] Our next group of thinkers, represented by such people as Ivan Pavlov and B. F. Skinner, Francis Crick and Richard Dawkins, hold the opposite view, namely, that man lacks free will. A person, they hold, is environmentally or genetically determined—or programmed, as Isaac Asimov once put it—to do as he does and to be as he is.

Still, both sets of thinkers and their distinctive mega-ideas do share a couple of common, unmistakable denominators. All these men would agree that values are relative because the universe, being governed by randomness and chance, is purposeless and meaningless, except as we humans give it purpose and meaning according to our own lights. Above all, these men, the best minds of the age, would agree that it's time to scrap Christianity.

12

"FREE WILL
IS AN ILLUSION"

Man has always asked, "What am I? Why do I exist? What is the meaning of life?" Over recorded time, from the Nile River to the Dead Sea to the Atlantic Ocean, the answers that have influenced Western civilization have varied. The Egyptians, Hebrews, Greeks, Romans, European Christians—all have offered answers. Until recent times, we have taken many of these answers seriously. Apparently, we no longer need to.

As the bright bulbs flash at award ceremonies for modern scientists, we are everywhere reassured that the old answers have been rendered obsolete. Richard Dawkins, recipient in 1990 of the Michael Faraday Award from the British Royal Society and lecturer in zoology at Oxford University, tells us so in *The Selfish Gene*. In this book he confidently pronounces his verdict on the traditional answers to the age-old questions asked by man: "There is such a thing as being just plain wrong, and that is what, before 1859, all answers to those questions were." In short, all "pre-Darwinian answers" are "worthless."[1] B. F. Skinner, once hailed by *Time* as the most influential psychologist of our era and long-time professor of psychology at Harvard University (1948-1970), confidently dismissed traditional answers as well. According to the prescientific view, he explains, "a person's behavior is at least to some extent his own achievement. He is free to deliberate, decide, and act, possibly in original ways, and he is to be given credit for his successes and blamed for his failures." But according to the new, superior scientific view, "a person's behavior is determined by a genetic endowment traceable to the evolutionary history of the species and by the environmental circumstances to which . . . he has been exposed."[2]

Under siege in these pronouncements is the very nature of man. Dawkins refers to humans as "gigantic lumbering robots" and "survival machines" for their "selfish genes."[3] Skinner concurs, in his own way, although he attributes more control to environment than heredity. He refers to "the human organism as a behaving system" and likewise says that "Man is a machine." In fact, "Man has . . . created the machine in his own image."[4] Skinner goes even farther by denying any existence to an inner man or inner agent within man. The "self" and its emotions are simply fictions: "the self is simply a device for representing *a functionally unified system of responses*," and "The 'emotions' are excellent examples of the fictional causes to which we commonly attribute behavior."[5]

"Science," says Skinner, "does not dehumanize man, it de-homunculizes him, and it must do so if it is to prevent the abolition of man."[6] To "de-homunculize" man is to divest him of "the imaginary person within the brain who perceives objects and events and makes decisions."[7] Francis Crick, winner of the Nobel prize in 1962 for his discovery with James D. Watson of the structure of DNA and distinguished research professor at the Salk Institute, reluctantly concurs. Sometimes he finds it hard "to avoid the idea of a homunculus." Nevertheless, he insists, his "Astonishing Hypothesis states that all aspects of the brain's behavior are due to the activities of neurons."[8] Again, men are machines, their brains, at best, bundles of neurons.

Also under siege, then, is the idea that humans have free will. We have always called the opponents of the idea of free will "determinists," but the scientists and social scientists of our era have stamped their imprimatur on a new brand of determinism. These thinkers hold that all that you or I happen to be or do can be explained by our environments, our genes, or a combination of both, sometimes along with other external factors. When we understand the truth about involuntary and so-called voluntary behavior, asserts Skinner, "we are likely to drop the notion of responsibility altogether and with it the doctrine of free will as an inner causal agent."[9] We have already seen hints of such a determinism in the writings of others we have examined—Hobbes, Darwin, Marx, Freud, Russell. From Hobbes to Skinner, Darwin to Dawkins, man has been viewed more and more as either an animal or a machine. According to this worldview, free will, as well as individual responsibility, is an illusion. Traditional moral norms, therefore, can have no objective basis (but they may, of course, have pragmatic value if they are employed to maintain social order and create a new world order). Any change in human behavior, moreover, must be initiated from without, not from within, although individuals (as Mill and Russell claimed) still deserve the right to happiness, not just to pursue it but to possess it.

Modern scientists have succeeded in convincing many people that human behaviors (homosexuality, alcoholism) and potentialities (IQ, ambition)—in animalistic or mechanistic ways—are determined solely by environment and heredity. Although many people would like to think of themselves as voluntarists, many think and act as determinists; so we find ourselves in a society today in which the senses of individual responsibility and accountability are diminishing and the senses of victimhood and entitlement are increasing. We who still believe that man has an inner self, a soul capable of free moral choice, have only one recourse before us in the face of the new determinism. With all our might, we must set out to oppose and refute this mega-idea.

A Programmed, Survival Machine on Two Legs

Shortly we will see how the two main lines of determinist thought have gradually converged since the 1950s, thus helping to extend the argument within our culture. One group, led by Skinner, we call behaviorists; the other group, led by such people as Asimov, Dawkins, and Crick, we call genetic (or biological) determinists. The behaviorists generally treat heredity as secondary to environment, and the genetic determinists generally treat environment as secondary to heredity, but noises of concession are made all around, although occasionally, as in the case of Francis Crick, a criticism aimed at another school may be direct.[10] In concert, however, these schools of thought have opened the back door to other types of determinism, "soft" and "hard," as they relate to technology, media, and language. The nature versus nurture debate has raged for centuries. Hobbes in *Leviathan* favored nature; Rousseau in *Émile,* nurture. As we shall see, the nature argument tends to hold the field today, in spite of, or perhaps because of, the considerable influence that Romanticism and existentialism have had on culture. Indeed, Skinner himself expressly pronounced Rousseau wrong.[11]

Environment Dictates What We Are

B. F. Skinner (1904-1990) was apparently inspired early in his career by an article written by Bertrand Russell on behaviorism. As a researcher, Skinner was influenced by such early behaviorist luminaries as J. B. Watson (1878-1958), who worked with rats; Edward Thorndike (1874-1949), who worked with dogs and cats; and Ivan Pavlov (1849-1936), who worked with a dog whose salivations at the jingle of a bell are by now famous. Pavlov, for his work, won the Nobel prize in physiology in 1904. Skinner followed these early pioneers, working with pigeons and rats and creating his famous Skinner Box for conditioning behavior.

From such behaviorists, we have derived a bevy of terms that we employ today: *learning curve, stimulus and response, conditioned reflexes, operant conditioning, survival value, passive resistance, positive reinforcement* (now *positive feedback*), and *behavior modification*. Don't we indeed today speak of our learning curve? Don't we want to give our children positive feedback? Don't we set out to condition our bodies? Of all these men, Skinner clearly emerged as the undisputed leader whose influence has been most felt in psychology and education, especially educational practice.

To grasp the direction of Skinner's thought, we must first grasp two of his basic premises. First, he held that man is merely an organism without freedom or ultimate responsibility:

> The hypothesis that man is not free is essential to the application of scientific method to the study of humans. The free inner man who is held responsible for the behavior of the external biological organism is only a prescientific substitute for the kinds of causes which are discovered in the course of scientific analysis.[12]

Science, to Skinner's mind, proved that the findings of philosophy and theology are erroneous and that the analysis of material causes and effects is sufficient for understanding the nature of man. Second, he held, like any good evolutionist, that the survival of the species is the prime directive in any kind of effort to improve humans or culture. "The current culture which . . . is most likely to survive is, therefore," he claims, "that in which the methods of science are most effectively applied to the problems of human behavior."[13] With proper observation and evolutionary insight, all we need to do is identify and apply the right methods, and we will end up with the ideal society—namely, the one with the highest "survival value."

Central to the thought of Skinner was that environment, more than any other factor, makes us what we are, dictating how we behave, think, and feel. He concedes that there are genetic factors, but "The most that can be said is that the knowledge of the genetic factor may enable us to make better use of other causes." Indeed, these *other* causes produce "quicker results." Even the causes "to be sought in the nervous system are . . . of limited usefulness in the prediction and control of specific behavior."[14] Therefore, he insists that if we are to apply the methods of science to human affairs, "we must assume that behavior is lawful and determined. We must expect to discover that what a man does is the result of *specifiable conditions* and that once these *conditions* have been discovered, we can anticipate and to some extent determine his actions" (italics mine). Even when a degree of indeterminacy appears—that is, when science can't explain all the causes—"It does not follow that human behavior is free. . . ." So complete is the environment's control of man that Skinner asserts, "The environment determines the individual even when he alters the environment." And he could have added that man only alters the environment because the environment has already dictated *ipso facto* that he do so. Environmental effects are everything. The truth, then, is simple: All series of behaviors "will lead us back to events outside . . . the organism."[15] Where human behavior is concerned, "A scientific analysis shifts the credit as well as the blame to the environment. . . ."[16]

Emboldened by this conviction, Skinner called on "culture designers" to "control" every aspect of society until a nearly Utopian society could be reached.[17] In his earlier work, *Science and Human Behavior*, Skinner speaks of cultural design and hints at a need for it. In his later work, *Beyond Freedom and Dignity*, however, he makes explicit the desirability of redesigning culture. He reiterates the idea that environment is everything, ridiculing the outmoded notions of "freedom" and "dignity." Then in a bold move, he asserts that science can show us what changes we need to make to improve society. The technology of behavior, he says, can make use of three "goods" based on the prime directive of survival: those "which are reinforcing because of the human genetic endowment," those "which are derived from personal reinforcers," and those which promote "the good of the culture" into perpetuity.[18]

In other words, with future generations in mind, as long as we make medical advances and practice birth control, satisfy our wants and needs in moderation without polluting the environment or wasting the world's resources, and preserve the world from violence, we will be following the right course.[19] The culture controllers must oversee this agenda. "We all control," he had said in *Science and Human Behavior*, "and we are all controlled. As human behavior is further analyzed, control will become more effective."[20] To help culture evolve, experimental methods must purposefully "strip away the functions previously assigned to autonomous man and transfer them one by one to the controlling environment." Obviously this transfer will leave "less and less for autonomous man to do."[21]

But one may ask, "Who will the 'culture designers' be?" Skinner would have answered, "Scientists and other sympathetic individuals under the guidance of science." Only scientists, who understand evolution's prime directive, survival, can understand what changes will be required.

Heredity Dictates What We Are

The genetic determinists often seem to be more moderate on the question of determinism. But this appearance of moderation, I believe, is false, even if sincere. They agree that other factors, and not only genes, influence human nature, making us what we do and are. But these men still express an almost blind faith in science and a reckless optimism about its potential for good.

Isaac Asimov bluntly reveals his genetic determinism in his book *Please Explain* (1973). He asserts that, just like computers, "human beings can only do what they are 'programmed' to do. Our genes 'program' us the instant the fertilized ovum is formed, and our potentialities are limited by that 'program.'" He believes that computers can be made as complex and creative as we are because he doesn't believe "that there is more to the human brain than the matter that composes it." Here he reveals not only his genetic determinism but also his atheistic naturalism. The brain is simply made up of cells, molecules, and atoms in their various arrangements. "If anything else [namely, a soul] is there, no signs of it have ever been detected." This last part of his argument is simply an appeal to ignorance, a logical fallacy that can be turned back against itself. Something else, a soul, may just as easily be there since "no signs" of its not being there "have ever been detected." Based on naturalistic assumptions, Asimov therefore optimistically concludes, "To duplicate the material complexity of the brain is therefore to duplicate everything about it."[22]

Francis Crick qualifies but can't conceal his genetic determinism. In chapters 7 and 8 of *The Astonishing Hypothesis*, he concedes that our knowledge of the brain and spine remains incomplete, indeed primitive. In terms of the neuron alone, we still "need to understand just how all these chemical and electrochemical processes interact." He even concedes "that genes . . . appear to lay down the broad structure of the nervous system, but . . . experience [throughout life] is needed to tune up and refine many details of the structure." Still, he holds firmly to his astonishing hypothesis throughout his book: "'You,' your joys and your sorrows, your memories and your ambitions, your sense of personal identity and free will, are in fact no more than the behavior of a vast assembly of nerve cells and their associated molecules." In the end, he concludes that such a machine as the brain "will *appear to itself* to have Free Will, provided it can personify its behavior—that is, it has an image of 'itself'" (italics mine). In fact, he is convinced that this so-called free will "is located in or near the anterior cingulate sulcus."[23] It's location resides in the brain because, for Crick as for Asimov, there is nothing beyond the brain.

Richard Dawkins, although he protests that certain critics have misunderstood him, casts a chilly shadow with his genetic determinism. He fairly chortles when describing the persistence of the selfish genes throughout evolutionary history, which began by necessity and chance in a prebiotic soup. Of the staying power of these genes, Dawkins declares:

> Now they swarm in huge colonies, safe inside gigantic lumbering robots, sealed off from the outside world, communicating with it by tortuous indirect routes, manipulating it by remote

control. They are in you and me; they created us, body and mind;
and their preservation is the ultimate rationale for our existence.
They have come a long way, those replicators. Now they go by
the name of genes, and we are their survival machines.[24]

We are "lumbering robots" and "survival machines" in his estimation.
Later he says that we must treat the individual "as a selfish machine, programmed to do whatever is best for its genes as a whole." "The genes,"
he tells us elsewhere, "are the immortals. . . ." Even altruism, parental
nurturance, and group cooperation, according to Dawkins, are part of
the selfish gene machine's plan for survival. He refers also to "Blind natural selection. . . ." He does, however, try to wriggle, Houdini-like, out
of his deterministic straightjacket several times. Genes that control
behavior, he says, act "indirectly like the computer programmer." All the
genes "can do is to set up beforehand; then the survival machine is on
its own, and the genes can only sit passively inside." After convincing
us that he believes we are machines, very much like computers, he
declares later, "We have the power to defy the selfish genes of our birth
and, if necessary, the selfish memes of indoctrination" in favor of what
he calls a "conspiracy of doves."

Obviously Dawkins, the liberal, can't dispense altogether with the
notion of free will. Or can he? In the notes section of the book, he
protests that Rose, Kamin, and Lewontin in *Not in Our Genes* falsely
accuse him of reductionism and determinism. But Dawkins can only
weakly defend himself by saying, "it is perfectly possible to hold that
genes exert a statistical influence on human behaviour while at the same
time believing that this influence can be modified, overridden or reversed
by other influences."[25] But none of his influences seem to presuppose the
existence of free will. The very word "influences" suggests other biological or environmental causes.

We can't overlook, as Phillip E. Johnson has pointed out in *Reason
in the Balance*, the naturalistic biases of such men. In a quest for pure science, they denounce philosophy and debunk religion. Asimov's atheism
is apparent, but so is Crick's and Dawkins's. Crick asserts that, if his
astonishing hypothesis proves true, it then "will be possible to argue that
the idea that man has a disembodied soul is as unnecessary as the old idea
that there was a Life Force."[26] Dawkins asserts that the God-idea survives

in the gene or meme pool only as a placebo that "provides a superficially plausible answer to deep and troubling questions about existence." It's an idea that is simply copied by "successive generations of individual brains."[27] Having spent too many years in formaldehyde-scented labs and at university teas, could these scientists be missing something? All science and no philosophy or theology, it seems to me, may make Ike, Frank, and Dick very dull boys. A naturalistic thesis can turn back on itself, making itself look ridiculous in the face of common sense.

Consider Johnson's rewording of Crick's Astonishing Hypothesis in the first-person singular: "I, Francis Crick, my opinions and my science, and even the thoughts expressed in this book, consist of nothing more than the behavior of a vast assembly of nerve cells and their associated molecules." If thoughts simply reflect the random collocations and automatic motions of assemblies of cells and molecules, then why should we take seriously the theories of Crick or any other determinist? Aptly concluding his analysis, Johnson says, "The plausibility of materialistic determinism requires that an implicit exception be made for the theorist."[28]

A Combination of Factors Dictates What We Are

Most recent determinists acknowledge that a complex mix of both genes and environment makes us what we are. With this complexity admitted, it's easy to see why others may be jumping on the bandwagon of determinism and cultural redesign. Hard determinists deny the existence of free will, human choice, in the areas of concern; soft determinists accept the significant role of influence, minimizing but not denying free will, human choice, altogether in the areas of concern.

Two schools of thought may be mentioned in passing. First, there is a group now called technological or media determinists. They believe that technology and media are advancing virtually autonomously and inevitably, altering culture forever as they do so. The advances may outstrip the ability of individuals to adapt, but adapt they *must*. In *Technopoly* (1992), Neil Postman, although not a determinist, speaks of "the deification of technology" as forcing a whole new anti-traditional mindset on our culture, which he labels "totalitarian technocracy."[29] Earlier books like *Autonomous Technology* (1977) by Langdon Winner and *The Social Shaping of Technology* (1985) by MacKenzie and Wajcman also address these concerns. But still other writers have been sounding alarms for decades. Among these writers are Jacques Ellul who has been warning us since 1964 that technology, instead of serving us, will force humanity to become more efficient, machinelike, as humans abandon themselves to the techniques and methods of technology. The fact that "human beings have to adapt to it and accept total change" Ellul finds dehumanizing.[30] He has expressed similar concerns about the shaping power of the media. Naturally, among these writers, too, must be included Marshall McLuhan. In *The Medium Is the Message* (1967), he says the new message of the media is "Total Change." And he speaks of our new "electrically-configured world" as forcing us to abandon old patterns of thought for new ones as we move "from the habit of data classification to the mode of pattern recognition."[31]

Second, there are the linguistic determinists. Basing their assumptions on the Sapir-Whorf theory of linguistics, they believe that language relativizes cultural awareness and molds individual thought. In 1929 Sapir wrote, "The worlds in which different societies live are distinct worlds, not merely the same world with different labels attached. . . ." And these worlds differ "because the language habits of [a] community predispose certain choices of interpretation."[32] In 1940 Whorf explained that "We dissect nature along lines laid down by our native languages." We perceive and interpret according to "the linguistic systems in our minds."[33] To such determinists, language dictates thought, perception, interpretation, and behavior. Some like Stanley Fish travel even farther down the dusty road of relativism: "it is impossible to mean the same thing in two (or more) different ways."[34]

I mention these forms of determinism, which include both soft and hard exponents, alongside the other types, to stress two points. First of all, determinism, in its denial of human free will and its attribution of control to other agencies, can take ever new and dangerous forms. Second, whenever free will is denied, social engineers of one kind or another can leap into any field, romping like wolves among sheep, as they try to redesign behavior or language as they see fit to further their own agendas. Ironically, in every case these agendas have been progressive and liberal—always pushing us away from tradition and Christianity and toward novelty and secularism.

INFLUENCE OF THE MEGA-IDEA

In today's world the ubiquitous influence of the determinists may seem curious, given that they are our contemporaries. Even so, this phenomenon is still explainable in terms of the trickle-down theory. As ideas pour down from earlier times—from Hobbes, Rousseau, and others—successive layers of silt, so to speak, are built up, with the topmost being most apparent. Or, looked at in another way, we stand at a point on a bank, watching the present streams pour down through channels that earlier streams carved. *Because of* the earlier mega-ideas and thinkers, the ideas of the determinists are having an even more immediate, powerful impact on current culture. Two modern trends, in particular, should alarm us.

Just Another Excuse for Bad Behavior

What is man if he lacks free will? The poor, the criminal, the immoral, the weak of will—all become victims. Without free will, nothing, internal or external, is really within the control of any human being. Isn't that what the determinists are telling us? Today, in response to modern determinism, a new trend has developed—namely, to blame everyone except oneself when one's life goes awry or one's behavior turns bad. Flip Wilson used to joke, "The devil made me do it," but today people aren't joking when they say that their genes or environment made them behave violently or insensitively. Maybe the thief's father was a criminal, or the pedophile's mother was an abuser. Maybe the crazed man with the Uzi ate Twinkies before he massacred his victims.

In general, this trend has fostered an attitude of irresponsibility within society. "A man's word used to be his bond," my dad likes to say. "A commitment required only a handshake." But who keeps his word these days, and how many are willing to make commitments? And how many practice self-sacrifice? If a headache is coming on or El Niño is heating up the Pacific Ocean, a man can always find a way out. Circumstances are beyond his control. So victims exist everywhere. If kids behave or perform badly, teachers, parents, or TV violence is at fault. In whatever area free will disappears, victimization takes its place, and whenever victimization is presumed, so seems to be entitlement. Although we are now attempting to reform the welfare system, consider the damage the Great Society, advanced by Lyndon Johnson, has done on this score. Chuck Colson, in his book *Why America Doesn't Work*, makes the harm all too plain:

> The Great Society was a disaster . . . not so much because of its ineffective programs as because of the emphasis on welfare as "entitlement" rather than need. Before long, welfare hearings became legal circuses where the poor were treated like zoo animals at feeding time, instead of women and men created with moral responsibilities. And the more time the victims of this process spent on the dole, the more their work skills deteriorated.[35]

And we might add, "the more the *victims*, stripped of their humanity, felt like victims, the more their senses of right and wrong deteriorated also." When a person feels like a victim who is entitled to certain rights and goods, he naturally concludes, like a spoiled child, that others are responsible for his misfortunes. Petulantly he will refuse to help himself, and he will resent others who help themselves. Out of anger and envy, he may then try to encourage others to adopt his attitude, applying peer pressure to others to scale down their dreams and slacken in their efforts. In this way, the irresponsible who shirk their duties and refuse to make personal sacrifices fulfill the words of Paul: "they not only continue to do these very things but also approve of those who practice them" (Rom. 1:32). Already we have seen how the entertainment industry reinforces this irresponsibility through depictions of casual sex, rationalized family ruptures, and glorified antiheroes. Irresponsibility breeds cynicism and apathy. Why care about anything, right? It's all meaningless anyway.

The attitude of irresponsibility is no more clearly evidenced than in our approaches toward crime and punishment during the past forty years. For years the pundits inveighed against punishment of any kind, preferring to reform the malefactors. All the maladjusted needed was a little behavior modification. The influence of Skinner, especially, is apparent in this area. If "the achievements for which a person himself is to be given credit seem to approach zero," as he says, then certainly the crimes a person commits for which he is to be blamed would seem to approach zero too.[36] There is little question that Skinner held that people weren't responsible for their behavior, good or bad. Therefore, he saw little value in punishment. Says he, "a man who has been imprisoned for violent assault is not necessarily less inclined to violence. Punished behavior is likely to reappear after the punitive contingencies are withdrawn."[37] Therefore, believing that crime is soluble behavioristically, he preferred that we try "to design a world in which behavior likely to be punished seldom or never occurs." If we can do it for "babies, retardates, or psychotics," then we can do it for everyone.[38]

But what has such social engineering achieved? As "The expected prison sentence for all serious crimes has decreased more than 60 percent since 1954,"[39] crime has been increasing dramatically among adults and juveniles. Whereas population has only increased by 41 percent since 1960, the number of violent crimes—aggravated assaults, robberies, rapes, and murders—has increased by more than 550 percent since then.[40] Perhaps more alarming, "Since 1965, the juvenile arrest rate for violent crimes has tripled."[41] We have a crime problem in America because we have listened for too long to the determinists, whom we have allowed to create social policy in the face of contrary common sense.

In this climate, then, we can't talk about sin anymore, let alone original sin. We can't even talk about right or wrong, virtue or vice, except as they relate to our prescientific aversions or neural programs, grounded as they are in thousands of years of primitive evolution. Thus we are caught in a whirling vortex of causes and effects—environmental, genetic, technological, linguistic—that boggle the mind and threaten to unravel the tapestry of society. So what is the solution? How can we rid our society of aggression, sexism, ethnocentrism, and racism? The social engineers, aided by the insights of the scientists, still claim that they can save us. The determinists haven't finished experimenting with us yet. After all, science, as we learned from Bertrand Russell, is the new savior. Through patient observation and experimentation, we can develop new "methods" by which "to *control* the inappropriate behavior" of others.

An Ever-Renewing Faith in the Power of Education

For this reason, many determinists are engaged in what I call The Great Educational Project—or what Dawkins might call a "conspiracy of doves." Modern education is built on the procrustean bed of John Dewey's exaltation of pragmatism and pluralism. By means of "instrumentalism," Dewey rejected the traditional notions of truth, conceiving instead of "thought as an evolutionary process," a process of discovery for every student in every classroom. To Dewey, "all reality is temporal, and the process, though evolutionary, is not . . . the unfolding of an eternal idea."[42] In short, Dewey regarded truth to be relative. If we add to the pragmatism of Dewey a layer of determinism, à la Skinner, Crick, and Dawkins (with a couple of shovelfuls of humanistic psychology heaped on), we end up with modern education. Through generalized reinforcers—attention, approval, affection, submissiveness to others (namely, "cooperation"), and tokens[43]—and positive reinforcement rather than punitive control, educators can modify the environment and behavior of children to produce better, more scientific, more modern people. The "culture designers" can then go to work, reprogramming minds as well as behavior by means of positive reinforcers and operant conditioning. They can advance their own progressive agenda and dismiss the claims of tradition, in particular, religion. These fossilized remnants must be consigned to the crematorium of history, for as Dawkins tells us, all thought before 1859 is wrong.

But this new methodology (and propaganda) is clearly bankrupting American education. The results of The Great Educational Project have been abysmal. In 1967 the U.S. Office of Education published a document by the Behavioral Teacher Education Project, which stated as its main goal the development of "a new kind of elementary teacher who . . . functions as a responsible agent of social change."[44] Since then, how successful have the new "culture designers" been? Behaviorally, our deterministically educated children have made little if any progress, despite our proliferation of Head Start programs and celebration of Sesame Street values. Discipline problems in the public schools have steadily increased over time. According to a ranking of public school behavioral problems that appeared originally in the *Congressional Quarterly*, "Talking out of turn," "Chewing gum," and "Making noise" ranked as the top three problems in 1940. By 1990, the top three problems were "Drug Abuse," "Alcohol Abuse," and "Pregnancy." Four other problems on the 1990 list—"Suicide," "Rape," "Robbery," and "Assault"—didn't even appear on the 1940 list.[45]

Academically, students haven't been performing any better. Scholastic Aptitude Test (SAT) "scores among all students dropped 73 points from 1960 to 1993."[46] In real terms, they continue to drop. Until recently many of us who teach English thought that verbal abilities were showing the greatest overall decline among American students. But a recent international study that compared the ability of U.S. students in math and science with the abilities of students from twenty-one other countries paints an equally grim picture. "U.S. 12th graders," according to a February 1998 article by Reuters, "outperformed only three countries—Lithuania, Cyprus and South Africa—among 21 nations that took part in the Third International Mathematics and Science Study (TIMSS)." Put less delicately, U.S. seniors finished eighteenth out of a field of twenty-one.[47] Back in 1988 when U.S. students finished last out of only five nations tested in science, they *did* finish first in one area: when asked if they were good in math, they said "yes" in greater numbers than the students did from the other four nations. Ironically, the Koreans, who finished first on the science test in 1988, finished last when asked to rate their own math abilities.[48] Apparently, with the help of self-esteem programs, American students feel good about doing badly.

Of course, a movement is now afoot—supported by the Department of Education, National Education Association, American Federation of Teachers, and several state governors—to raise American educational standards. The effort sounds benign and noble, but much of the enthusiasm, I fear, may be due to what is perceived as just another opportunity to redesign culture. Ideologically, the only contentless course is math. For all the others—science, literature, history, and so on—educators can establish standards that advance the new social agenda. Now a new test may require a student to demonstrate that he understands the evolutionary "fact" that there is no Creator. Now a new test may require a student to remember facts from *Annie John* by Jamaica Kincaid, a coming-of-age novel about an adolescent lesbian (already read by ninth graders in California). Or a new test may require mastery of historical data about the noble role of the Moslems during the Crusades and the ignoble role of Christians during the Inquisition. It would be easy to set new standards based on revisions of Western history and classical literary canons. Remember the values clarification movement pioneered in the late 1970s by Sidney Simon and Louis Raths in their book *Values Clarification* (1978). What values did the social engineers succeed in clarifying? The students subjected to this form of cultural design learned only to clarify their personal wants and to regard all values as subjective and relative.[49] They learned that the supreme virtue is toleration.

Capturing well the essence of the new value system, Alvin Toffler states, "Tolerance of diversity is the first commandment of the de-massified society, including tolerance of the intolerant—up to a point."[50] If led by progressives with scientific—as opposed to "prescientific"—attitudes, will the implementation of new standards be any more successful than the previous trendy reforms were in creating a better American society?

In a deterministic world, those who "know best" will feel it their duty to control human behavior and progress. C. S. Lewis warned us of these man-molders in his book *The Abolition of Man*, a book whose ideas Skinner contemptuously dismissed, declaring that the abolition of man—"the inner man, the homunculus, the possessing demon"—is long overdue.[51] Sagely, Lewis foresaw in 1947 that "the man-moulders of the new age will be armed with the powers of an omnicompetent state and an irresistible scientific technique: we shall get at last a race of conditioners who really can cut out all posterity in what shape they please."[52] Could Lewis have been overstating the case? Could Skinner have had in mind only modest plans for his cultural designers? No. Skinner had set his sights on reforming government too. As Skinner saw it, "By showing how governmental practices shape the behavior of those governed, science may lead us more rapidly to the design of a government, in the broadest possible sense, which will necessarily promote the well-being of those who are governed."[53] The determinists aren't content just to condition pigeons or manipulate genes. They want to condition and manipulate humans too.

The Judeo-Christian and classical traditions hold that humans do have free will. Free will and freedom aren't the illusions of a prescientific era. Christianity has always maintained that men can make moral choices for which they are to be held responsible. Before God, they are responsible for their choices and actions. Jesus said, "Not everyone who says to me, 'Lord, Lord,' will enter the kingdom of heaven, but only he who does the will of my Father who is in heaven" (Matt. 7:21). Even after a Christian has been saved by grace through faith, as Paul put it, he still must think and behave properly. True, the power of God will assist him, but he must fight the good fight and run a good race to receive the prize. Peter exhorted Christians, lest they become entangled in the world, to make every effort to grow in faith: "make every effort to add to your faith goodness; and to goodness, knowledge; and to knowledge, self-control; and to self-control, perseverance; and to perseverance, godliness; and to godliness, brotherly kindness; and to brotherly kindness, love" (2 Pet. 1:5-7). The culture designers, the modern determinists, may despise Christianity (though tolerating it "up to a point") because it's the last bastion of tradition within the culture, the last barrier between them and the achievement of their secularist agenda.

One sure way to deprive people of freedom is to deny the existence of free will. Another sure way is to convince them that all ethical values are relative. It's easy then to convince them that choices are accidental, subjective, and ultimately irrational. Although not the first relativist by any means (and certainly no determinist himself), our next writer, Aldous Huxley—of the august Huxley family—has probably done more than any other modern writer to popularize relativism, the most potent mega-idea of our time. Like Freud, Russell, Sartre, and Skinner, he too was an activist and reformer. He declared that the relativist is the true life-worshiper. He held that all religious philosophies, except biblical Christianity, are equally true, as beheld in the light of one's subjectivistic experience of the Ground of being. Finally, Aldous Huxley, not Timothy Leary, was the father of the modern drug craze. Leary was a "square" professor of psychology at Harvard University until he heard Huxley speak in 1960 on the "gratuitous grace" offered by mescaline and LSD.

The horror of relativism, like determinism, is that it makes people moldable, capable of believing that almost anything is true or false. In a moment of prophetic clarity, speaking of the potential misuses of "chemical euphoria," Huxley offered one caution that may be equally applied to the culture-designing determinists we have just examined: "The pursuit of happiness is one of the traditional rights of man; unfortunately, the achievement of happiness may turn out to be incompatible with another of man's rights—namely freedom."[54] Don't all culture designers just want everyone to be happy? "Can't we all just get along?" they have been pleading with us for decades.

"Everything Is Relative"

Like a stealthy U-boat, the term *relativism* has submerged and resurfaced several times in this book. Now we are prepared to examine how our cultural drift toward relativism spoken of in the first chapter—and alluded to in several later chapters—has reached an advanced stage. We are prepared to observe how the mission of the postmodern relativists is unfolding rapidly before our eyes as a few elitists deconstruct and reconstruct traditional values along new lines. In many ways the *avant garde* of relativism has already invaded the land and overpowered traditional thought and lifestyles. Many people already make daily pronouncements based on the theory of relativism, convinced that "all truth is relative to the individual and to the time or place in which he acts."[1] Uncritically, they embrace both cultural relativism and ethical relativism. Most people do so, however, without realizing the peril.

But most people are unfamiliar with the two main subdivisions within ethical relativism: *normative relativism* and *metaethical relativism*. The members of both camps deny that absolutes exist. The first group holds that each society has its own conventions, though they may differ from those of other societies, and therefore "everyone ought to act in accordance with his own society's code."[2] Surely, this recommendation merely has pragmatic or "survival value." The second group holds to an even more radical thesis: "the meanings of moral terms of appraisal such as 'right' and 'wrong' are themselves relative to one's society. Put metaphysically, there is no such property as rightness."[3] Both groups are dangerous because they declare that there are no absolute truths or morals.

But in asserting that "There are no absolute truths" or that "There are no absolute rights and wrongs," relativists contradict themselves. Their statements are self-refuting because they are affirming the absolute truth of relativism. But clearly if relativism is "true," then relativism must be regarded as relative too. Of course, such a position leaves us nowhere, but perhaps that is exactly where the relativists, hell-bent on cultural redesign, want to leave us—lost, disoriented, defenseless.

We have seen signs of relativism, along with subjectivism, creeping into the culture ever since our first modern thinkers set about reforming culture. Hobbes claimed that any interpretations of the words of Scripture would have to be relative, and so he was able to argue in behalf of the sole authority of an absolute monarchy. He also insisted that *good* and *bad* are but names that we assign to what we like or dislike. Hume and Rousseau, in different ways, urged us to trust our innate *feeling*s of right and wrong. Mill looked to utility for answers, not to absolutes. Darwin explained that right and wrong varied from culture to culture and age to age, according to men's approbation and disapprobation of certain kinds of behavior. Marx and Nietzsche, in different ways, subscribed to historical relativism. Marx believed that the bourgeoisie and their values would eventually be driven from the stage of history, and Nietzsche believed that his supermen would arise to overthrow the little people, the Christians, with their small morality. Sartre taught, like Nietzsche, that God is dead, but also concluded that absolutes can't exist and that life is meaningless. Freud, Russell, Skinner, Crick, Dawkins—all these writers have also raised serious doubts about traditional morality and exhorted us to look elsewhere for values. Believing that humans are machines, they have assented to the idea that values are relative because humans are driven by unseen, often primitive and selfish forces.

And other modern writers—from Max Weber (1864-1920), Oswald Spengler (1880-1936), and Ludwig Wittgenstein (1889-1951) to Jacques Derrida and Richard Rorty, who are still writing today—have continued to advance the cause of relativism. Oswald Spengler, for example, in *The Decline of the West* (1918, 1922), characterized cultures as living organisms that undergo birth, maturation, and decay. To Spengler, "thought and values are . . . always relative to a specific culture and have no universal validity."[4] Today Richard Rorty insists through his neopragmatism "that the test of philosophical truth [is] overall *coherence* rather than correspondence to objective reality or deducibility from universally granted principles." That means, says Phillip E. Johnson, "that there can be competing truths based on different first principles, mutually contradictory but equally coherent and hence equally 'true.'" For Rorty, the professor, "the purpose of university teaching is political transformation of the students, those persons whom it is not too late to acculturate into 'our' historically contingent way of thinking."[5] In other words, Rorty wants to convert as many students as he can to relativism.

So why are we going to now examine Aldous Huxley (1894-1963) as our primary modern exemplar of relativism? Aldous Huxley, though by no means the father of relativism, offers the best example of a major modern relativist because he *popularized* relativism on many fronts—social, psychological, religious. Early in his career he held that everything is relative—values, morals, beliefs—because experience is relative, differing from moment to moment, even within the same person. A well-adjusted person can be a Buddhist one moment, a Christian the next; a pragmatist one moment, a mystic the next. And there is no contradiction. To "the life-worshiper," the one who truly affirms life and lives it to the full, says Huxley, it's all the same. Absolute, objective truth doesn't exist. Truth, he was to hold later in life, only exists subjectively, to be experienced as the universal Ground of being. In this way, as we will soon see, the ideas of Huxley form a bridge between modern relativism and the last mega-idea we will examine.

So Many Doors and Windows

We can only marvel at the popularity of Aldous Huxley, who was destined by birth, it seems, to be a mover and shaker in Western culture. Thomas Huxley, Darwin's bulldog, was his grandfather. Leonard Huxley, a writer and editor, was his father. Sir Julian Huxley, a world-renowned biologist, was his brother. Anthony Huxley, a Nobel laureate in physiology, was his half brother. Matthew Arnold, the great Victorian cultural critic, was his second cousin. In the 1920s he was a close friend of D. H. Lawrence; in the 1940s he hobnobbed with the glitterati of Hollywood. No slouch, Aldous graduated from Oxford with honors and wrote forty-seven books during his life, including his famous *Brave*

New World (1932), an anti-Utopian book, and *The Island* (1962), an Utopian antidote to *Brave New World*. In 1959 he was awarded by the American Academy of Arts and Letters the Award of Merit for the Novel (other winners had been Ernest Hemingway, Thomas Mann, and Theodore Dreiser).

He was also a respected essayist and the author of *The Perennial Philosophy* (1945), which made many Westerners rethink their allegiance to Christianity, and *The Doors of Perception* (1954), which made many professors and writers, including Timothy Leary, Alan Watts, Abraham Maslow, Jack Kerouac, and Allen Ginsberg, find hope in the promises of mescaline and LSD.[6] The late rocker Jim Morrison named his band, the Doors, after Huxley's book *The Doors of Perception*. Aldous Huxley, attended by his wife on the day of his death (the same day that John F. Kennedy and C. S. Lewis died), was injected with 100 milligrams of LSD as he slipped serenely through whatever portal and into whatever realm awaited him. Just recently, in 1994, Ram Dass, the former Dr. Richard Alpert and lecture partner of Timothy Leary, spoke glowingly of Aldous Huxley at the Celebration of his Birth Centenary, with Laura Huxley, Aldous's widow, looking on.[7]

Unfortunately, the ideas of Huxley have deceived many people. Like Alices caught in Wonderland, generations of individuals, influenced by his brand of relativism, have passed or peered through so many doors and windows of different dimensions since his day that they have come to expect the broad, rather than the narrow, road in life. Such freedom, they now believe, is their birthright. Huxley had a great deal to do with urging us to throw open, willy-nilly, these doors and windows of confusion. "*Simultaneous existence in a dozen parallel worlds*—this," claims his biographer, Sybille Bedford, "is what always exercised Aldous's mind."[8]

Throw Open the Doors of Relativism

In a compilation of essays published between 1923 and 1956, entitled *Collected Essays*, Huxley reveals his lifelong commitment to subjectivism and relativism. He proffers some unusual notions about love and sexual relations, subordinates knowledge to subjective experience, and almost seems to endorse inconsistency as a way of life. Like many writers of his day, he was experimenting with ideas and testing the boundaries of tradition.

The way he talks about love reveals his appreciation of not only cultural relativism but also social experimentalism. In "Fashions in Love" (1929), he speaks of the conventions of love between people as relative, depending on cultural conditioning. Although "love is the product of unchanging passions, instincts, and desires" in human nature, it's also the product "of laws and conventions, beliefs and ideals, which the circumstances of time and place, or the *arbitrary fiats* of great personalities, have imposed on a more or less willing" (italics mine). Even homosexuality is a mode of love. As always convention, not absolute standards of right and wrong, intervenes to mold the fashions of love in any age. "Convention and public opinion molded the material of love into forms which a later age has chosen to call 'unnatural.'"

In a much later essay, the "Appendix" to *Tomorrow and Tomorrow and Tomorrow* (1956), he urges us to look at the facts of sex and to consider sexual experiments in lifestyle worthy of serious examination. He speaks approvingly, in particular, of John Humphrey Noyes's Oneida Community, where group sex in the name of "Bible communism" was practiced, and of Tantric yoga, a practice that encourages the view that sexual union is a path to divine union. Both practices, says Huxley, make the act of sex a religious sacrament.[9]

The way he talks about knowledge, in an essay from his book *Tomorrow and Tomorrow and Tomorrow*, reveals his commitment to subjective experience as the true basis for understanding. Already influenced by his experimentations with mysticism and hallucinogens, Huxley subordinates knowledge—of uniform beliefs, doctrines, and "homemade systems of ideas and word patterns"—to "understanding." "Understanding," he claims, "comes when we liberate ourselves from the old and so make possible a direct, unmediated contact with the new, the mystery, moment by moment, of our existence." This understanding isn't conceptual, nor can it be acquired. It must be experienced directly and inwardly. Pseudo-knowledge and our overvaluation of words are responsible for at least two-thirds of human misery. But the understanding, or truth, Huxley advocates isn't only relative but nonrational. "Truth can be defined in many ways," he says. But if it's defined as understanding—subjective experience, "then it is clear that 'truth must be lived and there is nothing to argue about in this teaching; any arguing is sure to go against the intent of it.'" Here, Huxley is quoting Emerson.

A few lines later he quotes William Law to the same effect: "Away, then, with the fiction and workings of discursive reason, either for or against Christianity." Huxley's final formula urges us to embrace the experiential and nonrational: "Be aware impartially, realistically, without judging, without reacting in terms of remembered words to your present cognitive reactions. If you do this, the memory will be emptied, knowledge and pseudo-knowledge will be relegated to their proper place, and you will have understanding." And what is this understanding? Says Huxley, "you will be in direct contact with reality at every instant."[10] In other words, just go with the flow, and you will *experience reality* as it really is—whatever, of course, that may mean.

Finally, the way he talks about human personality and psychology is perhaps most radical in its advocacy of relativism because it makes virtues of inconsistency and eccentricity for their own sakes. In the essay "Pascal" (1929) he contrasts the creeds of two kinds of people: "the life-worshiper" and "the death-worshiper." Pascal, the Christian, is the epitome of "the death-worshiper" because he chose "an irrational abstraction to believe in—the God of Christianity" and because he practiced self-sacrifice. Such a consistent thinker, such a consistently moral man, "is either a walking mummy or else, if he has not succeeded in stifling his vitality, a fanatical monomaniac." The life-worshiper, the healthy individual, by contrast, is a kind of sense-oriented, energetic chameleon.

> The life-worshiper's philosophy is comprehensive. As a manifold and discontinuous being, he is in a position to accept all the partial and apparently contradictory syntheses constructed by other philosophers. He is at one moment a positivist and at another a mystic: now haunted by the thought of death . . . and now a Dionysian child of nature; now a pessimist and now, with a change of lover or liver or even the weather, an exuberant believer that God's in his heaven and all's right with the world. He holds these different beliefs because he is many different people. Each belief is the rationalization of the prevailing mood of

one of these persons. There is really no question of any of these
philosophies being true or false.

Huxley again reveals his relativism and subjectivism. Philosophies are
based on psychological moods and states only, with one no truer than
another. They are simply facts of experience. "And since one psychological state cannot be truer than another, since all are equally facts,"
concludes Huxley, "it follows that the rationalization of one state cannot be truer than the rationalization of another." A few pages later he
claims that the consistent and the moral are simply fools who are terri-
fied of freedom. Says Huxley, "morality is always the product of terror;
its chains and strait-waistcoats are fashioned by those who dare not trust
others, because they dare not trust themselves, to walk in liberty."[11]

Throw Open the Doors of Diversity

In *The Perennial Philosophy* Huxley sets out to prove that unity underlies the diversity within all religious traditions. In it he quotes mystics
from various traditions to prove that they all point to a *philosophia
perennis*, a term first used by Leibniz (1646-1716), says Huxley, to
describe a metaphysics that is "immemorial and universal," the
"Highest Common Factor" in all theologies and religions the world
over. It's "the metaphysic that recognizes a divine Reality substantial to
the world of things and lives and minds; the psychology that finds in the
soul something similar to, or even identical with, divine Reality; the ethic
that places man's final end in the knowledge of the immanent and transcendent Ground of all being."[12] Huxley wrote this book while he was
living in Hollywood and trading ideas with Gerald Heard, Christopher
Isherwood, and Swami Prabhavananda of the Ramakrishna Order of
India, all of whom espoused the belief that all "paths" lead to God. In
Hollywood Huxley discovered the broad way that accorded with his
earlier insights about the relativity of human experience and consciousness. As early as his essay on Pascal, he had been urging diversity on his
readers: For the life-worshiper, he explained, "the harmony of life—of
the single life that persists as a gradually changing unity through
time—is a harmony built up of my elements. The unity is mutilated by
the suppression of any part of the diversity."[13]

Because Huxley loved diversity and multiplicity so much, however, he failed to make his case for mystical unity. Trying to support his thesis, he quotes from books like the *Upanishads*, *Bhagavad Gita*, and *Dhammapada* (but never from the Bible, as he informs us in his "Introduction") and from mystics of every persuasion—Hindus, Sufis, Buddhists, Taoists, Christians. He keeps insisting, despite apparent contradictions between scriptures and mystics, that we can divine "the one within and beyond the many." If we accept the paradoxes and cease to quibble over trifles, we shall realize the ultimate good "in an eternal divine now," if we sufficiently desire it, "as a fact of immediate experience." After all, at best the Truth "can be hinted at in terms of *non sequiturs* and contradictions." Again, he is simply embracing the relative and the nonrational. He is also being misty, not mystical. Huxley's view of moral good and evil is perhaps most perplexing and unconvincing: "good," he claims, "is the separate self's conformity to, and finally annihilation in, the divine Ground which gives it being; evil, the intensification of separateness, the refusal to know that the Ground exists." In short, he can only know he is being good when he *feels* that he is drawing closer to the Ground of being. Universal application is impossible within such a moral framework.

Finally, for all his "tolerance," Huxley attacks Christianity mercilessly and subscribes to an exclusively Eastern view of God: Ultimate Reality is best understood as "impersonal and nonethical"; the law of *karma* does in fact operate in the world; men must annihilate their egos, becoming pure and selfless first, if they want to experience the Ground of being. He places his faith in a path of works because he despises historical details and all the nasty little particulars and distinctions. For this reason he seems to debunk any attempt at understanding a Jesus with an "I," a historical Jesus.[14] It's better, as far as Huxley is concerned, if God is whatever we want or need him to be in the course of our journey.

Therefore, he urges us to accept the rich diversity of faiths, drop our theological imperialism, which he sees as a sin of the first magnitude, and simply turn within to sink into the Ground of all being, pure is-ness (the *Istichkeit* of Meister Eckhart). "Like any other form of imperialism, theological imperialism is a menace to permanent world peace." By embracing this diversity, he holds, we will discover the unitary truth that will set us free. Only the triumph of the perennial philosophy can save the world.[15] We can only wonder what Huxley would have made of Jesus' words in Matthew 10:34: "Do not suppose that I have come to bring peace to the earth. I did not come to bring peace, but a sword." According to Jesus, the Truth always has a way of dividing rather than unifying people.

Throw Open the Doors of Perception

After a series of experiments with mescaline and LSD, Huxley published *The Doors of Perception* and then later *The Island*, one year before his death. Huxley took his first "trip" under the supervision of Dr. Humphrey Osmond, a Canadian psychiatrist, in 1953. Over the next few years he was to experiment with "psychedelics" several times. In 1960 he met Timothy Leary, a young psychologist eager to attach himself to Huxley's coattails. By 1961 he was speaking of the "Visionary Experience" at a conference in Copenhagen, where afterwards he met with Dr. Albert Hoffman, the discoverer of LSD (1943), the "*moksha-*medicine" as Huxley was to call it in *The Island*, published a year later. In Sanskrit *moksha* means liberation, specifically liberation through self-effort, from the rounds of births and deaths, and consequently the simultaneous full realization of one's True Self.

In *The Doors of Perception* Huxley describes eloquently, too eloquently, his experiences under the influence of mescaline. As usual we encounter his relativism: "From family to nation, every human group is a society of island universes."[16] Island universes, naturally, may have some things in common, but they will also differ in many ways. Perhaps mescaline, Huxley surmises before his drug trip, will provide him with the visionary experience that will enable him to enter and understand different "island universes." He speaks of mescaline as delivering him, for the moment, from "the world of selves, of time, of moral judgments and utilitarian considerations, the world . . . of self-assertion, of cocksureness, of overvalued words and idolatrously worshiped notions." As he reflects and examines objects, he believes that the "Mind at Large" occasionally breaks in, oozing "past the reducing valve of brain and ego." He expresses exhilaration mixed with reservations. "As a rule the mescaline taker discovers an inner world as manifestly a datum, as self-evidently 'infinite and holy,' as that transfigured outer world which I had seen with my eyes open."

Praising the Native American use of peyote, he sees in drugs the possibility of chemically opening doors into the Other World. But he realizes that what one can experience on mescaline isn't the same as the realization of the ultimate purpose of life—enlightenment. At best the drug offers "'a gratuitous grace,' not necessary to salvation but potentially helpful and to be accepted thankfully. . . ." Of course, he concedes that only those with healthy minds will experience the salutary effects of the drug. He knows that some unbalanced personalities might experience something more akin to purgatory or hell. In the end, however, Huxley expresses satisfaction with the experience: "the man who comes back through the Door in the Wall will never be quite the same. . . ." He will be wiser, happier, humbler, "yet better equipped to understand the relationship of words to things, of systematic reasoning to the unfathomable Mystery which it tries, forever vainly, to comprehend."[17] It certainly sounds like a "good trip" to me, one that might have inspired others to follow in the footsteps of his mescaline-laced moccasins.

In *The Island* Huxley describes an Utopia in which the denizens of the isle use *moksha*, a psychedelic concoction, for spiritual purposes. A few years earlier he had already subscribed to the development and use of physiologically harmless—that is, safe—"mind changers." Although he conceded to some dangers these drugs might bring, he felt they would help people by providing them, when administered in the right environment, with "a genuine religious experience," ultimately leading even to religious revival.[18] But *The Island* goes farther. The people of the island, Pala, live in a society founded by a Buddhist and a medical doctor and led by the Raja, who try to synthesize the best of Eastern and Western philosophies. The economy is driven by people's wish to be "happy" and "fully human." Children practice dance, study ecology, and live in as many as twenty homes, among adoptive families: "Whenever the parental Home Sweet Home becomes too unbearable, the child is allowed, is actively encouraged . . . to migrate to one of its other homes." People are to stop all their "pro-ing and con-ing" and to strive for enlightenment only. They are to take the "*moksha*-medicine" to have their eyes opened and their lives transformed into blessedness.

Especially instructive are the Raja's code of laws, "Notes on What's What, and What It Might Be Reasonable to Do about What's What." "In religion," he says, "all words are dirty words. Anyone who gets eloquent about Buddha, or God, or Christ, ought to have his mouth washed out with carbolic soap." And "the beings who are merely good are not Good Beings; they are just pillars of society." Apparently the islanders are to distrust words and appearances. Indeed, they are to distrust even reason: "We cannot reason ourselves out of our basic irrationality. All we can do is to learn the art of being irrational in a reasonable way."[19] All is paradox. All is irrational synthesis.

In this way, over the years Huxley has encouraged many sincere seekers of truth to strive for the perfect altered state of consciousness in which they might be set free from the limitations of their knowledge and their senses. He wanted people to achieve understanding—a direct experience of the Ground that transcended all categories of right and wrong. The best moral commandment that Huxley could lay down is of little help in the real world: "You shall realize your unity with all being."[20]

INFLUENCE OF THE MEGA-IDEA

The methods of relativists have always been the same. They attack traditional morality, ridicule reason and common sense, and promote "tolerance" for its own sake. Since the 1960s especially, society has been caught in a whirlpool of "moral" rationalizations of immorality. Now, therefore, only might—political muscle and the almighty buck—can make right as beliefs clash in the marketplace of ideas, in a post-Christian culture in which a moral consensus no longer exists. As we have found, social engineers create order by promulgating politically correct views to maintain their hold on the collective consciousness of the nation. Ironically, however, although relativism is the logical end point of extreme individualism, in the end it destroys the freedom it promises. Moreover, because it's self-refuting, it rejects the laws of rationality—the principles of logic. Christianity is unwelcome in this brave new world because it does make truth claims, does respect the principles of logic, and doesn't accept all lifestyles and paths as welcome guests at the banquet table of the Bridegroom.

The Quest for "Altered" States of Consciousness

In the 1960s, in the wake of Huxley's writings, the drug craze exploded with an almost evangelistic fervency. People like Timothy Leary and Ram Dass emerged as new heroes telling the young to turn on, tune in, and drop out. Tom Wolfe published *The Electric Kool-Aid Acid Test*, a travelogue that described his life on the road with Ken Kesey and his "magic bus" full of stoned hippies. Soon The Who were "talkin' 'bout my generation" and singing about the "magic bus," and the Beatles were soaring off to India to study under the Maharishi Mahesh Yogi, who by the way was the first guru of that modern medical guru Deepak Chopra. But of course Chopra, in helping us alter our consciousness and achieve happiness today, speaks of herbal remedies, not magic mushrooms. In the 1960s it was the mushroom or peyote that was to cure all our psychic ills. But the message remains essentially the same: alter your consciousness and live happily ever after.

The drug movement of the 1960s, of course, quickly degenerated into something ugly and also trivial. The signs of degeneration were already present in *The Electric Kool-Aid Acid Test*. When Kesey and his *ganja* gang held a love-in among the pines of California, another gang, Hell's Angels, crashed the party. Kesey decided to turn on the Angels with acid to mellow them, but they ended up "gang-banging" a few girls, who made themselves willing sacrifices, so to speak, to keep the lid on the event. Later in the 1960s the Hell's Angels again wreaked havoc at the Rolling Stones concert at the Altamont Speedway in California. The seedy elements we associate with drug use today crept into the movement slowly and soon displaced all the love-smitten seekers of peace and enlightenment. Then came the legions of hedonists who sought sense pleasures, especially of the "free love" kind, and longed for mindless self-expression. Stoned people got "the munchies" and "tripped out" on old Laurel and Hardy movies. Many got caught up in obsessions, like one friend of mine who meticulously collected baseball cards by day and compulsively stalked "chicks" by night in search of "free love." Then at last the defining turning point occurred—Woodstock, which was a hedonist's, not a mystic's, paradise. The few remaining East-turners and mystics ran off to India and stopped taking drugs altogether. So what are people getting today for all their "altered states"?

Today we see the wreckage, more and more of which keeps washing ashore, of the Huxley-inspired experiments. At local raves across the nation, TV news shows tell us, LSD and Ecstasy are being brazenly sold to teens who "just want to have fun." My college-aged students tell me they have many friends who smoke marijuana, often daily, as part of their lifestyle. I can spot the glassy-eyed seated along the back walls. Sadly, the facts support these observations. According to a survey released in 1996 by the Partnership for a Drug-Free America (PDFA), marijuana use by adolescents is again increasing after a ten-year decline. Among eighth graders between 1991 and 1995 marijuana use rose from 6.2 to 15.8 percent; among tenth and twelfth graders between 1992 and 1995 marijuana use increased from 15.2 to 28.7 to 34.7 percent. Thirty-five percent of young people say they are hearing "more and more talk about legalizing marijuana." And this marijuana contains more of the active ingredient in marijuana, THC, than the marijuana thirty years ago did.

Attitudes toward drug use are becoming more tolerant, says the PDFA, because of the glorification of drug use "by music groups, television, and movies and a drop in anti-drug information in the media."[21] Surely, we can see that the "enlightenment" that one generation naively sought has resulted in the "benightedness" that another generation has found. Today teens pierce their tongues and go "kickin'" at orgiastic raves, or cease to have dreams and distrust even benign authority, because they believe they are in bedlam, not heaven.

Yet they keep seeking. We forget that the kid who is sniffing glue in a garage is also looking for an altered state of consciousness, though by another name. He simply wants to get high so he can escape the existential meaninglessness of life or his overscrupulous parents and teachers, who he feels shouldn't be hassling him so much about his behavior and his grades. We can thank Huxley and his cohorts, in part, for this sad state of affairs, for they encouraged people to open the doors of perception with drugs. As more and more people decided, as Timothy Leary put it, that our culture was "a 'fake-prop-set society,' they . . . turned to drugs."[22]

The Adoration of the Nonrational

Through *The Perennial Philosophy* Huxley opened a great many doors, most especially the ones that have fostered a renewed respect for pagan spiritual experience and *praxis*. The Vedantins, Sufis, and Buddhists have benefited, but so have the WICCANS, Scientologists, Moonies, Eckankarians, Rastafarians, Divine Light Mission, and Brotherhood of Urantia. Since Huxley's time, a spate of books and gurus has appeared on the scene to tell us how to tap into our subconscious storehouse of wisdom, discover the secret of the ages in the stars, or plunge within to find the True Self. In my day names like Gurdjieff and Ouspensky and Carlos Castaneda were new. Now we have Deepak Chopra, Frederick Lenz, Nick Bunick, Andrew Cohen, and Peter Novak. And the books keep coming: *Seth Speaks, A Course in Miracles, The Celestine Prophecy, Snowboarding to Nirvana, The Messengers, The Way of the Wizard, The Seven Spiritual Laws of Success, Conversations with God,* and *DivisionTheory*. What do these movements, people, and books have in common? They take advantage of the tendency in our times to prefer the nonrational (even irrational) over the rational, the objective over the subjective, the relative over the absolute when it comes to faith and religious insight.

Several years ago in *Escape from Reason*, Francis Schaeffer elaborated on the modern tendency to seek "Upper Story" experiences. If people cease to believe that rationality and logic can make sense of life, or that words can capture truths, they then will turn to the nonrational or suprarational. "Aldous Huxley," Schaeffer observes, "made a titanic addition to this way of thinking" by encouraging people to seek "a first-order experience" through drugs.[23] Huxley, as we have seen, also added to this way of thinking by advocating relativism and diversity, with the Ground of being experience serving as the only valid test of truth for each person. If everything here below is relative, then each individual will have to uncover his own meaning, looking within himself or hearkening to "channeled" messages. In this way, this search for nonrational, nonlogical, nonlinear modes of experience—mystical, pharmacological, even sexual—has become valid and indeed imperative for many people, especially those who find themselves reeling in the midst of the modern chaos of voices.

So as Schaeffer contended in *The God Who Is There*, "Whether it is the existentialist speaking, or Aldous Huxley, or Eastern mysticism, we find a uniform need for an irrational experience to make some sense of life."[24] Today the irrational rules. If we try to reason with someone about truth or morality, he is likely to turn away in disgust, glibly ending the exchange with "That's just *your* opinion."

I have encountered the biases of nonrational relativism many times. I could relate the story of a high school vice-principal who chided me for protesting the selection by an English teacher of a novel that made homosexuality seem normal, even desirable. After telling me that the book is on the state's approved reading list, he smugly added, "Well, everyone knows that values are all relative anyway." I could cite the responses of young students when I argue that relativism isn't only self-refuting but barbarous. "Who," I ask, "could ever say that the sexual abuse of a two-year-old child is neither right nor wrong, just relative?" Some are silenced by the question, but others aggressively appeal to cultural relativism. Well, they say, the Spartans used to expose their infants . . .

But one example will suffice to illustrate that the nonrational is more respected today than the rational. To my speech classes, in which the ages of students range from twenty-five to fifty, I have several times delivered a persuasive speech on astrology, based on my refutation of it in my book *Embraced by the Darkness: Exposing New Age Theology from the Inside Out* (Crossway 1996). Using reason, scientific evidence, and ample visuals, I assail the "science" of astrology. I prove that the zodiac of twelve signs isn't even a plausible fiction and that the planets shed no measurable influences on the earth. I concede that electromagnetic storms and gravitation are measurable, but I prove that these solar and lunar influences are so strong that they would block out any alleged "influences" from the planets.

I argue finally that the last refuge of astrologers is subjectivism. When defeated by science and reason, they claim—appealing to ancient myths and Jungian archetypes—that astrology has a symbolic validity. I point to the arbitrariness of the symbols, the want of proof as to causality, and the fuzziness of the nonrational gibberish that forms interpretations. In no class have I ever convinced a believer in astrology, serious *or* casual, to disbelieve, or even to reconsider his belief. Students explain to me that "proof" makes no difference where their belief is concerned. If it "works" for them or for others, it's valid on that basis alone. It's all relative, right?

The New Litmus Test of Toleration

Alvin Toffler, as we noted in the last chapter, declared that "Tolerance of diversity is the first commandment of the de-massified society, including tolerance of the intolerant—*up to a point*" (italics mine). In terms of religions, the exceptions, he notes, are those faiths "that combine totalitarianism with universalism." He calls them "agents of the Dark Age."[25] Unfortunately, Christianity is totalitarian and universalistic in that it holds that Christ is the only way to salvation and that the world will be better off when Christ returns to reign over the earth. A Christian state, we believe, is better than a non-Christian state, and the way of Christ is preferable to the path of the Hindus or the Buddhists. Toffler was probably thinking of Islamic Fundamentalists, but a great many people will slip Christianity into the same category. And perhaps we Christians should realize that we are already, in the minds of many, in that same category—at least in the sense that just below the "point" of the Christian Faith most secularists draw their Maginot line of tolerance.

This new brand of toleration—*up to a point*—is the new litmus test for cultural sensitivity. Everyone is tolerated as long as he doesn't believe in absolute truth or permanent standards of right and wrong or promote rational formulations of faith. Anyone who seeks to engage in reasoned discourse—that is, argument—is regarded as divisive. To be labeled "intolerant" is tantamount to being branded as a heretic. It means a scarlet letter for anyone in the spotlight of the media. Just think of the public figures who committed a politically incorrect *faux pas* and then rued the day they ever cracked open their lips. With every other moral value being relative, it's curious that toleration should become today an absolute virtue, carrying the onus of sin with it should it be violated. Certainly not only Aldous Huxley but a great many thinkers have led us to this pass. If a modern philosopher as prominent as Richard Rorty claims that the quest for truth is over, surely tolerance is no more true than intolerance. And yet the truth is apparent: A well-practiced toleration, when brought to perfection in the public or private sphere, will throw open the doors of opportunity for any simpering sycophant.

More importantly, this new litmus test of toleration effectively shuts down debate. It keeps the lips of Americans sealed in the face of the agendas of radical feminists, gay rights advocates, and environmentalists. With impunity, the young can be easily recruited, believing, as they are told, that diversity leads to unity and intolerance to division. It keeps the lips of parents sealed in the face of the rampant permissiveness and hedonism in the culture. If they dare to speak out against some "lifestyle" or "choice" made by the enlightened young, reared on subjectivism and relativism as taught in the schools and broadcast by means of TV, movies, and music, they will be ignored the way one ignores a gnat or brushed aside the way one brushes aside a mosquito. Traditional arguments as well as appeals to logic and reason are empty in the face of the new relativistic value of toleration. Who has time for distinctions? For nagging contradictions? Everyone wants to feel good.

Finally, and worse, the new litmus test of toleration keeps the lips of Christians sealed in the face of the many onslaughts on traditional Christian belief and culture (onslaughts that began with Hobbes and continued through Huxley). Christians, backed into the corner of their churches, lashed to their pews, can always take refuge in piety. The hymns rise melodiously, hanging in the air, while only four blocks away a kid is smoking pot or two unmarried lovers are making a baby. Shushed by the new tolerance, Christians no longer speak of hell or judgment, not even in sermons, much less in public. It would be indelicate and unwise.

In this climate we Christians, fearful of censure and ridicule, often reflexively shrink from any confrontation, but we mustn't. In the face of the moral chaos around us, for the sake of all those whose hearts and lives are being broken, we must speak out. To step out of our comfort and safety zones, however, we may need to renew our courage by remembering constantly our true lots in life as servants of Christ. "If they persecuted me," declared Jesus, "they will persecute you also" (John 15:20). He told us, too, to count the cost of discipleship before putting our hands to the plow and never looking back. Later Paul warned, "In fact, everyone who wants to live a godly life in Christ Jesus will be persecuted, while evil men and impostors will go from bad to worse, deceiving and being deceived" (2 Tim. 3:12-13). Paul wrote "everyone," not "everyone in the first century" or "everyone under Roman rule." "Dear friends," wrote Peter, "do not be surprised at the painful trial you are suffering. . . . But rejoice that you participate in the sufferings of Christ . . ." (1 Pet. 4:12-13).

We might as well face it: we are going to have to live, as Peter says, as "aliens and strangers in the world" (1 Pet. 2:11)—in the world but not of it—if we are going to carry out the mission of Jesus Christ. If Christ predicted that we would suffer persecution for his sake, then we must gird up our loins to confront bravely and lovingly our inevitable conflicts with the world, taking the side of Christ in the power of the Holy Spirit. The sophisticated—from Hobbes to Huxley and beyond— might like to silence us, but we dare not surrender before their censure and ridicule. We should be willing to die for the one who died for us, not only for us but for everyone else too, innocents and enemies alike.

As we have seen, Huxley threw open several doors, wide enough to be French doors, that made it possible for relativism to blow into every corner of society. The doors he threw open, however, also helped create wide openings for the last mega-idea, doors, sad to say, that have been cracked even farther open by many who call themselves Christians. Like us, they have been grazing within the sheepfold of Christendom. Unlike us, they have been fiddle-faddling for years with the fundamentals of the Faith. Just now the influence of their mega-idea is beginning to pour down the mountainsides into the rivers and valleys. It's particularly frightening because it has already infiltrated a large part of Christendom and soon will have far-reaching effects on not only the Faith but also the fate of the world in the new millennium.

Aldous Huxley can help us get a glimpse of this last mega-idea. In 1937 he edited *The Encyclopedia of Pacifism.* He was also involved during World War II in the Peace Pledge Union. Like Russell, Huxley was a pacifist, but he went a step further by making an odd request of the soldiers in Europe. He urged them to meet the tanks of the enemy, the Nazis, "with the redeeming power of love."[26] Of course, with the *Russell-Einstein Manifesto*, Russell carried the call to pacifism into the 1950s. But the message remained alive—and took popular form—when John Lennon sang "All You Need Is Love" during the Vietnam era. While the Cold War was still raising goose bumps on the backs of our necks, artists in the eighties on behalf of the hungry sang, "We are the World. We are the children." The new mega-idea, inspired by these sentiments and aided by the work of liberal theologians, is leading to a new faith in a new world order, in which all divisions will vanish and peace will reign forever. For such to occur, however, Christianity and other "dark age" religions must be discredited and dismantled in favor of a one-world generic religion that appeals to masses of people and yet also satisfies the scientists and secularists.

FIFTH STAGE

IN THE SLIDE TOWARD RELATIVISM

Today, with relativism almost fully in place,

the new millennium may well be marked by a kind of

New Age optimism and antirationalism, a postmodern

globalism that sees "love"—a generic, sanitized

version—as the only answer in a world more

and more torn by conflict over beliefs.

"ALL WE NEED IS LOVE"

On a November 1997 broadcast of *Touched by an Angel*, the angel Tess reassures a homosexual that God loves him the way he is, behavior and all, because God made him the way he is. He is God's "beautiful child." God, says the angel Monica, doesn't make anything that is "queer." On a February 1998 broadcast of *Nothing Sacred*, the priestly main character fights for the right of a nun to become a priest because she *feels* called to the priesthood. In 1998 one of Deepak Chopra's books, *The Path of Love: Renewing the Power of Spirit in Your Life*, became a best seller. Meanwhile, other New Age books remain popular: *Embraced by the Light*, *The Celestine Prophecy*, *A Course in Miracles*, *The Messengers: A True Story of Angel Presence and a Return to the Age of Miracles*, and *Conversations with God: An Uncommon Dialogue*. Even the late nineteenth-century channeled work of Levi Dowling, *The Aquarian Gospel of Jesus the Christ*, still gets circulated in New Age circles as an authentic "spiritual" work.

So what can we infer from these multifarious expressions of religious sentiments and inclinations in America? All this renewed interest in spirituality, according to pollster George Barna, is leading us more and more to become not a Christian nation but "a syncretistic, spiritually diverse society." America is perceiving religion in a new way—as "a personalized, customized form of faith views which meet personal needs, minimize rules and absolutes, and . . . bear little resemblance to the 'pure' form of any of the world's major religions."[1] "All we need is love," John Lennon promised us in one song, later encouraging us in another to "imagine" a world where there will be "no more religion" and "the world will be as one."

All these modern expressions tout love—love without conflict, judgment, and division—as the saving power for humanity. Ironically, all are made possible not just by ethical relativism, New Age influences, and the many mega-ideas we have examined so far, but by something far more insidious: high treason within the ranks of Christendom. The sabotage began in the eighteenth century with J. S. Semler (1725-1788), who asserted that the New Testament canon was the work of men and that scholars should independently investigate the matter of authenticity, and Friedrich Schleiermacher (1768-1834), who denied the authenticity of the pastoral epistles. Then came the University of Tübingen school of theology led by F. C. Baur (1792-1860), who inaugurated "Higher Criticism," called today the "historical-critical method." Higher Critics insisted that the Bible be approached without presuppositions and be examined scientifically, historically, and rationally as any other text would be. Unfortunately, most Higher Critics have been skeptics and progressives who have continually challenged the traditional scriptural notions of authority, canonicity, authorship, inspiration, and inerrancy.

Later came such figures as J. E. Renan (1823-1892), who wrote a humanizing biography of Jesus Christ; David Strauss (1808-1874), who argued that the New Testament story is myth; Bruno Bauer (1809-1882), who doubted the historicity of Paul and Jesus; and Julius Wellhausen (1844-1918), who denied the Mosaic authorship of the Pentateuch and thus helped develop modern "form criticism."[2] Thereafter, the floodgates of criticism opened, and such liberal theologians as Paul Tillich (1886-1965), Reinhold Niebuhr (1892-1971), and Rudolf Bultmann (1884-1976), among others, began to dominate the thinking in mainline seminaries in America. They worked existentialism and subjectivism into their theology, or favored "Christian socialism" and ethical relativism, or demythologized Scripture in a compromise with scientific rationalism. Such men have served as saboteurs within the Christian fold itself.

Unfortunately, the work of a still newer breed of saboteurs continues today. Such major theological figures, who by all appearances are benign and friendly toward theism, are steering Christendom ever closer to emasculation and destruction. Having begun as Christians or still bearing the name *Christian*, they are misleading millions, fulfilling, perhaps unwittingly, a global New Age agenda. They aren't just heretics anymore, but apostates who are happily promoting our last, most dangerous mega-idea under consideration. Namely, *in a pluralistic and relativistic world, universal, unconditional, unifying, nonjudgmental love alone can reconcile all our differences and bring us peace*—especially if we can "look past our differences," celebrate "our unity-in-diversity," and allow everyone to coexist "on a level playing field." Christianity doesn't hold all the truth. Christ was just one of many world sages. Creedal religion always results in ignorant, divisive dogmatism and warfare. Truth is universal, existing in every religion and evolving as humans evolve. We need to become one world and one people, joined one to another by our appreciation of "unity in diversity." In one sense this synthesis represents the "higher" truth of postmodern relativism; in another, however, it may well foreshadow the end of Christianity as we know it.

THEOLOGIANS OF A NEW PARADIGM

Paradigm, a trendy word that simply means model or example, is one of the chief buzzwords of the postmodern era. As used originally in 1962 by Thomas S. Kuhn, physicist and historian of science, it appeared in the phrase "paradigm change." Presumably, scholars now say, we are in an era of unprecedented "paradigm shifts." In other words, people's models of the world, or mental frameworks, are changing drastically. If this thirteenth presupposition—or "paradigm shift"—takes hold, it may well lead to the ruination of Western civilization, if not the whole world. It most certainly will greatly impede, more and more, the work of the church. In a world where paradigm shifting is seen as a virtue, there will be no room for exclusive truth claims or doctrines. As many writers prove today, the trend is toward synthesis in relation to world religions and ideologies. As the mega-idea of this chapter relates to the work of the saboteurs within the sheepfold, it has three main components that should throw orthodox Christians into a tizzy of concern for the fate of future generations.

We Must Grant That Truth Resides in Every Religion

Harvey Cox, professor of divinity at the Harvard Divinity School, former protégé of Paul Tillich, and a leader within the World Council of

Churches, proposes that we not only dialogue with the practitioners of other faiths but realize that they, too, will be provided rooms in Jesus' many mansions. Every religion, in short, contains enough truth so that Jesus can say to the faithful of that religion, "I am going . . . to prepare a place for you" (John 14:2). Thus set free to be as broad-minded as a multilaned superhighway, he appreciates "in a new way," when strolling through the temples of Vrindivan, "the infinite forms the love of God takes and the myriad vehicles through which it touches people." Apparently, he wasn't thinking of images of Shiva lingams (carved phalluses) and the goddess Kali with her protruding tongue, a severed head in one hand and a sword in the other. Or was he? If the love of God takes "infinite forms," then mustn't Cox see it also in a ragtag voodoo doll or a glossy snapshot of the Sears Tower? Cox can only hope, he says, that we will try "to doxologize the fragile oneness of the whole earth and all her inhabitants." We need only to study "the sacred stories by which we hymn the unity of our species and its animal and cosmic neighbor. . . ." In doing so, we shall be able "to claim these reminders of our common destiny from within the desperate sources that first gave them voice."

If we don't recognize that the mansions of Christ are numerous enough (perhaps as Motel 6s) to hold people of all faiths, we may, Cox believes, end up annihilating ourselves. So what must we do to speed the development of a unity-in-diversity mind-set? "We cannot," he says, "merely speculate on whether rites and myths will someday cease to divide and stupefy people; we must so shape and reconceive them that they unite and enlarge us."[3] Cox seems to assume that religions, including Christianity, consist of divisive myths and rites that need to be redesigned so each can synthesize with the other or so everyone can at least find a common ground.

Another approach, taken by Harvey Cox as well as by Hans Küng, Catholic theologian and professor of dogmatic and ecumenical theology at the University of Tübingen, attempts to apply a pragmatic test to a religion to assess its validity. Cox believes that, in the spirit of Christ, religious people, whatever their persuasion, should be judged by their fruits. It isn't doctrinal or ritualistic correctness that matters but "spiritual commitment." Cox claims, "Jesus' example also reminds us that the search for oneness-in-diversity in interreligious dialogue is not only a matter of making judgments" but of refraining from judgment.[4] It's hard to see the source of the example here since Jesus didn't engage in "interreligious dialogue," nor did he seek "oneness-in-diversity." After all, Jesus chided the Samaritan woman at the well and expected her to adopt his faith. He also told the seventy-two he sent out to shake the dust off their feet when leaving a town that wouldn't accept the Gospel. The pragmatic test for Küng, as it is for Cox, is whether someone is becoming more of a human being. Says Küng, "The basic question in our search for [truth] criteria reads: What is *good* for the individual?" He then provides the answer: "What truly helps him or her to be a human being. Accordingly, the basic ethical norm is Man should live in a human, not an inhuman, fashion. . . . The moral good is what allows human life in its individual and social dimension to succeed and prosper in the long run."

A true religion heals and protects rather than destroys and denigrates humans and their humanness. "We must not forget," asserts Küng, "that followers of other religions are to be respected as such, and not to be subsumed in a Christian theology." We therefore need more *"indifference* toward supposed orthodoxy,"* more "sense of *relativity* toward all human establishing of absolutes," more *"synthesis* in the face of all denominational and religious antagonisms. . . ." Thus, as Küng claims earlier, "Even the non-Christian religions can be . . . ways to salvation."[5] Küng's pragmatism sounds a lot like utilitarianism and a general advocacy of the "greatest-happiness principle" recast in theological language. Moreover, it's hard to see how mere virtue—doing good and feeling good as opposed to doing harm and feeling bad—have anything to do with the principle of truth.

Huston Smith, a former professor at MIT and Syracuse, takes a more abstract approach, based on his knowledge of Western philosophy and his experience with the religions of the world. Despite being raised by two generations of Christian missionaries to China and being a Christian for a number of years, Smith aligns himself with Eastern mysticism (he studied under a swami of the Ramakrishna Order for ten years), the Theosophical Society, and his late friend Aldous Huxley. Like Huxley, he has been speaking for years of the common Ground in all religions, as he did in his best-selling book (1.5 million copies) *The World's Religions: Our Greatest Wisdom Traditions*, written forty years ago, and has done more recently in *Forgotten Truth: The Common Vision of the World's Religions* (1993). After all, he says, he has trained "under swamis, Zen masters, and

Sufi shaikhs; encountering Tiwis and Aruntas in the Australian bush; sitting in total harmony with Thomas Merton, the Dali Lama, and a remarkable Native American chief. . . ." In all these cases he has felt the same still presence. In *Beyond the Post-Modern Mind*, he praises the idea of "primordial connectedness" by speaking of the pre-Cartesian philosophers who "started with unity and then went on to diversity. . . ." To these, "thinking was regarded as the activity of beings (ourselves) who were theomorphic; human nature was . . . the *imago dei*, or Buddha-nature, or Atman. As 'Divinity' is but another word for 'Reality,' to say that we are born of its likeness is to affirm our affinity with it from the start."[6] Here again we find the idea of unity in diversity. All spiritual traditions are grounded in the same ultimate sense of "Reality."

Unfortunately, Cox's and Küng's definitions of truth don't hold water very well, nor does Smith's. Cox argues that he has uncovered a paradox in two of Christ's sayings, making both "true." He cites, "I am the way and the truth and the life. No one comes to the Father except through me" (John 14:6), and he also quotes, "In my Father's house are many mansions" (John 14:2, KJV). In explaining the thesis of his book *Many Mansions*, he ignores the absolutism of the first saying by misinterpreting the second, ignoring the context and reading it symbolically, apparently as his mentor Tillich would have done. Jesus explicitly says that he is preparing the many "rooms" (NIV) in heaven for his sorrowful apostles, not for every Tom, Dick, or Hari who believes that God exists. Küng simply resorts to self-contradiction. He handles the truth in such a way, as Mortimer Adler puts it, "that all religions are true and, on the other hand, that for a person of any one religious faith, there is only one true religion, his own." Such a view must relativize spiritual and propositional truth. According to Adler, "Hans Küng's book is no better than Cox's with respect to the logic of truth."[7]

As for Smith, he is simply taking refuge, as Huxley did and as Hindus do, in the subjective nature of Ultimate Reality. Thus Smith doesn't present an argument at all, but an Eastern worldview that holds that all paths are true simply because God is defined as absolute existence, consciousness, and bliss, both transcendent and immanent, in its ultimate nature impersonal and always changeless. Cox acknowledges this Hindu view—and perfectly captures Smith's idea of unitary truth—when he says, "For the Hindu . . . change usually means decline from a more perfect state and is largely illusory in any case. God never changes. We do."[8] This form of argument sways the imagination, not the intellect.

We Must Transcend the Flawed Particulars and Historical Details

Although Cox believes in balancing the "particulars" of faiths with the "universal" within all faiths, other theologians aren't so naive. Cox seems enamored by the delights of paradox and is thus caught in a whirlpool of spiritual subjectivism as he searches for a "crazy wisdom": "the ultimate union of what appear to be opposites."[9] By contrast, Hans Küng, Huston Smith, and the scholars of The Jesus Seminar seem to recognize that the particulars, those nasty little distinctives that vary from faith to faith, will inevitably clash. Therefore, they search for ways to mitigate the differences, transcend the particulars, and discount as fabrications the historical details. In one way or another they must confirm the truth of their universalism and ecumenism.

Küng's view shows some moderation but not so Smith's. Küng is committed to an ecumenism, based on the work of "the theologians of a new paradigm," that moves in two directions: "*inwards*, for the domain of the ecumene between the churches, among Christians; and *outwards*, for the domain of world ecumene outside the Church [and] Christianity. . . ." Says Küng, "This kind of ecumenism corresponds to the transcultural or universalist aspects of paradigm analysis in theology and in other fields."[10] He seems to approve of the new "encounter between Christianity and the other religions on the level of roughly equal rights" and the tendency among people today "to listen and to learn from the other religions."[11] Küng demonstrates universalist as well as ecumenical leanings, but he doesn't seem to be disillusioned as yet with his Christian heritage.

So intense is Smith's universalism, however, that he approvingly paraphrases and quotes a Theosophical writer, Frithjof Schuan. Despising the "scandal of particularity," Smith argues that a loving God would not have left the vast majority of humanity for thousands of years to stagnate without hope, "in the darkness of mortal ignorance until he chose to disclose his truth to a rivulet of humanity concentrated in a tiny locale. . . ." The idea, he says, is too monstrous to abide and then approvingly quotes Schuan again: "'To suppose that God could act in such a manner . . . flagrantly contradicts [his] nature, the essence of which is Goodness and Mercy. This nature, as theology is far from being unaware, can be "terrible" but not monstrous.'"[12] We can only conclude from Smith's position that he conceives of God as a being who favors universals over particulars. The sooner religions unite, discovering unity in diversity within the transcendental Ground of all being, the better off humanity will be, for only then will men truly understand the "mercy and goodness" of the one true, impartial God.

Perhaps those most radically opposed to the particulars of Christianity are the seventy-four scholars of The Jesus Seminar, a number of whom—notably Robert W. Funk, J. Dominic Crossan, and Marcus Borg—are "Christians." Since the inception of The Jesus Seminar in 1985, the group has received scads of media coverage by way of cover stories in *Time*, *Newsweek*, *Life*, and *U.S. News and World Report* (as recently as Easter week 1996), on radio and TV talk shows, including *Larry King Live*; and in a mini-series, *The Life and Times of Jesus*.[13] Robert W. Funk, director of the Westar Institute, launched the Seminar, he says modestly, "to assess the degree of scholarly consensus about the historical authenticity of each of the sayings of Jesus."[14] Actually, the agenda of the Seminar is more radical, as Funk has admitted: "We want to liberate Jesus. The only Jesus most people know is the mythic one. They don't want the real Jesus, they want the one they can worship. The cultic Jesus."[15]

And the scholars have succeeded in doing so. After voting on over 1,500 sayings of Jesus in the Gospels, using colored beads (ranging from red for authentic to black for inauthentic), they concluded that only "Eighty-two percent of the words ascribed to Jesus in the gospels were not spoken by him. . . ."[16] Of the 18 percent that may be "ascribed" to him, only 2 percent received mostly red beads. Indeed, once all the beads had been counted and consigned to the macramé pile, the Gospel of John had been adjudged inauthentic—in effect, non-canonical—and the view it presents "alien to the real Jesus."[17] Yet the dubious Gnostic Gospel of Thomas had been added to their new canon, having received a sufficient number of red ("That's Jesus!") and pink ("Sure sounds like Jesus") votes.[18]

The Jesus who thus remains is unrecognizable to most Christians. In *The Five Gospels*, Funk and his fellows conclude that Jesus was just a laconic sage: "slow to speech, a person of few words," "self-effacing, modest, and unostentatious." Therefore, "it is difficult to imagine Jesus making claims for himself—I am the son of God, I am the expected One, the Anointed. . . ."[19] Crossan claims that Jesus was less interested in ushering in the Kingdom of God than in challenging "political normalcies of power and privilege, hierarchy and oppression, debt and foreclosure . . . imperial exploitation and colonial collaboration." To Crossan, then, Jesus was a pre-Marxist revolutionary whose primary message was simple: "God says, 'Caesar sucks.'"[20] Jesus, moreover, never rose from the dead, but instead "his body was probably buried in a shallow grave and may have been eaten by dogs."[21] And Marcus Borg holds that "the image of the historical Jesus as a divine or semi-divine figure, who saw himself as the divine savior whose purpose was to die for the sins of the world . . . is simply not historically true."[22]

To the scholars of The Jesus Seminar, the Gospels recount myths. The Gospel writers simply superimposed their own memories on a tradition of sayings and parables, thus making Jesus say what they wanted him to say.[23] Even repentance wasn't part of Jesus' message. In the gospels according to The Jesus Seminar, "Jesus is rarely represented as calling on people to repent." In fact, "the call to repentance may well have been derived from John [the Baptist] and then attributed to Jesus."[24] If we believe the scholars of The Jesus Seminar, Jesus was simply a warm, fuzzy sage who mainly preached love and compassion, at one and the same time a political radical (liberation theologian) and a tolerant universalist (postmodern theologian of the "new paradigm").

We Must Embrace the Cosmic Christ in All Creation

With this conception of Jesus in place, we are ready for the mystical revisionism and reductionism of people like Matthew Fox and Huston Smith. The last refuge of the ecumenical universalist, as Aldous Huxley illustrated in his *Perennial Philosophy*, is mysticism. And so to render Jesus palatable to millions, the new religious engineers—global "culture designers"—must make him transcend particularity and history and evaporate into universality and mystery. He then can become a universal, unifying personification of omnipresent Love, capable of satisfying every taste and offending no one.

Matthew Fox, in *The Coming of the Cosmic Christ*, proceeds from where The Jesus Seminar leaves off, catapulting us into a cosmic vision of Jesus as a kind of generic pantheistic Presence. Fox, a former Dominican and now Episcopalian priest who directs the Institute in Culture and Creation Spirituality at Holy Names College, also subscribes to "a paradigm shift in theology and religion itself. . . ." He knows that such a shift, although necessary, won't be easy. "To move from a 'personal Savior' Christianity—which is what an anthropocentric and antimystical Christianity gives us—to a 'Cosmic Christ' Christianity calls," says Fox, "for *metanoia*, a change of perspective. . . ." He longs for a new symbolism: "the appropriate symbol of the Cosmic Christ . . . is that of Jesus as Mother Earth crucified yet rising daily." He sees the Cosmic Christ pantheistically, as omnipresent already in every creature: "The Cosmic Christ is the 'I am' in every creature." He envisions the Cosmic Christ as the great unifier, the great underground river that unites all traditions, as though they were so many wells: "Buddhist wells, Native American wells and Christian wells, Islamic wells and Judaic wells." He speaks of Jesus as "a perfect bridge" of wisdom. Surely, as a mystic, Fox realizes that this Christ who pervades every object, person, and tradition (including goddess religions) can only be grasped generically and egocentrically. "'Christ,'" he admits, "is a generic name. In that sense we are all 'other Christs.'"[25]

Huston Smith's approach, although more intellectual, appeals equally to the mystical element, the Ground of being. First, he reiterates the guidelines of a perennial philosophy that remains "open to better beliefs and what lies beyond belief altogether. . . ." This philosophy insists "that the final reality, the infinite, is radically ineffable" and therefore "it relativizes all concepts, formulations, and systems"—hence all particulars and distinctives. Answers to the "whys" of God and creation come through direct subjective experience: eternal religion "ranges time and space for insight—*prajna*, vision, a revelation which, by-passing words, will disclose directly why we exist and why the world is the way it is. . . ." How convenient it is for the mystic to claim private experience as his authority, a state beyond words (particulars and distinctives), where discord and disagreement may occur! In the end, like Fox, Smith must characterize the truth as mystical, generic, and universal. Isaiah, Christ, Paul, Buddha as well as Copernicus, Newton, and Kepler all tell us the same thing about the universe: "They tell us of depth upon depth of value falling away from this visible world. . . . They tell us that this universe in all its vastness is permeated to its very core by love."[26] In all our questing, no matter what path we follow, all we need and find is love.

INFLUENCE OF THE MEGA-IDEA

If love unites everything, people ask, then why can't we always perceive love behind and within our "differences"? What's wrong with humankind? The universalists and ecumenists believe we can achieve world peace if only we will learn to practice universal, unconditional, nonjudgmental toleration and love. It would seem that relativists, proponents of diversity, and determinists, opponents of free will, would balk at such an agenda. Actually, however, they agree wholeheartedly with the agenda, if not always the vision, because they are joined at the hip with the universalists and ecumenists by one shared goal and two shared beliefs. They all *seek* global peace and unity, of the classless, genderless, nonsectarian variety. They all *believe* in the "fact" of evolution, whether of humanity, consciousness, or social systems, *and* in the essential role of education or "culture design" in securing a bright future for humankind. As Fox puts it, "Reeducation is greatly needed during the era of a paradigm shift. It will require different roles of different persons—indeed it may require an entirely different kind of person."[27] This mega-idea, along with the agenda I foresee, is so new historically that it's difficult to make out, in detail, through the haze of pronouncements and technicalities, the full range of effects that are inching toward us. At best, for now, we may only be able to see the influences as minute droplets, like a fine mist falling about us, just beginning to form pools at our feet. In this spirit of tentativeness, I still think we can glimpse three effects of this mega-idea now beginning to form.

The Birth of a One-World Generic Natural Religion

Through mysticism, says Fox, we can achieve "deep ecumenism," the "unleashing of the power of wisdom from all the world's religious traditions." Without such global ecumenism, he asserts, "there will never be global peace or justice. . . ." He reiterates his point by declaring that the Second Vatican Council in the 1960s already declared as much. "The Catholic Church," says the document *On Non-Christian Religions*, "rejects nothing which is true and holy in these religions."[28] But Fox is no lone Christian voice crying in the wilderness. The World Council of Churches (WCC), in the policy statement they prepared for their Eighth Assembly on the occasion of their fiftieth anniversary, lapses into sheer vagueness but makes their emphasis clear enough. They approve of interreligious dialogue. As they watch the "process of growing global-ization," they remain committed to "the quest for unity in its universal dimension, *embracing the human community* as well as the church" (italics mine). They acknowledge and welcome the growing number of voices among their ranks who have called for "macro-ecumenism," opening "the ecumenical movement to other religious and cultural tra-ditions beyond the Christian community." They want to remain "Christian," but they also want to "heal" humanity and creation and work "for justice, peace and the integrity of creation" throughout the world, especially "insisting on justice and full participation for women in church and world." They want "to arrive at new understandings of reality" and to embody unity so that "the world may believe," but they never say what they want the world *to* believe as regards Jesus Christ.[29] The agenda of the WCC sounds leftist, feminist, socialist, and vague enough to satisfy the exuberance of universalists of any stripe.

Other groups also support this agenda. Not just the WCC but the United Nations has its "culture designers."[30] Tal Brooke says that "Robert Muller, assistant secretary general to the United Nations and author of the key New Age book entitled *New Genesis: Shaping a Global Spirituality*, is a key voice among political VIPs of the New Age Movement." The United Nations, according to Muller, is "a key catalyzer of globalism."[31] It's Muller, in fact, who declares in his book, "The next stage will be our entry into a moral global age—the global age of love—and a global spiritual age. . . . We are now moving fast towards the fulfillment of the visions of the great prophets who . . . saw the world as one unit. . . ."[32] The Parliament of Religions, which met for its centennial celebration in 1993, has been making the same pitch for a century, ever since Swami Vivekananda mounted the podium in 1893 in Chicago in behalf of Vedanta.

Only two years ago, on January 23, 1997, an organization calling itself the GaiaMind Project sponsored a global meditation day, called GaiaMind, based on a rare alignment of the planets. They were hoping their meditations would help promote "the emergent unified planetary consciousness—to affirm that we are all one," all striving for "the healing transformation of the Earth."[33] Gaia is the goddess—the unitary con-sciousness—of a personified earth. I found the ad for this seemingly obscure "global meditation day" in an unusual place. Ironically—and alarmingly—it was listed among links on the WCC's home page under "Other Resources" and then "Religions of the World." A hop, skip, and jump into the search engine Yahoo brought me to such topics as "Events," "Lesbians, Gays, and Bisexuals," and "Theosophy." After selecting "Events" and then "New Age" (I could have selected "Paganism"), I found the GaiaMind site. Are we to assume that the WCC tacitly supports the efforts of New Agers and paganists as long as they "are all on the same page" as the WCC, all promoting global peace and unity?

The transformation of people has already begun, apparently, and Fox's "different kind of person" is already developing. This new kind of person seems to be oriented toward mysticism, pantheism, and paganism. Fox even claims that "One of the more surprising areas of deep ecumenism may well prove to be that between goddess religions and Christian mysticism." He even waxes eloquent about Gaia and goddess worship for a full page.[34] In a recent article written in the *SCP Journal*, Peter Jones, professor of theology at Westminster Seminary in California, argues that this transformation, occurring inside and outside the church, is already upon us. He refers to several influential nuns who have fled convents for covens. One, Mary Daly, tenured professor of theology at the Jesuit Boston College, denounces the Christian faith and "describes herself as an eco-feminist lesbian witch." Jones refers to a mainline denomination that sponsored a "RE-Imagining Conference" attended by 2,000 "mostly middle-class, middle-aged women from middle-of-the-road, mainline Christian churches." The women ended their event blessing some "sacramental milk and honey in a sort of Lady's Last Supper, with a hymn [quoted by Jones in full] to the goddess that bordered on lesbian pornography." He also cites the case of Virginia Mollenkott, a former "evangelical author," who turns for wisdom to the occultic *A Course in Miracles* as well as tarot cards and has committed herself to the noble call of the downfall of "the heteropatriarchal culture." He refers to James M. Robinson, another Jesus Seminar scholar and former president of the Society of Biblical Literature, who urged "fellow Bible scholars to deconstruct their discipline in order to 'lay bare [its] . . . biblicistic presuppositions.'"

Apparently Robinson's appeal didn't fall on deaf ears. In 1995 at the annual conference of the Society of Biblical Literature, reports Jones, "Leading New Testament scholars rejoiced that the heretical Gnostic

Gospel of Thomas had finally made it into the club, and that now we could disband the club"—namely, "the New Testament canon of Holy Scripture."[35] As such pagan and pantheistic heresy enters the church, it offers the world a false testimony of Christianity, leaving many with the impression that the Faith is so anemic that it's open to "new paradigms." Actually, this effort to transform beliefs may already be working well in America. As George Barna points out, although 93 percent of adults say they believe in God, three of ten when asked to define God describe a God different from the one depicted in the Bible. Fifty-three percent believe that "all people pray to the same god or spirit, no matter what name they use for that spiritual being." And finally, most people believe that "good people" will *earn* a place—a mansion, I suppose—in heaven.[36]

Clearly such an approach to God and Christ isn't only generic, stripping Christ of his uniqueness, but *natural*. The exponents of *natural* religion have always held—from the Greeks to the Hindus, Rousseau to Huxley—that one may reach God (union with the inner Divinity) by means of self-effort. Through spiritual exercises, inner experimentation, reason, and direct intuitive experiences, the natural religionist believes he can discover the one true God. This view contradicts the Christian view. Orthodox Christianity maintains that we are saved by grace through faith (not by self-effort), that truth comes by means of revelation as confirmed by Holy Scripture, and that Christ, the narrow path and gate, is the only way to God. Natural religion always advocates the broad path and the way of self-effort. Huston Smith states this position best. He refers to Aldous Huxley's belief that the Ultimate Reality—the Ground of being—is only apprehended "clearly and immediately" by those "who have *made themselves* loving, pure in heart, and poor in spirit" (italics mine). Then Smith adds, "Perhaps such purity of heart is the indispensable instrument for disclosing the key perceptions on which religion's incredible assumption is grounded."[37] In other words, if we make ourselves pure in heart first, then we will experience the Ultimate Reality. Then we will find, as Smith says, that the universe "is permeated to its very core by love." The one-world generic religionists continue to miss the critical point: humans can't meet this condition. As Christians have been trying to explain for two millennia, all the herculean self-effort of a lifetime—or a billion lifetimes—will never make a person pure.

The Demise of Evangelicalism

Such a universalizing of "love" leads to a generalizing of Jesus Christ. As a result, Christ is stripped of his historical distinctives, and Christian theology is rendered inoffensive—and ineffectual—by becoming generic. Jesus stories become myth, as the Christian Rudolf Bultmann and the non-Christian Joseph Campbell have both held, on a par with all the other religious myths of the world.[38] Jesus can thus be fitted into anyone's agenda. According to this revision of history, dogmatism—read "intolerance"—becomes the only sin.

As Huxley put it in 1956, "zeal, dogmatism and idealism exist only because we are forever committing intellectual sins. We sin by attributing concrete significance to meaningless pseudo-knowledge. . . ."[39] Creedal Christianity becomes the enemy of progress because by insisting on certain distinctives and imperatives it creates divisions in the world. Thus, many mainline denominational leaders are willing to deny the historic distinctives of the faith, as though doing so will create dialogue and call fresh sheep into the fold. For example, the recently appointed United Church leader of Canada, Rev. Bill Phipps, thinks it good that he doesn't believe in the divinity or resurrection of Christ. By encouraging "tolerance of divergent views," he thinks hundreds of thousands of unchurched people will be hearing and talking about Jesus, offering the church a "marvelous opportunity to evangelize."[40]

Such twisted logic can only lead to the end of evangelicalism. Without a belief in the divinity and resurrection of Christ, there can be no faith. "And if Christ has not been raised," asserts Paul, "your faith is futile; you are still in your sins" (1 Cor. 15:17). The foundation of the Christian Faith is the Resurrection. If Christ, wholly man and wholly God, without blemish or stain, didn't die for the sins of the world and rise from the dead as a sign and promise to all believers, then Christianity becomes meaningless—indeed, "useless" (1 Cor. 15:14). It becomes a myth that one can take or leave at his own discretion; and certainly no one bases his life on myth. Moreover, if by self-effort one could become pure in heart—overcoming his own "sins"—there would be no need for repentance. In fact, sin would be tolerable; only ignorance would be unacceptable. Ignorance of unity in diversity leads to division, separation from Ultimate Reality and from humanity, disintegration within the human psyche, *dis*-ease of mind and body. If people were to hold this view, Christians wouldn't be able to evangelize those who need evangelizing. All that would remain, in place of the alpine air of the historic Faith, would be a great smog that would blow hither and thither across the globe as the "Cosmic Christ."

True, Jesus had much to say about mercy and love, but he also didn't preach a generic, nonjudgmental, nondivisive, relativistic faith. He declares, in the Gospel that the Jesus Seminar conveniently rejects, "I am the way and the truth and the life. No one comes to the Father except through me" (John 14:6). He also proclaims that he came into the world to bring fire, sword, and division: "Do not suppose that I have come to bring peace to the earth. I did not come to bring peace, but a sword" (Matt. 10:34). He warns that he has come to divide. "From now on there will be five in one family divided against each other, three against two and two against three" (Luke 12:52). If he won't spare one family from divisions, then why should we think he will spare the family of man from conflict? Or put another way, although the truth *does* set us free, it also *must* divide. If the truth doesn't divide, it isn't the truth. Therefore, sad to say, those who seek peace at any price—through universalism or ecumenism—must be counted among the enemies of Christ.

The Construction of the Stage for the Antichrist(s)

In *When the World Will Be as One,* Tal Brooke, president of Spiritual Counterfeits Project and graduate of the Princeton Divinity School, presents a convincing, well-documented case for the existence of a worldwide conspiracy to create a one-world government. The conspiracy, according to Brooke, is at least 200 years old and involves many major world banks as well as collaborators from the United Nations. Such speculation may not be at all far-fetched. Speaking of the need to "cooperate" with international non-governmental and governmental agencies, including the United Nations, the framers of the WCC's policy statement for their Eighth Assembly in 1998 say, "The challenges of globalization and *the search for an international order of justice and peace* necessitate close contacts between the WCC and such organizations" (italics mine).[41]

On March 16, 1998, *Ecumenical News International* reported that a senior French official was urging Protestant churches to support

European unity. "The construction of Europe is an important arena for ecumenism," he says, "and the rapprochement between churches is an important factor in European integration."[42] Even someone as moderate and well-intentioned as the philosopher Mortimer Adler speaks approvingly of the idea of a "world federal constitution," which would include "a bill of human or natural rights," and a "world community" founded on the principles of truth of Western mathematics and science.[43]

Such globalism, however, is naive and unworkable. It's unrealistic and ultimately cruel. Unity in the midst of diversity may, in fact, be achieved for a time, as history proves, but only by violence and persecution. Over time if such a view gains currency, we may well find ourselves returning to tribalism and barbarism, under the authority of a dictatorship, not advancing toward world peace and unity. Surely, those who can't and won't conform to the global universal vision will pose a knotty problem for the "culture designers," a problem they may only be able to solve through concentration camps and mass exterminations. Indeed, we might imagine something like the futuristic world in H. G. Wells's *The Time Machine*. The gentle Eloi of the new millennium will find themselves answering, zombie-like, the siren calls of an elite group of hidden powerbrokers, like the bloodthirsty Morlocks, the few who "cannibalize" the unsuspecting many.

But Christ and his apostles warned us Christians of the Antichrist 2,000 years ago, so we can't plead ignorance. There will be wolves—false teachers and prophets—inside and outside the sheepfold, Jesus tells us (Matt. 7:15; 10:16). Jesus, the Good Shepherd, is the only one who has laid down his life to protect his flock from ravenous wolves (John 10:11-18). Paul speaks of "the man of lawlessness" (2 Thess. 2), but John refers to the *spirit* of antichrist in the world (1 John 4:3) and to one Antichrist as well as many antichrists (1 John 2:18-19). Those who deny that Jesus is the Christ, the Son of God, and that Jesus Christ came in the flesh, as the Word, are deceivers, he says, and thus antichrists (1 John 2:22; 4:2-3; 2 John 7).

John also applies a telling *test* that should put on notice ecumenists and universalists like Cox, Küng, Smith, the Fellows of The Jesus Seminar, the WCC, and the multitudes of New Age sympathizers. Speaking as an apostle and of the apostles (and possibly of other teachers who adhere to the original Gospel), John says, "We are from God, and whoever knows God listens to us; but whoever is not from God does not listen to us. This is how we recognize the Spirit of truth and the spirit of falsehood" (1 John 4:6). Peter warns us that false prophets will appear among us. "They will," he says, "secretly introduce destructive heresies, even denying the sovereign Lord who bought them" (2 Pet. 2:1). Aren't the ecumenists and universalists today, in fact, rejecting not only the words of Holy Scripture, the words of Christ and the apostles, but the historical Christ "who bought them"? Then, sadly, mustn't we call them antichrists?

Are we on the brink of the Second Coming? I wouldn't dare try to speculate. If Jesus declared that not even the Son of Man knows the details of his return (Matt. 24:36; Mark 13:32), and if the apostles, echoing their Lord (Luke 12:39), preached that he would return like "a thief in the night" (1 Thess. 5:2; 2 Pet. 3:10), I won't prophesy out of turn, even if I make bold, in private, to mark certain signs. Yes, mystery Babylon may exist already, and the beast and false prophet may soon enter the world (see Rev. 13—17). But I *can* say that we should die daily and that we should so live each moment that we are prepared for Jesus should he return with the next breath we take.

And I *can* assert one thing more with certainty. Clearly, the mega-idea of this chapter, like those of the previous twelve chapters, promises to do our culture and humanity more harm than good. Nevertheless, as realists we must recognize that the message of the universalists and ecumenists is spreading throughout the world today, all too apparent in its allure: forget the distinctions, forget the differences, "come together." Like a kaleidoscope of colors, all the mega-ideas in concert swirl together and becloud our judgment. Or they collide as in a cyclotron, bouncing all around us, distracting and disarming us, leading many to fall away from not just tradition but absolutes—toward chaos. Or they simply inundate us like the waters of a floodtide.

What answer does Christianity offer amid this Babel of paradigms? A very satisfying one indeed. Christianity needn't be revised, for it remains as true and relevant today as it was in past ages. Whatever the various modern voices claim, there is enough evidence for the validity and practicability of the Christian Faith to make belief in it philosophically permissible, if not obligatory. In the next chapter, I shall endeavor to put the ever new, though ageless, wine of the Gospel into new wineskins—or, should I say, new glass carafes with redemption value. Ironically, as we shall find, love—when it's turned right-side-up again—really *is* all we need.

A Defense of
Christian Absolutism

In late March 1998, armed with pistols and rifles, garbed in camouflage, two boys, eleven and thirteen, opened fire on a junior-high schoolyard in Arkansas. Calculatingly, one of them had tripped the school's fire alarm, and so kids and teachers poured out of the school, and a number of them were then caught in the crosshairs of a deer rifle. After the melee, five lay dead and eleven wounded on the school grounds. Of the five who were murdered, four were preteen girls, one a teacher. What was the cause of the massacre? One of the boys, the news reported, was distraught over having been rejected by his girlfriend. Many of us were sickened by yet another senseless act of violence perpetrated by kids against kids. Across the nation people were shocked.

But having examined the mega-ideas that have reshaped our culture over the past 300 years, should we really be surprised that such incidents are occurring? In this era, when children assassinate children, parents kill children, and children execute parents, we should instead be surprised that more incidents of this kind *aren't* occurring. To many great thinkers, remember, emotion, even passion, is more trustworthy than reason; pleasure, not just "happiness," is a "right" of every citizen; humans are simply "survival machines"; life is meaningless; moral values are relative. By becoming the freethinkers envisioned by progressives from the Enlightenment onward, we have become less free than we were when we practiced Judeo-Christian moral codes. Today many not only blindly succumb to their passions but, worse, prey on others. Their beliefs—the presuppositions that lie scattered like refuse on the "Ground of being"—lead them to behave antisocially and then to rationalize irrationally their immorality.

No, we shouldn't be surprised by senseless acts of hatred and violence, by daily examples of perversion and molestation. Many people are simply running amok. As one Christian leader has said of people today, "Losing the conviction that they are made in the image of God, people will tend to treat each other as animals or machines. People are what they believe."[1] And people will also act as they believe.

Of course, progressive as well as orthodox Christians want to stanch evil and champion righteousness and compassion in the world. But as we found in the last chapter, the progressives, though no doubt sincere, have it all wrong. They want global peace at any price, including the price of their faith. Seeking unity in diversity, attempting to tolerate as many values and views as possible, they have compromised with the purveyors of modern rationalism and postmodern relativism. Yet in seeking unity, they mishandle diversity, refusing to render judgments when judgments are required. In denying the existence of universals—namely, traditional absolutes—they juggle countless particulars, hoping to find through "toleration" and "appreciation" a unity that can never exist. In the end, however, all such people "are left with are particulars," says Francis Schaeffer; the "universals are lost. . . ." Subscribing to a "diversity" mind-set, Christian progressives become loath to defend the Faith. Instead, they retreat from the pitched battle over presuppositions and join the drift toward naturalism and cynicism, the result of which today is that "nature is eating up grace in the area of morals . . . [and] epistemology. . . ."[2]

Thus we find that, aided by Christian progressives, naturalism and natural religion are allowed to reign in the field of ideas. Perhaps out of a need for approval and acceptance, these relativistic universalists fail to welcome their lot as Christians. "If you belonged to the world," says Jesus, "it would love you as its own. As it is, you do not belong to the world. . . . That is why the world hates you." Then he adds, "If they persecuted me, they will persecute you also" (John 15:19-20). Afraid of conflict, ashamed of the historic Faith, the progressives have lost their nerve. False presuppositions, as we have seen, have a way of separating the sheep from the goats, the apostles from the apostates.

Yes, Christianity does divide people, with the fire of the Spirit and the sword of the Scriptures; but every other ideology in the world also divides.

The Hindus believe in many gods but abide, so they believe, in the impersonal Brahman. Classical Buddhists don't believe in any gods or God. Christians believe in a Trinitarian personal God, the Father of Jesus Christ, who was God incarnate, fully God and fully man. Each view works itself out in differing—often morally, logically, and epistemologically contradictory—particulars. Such distinctives must exist in the world because every person as well as every culture possesses a governing worldview, a set of beliefs, a code of right and wrong, grounded in presuppositions. The human enterprise should be to find the worldview that is true—truest to life in every particular, most coherent in every respect—and adopt it fully. Orthodox Christianity, I maintain, is that one true, coherent worldview.

At this critical stage in the history of Western culture, I intend to argue in this final chapter, we in the West must elect to return to a Christian worldview and moral consensus, collectively and individually. For our only other two alternatives would be imprudent, even suicidal—to continue to advance along the lines of relativism, or to try to create the impossible, a secular moral consensus from out of the confusion of tongues called pluralism or postmodern relativism. After readopting the way of Christ, we will understand that global unity and peace can only be achieved through the unconditional, unifying love of Jesus Christ. The path of love is the path of Jesus Christ who, having sacrificed himself for humanity, will return to establish his Kingdom on earth, for the eventual foundation of a new heaven and earth (Rev. 21).

TWO CONCESSIONS ABOUT THE FAITH

Before advancing my thesis, I would like to make two concessions aimed at those, Christian and non-Christian, in whose craws such words as *orthodox*, *evangelical*, and *church* get stuck. I trust that those for whom these words aren't anathema will bear with me.

First, *orthodox Christianity is frankly presuppositional.* Recognizing that people live and die by their presuppositions, we orthodox Christians freely acknowledge and reveal ours. To us, they are so reasonable and salutary that we base our lives upon them. Through general revelation, natural observation, we infer, like other theists, that God exists, eternal and infinite, as the sole uncaused Cause, Designer, and Regulator of the universe. All, we believe, can ascertain through the handiwork of God his natural laws, but *not* his spiritual laws. Through special revelation, Scripture, therefore, we derive our particular presuppositions about God, creation, and God's plan for creation. Our trust in special revelation is grounded in our certain belief, based on evidence and reason, that the sixty-six books of the Bible are inerrant in their original autographs and fully trustworthy and authoritative in all matters upon which they touch.

Through Scripture, we believe that God communicates with mankind, offering us his "propositional revelation" and speaking to us personally and truly, though "not exhaustively," of himself.[3] God reveals that he is Trinitarian, one divine essence existing in three Persons, and personal, the Maker of all things, seen and unseen, including moral and spiritual laws. He reveals that his creation is real and good, not illusory or evil, and that he invades human history and overrides natural law whenever he chooses. Because God is righteous yet compassionate, he sent into the world his only Son, the only mediator between God and man, the second Person of the Trinity. Fully God and fully man, Jesus Christ, who was born of a virgin, lived in first-century Palestine, preached the Gospel, performed miracles, and died under Pontius Pilate a sacrificial death on a cross. After three days, he arose from death in fulfillment of Scripture. In heaven and in believers' lives, he now lives and reigns spiritually but will return one day physically. The Holy Spirit, the third Person of the Trinity, assists him in his work.

We believe that, according to God's plan, we have been saved by the grace of God through faith in Jesus Christ. Formerly, through disobedience, we were God's enemies; now we are his adopted heirs. Because of Jesus' final Great Commandment, we also, admittedly, adhere to an evangelistic agenda: we must preach the Gospel to the world and "make disciples of all nations" (Matt. 28:18-20). Yes, we do want the Word to *trickle down* into every mind and heart. For we believe that Christ alone died for the whole world (John 3:16; 1 John 2:2) and that he doesn't want "anyone to perish, but everyone to come to repentance" (2 Pet. 3:9). Nevertheless, in all our evangelizing we wish to win others over by love, not fear—by reason, not coercion.

Second, the church throughout history has indeed harbored lunatics and committed atrocities. Inquisitors were often callous ruffians and corrupt toadies; bearers of the Gospel, lay and clerical, Catholic and

Protestant, were sometimes bad to the bone. They skewered non-Christians and roasted fellow Christians. But if the history of Christianity is considered as a whole, the lunatics will appear to be aberrations and most often enemies of the Word. Historically speaking, they are frayed threads on an otherwise magnificent tapestry of faith, hope, and charity. Jesus, foreseeing the future of the church, warned his followers of sheep in wolves' clothing; and the apostles John, Peter, and Paul warned of false prophets. Jesus also instructed his disciples to follow the narrow way. He declared that many would be called but few chosen. Until he returned, he said, tares would exist among the wheat. The Faith, therefore, mustn't be judged by those unfaithful to it—by the fanatical, hypocritical, and insincere of the past or present.

Naturally, we don't excuse the excesses of the church. We own up to them and ask for forgiveness, for they are inconsistent with the teachings of our Lord. We know it, and the world knows it. So we readily confess our sins. We can always serve our Lord more fully and completely. But we must also insist that the church isn't comprised of perfect people, just saved people. Some Christians are immature in the Faith, some mature. Even then all have different personalities and aspirations. Some like Peter may begin rough and need refining; others like John may begin timid and need encouraging. The church is the body of Christ, with weaker and stronger, attractive and less attractive parts. One of the beauties of Christianity is precisely that Jesus is an equal opportunity, nondiscriminatory Master. To enter his body, one need only believe in him and receive his everlasting life (John 20:31). Everyone must recognize, too, as Charles Williams aptly put it, that "The history of Christendom is the history of an operation. It is an operation of the Holy Ghost towards Christ, *under the conditions of our humanity . . .*" (italics mine).[4] When looked at from one angle, the church consists of faithful but flawed individuals. When looked at from another, it reveals the purpose of God working itself out in a people.

In fact, had it not been for the advent and advance of Christianity in the West, we would still be barbarians. Indeed, to the extent that the influence of Christianity is diminishing in the West today, we seem to be descending into barbarism again. Indecency and selfishness are increasing; decency and unselfishness, declining.

THREE ARGUMENTS FOR CHRISTIAN ABSOLUTISM

Reason is always an insufficient instrument in matters of faith, for Christianity is, first, revelational and, second, propositional. We can't really convince anyone to believe, but we can try to remove obstacles to belief, as I have been trying to do in this book. In this spirit I shall now offer three rational, though not foolproof, arguments suited to modern men and women. Here I'm using the term *rational* as Christian philosopher J. P. Moreland has used it. "A belief can be rational," he says, "in the sense that it is a rationally *permissible* belief. A belief *P* is permissible in case believing *P* is just as warranted as believing not-*P* or suspending judgment regarding *P* in light of the evidence." A belief can be rational in another, more certain sense too. "A belief *P*," Moreland goes on to say, "can also be rational in the sense that it is a rationally *obligatory* belief. A belief *P* is obligatory if believing *P* has greater warrant than believing not-*P* or suspending judgment regarding *P* in light of the evidence."[5] If we Christians can demonstrate to postmodern people that Christianity is at least rationally *permissible*, then I suspect we can leave it to the Holy Spirit to convince them that belief in Christ is rationally *obligatory* as well.

The Moral or Pragmatic Argument

This argument has some of the defects of pragmatism and utilitarianism. To say that Christianity *works* in the practical sphere may strike one as being as trite as a billboard ad of several years ago that simply said of the car it advertised, "It works." But there is more to the argument than first meets the eye. Once again we are really considering the implications and consequences of certain held and lived presuppositions. Most people today can appreciate this argument, I believe, because they can acknowledge that media moguls, politicians, and educators seem to have a "palpable design" upon us and that each of us needs to be alert to these designs. Speaking of technology, Neil Postman says, every one that arises "is a product of a particular economic and political context and carries with it a program, an agenda, and a philosophy that may or may not be life-enhancing and that therefore requires scrutiny, criticism, and control."[6] As we have found, the same may be said of the mega-ideas that form various worldviews. People need to recognize that they operate daily on such presuppositions far more than they may realize. Then the pragmatic or moral argument acquires new meaning: "The problem is having, and then acting upon, the right world view—the world view which gives men and women the truth of what is."[7] Today we desperately need a truth-bearing, "life-enhancing" worldview.

Thus, from the practical standpoint of morals, we need to examine our presuppositions, not just individually but collectively, then act decisively to reform society. Considering the detrimental effects of the thirteen mega-ideas, we can see that culturally we aren't progressing but retrogressing. The values—actually, the valuelessness—of subjectivism and relativism, naturalism and determinism in all their forms are bankrupting us morally. Doubtless, as certain pundits argue, we could *try* to forge a new pluralistic consensus. But we wouldn't succeed. Pluralism—ethical relativism, multiculturalism, religious syncretism—can offer neither consensus nor synthesis. It can only lead to contradiction and conflict. Representing various groups, pluralists, like all humans, already advance their own competing agendas, often resulting in unnatural divisions among themselves along racial, cultural, religious, and ethical lines.

Perhaps, one may argue, pluralists *will* agree one day on fundamentals, the general "oughts." For example, they may come to agree that "it's always better to respect than disrespect others who are different from oneself." But who will interpret this generalization? How will it be applied? *Ought* I to respect drug dealers? *Ought* I to respect crackheads? What does it mean to "respect" another? Is "respect" agreement or just toleration? Am I ever warranted in expressing disapproval, even censure? The problem with pluralism, which avoids imposing specific "oughts" on others, is that it's so allied to relativism as to make the two identical in effect. Saying that all cultures, lifestyles, or paths are equally valid is just as self-defeating as saying that everything is relative.

But unquestionably, in light of recent trends, we do need a moral consensus to restore our sense of shared community and shore up the ruins of society. But how shall we obtain it in a "pluralistic" society? If we really want unity and order, our best hope lies in the direction of Christianity. Instead of inventing wheels within wheels of ideology, we need to reaffirm the most successful moral consensus in Western history, the Christian one. This plan is indeed sensible and feasible, given the way

a community—that is, a culture—thrives and survives. "The psychological unity of many selves in one community," explains the philosopher Josiah Royce, "is bound up . . . with the consciousness of some
lengthy social process which has occurred. . . . And the wealthier the
memory of a community is, and the vaster the historical processes which
it regards as belonging to its life, the richer . . . is its consciousness that
it is a community, that its members are somehow made one in and
through and with its own life."[8]

Christian culture fulfills these criteria. Its history has been lengthy,
vast, and abundantly memorable. Despite the claims of its cynical
detractors, its accomplishments and contributions in the past 2,000
years have been far more constructive than destructive. Virtues like honesty, decency, diligence, charity, simplicity, fidelity, to be sure, aren't the
exclusive property of Christians, but throughout the West these and
other virtues have always been grounded in the Old and New
Testaments and the life of Christ. Thus, presuppositionally they have
always been distinctively and particularly related to the Christian worldview. A return to normative values can only be effected through a return
to Christianity. Let's not demolish the work of centuries just because in
the church there have always been—and always will be—a few loose
screws in the pews. All in all, a return to Christian virtues will have a
salubrious effect on society.

This appeal to the historical efficacy and continuity of Christian tradition, then, represents a pragmatic and moral argument in favor of
Christianity. By itself, however, the argument probably won't satisfy most
ecumenists and universalists, nor will it justify for many pluralists a return
to a Christian consensus over and above other religious or cultural traditions. It may well only satisfy those people who, disenchanted by
today's moral decadence and unaffiliated with any alternative "spirituality," long for a simpler, more coherent moral frame of reference.
Therefore, in addition to establishing the need for absolute truths, we
must demonstrate that Christianity does in fact embody absolute truth,
"true truth," as Francis Schaeffer used to say. Otherwise, many will still
perceive the call for a return to Christianity as arbitrary and subjective,
a matter of taste or opinion that a few want to impose on others against
their wills. In a relativistic world it will always boil down to "our" will
against "theirs." "Where there are no absolute truths," says Gene

Edward Veith, Jr., "the intellect gives over to the will."[9] Clearly, in the spirit of our Lord, we Christians don't want to willfully *impose* our Faith on others. We want them to accept of their own accord the irresistible appeal of Christian absolutism, as well as the invitation of Christ.

The Historical or Objectivistic Argument

What are the particulars of this formerly acceptable moral consensus? What does Christianity teach about morality and duty—in regard to God, work, relationships, community, and so on? Are the teachings consistent and applicable? What does Christ require of his followers? We can only answer these questions by encountering the person, words, and works of the historical Jesus Christ and by studying Scripture in the right frame of mind. Unreasonably and unfairly, critics are challenging the Faith on two battlefronts today. One is the historicity and nature of Jesus Christ; the other, the reliability and authority of Scripture. Christians must therefore be prepared to address these two points of tension. As Martin Luther put it, "If I profess with the loudest voice and clearest exposition every portion of the truth of God except precisely that little point which the world . . . [is] at that moment attacking, I am not confessing Christ, however boldly I may be professing Christ. Where the battle rages, there the loyalty of the soldier is proved." It's "mere flight and disgrace if he flinches at this point."[10]

Historically, Jesus Christ really existed as he is depicted in the New Testament. A few sources external to the Bible do refer to Jesus. Josephus, a Jewish historian of the first century, refers to Jesus twice in his *Jewish Antiquities*. Of Jesus, he says, "At this time there appeared Jesus, a wise man. . . . For he was a doer of amazing deeds, a teacher of persons who receive truth with pleasure," many of whom were Jews and Greeks. "And when Pilate condemned him to the cross . . . those who loved him from the first did not cease to do so." When speaking of Ananus, a high priest, Josephus mentions in passing the unjust stoning of James, "the brother of Jesus."[11] Tacitus (ca. A.D. 60-ca. 120), the Roman historian, and Pliny the Younger (A.D. 62-ca. 113), the Roman statesman, both refer to "Christus" or "Christ" and to the persecutions of early Christians. Pliny even refers to the worship practices of Christians: "on an appointed day they had been accustomed to meet before daybreak, and to recite a hymn antiphonally to Christ, as to a god, and to bind themselves by an oath, not to commit any sins."[12]

But it's to the biblical accounts of Jesus that we must turn if we want to understand his personality, words, and works aright. Luke perhaps best understood the historical method. From the start he tells us that because many had tried to recount the testimony of eyewitnesses, he also, having "carefully investigated everything from the beginning," would "write an orderly account" so that the reader "may know the certainty" of everything he has been taught (Luke 1:1-4). But the other Gospel writers were no less fastidious in recording details. Matthew not only records the Beatitudes but vividly describes Jesus' reactions. Jesus was "astonished" at the faith of a centurion (Matt. 8:10); he placed his hands on children and touched the eyes of blind men. And "all who touched him were healed" (14:36). In Mark, claiming the prerogative of God, Jesus forgave the sins of a paralytic after he was moved by the faith of those who lowered the man through a hole in a roof. Then some teachers of the law sitting nearby accused Jesus of blasphemy (Mark 2:6-7), for they realized that he was making himself equal with God: "Who can forgive sins but God alone?"

In John, Jesus declares his divinity in many settings—for example, "I and the Father are one" (10:30)—while still revealing his humanity at every turn, for example, sitting down at a well because he was "tired . . . from the journey" (4:6), there taking time to speak to a simple Samaritan woman. In John, too, the shortest, most poignant verse in the New Testament appears: "Jesus wept" (11:35). C. S. Lewis, the great Cambridge Medieval and Renaissance scholar, said that, having studied myths all his career, he was certain that the Gospels record history not myth.[13]

Despite the efforts of progressive Christians, with their anti-supernatural biases, to minimize the grandeur of Scripture, an abundance of evidence exists confirming the reliability of the records. Progressives have tried to demythologize and relativize Scripture. Many not only deny the reality of the historical Jesus Christ but also dismiss all the signs and miracles in the New Testament, including the virgin birth and the Resurrection, claiming that overzealous Christians of the second century added such details later. The Jesus Seminar, as we saw in the last chapter, has gone so far as to reinvent Jesus along these new lines. Yet archaeological and bibliographical evidence more and more supports an early dating of the New Testament, placing the composition of it between A.D. 50 and 75 but no later than A.D. 80,[14] with Paul's works written between A.D. 50 and 57 and the epistle of James possibly as early as the late 40s.[15] Scholars, moreover, have confirmed numerous historical details mentioned in the scriptural records. Through digs, they have found locations in the temple (destroyed by the Romans in A.D. 70) that are described in detail in the Gospels. They have also mostly confirmed the chronology of Acts, especially as it relates to the trials and journeys of Paul.[16]

True, scholars don't have access to extant manuscripts from the first century, but they do possess about 32,000 New Testament citations from the writings of the early Church Fathers (ca. A.D. 95-325) and numerous reliable manuscripts and fragments of the Gospels. The citations in the writings of the early Church Fathers are so numerous that, when compiled, they virtually reconstruct the entire New Testament.[17] The earliest extant manuscript is the Rylands Papyrus 457, a fragment of the Gospel of John (ca. 130). Scholars also possess, dated from the second century on, over 20,000 manuscripts in Greek, Syriac, Coptic, and Latin (North African and European).[18] Indeed, this evidence is so abundant that the evidence we possess for other ancient texts pales beside it. "There is far more textual support for the text of Holy Scripture," says Gleason L. Archer, "than there is for any other book handed down to us from ancient times, whether the works of Homer, the Attic tragedians, Plato, Cicero, or Caesar."[19] As for variants in the texts, say Geisler and Nix, only about one eighth have any weight, with most amounting to "mechanical matters such as spelling or style." Of all the variants, "only about one-sixtieth rise above 'trivialities,' or can in any sense be called 'substantial variations.' Mathematically this would compute to a text that is 98.33 percent pure."[20] With so many available manuscripts of the New Testament, biblical scholars can compare texts and collate data until they find the most accurate, authoritative reading possible. It would seem therefore that the same God who inspired the Bible has also ensured its accurate transmission.

The Bible itself bears witness to its divine origin, reliability, and authority. In the Old Testament alone, Harold Lindsell points out, "The writers . . . professed more than 2,000 times that the words they wrote were given them directly from God."[21] Jesus and his apostles taught that Scripture is to be regarded as not only reliable but authoritative. Jesus referred to incidents from the Old Testament as real events: the creation of man and woman (Matt. 19:4-5), the Flood (Luke 17:26-27), the snake in the desert (John 3:14), David as an author of the Psalms (Mark 12:36), and so on. He referred to Moses as the giver of the Law (Matt. 19:8; Mark 10:5; Luke 20:37; John 5:46). He also said that Scripture (here, primarily the Old Testament) can't be broken (John 10:35) and must be fulfilled in every detail (Matt. 5:18), and he cited Scripture, as God's Word, in his arguments against the Pharisees (Mark 7:6-13; Luke 16:29-31).[22]

Most importantly, Jesus claimed to be speaking the words of God. After saying that he is "from above," he says of his relationship with God, "what I have heard from him I tell the world" (John 8:23, 26). And a few lines later he says, "When you have lifted up the Son of Man, then you will know who I am and that I do nothing on my own but speak just what the Father has taught me. The one who sent me is with me; he has not left me alone, for I always do what pleases him" (John 8:28-29.; see also 6:63; Matt. 24:35).

Among the apostles, Paul wrote of Scripture, "All Scripture is God-breathed and is useful for teaching, rebuking, correcting and training in righteousness" (2 Tim. 3:16). And Peter wrote, "prophecy never had its origin in the will of man, but men spoke from God as they were carried along by the Holy Spirit" (2 Pet. 1:21), and he referred to the epistles of Paul as Scripture (2 Pet. 3:16).

Scripture, having its origin in God, must therefore always be taken seriously. Augustine rightly observed, "It seems to me that the most disastrous consequence must follow upon our believing that anything false is found in the sacred books," for "if you once admit into such a high sanctuary of authority one false statement . . . there will not be left a single statement of those books which . . . if appearing to anyone difficult in practice or hard to believe, may not by the same fatal rule be explained away."[23] Until the Enlightenment, this high view of Scripture was universally held by the church, for the implications of Augustine's words have always been plain to anyone with common sense. "One cannot logically claim to be a Christian," argue two contemporary scholars, "and, at the same time, deny the authority of the Bible." Then they add just as forcefully a page later, "We believe that consistent Christianity requires us to affirm the inerrancy of the Scripture."[24] To affirm less is to be inconsistent or, worse, heretical.

Finally, despite the ad hominem attacks of progressives, orthodox Christians aren't daft bibliolaters, Bible-thumpers, or "wooden-headed literalists." We don't interpret Scripture willy-nilly, as taste or emotion dictates (although we may disagree among ourselves on fine points). Instead we adhere to the principles of a sound interpretative practice, called hermeneutics, just as scholars and thoughtful readers have always attempted to do. Our methodology isn't so different from that recommended by E. D. Hirsch, Jr., who asks fellow literary critics to consider "authorial intent." Says Hirsch, "If the meaning of text is not to be the author's, then no interpretation can possibly correspond to the meaning of the text."[25] "To interpret," claims Walter C. Kaiser, "we must in every case reproduce the sense the Scriptural writer intended for his words."[26]

In understanding scriptural truth and submitting to the authority of Scripture, then, we practice *exegesis* rather than *eisegesis*. We search for "what the text means" rather than "what I *feel* the text means." In practice, we try to follow definable steps when interpreting Scripture. We analyze the historical-cultural milieu in which the writer wrote, consider the context of a passage in relation to the rest of the work in which it's found (and all the author's other works), perform an analysis of words and sentences (ideally in the original language), consider the theological understanding of the original audience, analyze the literary form or method used in a passage, and compare our interpretation with what other qualified interpreters have said. Last, we *apply*—as surely and eventually we must—the text in question to ourselves in our time and culture.[27]

Jesus, though divine, once lived as a historical person. As we have seen, the only source of what we can know about Jesus, the Bible, is reliable and intelligible. The historical or objectivistic argument simply asks that a person take the next logical step in belief, accepting that he can also count on the words of Jesus and his apostles as recorded in the Bible to be divinely inspired and authoritative. In the face of such abundant evidence, a person needn't trust his own faltering lights. If he really wants to know Jesus Christ and the will of God, he need only embrace the Word of God as his sole *authority* in all matters of faith and practice. "Don't be scared by the word authority," said C. S. Lewis sensitively and reassuringly. "Believing things on authority only means believing them because you have been told them by someone you think trustworthy. Ninety-nine percent of the things you believe are believed on authority."[28] The Bible, as a careful historical and objective examination amply proves, is indeed trustworthy.

The Relational or Dualistic Argument

In one sense the universe, as well as the world we occupy, is comprised exclusively of relationships. Slowly, imperceptibly constellations rotate above us. Within reach—indeed within our very cells—electrons and protons whirl around the nuclei of atoms. In space-time, threads of communication spider the globe, cars jockey on freeways but find their destinations, a couple snuggles on a park bench, and a father bats a balloon with his toddler. Even within the mind, thoughts race, colliding, causing, effecting, merging, separating, extending, thousands of associations appearing and disappearing each day. In all of life, we search for order and meaning. We are liars if we don't.

Even Einstein sought a Unified Field Theory, one that would explain the disparate phenomena of the universe. At best he could only arrive at a unifying pantheism: "a belief bound up with deep feeling, in a superior mind that reveals itself in the world of experience. . . ."[29] Orthodox Christians also believe that God reveals himself "in the world of experience," but in a dualistic, not a pantheistic sense. Just as objects and people are existent *others*, God is for us the ever-existent *Personal Other*. We reject pantheism because it leads to impersonality—one ends up talking about impersonal force, substance, or abstract love, not the God of Christianity.

In Christianity, therefore, if anything really matters within the space-time-matter nexus, it's relationships. We exist in relationship to nature and objects in general. Therefore, we have awesome environmental and material responsibilities, for we respect all that God has created or permitted us to create. Whatever is good, we are to nurture and preserve. In Genesis, God told our first parents, "Be fruitful and increase in number and fill the water in the seas, and let the birds increase on the earth" (1:22), and "I now give you everything" upon the earth (9:3). More importantly, however, we exist in relation to other humans, starting with our families, according to Augustine's circle of charity, and extending out to the family of man. Christians must honor parents and elders, and they must provide for their families: "If anyone does not provide for his relatives, and especially his immediate family, he has denied the faith and is worse than an unbeliever" (1 Tim. 5:8). We must, following Christ's example, be loyal and true to our friends, even to the extent of laying down our lives for them: "Love each other as I have loved you. Greater love has no one than this, that he lay down his life for his friends" (John 15:12-13). We are to help even strangers, as the story of the Good Samaritan illustrates, and to love our enemies as ourselves, as impossible as such love may at times seem. First and foremost, then, right relationships are a priority for us. The universe we occupy is real, not illusory, as Hindus and Buddhists believe. If it were illusory, our love wouldn't need to extend any farther than the fringes of our meditation cushions.

But right relationship extends beyond nature and man to God. We love God because he first loved us, having created us in his own image so that we could—in the original, pre-Fall sense—commune with him. At the heart of this relationship isn't only adoration or obedience but *communication*. The personal God, who cares about our relationships with creatures and with him, endowed us from the beginning with language. At God's prompting, Adam named the creatures. Prophets spoke on behalf of God. Jesus was the incarnated *Logos*, the Word. The Gospel took the form of words. Within this framework, it's reasonable to conclude "that this personal God who is there," who "made man in His own image as a verbalizer in such a way that he can communicate horizontally to other men on the basis of propositions and languages," can also communicate to men "on the basis of verbalization and propositions."[30] In this way a loving God communicates vertically and veridically to men through objective, unalterable Scriptures.

If God hadn't created an objective and unalterable Scripture, two problems would result in our relationship with him. First, without his *objective* Word, people would rely on general revelation only, God's revelation of himself in nature as cause and designer. Thus they would trust fallen reason, emotion, and intuition alone, all faulty and wayward faculties at best, more prone to pride than humility. They would strive for purity and liberation, as Hindus and Buddhists do, through self-effort alone. Special revelation—the Gospels, for example—would carry little weight. Second, if Christians didn't hold to an *unalterable* canon of inspired Scripture (fixed after the death of the apostles), then anyone could create new scripture, and confusion would ensue. The Book of Mormon exemplifies this problem well. No one has ever found the tablets that Joseph Smith translated, and no one has ever verified any of the history "recorded" therein; yet millions follow the Book of Mormon and even use it to reinterpret the canonical Scripture of orthodox Christianity.

Therefore, God, who has made us verbalizers in his image, relational creatures who love and want to be loved,[31] has provided a way, Scripture, for us to understand him and his will, a way more certain than intellect, intuition, or passion. If he hadn't provided this means of communication, how could we say that he cared *personally* about our relationship with him and his creation? A loving God wouldn't require that we muddle along, fending for ourselves.

Jesus Christ, of course, testifies to the emphasis on relationship most humanly and fully as God's best exemplar and spokesman, as God's very Word. For this reason, Christ's leadership is critical to a Christian. We trust his claims about himself and contemplate his actions as recorded in Scripture and written in our hearts, where he lives as surely as he lives and reigns in heaven. When Jesus asked Peter, "Who do you say I am?" Peter replied, "You are the Christ, the Son of the Living God." Far from rebuking Peter, Jesus declared, "Blessed are you . . . for this was not revealed to you by man, but by my Father in heaven" (Matt. 16:15-17). When during Christ's trial, Caiaphas, the high priest, demanded of Christ, "Tell us if you are the Christ, the Son of God," Jesus didn't hedge his claim. He frankly stated, "Yes, it is as you say" (Matt. 26:63-64), and "I am" (Mark 14:62), designating himself to be the I AM of the Old Testament.

As God and man, he loved needy sinners, healed the sick, railed against hypocrisy and injustice, and bravely, uncomplainingly faced his own crucifixion (on a charge no less flimsy than blasphemy). No better exemplar of the best of humanity and the beauty of relationships has ever existed in the history of the world. Not Buddha (who beat a cowardly retreat from life), not Krishna or Rama (who are both mythical characters at best), not Mohammed (who preferred to wage war rather than die for the sins of others). In relationships, Jesus Christ is the standard and measure of all things for orthodox Christians. As Thomas à Kempis put it, "Whoever desires to understand and take delight in the words of Christ must strive to conform his whole life to him."[32]

Christianity, then, is ultimately relationship-centered—in the Personhood of God and, most especially, in the Person of Jesus Christ. Through Christ, the bridge between God and man, we can approach God. Through Christ, the true vine, we can enjoy the power of God and know his will. Through Christ, *fully* God and *fully* man, we can communicate not only with the Other but with others in community. First, we embrace the community of believers, the body of Christ, the unity of believers for whom Christ himself prayed (John 17:20-26), remembering always that "the perfection of this unity will only be reached so long as the believers keep in touch with their exalted Lord and contemplate the glory which has been His from eternity."[33] Then in compassion, balancing mercy and justice, never compromising the Word of God or denying the sole sonship of our Lord, we can embrace ever larger communities. In every context we can exemplify the peace, hope, and love that others so desperately crave by means of the unity we have in Christ. Others may experience this unity too, if they will join us in following Christ and in reestablishing the Christian traditions and sensibilities that made our culture, until very recently, a *community* with shared presuppositions and a shared history, both a real past and an envisioned future. Perhaps when we have achieved such a unity of community, we will at last be able to pursue successfully what Royce called "the Christian doctrine of life"—"the ideal of the Universal Community."[34]

Thus gripped as individuals by the love of Christ and by "true truth," we will find that God will happily reach into our lives, privately and publicly. The more we love God, the Other, with all our hearts, minds, souls, and strength, and our neighbors as ourselves, the more he will surely bless us with what Rudolf Otto has called "numinous experiences"—the recurrent, "direct apprehension of a personal Being who is holy, good, awesome, separate from [us]," a Being upon whom we can depend for "life and care."[35] The more we depend on the Father, the more he will also surely steer us clear of the rocky shoals of cynicism, loneliness, and selfishness, toward the safe port of abundant life in Christ. Relationships, earthly and spiritual, will then be our greatest delight and highest priority, and the world will always be meaningful to us.

THE CHOICE OF NORMATIVE AUTHORITY

When speaking to the Israelites at Shechem, Joshua laid a choice before the tribes: "But if serving the LORD seems undesirable to you, then choose for yourselves this day whom you will serve . . ." (Josh. 24:15). Then he added two lines later, "But as for me and my household, we will serve the LORD." Everyone faces this choice, both as a life decision and as a daily exercise. If we want to understand and serve God, we must first *choose* the one true God—and accept no substitute. In the Christian context, then, one must choose the leadership of Jesus Christ and the absolutes of Scripture or the leadership and authority of someone else, either oneself, another religion, or an eclectic blend of mega-ideas. As I have been arguing, the right choice—for Western culture and for everyone—is Christianity.

If we consider the claims of Jesus Christ that he is God and the only way, we must see that he demands that we choose him. "I am the way and the truth and the life," he insists. "No one comes to the Father except through me. If you really knew me, you would know my Father as well" (John 14:6-7). In using the terms "no one" and "except," he leaves no alternatives. In fact, he says, "He who is not with me is against me" (Matt. 12:30). If we want to know God, he tells us, we must believe in him: "The work of God is this: to believe in the one he has sent" (John 6:29). Otherwise, we remain lost and condemned: "Whoever believes in [me] is not condemned, but whoever does not believe stands condemned already because he has not believed in the name of God's one and only Son" (John 3:18). Surely, these words can't be taken to be those of simply a New Age "wise man" or "a great moral teacher." As C. S. Lewis points out, such claims, "if not true, are those of a megalomaniac, compared with whom Hitler was the most sane and humble of men." A person who makes such claims, Lewis continues, "is either God or a complete lunatic. . . ."[36] Or as Josh McDowell points out, a person who makes such claims, if not true, is a liar and hypocrite (for he taught others to be honest), a demon (for he told others to trust their eternal fates to him), and a fool (for he was crucified for calling himself God).[37]

Thus, if the claims of Jesus are true, we would have to accept him as the Lord himself, rejecting the notion that he is simply a great moral teacher. Jesus in his time, says Lewis, "produced mainly three effects—

Hatred—Terror—Adoration."[38] We face the same choice today as people did 2,000 years ago in Palestine. Speaking across the ages, Jesus Christ still insists that we choose him.

Either Jesus was a lunatic, a liar, or the Lord himself. We can't wriggle out of this tri-lemma by arguing that the scriptural record of the words and works of Jesus Christ is flawed, for clearly it isn't. Nor can we argue that Jesus Christ was simply a time-bound man of his times, and so reflected the messianic and apocalyptic thinking of his day. If such were true, then Jesus' claims about himself would, once again, be false, and his works would be enigmatic and incongruous. How could a mere human perform miracles? It won't do to say that he was simply an advanced yogi or occultic master who adapted his message to the ignorance of his hearers either. If such were the case, he would again be a liar and deceiver, for he claimed to teach *timeless truth*—"my words will never pass away" (Matt. 24:35)—not relative truth. He said that this truth would set people free. Why would he dumb down his message for the multitudes but stir up the hatred of the scribes and Pharisees against him? This line of thought must lead us away from Scripture and orthodox Christianity toward an idiosyncratic revision of Jesus Christ. Therefore, we would be denying, not choosing, Christ. A *particular* Christ, the Christ of the New Testament, asks us to choose him before we take to universalizing and generalizing his message. There can be no faith in a universal—or "cosmic"—Jesus Christ without faith in the particular Jesus Christ of the Bible.

We face a similar choice in regard to Christian absolutism. We can choose relativism, subjectivism, or naturalism, but we risk the safety and security of future generations as we, helter-skelter, embrace progress and every experiment that strikes our fancy. We can live according to our own lights and let everyone else do the same, but we will have to deal with the inevitable knotty conflicts and contradictions that will ensue at the social level. We can follow an imported religion, foreign to Western thought, but we will have to live, in many respects, at odds with ourselves, our family heritage, and our culture. We can devote ourselves to helping to invent a new consensus, but we will have to resort to conflict with others as we try to impose on them new values, views, and lifestyles. Cultural life will then simply involve a fierce struggle of disparate, desperate wills, a struggle for ascendancy in which victory will go to the mighty. Many will simply fall prey to the might of the media elite, the academicians and their trained cadre of "communications experts," and the moneyed, the corporate giants and wealthy individuals who can manipulate public education and opinion. In the end the mega-ideas will win, and only God knows what will remain of Western—indeed American—culture after the dust settles.

On the other hand, as I have argued, we can return to a Christian consensus, of the kind that prevailed up until forty years ago. Using Holy Scripture as our authority, guided by tradition and reason, we can return to a set of commonly held presuppositions and reduce the amount of wasted dialogue. People will assume that premarital sex is wrong, among teens or adults. Passing out condoms to teens in high school, AIDS or no AIDS, will seem unconscionable. People won't countenance adultery either, and they will frown on divorce, except in those instances permitted by God in Scripture. We can still debate some of the particulars, naturally. For instance, what constitutes abandonment as a permissible reason for divorce? With common assumptions about the undesirability of divorce, legislators, theologians, and everyday citizens will be prepared to grapple with such matters. In this way, stability will return to our culture and democracy. Freedom of choice will remain; dialogue will continue. And people, once biblically literate again, will be able to distinguish right from wrong more readily. It won't just be wrong to slaughter baby seals and whales. It will obviously be wrong for homosexuals to practice their "lifestyle" and receive political support as a mistreated minority. As it was forty years ago, no one will think twice about allowing homosexuals to marry. Nor will anyone question the appropriateness of posting the Ten Commandments on a classroom or courtroom wall.

Christianity (that is, Christians), it's true, hasn't always followed well the instructions of the Lord. Yes, we have had our Richelieus and Rasputins, our Crusades, Inquisitions, and witch-hunts, but all that history is part of the past from which we can learn under the continued tutelage of God. Whether everyone ultimately bends his knee before Christ won't really matter, even though we would like to see everyone do so, as long as the Christian worldview predominates in the West. Christianity stands at the apex of all the moral, social, and religious options because it's the only message that teaches so passionately, through the demonstrable actions of the Savior, that human life matters and that love must be extended to all, ally and enemy alike. Christianity is also at once the most fully human and humane, least elitist and least exclusive of all the religions in the world. It's the only religion that comprehends and appreciates the needs, hopes, and desires of every human being in the world, unyielding in its sense of justice, unstinting in its compassion, uncompromising in its faith, all-embracing in its fellowship.

Christianity is indisputably a moral as well as a spiritual way of life. It's also logically permissible because it answers, if given the chance through study and prayer, the ageless questions man has asked about man, morality, nature, and God. It's tragic that today Christians, having been ghettoized by popular and elitist culture, can't as readily share these answers with a culture that daily slides toward relativism and chaos, toward confusion and pain for millions—most especially children. Yet Christians can't and won't forget these innocent ones, for whom politically correct Pocahontas and Shopper Barbie, equipped with her new Master Card, represent "truth," for whom rap and rock "artists" like "2" Live Crew and Nine Inch Nails as well as TV shows like *Beverly Hills 90210* and *Melrose Place* represent "values."

When will the lion lie down with the lamb or the new heaven and earth appear? No one can say. Nevertheless, we Christians can be certain of one thing. As witnesses and apologists, as parents and citizens, we must ground our lives, moment by moment, in the life of Christ and submit to the unfoldment of his Love within us. Because Christ is our Way, we mustn't wait for the "evolution" of a new man or new culture. Says C. S. Lewis, "it has happened already. In Christ a new kind of man appeared: and the new kind of life that began in Him is to be put in us."[39] And with this Christ-life abiding and growing within us, we mustn't merely wait for progress to run its course, in the meantime retreating from the fray or taking refuge in pietism. Until the Lord returns, it may be up to us—and us alone—to reform the culture and rescue the innocent. The culture—propelled hurly-burly by all its progress without reason—has been hurtling toward a grim, uncertain future for far too long.

APPENDIX

Table 1: The Clash of Worldviews: Anti-Christian Versus Christian

The Secularist, Postmodern View	The Orthodox Christian View
Man makes right, not God	God makes right, not man, for God makes man
Man possesses within him an innate, trustworthy moral sense of good and bad, right and wrong	God endows man with a conscience, but it's imperfect and corruptible—too easily deluded
Man is good by nature in his free, primitive state but corrupted by society	Man is flawed by nature but salvageable by God, in whom he may find goodness and freedom
Happiness—an increase in pleasures and decrease in pains—is the measure and goal of a good life	Love of God, along with conformity to his will, is the measure and goal of a good life
Man too is an animal, having climbed by chance and necessity from paramecium to homo sapiens	Man is neither animal nor angel but is made in God's image, endowed with reason and a soul
Material and economic causes alone produce social change: existence precedes essence	Man proposes: God disposes. The material is a dead letter; the spirit animates and empowers
Only slaves and fools restrain their wills and desires; geniuses heed the call of their passions	Wise men, who love God and his precepts, find happiness in restraining their wills and desires
There is no God, only unconscious, mechanistic forces and causes—faith in God is infantile	"Grown" men know that God, the Creator and Cause of the seen and unseen, really exists
Christianity is crude; even Christ is flawed. Only science can save us	Christianity is simple yet sophisticated; Christ, who is perfectly human and divine, can save us
Life is meaningless apart from man's self-initiated, self-assertive actions	Life is only meaningful in subservience to the grace, love, and Word of God
Free will and responsibility are illusions when considering human thought and practice	Free will and responsibility are problematic but necessary in thought and practice within society
All standards, values, and beliefs are relative to one's nature, circumstances, era, and culture	God teaches propositional, absolute truth and eternally upholds absolute moral standards
A universal, unifying, generic, nonjudgmental love alone can bring peace to the world	The love of Christ, the Savior and Light of the world, can alone bring peace to the world

Table 2: The Three-Century Slide Toward Relativism—and Beyond

1651 to 1859

Five Stages of Development of 13 Mega-Ideas	Some Major Movers and Shakers
Western man declared his autonomy, emancipating himself from tradition and revelation, the objective authority of God	T. Hobbes; G. Leibniz; *philosophes* (D. Diderot, Voltaire, d'Holbach), D. Hume, T. Paine, J.-J. Rousseau and Romantics (J. W. Goethe, Byron), A. Comte, J. Lamarck, I. Kant, G. Hegel, R. W. Emerson, Higher Critics (F. C. Baur, D. Strauss, E. Renan), J. S. Mill and utilitarians

1859 to 1900

Man declared himself to be an evolving, progressing animal, possessed of unlimited potential. From then on, existence was *presumed* to precede essence, and naturalism began to reign supreme among the leading intellectuals	C. Darwin, T. Huxley, E. Haeckel, H. Spencer, J. Tyndall, G. Mendel, G. F. Romanes, K. Marx and F. Engels, W. James, F. W. Nietzsche ("God is dead")

1900 to 1946

Man decided that he didn't need the "dead" God of his fathers any longer, for now he had Science and the Greatest-Happiness Principle to guide him toward a more enlightened future for humankind. Sense-bound reason was now cut loose from God	M. Weber, S. Freud, A. Adler, B. Russell, A. N. Whitehead, C. Jung, J. Huxley, H. Bergson, O. Spengler, L. Wittgenstein, J. Dewey, A. Maslow, F. Pearls (Gestalt)

1947 to 1999

Man has asserted that all truth and moral norms are relative—indeed, meaningless—while an elite few have taken advantage of the situation to promote various progressive agendas. Now intuition has been cut loose from God	Existentialisits (M. Heidegger, J. P. Sartre, A. Camus), A. Huxley, C. Lévi-Strauss, B. F. Skinner, R. Barthes, R. Dawkins, F. Crick, M. Foucault, J. Derrida, T. Kuhn, R. Rorty

2000 to ?

With relativism almost fully in place, the new millennium may well be marked by a kind of New-Age optimism and antirationalism, a postmodern globalism that sees "love"— a generic, sanitized version—as the only answer in a world more and more torn by conflict over beliefs	M. Gandhi (d. 1948), Carl Rogers and some humanistic psychologists, Ram Dass (aka, Gordon Alpert), Eastern gurus, T. Merton, H. Küng, H. Cox, H. Smith, M. Fox, J. Campbell, World Council of Churches, The Jesus Seminar, process theologians

Table 3: Toward a Return to a Christian Moral Consensus in the New Millennium

Category of Life	A Few Timeless Judeo-Christian Principles for Living
Other Peoples and Cultures	Because we are all strangers in the world (Lev 25:23-24; 1 Pe 2:11), we must treat strangers and foreigners respectfully (Ex 22:21; Lev 19:33-34)—and love our enemies (Pr 25:21; Mt 5:44; Ro 12:20-21). God is the Lord—ruler, provider, and judge—of all peoples (Ps 9:8, 24:1, 33:8-10, 110:6; Mal 1:11; Mt 5:45, 12:17-21, 28:18-20; Ro 3:29-30). If we *must* fight evildoers, God fights with and for us (2 Ch 32:8; Ne 4:20; Ps 35:1-6, 92:9; Mal 4:1-3). God, should we forget him, can judge us through the actions of other nations until we repent (Dt 8:19-20; Isa 1:1-31; Mt 11:20-24, 23:37—24:2).
Civic Responsibilities	Seek justice (Isa 1:17). Render justice to the poor, weak, innocent, and oppressed, and don't pervert justice or show partiality to the rich (Ex 23:2-8; Lev 19:15; Dt 16:18-20; Ps 106:3). Obey the laws of God (Dt 5:1-22; Ecc 12:13-14; Eze 18:4-9; Mt 19:18-19) and the governing authorities if you wish to live and prosper (Mt 22:21; Ro 13:1-7; 1 Pe 2:13-17). Pay the laborer his just wage (Jer 22:13-16; Mal 3:5; Lk 10:7; 1 Ti 5:18), and don't withhold good from those who deserve it (Dt 24:14-15; Pr 3:27-28). Seek the peace and prosperity of your city; if it prospers, you prosper (Jer 29:7). As much as it depends on you, live at peace with everyone (Ro 12:18); show kindness to your neighbors (Lk 10:30-37).
Family Obligations	Marry and beget children (Jer 29:6) if you choose and God approves (1 Cor 7:8-9). Wives, be submissive to your husbands and respect them; husbands, be considerate to your wives and love them as you love your own bodies (Eph 5:22-33; Col 3:18-19; 1 Pe 3:1-7). Don't divorce except for the causes of infidelity or, in rare cases, desertion by an unbelieving spouse (Mt 5:32; 1 Co 7:10-16). Raise your children in the fear of the Lord and discipline them firmly and fairly (Pr 13:24, 23:13-14, 29:15-17; Eph 6:1-4; Col 3:20-21); it's a great evil to cause the "little ones," the innocent, to sin (Lk 17:2). Provide for your relatives, most especially your immediate family (1 Ti 5:8). Together give generously, freely, cheerfully to the needy and to the work of God (Mt 6:3-4; 2 Co 9:6-13).

Table 3: Toward a Return to a Christian Moral Consensus in the New Millennium—Continued

Category of Life	A Few Timeless Judeo-Christian Principles for Living
Sexual Morality	God detests prostitution, female and male (Dt 23:17-18; Pr 23:26-27; 1 Co 6:9-10, 15-16). God detests homosexuality (Lev 18:22; Ro 1:26-27; 1 Co 6:9-10). God detests premarital sex (fornication, "immorality" in NIV), adultery, and pornography (Dt 5:18, 22:13-24; Pr 6:23-7:27; 1 Co 6:18-19; Col 3:5-8; 1 Th 4:3-8; Mt 5:27-28, 19:18). God regards the marital union to be inviolable and sacred (Gen 2:24; Mt 19:4-6; 1 Co 6:15-16). Let a married couple enjoy each other (Pr 5:18-19; Ecc 9:9; SS 7:1-13) or refrain only by mutual consent for a while, for the body of each belongs to the other (1 Cor 7:2-5).
Work and Duty	Serve God and the cause of righteousness, not money and security (Ps 37; Mt 6:24, 33; Jn 6:27; Col 3:23-25). Work diligently, skillfully, and honestly (Pr 6:6-11, 10:16, 22:29; Ecc 9:10; Jer 17:10-11; Lk 16:10-12), doing something useful and good (Eph 4:28), never being a burden on anyone if you are capable of working (Ac 20:34-35; 2 Th 3:6-13). Find satisfaction and happiness in the work that you have to do (Ecc 5:18-20). Trust God for all provision and don't worry (Ps 37; Ecc 11:10; Jer 17:5-8; Mt 6:25-34; 1 Pe 5:7). Give thanks to God and praise him in all that you do (Ps 107, 138—139, 145; Isa 12:1-6; Php 4:4-8; 1 Th 5:18; Heb 13:15). Strive to live a quiet life; mind your own business; live above reproach (1 Th 4:11; 1 Pe 2:11-12).
Personal Character	Live a balanced life devoted to truth (Pr 30:7-9; Jn 8:31-32), improving always in wisdom (Pr 2—3; Jas 1:5, 3:13-18) and virtue (Php 2:12-15; 2 Pe 1:5-7). Fear the Lord and delight in his commands (Dt 4:6-22) to secure a stable, fearless heart (Ps 23, 112:1-9). Forgive rather than resent; give rather than receive (Lk 6:37-38); strive to imitate the love of Christ (Jn 14:6, 15:12-13; Ro 12:17-21). Humble yourself under God's mighty hand that he may lift you (Lk 18:14; Jas 4:10; 1 Pe 5:6). Love the Lord your God with all your heart, soul, and mind, and love your neighbor as yourself (Lev 19:18; Dt 6:4-5; Mt 22:37-40). Pray unceasingly (1 Th 5:17).

Figure 1: Two Paths to Postmodern Relativism & Cultural Redesign

**The Humanistic Rationalism
of Autonomous Man
(Atheistic, Deistic, or Pantheistic)**

KEY VIEWS

1. empiricism
2. Darwinism (social, scientific)
3. pragmatism
4. logical positivism
5. Marxism
6. behaviorism

*materialism
(naturalism, scientism)*

*subjectivism
(Romanticism)*

KEY VIEWS

1. transcendentalism
2. utilitarianism
3. vitalism (Bergson)
4. existentialism
5. humanistic psychology
6. neo-paganism

Cultural & Ethical Relativism

pluralism — sexual revolution
deconstructionism — feminism
determinism — multiculturalism
globalism

**The Four M's of the New Millennium:
Money, Might, Magic & Magnetism Make Right**

NOTES

Chapter 1: The "Hydroelectric" Power of Unquestioned Assumptions

1. This information may be readily found in the following source: United States, Department of Commerce, *Statistical Abstract of the United States*, Washington, D.C.: GPO, 1996 and 1970. In light of the long-term influence of the mega-ideas discussed in the remainder of the chapter, it's also interesting to note that birth rates among unwed mothers in general, of all ages, have increased dramatically since 1940. By comparing the data in the 1970 and 1996 volumes, one finds that from 1940 to 1993 such births increased per 1,000 from 89.5 to 357, representing nearly a 400 percent increase in the number of illegitimate births during this fifty-three-year period.

2. Josh McDowell and Bob Hostetler, *Right from Wrong* (Dallas: Word, 1994), 258, 269, 260.

3. Modernism is characterized by "scientific rationalism, humanism, and bias against the past," as Gene Edward Veith, Jr., puts it in *Postmodern Times* (Wheaton, Ill.: Crossway Books, 1994). "Modernists," says Phillip E. Johnson in *Defeating Darwinism* (Downers Grove, Ill.: InterVarsity, 1997), "believe in a universal rationality founded on science. . . ." More and more, scholars today are referring to the present era as being dominated by postmodernism. Harold O. J. Brown in *Sensate Culture* (Dallas: Word, 1996) claims that "Today there is a growing trend to dismiss even the assured facts and scientific evidence of the natural sciences as interpretations that will naturally vary from observer to observer. This gives rise to a skepticism that denies truth exists at all or, if it does exist, that it can be known—or, even if it can be known, that it can be expressed and communicated." Or once again Phillip E. Johnson in *Defeating Darwinism* explains that "postmodernists believe in a multitude of different rationalities and consider science to be only one way of interpreting the world. In other words, modernists are rationalistic; postmodernists are relativists." We shall deal with the former group in the earlier chapters of this book, the latter in the later chapters.

4. I owe a debt of gratitude for this insight to Mortimer Adler, who in his book *Ten Philosophical Mistakes* (New York: Simon & Schuster, 1985) begins his unveiling and refuting of the ten errors with Thomas Hobbes, John Locke, and the British empiricists.

5. Again according to the *Statistical Abstract of the United States* (1996), the suicide rate among teens, as shocking as it seems, has risen by more than 200 percent in the last ten years alone. (Consider by how much it has probably risen since 1940!)

6. Adler, *Ten Philosophical Mistakes*, 25.

7. C. S. Lewis, "Christian Apologetics," *God in the Dock: Essays on Theology and Ethics*, ed. Walter Hooper (Grand Rapids: Eerdmans, 1970), 92-93.

Chapter 2: "Man Makes Right, Not God"

1. William H. Marnell, *Man-Made Morals: Four Philosophies That Shaped America* (Garden City, N.Y.: Doubleday, 1966), 9.

2. From "Biographical Note" to Thomas Hobbes, *Leviathan, Or, Matter, Form, and Power of a Commonwealth Ecclesiastical and Civil*, ed. Nelle Fuller, in *The Great*

Books of the Western World, Vol. 23 (Chicago: Encyclopedia Britannica, 1952), 41-42.

3. Bertrand Russell, *A History of Western Philosophy* (New York: Simon & Schuster, 1945), 547.

4. Hobbes, *Leviathan, Great Books of the Western World*, Vol. 23, 82.

5. Ibid., 49, 47.

6. Ibid., 59-60.

7. Ibid., 61.

8. Ibid., 76, 96.

9. Ibid., 79.

10. Russell, *A History*, 549.

11. Hobbes, *Leviathan*, 86-87, 99.

12. Ibid., 99.

13. Ibid., 61-62, 56, 56.

14. Ibid., 96.

15. J. P. Moreland, *Scaling the Secular City: A Defense of Christianity* (Grand Rapids, Mich.: Baker, 1987), 244.

16. Hobbes, *Leviathan*, 65.

17. Ibid., 61-62.

18. Ibid., 245.

19. Ibid., 193, 66, 199.

20. Ibid., 246.

21. Russell, *A History*, 557.

22. Mortimer J. Adler, *Adler's Philosophical Dictionary: 125 Key Terms for the Philosopher's Lexicon* (New York: Touchstone, 1996), 151-152.

23. Francis Bacon, *Novum Organum*, ed. Edwin A. Burtt, *The English Philosophers from Bacon to Mill* (New York: The Modern Library, 1967), 28.

24. See the *Statistical Abstract of the United States 1994*, 134th ed., U.S. Department of Commerce, 189. From 1971 to 1991, even with an increase in college student population of a quarter of a million, majors in foreign languages and letters dropped significantly, while majors in business and management, computer and information sciences, engineering, and health science rose significantly (by 100 percent in business and management, by nearly 1,000 percent in computer and information sciences). One must admit, however, that professors in the humanities have played a large part in scaring students away from their discipline, as Roger Kimball has pointed out in his book *Tenured Radicals: How Politics Has Corrupted Higher Education* (1990).

25. Hobbes, *Leviathan*, 162.

26. In the twentieth century the empiricism of Hobbes appears as logical positivism. A. J. Ayer, former Wykeham Professor of Logic at the University of Oxford, argues, as Hobbes did, that theological statements are meaningless in *Language, Truth and Logic* (New York: Dover, 1946), 114-120. In *Ten Philosophical Mistakes* (New York: Touchstone, 1985), 119-120, Adler cites a passage from Ayer to the same effect:

> If a sentence makes no statement at all, there is obviously no sense in asking whether what it says is either true or false. And as we have seen, sentences which simply express moral judgments do not say anything. They

are purely expressions of feeling and as such do not come under the category of truth and falsehood. They are unverifiable for the same reasons that a cry of pain or a word of command is unverifiable—because they do not express genuine propositions.

Today this philosophical position with regard to moral statements is called noncognitive ethics.

27. William Barrett, *Death of the Soul from Descartes to the Computer* (Garden City, N.Y.: Doubleday, 1986), 75.

28. Saul K. Padover, ed., *The Complete Jefferson*, Query XVII (New York: Tudor, 1943), 677, cited in a June 1996 letter written by Dr. James Dobson of Focus on the Family.

29. Thomas Jefferson letter to John Adams, April 11, 1823, as quoted by E. S. Gauslad, "Religion," in Merril D. Peterson, ed., *Thomas Jefferson: A Reference Biography* (New York: Charles Scribner's Sons, 1986), 287.

30. George Barna, *The Index of Leading Spiritual Indicators: Trends in Morality, Beliefs, Lifestyles, Religious and Spiritual Thought, Behavior, and Church Involvement* (Dallas: Word, 1996), 18, 55, 33, 36.

31. James I. Packer, "God: From the Fathers to the Moderns," Robin Keeley, ed., *Exploring the Christian Faith* (Nashville: Thomas Nelson, 1996), 100.

32. Adler, *Ten Philosophical Mistakes*. See prologue and chapters 1-3 in particular.

33. Will and Ariel Durant, *The Lessons of History* (New York: Simon & Schuster, 1968), 93.

Chapter 3: "Every Man Possesses an Innate Moral Sense"

1. Will and Ariel Durant, *The Age of Voltaire*, Vol. IX of *The Story of Civilization* (New York: Simon & Schuster, 1965), 159.

2. Bertrand Russell, *A History of Western Philosophy* (New York: Simon & Schuster, 1945), 546.

3. Ibid., 659.

4. Durants, *The Age of Voltaire*, Vol. IX of *The Story of Civilization*, 160.

5. J. P. Moreland, *Scaling the Secular City: A Defense of Christianity* (Grand Rapids, Mich.: Baker, 1987), 62-67.

6. Durants, *The Age of Voltaire*, Vol. IX of *The Story of Civilization*, 142.

7. Mortimer Adler, *Ten Philosophical Mistakes* (New York: Simon & Schuster, 1985), 37.

8. David Hume, *A Treatise of Human Nature* (New York: Penguin, 1985), 257.

9. David Hume, *An Enquiry Concerning Human Understanding*, Robert Maynard Hutchins, ed., *Great Books of the Western World*, Vol. 35 (Chicago: Encyclopedia Britannica, 1952), 456.

10. Ibid.

11. Durants, *The Age of Voltaire*, Vol. IX of *The Story of Civilization*, 143.

12. Hume, *An Enquiry*, 483.

13. Ibid., 483-484 (as well as Hume's note).

14. Durants, *The Age of Voltaire*, Vol. IX of *The Story of Civilization*, 143-144.

15. Russell, *A History of Western Philosophy*, 663.

16. Hume, *A Treatise*, 16.

17. Hume, *An Enquiry*, 459.

18. Hume, *A Treatise*, 153.

19. Hume, *An Enquiry*, 305.

20. Russell, *A History of Western Philosophy*, 671.

21. See Adler, *Ten Philosophical Mistakes*, 91-94.

22. Hume, *A Treatise*, 462.

23. Ibid., 520, 509, 510, 520.

24. Ibid., 527.

25. Hume, *An Enquiry*, 486.

26. Hume, *A Treatise*, 521.

27. Ibid., 668-669.

28. *The Encyclopedia of Philosophy*, Vol. IV, ed. Paul Edwards (New York: Macmillan, 1967), 87.

29. Durants, *The Age of Voltaire*, Vol. IX of *The Story of Civilization*, 146, speaking of *A Treatise*, III.iii.6.

30. Hume, *A Treatise*, 318.

31. Ibid., 320, 268.

32. Durants, *The Age of Voltaire*, Vol. IX of *The Story of Civilization*, 160.

33. Mortimer Adler in *Ten Philosophical Mistakes*, 181-183 explains this view and relates his shock as a young man when he first encountered it in Sir Arthur Eddington's Gifford Lectures, *The Nature of the Physical World*.

34. C. S. Lewis, "The Poison of Subjectivism," *The Seeing Eye: And Other Selected Essays from Christian Reflections*, ed. Walter Hooper (New York: Ballantine, 1967), 99-100.

35. Moreland, *Scaling the Secular City*, 194.

36. Hume, *An Enquiry*, 489.

37. Ibid., 497.

38. Ibid., 509.

39. David Hume, *Dialogues Concerning Natural Religion*, in *The English Philosophers from Bacon to Mill*, ed. Edwin A.. Burtt (New York: The Modern Library, 1967), 752-753, 764.

40. Phillip E. Johnson, *Reason in the Balance: The Case Against Naturalism in Science, Law & Education* (Downers Grove, Ill.: InterVarsity, 1995), 198.

41. Russell, *A History of Western Philosophy*, 673.

42. Johnson, *Reason in the Balance*, 40.

43. Durants, *The Age of Voltaire*, Vol. IX of *The Story of Civilization*, 145.

Chapter 4: "Man Is Good by Nature but Corrupted by Society"

1. Allan Bloom, *The Closing of the American Mind* (New York: Simon & Schuster, 1987), 170.

2. Bertrand Russell, *A History of Western Philosophy* (New York: Simon & Schuster, 1945), 684.

3. Will and Ariel Durant, *Rousseau and Revolution*, Vol. X of *The Story of Civilization* (New York: Simon & Schuster, 1967), 1-5, 152-214, 211.

4. Jean-Jacques Rousseau, *Discourse on the Origin and Basis of Inequality Among*

Men, in *The Essential Rousseau,* trans. Lowell Bair (New York: Meridian, 1983), 190.

5. Ibid., 166, 171, 171-172.

6. Ibid., 178, 181, 182.

7. Ibid., 186.

8. Ibid., "The Creed of the Savoyard Priest," 243, 252-253, 255-256, 275.

9. Ibid., 270, 258, 271, 262, 287.

10. Russell, *A History,* 691.

11. "To undo the evil," says Russell, summarizing the thought of Rousseau, "it is only necessary to abandon civilization" (*A History,* 688).

12. Jean-Jacques Rousseau, "Appendix," *On the Origin of Inequality,* in *Great Books of the Western World,* ed. Robert Maynard Hutchins, Vol. 38 (Chicago: Encyclopedia Britannica, 1952), 363.

13. Rousseau, *Discourse on Inequality,* in *The Essential Rousseau,* 114-145, 200.

14. Ibid., 155, 164-165, 199, 200.

15. Ibid., 153.

16. Ibid., 153-154.

17. Robert Wokler, *Rousseau* (Oxford: Oxford University Press, 1995), 44.

18. Rousseau, *Discourse on Inequality,* in *The Essential Rousseau,* 154, 179.

19. As cited in Will and Ariel Durant, *Rousseau and Revolution,* 4.

20. For an interesting trip down memory lane, consult Tom Wolfe's *The Electric Koo-Aid Acid Test,* in which Wolfe chronicles his adventures on the original "magic bus." The cult-like status of this book was largely responsible for much of the 1960s experimentation that followed in the wake of its publication.

21. Wokler, *Rousseau,* 88.

22. Ralph Waldo Emerson, *Selections from Ralph Waldo Emerson: An Organic Anthology,* ed. Stephen E. Whicher (Boston: Houghton Mifflin, 1957), 148-150.

23. Russell, *A History,* 692, 693.

24. Ibid., 694.

25. Ibid., 687.

26. Durants, *Rousseau and Revolution,* 185.

27. Wokler, *Rousseau,* 88.

28. "Glossary," *Exploring the Christian Faith,* ed. Robin Keeley (Nashville: Thomas Nelson, 1996), 342.

Chapter 5: "Happiness Is the Measure and Goal of a Good Life"

1. Bertrand Russell, *A History of Western Philosophy* (New York: Simon & Schuster, 1945), 723.

2. Edwin A. Burtt, ed., *The English Philosophers from Bacon to Mill* (New York: The Modern Library, 1967), 893.

3. Will and Ariel Durant, *The Age of Napoleon,* Vol. XI of *The Story of Civilization,* Vol. XI (New York: Simon & Schuster, 1967), 407.

4. E. D. Hirsch, Jr., Joseph F. Kett, and James Trefil, *The Dictionary of Cultural Literacy* (Boston: Houghton Mifflin, 1988), 109.

5. Will Durant, *The Pleasures of Philosophy: A Survey of Life and Destiny* (New York: Simon & Schuster, 1929), 18.

6. M. H. Abrams, ed., *The Norton Anthology of English Literature*, Vol. 2 (New York: W. W. Norton, 1968), 733-734.

7. John Stuart Mill, *Utilitarianism*, in *The English Philosophers from Bacon to Mill*, ed. Edwin A. Burtt (New York: The Modern Library, 1967), 897.

8. David Hume, *A Treatise of Human Nature* (New York: Penguin, 1985), 521.

9. Russell, *A History*, 775.

10. John Gay, "Dissertation Concerning the Fundamental Principle of Virtue or Morality," *The English Philosophers from Bacon to Mill*, ed. Edwin A. Burtt (New York: The Modern Library, 1967), 771, 777, 779, 785.

11. Jeremy Bentham, "Introduction to the Principles of Morals and Legislation," *The English Philosophers from Bacon to Mill*, ed. Edwin A. Burtt (New York: The Modern Library, 1967), 791.

12. Russell, *A History*, 774-775.

13. Bentham, "Introduction to the Principles of Morals and Legislation," 805.

14. Ibid., 793.

15. Russell, *A History*, 723.

16. Durants, *The Age of Napoleon* , Vol. XI, 405.

17. Bentham, "Introduction to the Principles of Morals and Legislation," 798.

18. Ibid., 799.

19. Mill, *Utilitarianism*, 900, 901, 903-904.

20. Ibid., 903, 912, 926.

21. John Stuart Mill, *On Liberty*, in *The English Philosophers from Bacon to Mill*, ed. Edwin A. Burtt (New York: The Modern Library, 1967), 956.

22. Ibid., 998, 1004.

23. Ibid., 988.

24. See C. S. Lewis's essay "We Have No 'Right to Happiness'" for an intelligent discussion of this idea in *God in the Dock*, ed. Walter Hooper (Grand Rapids, Mich.: Eerdmans, 1970), 317-322.

25. Mortimer Adler, *Ten Philosophical Mistakes* (New York: Macmillan, 1985), 133, 115.

26. Russell, *A History*, 900.

27. Ibid., 778.

28. Mill, *Utilitarianism*, 904.

29. Ibid., 918.

30. Mill, *On Liberty*, 1000-1001.

31. Anne Moir and David Jessel, *Brain Sex: The Real Difference Between Men and Women* (New York: Dell, 1991).

32. Christopher Lasch, *The Revolt of the Elites and the Betrayal of Democracy* (New York: Norton, 1995), 176, 5, 28-29.

33. Adler, *Ten Philosophical Mistakes*, 176.

Chapter 6: "Man, Too, Is an Animal"

1. Bertrand Russell, *A History of Western Philosophy* (New York: Simon & Schuster, 1945), 725.

2. Michael Denton, *Evolution: A Theory in Crisis* (Bethesda, Md.: Adler and Adler, 1986), 37.

3. Charles Darwin, *The Origin of Species by Means of Natural Selection* and *The Descent of Man and Selection in Relation to Sex*, in *The Great Books of the Western World*, ed. Robert Maynard Hutchins, Vol. 49 (Chicago: Encyclopedia Britannica, 1952), 7. All quotations of Darwin will be drawn from this volume, unless otherwise noted.

4. Darwin, *The Origin*, 232.

5. Darwin, *The Descent*, 590.

6. As cited in Denton, *Evolution: A Theory in Crisis*, 54-55.

7. See *The Origin*, 239. Notice how Darwin tries to explain why his views shouldn't disturb the religious sentiments of anyone by citing the words of "A celebrated author and divine" who had written to him. To this day, using the words of a liberal theologian to deny that there is any contradiction between Christianity and evolutionary theory is a common defensive tactic used by evolutionists.

8. See Phillip Johnson's eye-opening analysis of the movie based on the Scopes Trial, *Inherit the Wind* (1960), in *Defeating Darwinism by Opening Minds* (Downers Grove, Ill.: InterVarsity, 1997), Chaps. 2 and 7.

9. Alan Hayward, *Creation and Evolution: Rethinking the Evidence from Science and the Bible* (Minneapolis: Bethany House, 1995), 13-53.

10. See Phillip E. Johnson, *Darwin on Trial* (1991), *Reason in the Balance* (1995), and *Defeating Darwinism* (1997); Alan Hayward, *Creation and Evolution* (1995); Del Ratzsch, *The Battle Over Beginnings* (1996); Michael Behe, *Darwin's Black Box: The Biochemical Challenge to Evolution* (1996).

11. Phillip E. Johnson, *Defeating Darwinism by Opening Minds*, 113.

12. Darwin, *The Origin*, 243.

13. Denton, *Evolution: A Theory*, 44.

14. Ibid., 44.

15. Darwin, *The Origin*, 40, 65, 78-79.

16. Ibid., 63.

17. Ibid., 96.

18. Ibid., 233.

19. See Chapter 5 in Johnson's *Defeating Darwinsim by Opening Minds*; J. P. Moreland, *Scaling the Secular City: A Defense of Christianity* (Grand Rapids, Mich.: Baker, 1987), 70-75; Chapters 10-13 in Denton's *Evolution: A Theory in Crisis*.

20. Darwin, *The Origin*, 52.

21. Ibid., 92.

22. Phillip E. Johnson, *Darwin on Trial*, 2nd ed. (Downers Grove, Ill.: InterVarsity, 1993), 32-33.

23. Darwin, *The Origin*, 152.

24. Ibid., 232. The language in the 1872 edition is even stronger than that in the 1859 edition. See Denton, *Evolution: A Theory*, 58: The deficient record "is probably the gravest and most obvious of all the many objections which may be urged against my views."

25. Darwin, *The Origin*, 162.

26. Ibid., 164.

27. Denton, *Evolution: A Theory*, 56.

28. Ibid., 189.

29. Darwin, *The Descent*, 590-591.

30. Darwin, *The Origin*, 241.

31. Darwin, *The Descent*, 597.

32. Denton, *Evolution: A Theory*, 70.

33. Alvin Toffler, *Powershift* (New York: Bantam, 1990), 389.

34. Will Durant, *The Pleasures of Philosophy* (New York: Simon & Schuster, 1953), 90-91.

35. Darwin, *The Descent of Man*, 592-593.

36. Russell, *A History*, 780-781.

37. Darwin, *The Descent of Man*, 596.

38. Ibid., 562, 566, 596-597.

39. Ibid., 592.

40. Harold O. J. Brown, *The Sensate Culture: Western Civilization Between Chaos and Transformation* (Dallas: Word, 1996), 80, 84, 97.

41. Johnson, *Defeating Darwinism*, 104.

42. Brown, *The Sensate Culture*, 171.

43. Allan Bloom, *The Closing of the American Mind* (New York: Simon & Schuster, 1987), 205.

44. Brown; also see footnote, 174.

45. James H. Jones, "Annals of Sexology: DR. YES," *The New Yorker*, August 25 and September 1, 1997, 98-113, 100, 107.

46. As cited in Carl Cohen, "The Case for the Use of Animals in Biomedical Research," eds. Sylvan Barnet and Hugo Bedau, *Current Issues and Enduring Questions* (New York: St. Martin's, 1996), 251.

47. In ibid., Peter Singer, "Animal Liberation," 244.

Chapter 7: "Material and Economic Causes Alone Produce Social Change"

1. "Blood Red," *Heterodoxy*, http://www.cspc.org/bloodred.htm, December 15, 1997.

2. Karl Marx, "Introduction" to *A Contribution to the Critique of Hegel's Philosophy of Right* (1844), http://english-www.hss.cmu.edu/marx/1844-intro.hegel.txt, January 1, 1998, 1.

3. Will and Ariel Durant, *The Age of Napoleon,* Vol. XI of *The Story of Civilization* (New York: Simon & Schuster, 1975), 657-658.

4. Karl Marx, *Capital,* in *Great Books of the Western World*, ed. Robert Maynard Hutchins (Chicago: Encyclopedia Britannica, 1952), 11.

5. Ibid., 35.

6. Karl Marx and Friedrich Engels, *Manifesto of the Communist Party,* in *Great Books of the Western World*, ed. Robert Maynard Hutchins (Chicago: Encyclopedia Britannica, 1952), 428.

7. James Q. Wilson, *The Moral Sense* (New York: Simon & Schuster, 1993), 3.

8. Bertrand Russell, *A History of Western Philosophy* (New York: Simon & Schuster, 1945), 784-785.

9. Marx and Engels, *Manifesto*, 419.

10. Marx, *Capital*, 128. See also 150, and note how Marx responds to J. S. Mill's view of machinery on 180-181.

11. Ibid., 378.

12. Marx and Engels, *Manifesto*, 434.

13. Ibid., 416.

14. Ibid., 420.

15. Durants, *The Age of Napoleon*, 649.

16. Marx and Engels, *Manifesto*, 428.

17. Ibid., 428.

18. Karl Marx, "Marx's Letter to Ruge," September 1843, http://english-www.hss.cmu.edu/marx/1843-. . .arnold.ruge/1843.09-ruthless,critique.txt, January 1, 1998.

19. For penetrating analyses of this politically correct bent, consult Allan Bloom, *The Closing of the American Mind* (1987); Dinesh D'Souza, *An Illiberal Education* (1991); Gene Edward Veith, Jr., *Postmodern Times: A Christian Guide to Contemporary Thought and Culture* (1994); and David Thibodaux, *Beyond Political Correctness* (1994).

20. Richard Abcarian and Marvin Klotz, eds., *Literature: The Human Experience, Shorter Sixth Edition with Essays* (New York: St. Martin's, 1996), 925.

21. For more details, see "Demystifying Multiculturalism" by Linda Chavez, director of the Center for the New American Community and John M. Olin, Fellow at the Manhattan Institute, *National Review*, February 21, 1994.

22. Gene Edward Veith, Jr., *Postmodern Times: A Christian Guide to Contemporary Thought and Culture* (Wheaton, Ill.: Crossway Books, 1994), 148-149.

23. Harold O. J. Brown, *The Sensate Culture: Western Civilization Between Chaos and Transformation* (Dallas: Word, 1996), 146.

24. Christopher Lasch, *The Revolt of the Elites and the Betrayal of Democracy* (New York: W. W. Norton, 1995), 17.

25. Aristotle, *On Sophistical Refutations,* in *Great Books of the Western World,* ed. Robert Maynard Hutchins, Vol. 8 (Chicago: Encyclopedia Britannica, 1952), 228.

26. Aristotle, *Logic (Organon),* in *Great Books of the Western World,* ed. Robert Maynard Hutchins, Vol. 8 (Chicago: Encyclopedia Britannica, 1952), 25.

27. Francis A. Schaeffer, *The God Who Is There* in *The Francis A. Schaeffer Trilogy* (Wheaton, Ill.: Crossway Books, 1990), 6.

28. Ibid., 8.

29. Allan Bloom, *The Closing of the American Mind* (New York: Simon & Schuster, 1987), 209.

Chapter 8: "Only Slaves and Fools Restrain Their Wills and Desires"

1. Friedrich Nietzsche, *On the Genealogy of Morals,* trans. with an introduction by Douglas Smith (New York: Oxford University Press, 1996), 16, 20-21, 19, 36, 75-76.

2. Allan Bloom, *The Closing of the American Mind* (New York: Simon & Schuster, 1987), 206.

3. Ibid., 206.

4. Nietzsche, *On the Genealogy of Morals*, 41.

5. Ibid., 27.

6. Friedrich Nietzsche, *Thus Spoke Zarathustra*, trans. with an introduction by R. J. Hollingdale (New York: Penguin, 1969), 41.

7. Ibid., 110.

8. Ibid., 190-191.

9. Ibid., 14.

10. Bertrand Russell, *A History of Western Philosophy* (New York: Simon & Schuster, 1945), 765.

11. Will Durant, *The Pleasures of Philosophy* (New York: Simon & Schuster, 1929), 312.

12. Bloom, *The Closing of the American Mind*, 196.

13. Nietzsche, *Zarathustra*, 61.

14. Nietzsche, *Genealogy*, 19-21.

15. Ibid., 7.

16. Ibid., 79.

17. Ibid., 135.

18. Nietzsche, *Zarathustra*, 115.

19. Nietzsche, *Genealogy*, 20.

20. Nietzsche, *Zarathustra*, 116-117.

21. Ibid., 299.

22. For further evidence of such sentiments, see also Nietzsche's *The Antichrist* (1894).

23. Nietzsche, *Genealogy*, 134.

24. Nietzsche, *Zarathustra*, 237-238.

25. Durant, *The Story of Philosophy* (New York: Simon & Schuster, 1926), 315.

26. Nietzsche, *Genealogy*, 26.

27. Ibid., 136. Consult the entire "First Essay."

28. Douglas Smith, introduction to *Genealogy*, xv.

29. Nietzsche, *Genealogy*, 33.

30. Smith, introduction to *Genealogy*, viii.

31. Nietzsche, *Zarathustra*, 214.

32. Ibid., 138.

33. Smith, introduction to *Genealogy*, xiii.

34. Nietzsche, *Genealogy*, 41.

35. Nietzsche, *Zarathustra*, 215.

36. Ibid., 296-299, 51, 219, 222, 51, 230.

37. Russell, *A History of Western Philosophy*, 761.

38. Nietzsche, *Zarathustra*, 46, 85.

38. Nietzsche, *Genealogy*, 75-76.

40. Nietzsche, *Zarathustra*, 74, 138, 229, 299, 216, 109.

41. Friedrich Nietzsche, "On the Prejudices of Philosophers," *Beyond Good and Evil*, http://www.cwu.edu/-millerj/nietzsche/bge1.html, 2.

42. Friedrich Nietzsche, "The Free Spirit," *Beyond Good and Evil*, http://www.cwu.edu/-millerj/nietzsche/bge2.html, 1.

43. Smith, introduction to *Genealogy*, xxii.

44. Durant, *The Pleasures of Philosophy*, 329.

45. Ibid., 301-302.

46. Allan Bloom, *The Closing of the American Mind*, 79.

47. Joe Szimhart, "Snowboarding to Nirvana: Another Occult *New York Times* Bestseller, *SCP Newsletter*, Vol. 22:1 (Summer 1997), 1, 4-7.

48. Harold O. J. Brown, *The Sensate Culture: Western Civilization Between Chaos and Transformation* (Dallas: Word, 1996), 155.

49. Nietzsche, *Thus Spoke Zarathustra*, 91-93.

50. Christopher Lasch, *The Culture of Narcissism* (New York: W. W. Norton, 1979), 64-65.

51. Smith, introduction to *Genealogy*, xxviii.

52. Gene Edward Veith, Jr., *Postmodern Times: A Christian Guide to Contemporary Thought and Culture* (Wheaton, Ill.: Crossway Books, 1994), 54.

53. Ibid., 210.

54. Francis A. Schaeffer, *The God Who Is There*, in *The Francis A. Schaeffer Trilogy* (Wheaton, Ill.: Crossway Books, 1990), 61.

Chapter 9: "There Is No God, Only Unconscious, Mechanistic Causation"

1. Allan Bloom, *The Closing of the American Mind* (New York: Simon & Schuster, 1987), 136.

2. *The Freud/Jung Letters: The Correspondence Between Sigmund Freud and Carl Jung*, ed. W. McGuire (Princeton, N.J.: Princeton University Press, 1974), 534-535.

3. Sigmund Freud, *Why War,* in *The Standard Edition*, ed. James Strachey, Vol. XXII (London: Hogarth Press), 211.

4. Sigmund Freud, *The Origin and Development of Psycho-Analysis*, in *Great Books of the Western World*, ed. Robert Maynard Hutchins, Vol. 54 (Chicago: Encyclopedia Britannica, 1952), 13. All quotations from the works of Freud are drawn from this volume, unless otherwise noted.

5. Ibid., 19.

6. Freud, *Civilization and Its Discontents*, 772.

7. Freud, *Inhibitions, Symptoms, and Anxiety* (1926), 739, and *New Introductory Lectures on Psycho-Analysis* (1932), 840.

8. Freud, *The Origin and Development of Psycho-Analysis*, 14.

9. Freud, *The Ego and the Id*, 705-706.

10. Freud, *The Origin and Development of Psycho-Analysis*, 13

11. Freud, *Civilization and Its Discontents*, 791, 776, 791, 785n.

12. Freud, 790, 792-796.

13. Freud, *The Origin and Development of Pyscho-Analysis*, 20.

14. Freud, *Civilization and Its Discontents*, 784.

15. Freud, *The Ego and the Id*, 714.

16. Freud, *Civilization and Its Discontents*, 800.

17. Freud, *The Origin and Development of Psycho-Analysis*, 20.

18. Freud, *New Introductory Lectures on Psycho-Analysis*, 874, 884.

19. Ibid., 880.

20. Freud, *Civilization and Its Discontents*, 772, 778.

21. Ibid., 771, 776.

22. C. S. Lewis, "'Bulverism,'" *God in the Dock: Essays on Theology and Ethics*, ed. Walter Hooper (Grand Rapids, Mich.: Eerdmans, 1970), 271-273.

23. Freud, *Civilization and Its Discontents*, 800-801.

24. Freud, *The Ego and the Id*, 709.

25. Bloom, *The Closing of the American Mind*, 155.

26. Christopher Lasch, *The Revolt of the Elites and the Betrayal of Democracy* (New York: W. W. Norton, 1996), 217-219.

27. Harold O. J. Brown, *The Sensate Culture: Western Civilization Between Chaos and Transformation* (Dallas: Word, 1996), 88.

28. Irving Yalom, *The Theory and Practice of Group Psychotherapy* (New York: Basic Books, 1975), 85.

Chapter 10: "Christianity Is Primitive, and Even Christ Is Flawed"

1. Will Durant, *The Story of Philosophy* (New York: Simon & Schuster, 1926), 359.

2. Paul Edwards, "Appendix: How Bertrand Russell Was Prevented from Teaching at the College of the City of New York," in Bertrand Russell, *Why I Am Not a Christian and Other Essays on Religion and Related Subject*s (New York: Simon & Schuster, 1957), 207-259.

3. Durant, *The Story*, 357-358.

4. Bertrand Russell, "Am I an Atheist or an Agnostic? A Plea for Tolerance in the Face of New Dogmas" (1947). http://www.geocities.com/Athens/Delphi/2795/atheist_or_agnostic.htm

5. Bertrand Russell, "Prologue," *The Autobiography of Bertrand Russell*, Vol. I (London: Allen and Unwin, 1967), n.p.

6. Bertrand Russell, *A History of Western Philosophy* (New York: Simon & Schuster, 1945), 834.

7. Bertrand Russell, *Why I Am Not a Christian and Other Essays on Religion and Related Subjects* (New York: Simon & Schuster, 1957), 50, 55, 60.

8. Ibid., 49-50, 40, 71-72, 22.

9. Russell, *A History of Western Philosophy*, 834-836.

10. For extended arguments against the church and Christianity's view of marriage, see Bertrand Russell, *Marriage and Morals* (New York: Horace Liveright, 1929).

11. Russell, *Why I Am Not a Christian*, 19, 22, v-vi.

12. Ibid., 6.

13. Ibid., 10.

14. "A Debate on the Existence of God: Bertrand Russell and F. C. Copleston," in *The Existence of God*, ed. John Hick (New York: Macmillan, 1964), 183, 188.

15. Russell, *Why I Am Not a Christian*, 16.

16. Ibid., 16-19.

17. Ibid., 21-22.

18. Ibid., 47.

19. Ibid., 70.

20. Russell, *Marriage and Morals*, 98.

21. Russell, *Why I Am Not a Christian*, 171.

22. Study any current *Statistical Abstract of the United States*, published by the U. S. Department of Commerce, or consult William J. Bennett, *The Index of Leading Cultural Indicators: Facts and Figures on the State of American Society* (New York: Simon & Schuster, 1994).

23. C. S. Lewis, "We Have No 'Right to Happiness,'" *God in the Dock: Essays on Theology and Ethics*, ed. Walter Hooper (Grand Rapids, Mich.: Eerdmans, 1970), 317-322.

24. Russell and Copleston, "A Debate on the Existence of God," 188.

25. Russell, *Why I Am Not a Christian*, 62.

26. Bertrand Russell, *The Autobiography of Bertrand Russell, 1944-69*, Vol. III (London: Allen and Unwin, 1969), 71-72.

27. S. Robert Lichter, Stanley Rothman, and Linda Lichter, *The Media Elite* (New York: Adler and Adler, 1986).

28. Steven Allen, "The News Media Reflect a Liberal Bias," *Mass Media*, ed. William Barbour (San Diego: Greenhaven Press, 1994), 19, 22, 21, from "The Search for the Smoking Gun" by Steven Allen, in *And That's the Way It Isn't*, eds. L. Brent Bozell and Brent H. Baker (Alexandria, Va.: Media Research Center, 1990).

29. Dinesh D'Souza, *Illiberal Education: The Politics of Race and Sex on Campus* (New York: Random House, 1992), 172.

30. Consider viewing the following website: http://www.envirolink.org/orgs/cco

31. D'Souza, *Illiberal Education*, xviii.

32. Julia Ingram and G. W. Hardin, *The Messengers: A True Story of Angelic Presence and the Return to the Age of Miracles* (New York: Pocket Books, 1996).

33. For sustained arguments against New Age theology, see Brad Scott, *Embraced by the Darkness: Exposing New Age Theology from the Inside Out* (Wheaton, Ill.: Crossway Books, 1996).

34. Russell, *A History of Western Philosophy*, 834.

Chapter 11: "Life Is Meaningless"

1. David E. Cooper, *Existentialism* (Oxford: Blackwell, 1990), 1.

2. Walter Kaufmann, *Existentialism from Dostoevsky to Sartre* (New York: Meridian, Penguin, 1989), 11.

3. Cooper, *Existentialism*, 6.

4. "Philosophy Quick Guide No. 1: Existentialism," Hoose Library of Philosophy, http://www-lib.usc.edu/Info/Phil/Guides/ps-106.html.

5. Jean-Paul Sartre, *Essays in Existentialism*, ed. with a foreword by Wade Baskin and intro. by Jean Wahl (Secaucus, N.J.: Citadel Press, 1997), 34.

6. Cooper, *Existentialism*, 167.

7. For a full treatment of Heidegger's existentialism, refer to Michael Inwood, *Heidegger* (New York: Oxford University Press, 1997).

8. Cooper, *Existentialism*, 12.

9. Sartre, *Essays in Existentialism*, 35-36.

10. Martin Heidegger, *Being and Time*, trans. J Macquarrie and E. Robinson (Oxford: Oxford University Press, 1962), 42, as cited in Inwood, *Heidegger*.

11. Inwood, *Heidegger*, 19.

12. Jean Wahl, introduction, "The Roots of Existentialism," to Jean-Paul Sartre, *Essays in Existentialism* (Secaucus, N.J.: Citadel, 1997), 19.

13. Sartre, *Essays in Existentialism*, 37.

14. William Barrett, *Irrational Man* (Garden City, N.Y.: Doubleday, 1962), 217.

15. *The Norton Reader: Eighth Edition* (New York and London: W. W. Norton, 1992), which is used in many undergraduate composition classes across the U. S., features a portion of "Existentialism and Humanism," entitling it "Existentialism" and noting that it was taken from Sartre's book *Existentialism* (1947).

16. Sartre, *Essays in Existentialism*, 38.

17. Ibid., 39-40, 60.

18. Cooper, *Existentialism*, 89.

19. Sartre, *Essays in Existentialism*, 40-41.

20. Ibid., 41, 42-45.

21. Albert Camus, "The Wager of Our Generation," *Resistance, Rebellion, and Death*, trans. Justin O'Brien (New York: Vintage, 1995), 246-247.

22. Ibid., 58.

23. Blaise Pascal, *Pensées*, in *Great Books of the Western World*, ed. Robert Maynard Hutchins, Vol. 33 (Chicago: Encyclopedia Britannica, 1952), 179.

24. Sartre, *Essays in Existentialism*, 51.

25. Ibid., 45-46.

26. Inwood, *Heidegger*, 59.

27. Sartre, *Essays in Existentialism*, 47-49.

28. Ibid., 46-47.

29. Ibid., 53, 55-56, 62.

30. Ibid., 34.

31. Cooper, *Existentialism*, 95-96.

32. Ibid., 139.

33. Ibid., 141.

34. Ibid., 171.

35. Heidegger, *Being and Time*, 227, as cited in Inwood, *Heidegger*, 42.

36. Inwood, *Heidegger*, 74.

37. Ibid., 73.

38. Sartre, *Essays in Existentialism*, 166.

39. Ibid., 172-173.

40. Ibid., 72.

41. By the publication of the second play, Sartre had already published his Marxist work, *The Critique of Dialectical Reason* (1960).

42. Sartre, *Essays in Existentialism*, 147.

43. Viktor Frankl, *Man's Search for Meaning*, rev. ed. (New York: Washington Square Press, 1984), 128. Interestingly, Frankl, a Jew who served time in a Nazi concentration camp, originally published this book in 1946.

44. See the fact sheets "Mental Illness in the Family: Mental Health Statistics" and

"Suicide: Teen Suicide," published on the Internet by the National Mental Health Association (1998), http://www. nmha.org/infor/factsheets.

45. See the press release "National Data Show Drop in Homicide and Increase in Youth Suicide," published on the Internet by the Department of Health and Human Services, October 23, 1995, http://www.hhs.gov/cgi-bin/waisgate? WAISdocID= 1948319321+0+0+0&WAISactioon= retrieve.

46. See "Warning Signs of Suicide," *Mayo Health Oasis* (September 2, 1997), published by the Mayo Clinic on the Internet, http://www.mayohealth.org/ mayo/9709/htm/suicide.htm

47. Ibid., "Mental Illness in the Family: Mental Health Statistics," National Health Association.

48. Sartre, *Essays in Existentialism*, 49.

Chapter 12: *"Free Will Is an Illusion"*

1. Richard Dawkins, *The Selfish Gene*, 1989 ed. (Oxford: Oxford University Press, 1976), 267.

2. B. F. Skinner, *Beyond Freedom and Dignity* (New York: Knopf, 1971), 101.

3. Dawkins, *The Selfish Gene*, 19-20.

4. B. F. Skinner, *Science and Human Behavior* (New York: Macmillan, 1953), 10, 46 and *Beyond Freedom and Dignity*, 202.

5. Skinner, *Science and Human Behavior*, 285, 160.

6. Skinner, *Beyond Freedom and Dignity*, 200.

7. Francis Crick, *The Astonishing Hypothesis: The Scientific Search for the Soul* (New York: Simon & Schuster, 1995), 274.

8. Ibid., 258-259.

9. Skinner, *Science and Human Behavior*, 116.

10. Crick, *The Astonishing Hypothesis*, 15.

11. Skinner, *Beyond Freedom and Dignity*, 124.

12. Skinner, *Science and Human Behavior*, 447.

13. Ibid., 446. In *Beyond Freedom and Dignity*, Skinner maintains that "Survival is the only value according to which a culture is eventually to be judged; any practice that furthers survival has survival value by definition," 136.

14. Skinner, *Science and Human Behavior*, 26-27, 28-29.

15. Ibid., 6, 17, 448, 26.

16. Skinner, *Beyond Freedom and Dignity*, 21.

17. See the precedent for this kind of thinking in B. F. Skinner's *Walden Two* (New York: Macmillan, 1976). This book was a novel, originally published in 1948, in which Skinner describes an ideal society governed by the principles of behavioral control.

18. Skinner, *Beyond Freedom and Dignity*, 134.

19. Ibid. See 163-164, 213-214 to get further intimations of Skinner's liberal Utopian vision.

20. Skinner, *Science and Human Behavior*, 438.

21. Ibid., 198.

22. Asimov, "What Is Intelligence, Anyway?" in *Please Explain* (Boston: Houghton

Mifflin, 1973), as cited in Mary Lou Conlin, *Patterns Plus*, 5th ed. (Boston: Houghton Mifflin, 1995), 205.

23. Crick, *The Astonishing Hypothesis*, 104-105, 3, 266, 268.

24. Dawkins, *The Selfish Gene*, 19-20.

25. Ibid., 66, 34, 196, 52, 200, 331.

26. Crick, *The Astonishing Hypothesis*, 261.

27. Dawkins, *The Selfish Gene*, 193.

28. Phillip E. Johnson, *Reason in the Balance: The Case Against Naturalism in Science, Law & Education* (Downers Grove, Ill.: InterVarsity, 1995), 64.

29. Neil Postman, *Technopoly: The Surrender of Culture to Technology* (New York: Vintage, 1992), 71, 48. In this genre, see also Alvin Toffler's *Powershift* (New York: Bantam, 1990).

30. Jacques Ellul, *What I Believe* (Grand Rapids, Mich.: Eerdmans, 1989), 136, 140. Readers may also want to consult Ellul's very early book *The Technological Society* (New York: Vintage, 1964).

31. Marshall McLuhan and Q. Fiore, *The Medium Is the Message* (New York: Bantam, 1967), 16, 63.

32. E. Sapir, "The Status of Linguistics as a Science," in *Culture, Language, and Personality*, ed. D. G. Mandelbaum (Berkeley, Calif.: University of California Press, 1958), 69.

33. B. L. Whorf, *Language, Thought, and Reality*, ed. J. B. Carroll (Cambridge, Mass.: MIT Press, 1956), n.p.

34. Stanley Fish, *Is There a Text in This Class? The Authority of Interpretative Communities* (Cambridge, Mass.: Harvard University Press, 1980), 32.

35. Chuck Colson and Jack Eckerd, *Why America Doesn't Work* (Dallas: Word, 1991), 75.

36. Skinner, *Beyond Freedom and Dignity*, 44.

37. Ibid., 62.

38. Ibid., 66.

39. William Bennett, *The Index of Leading Cultural Indicators: Facts and Figures on the State of American Society* (New York: Simon & Schuster, 1994), 34.

40. Ibid., 22.

41. Ibid., 29.

42. Bertrand Russell, *A History of Western Philosophy* (New York: Simon & Schuster, 1945), 820-821.

43. Skinner, *Science and Human Behavior*, 77-80.

44. David Thibodaux, Ph.D., *Beyond Political Correctness: Are There Limits to This Lunacy?* (Lafayette, La.: Huntington House, 1994), 189-190.

45. Bennett, *The Index of Leading Cultural Indicators*, 83.

46. Ibid., 84.

47. "Study: U.S. Science Students Lag Behind World," copyright 1998 by Reuters (via ClariNet), February 24, 1998, http://www2.netcom.com/bin/webnews?a= Top_Stories:OF8_ 18YRUnoitac.

48. Bennett, *The Index of Leading Cultural Indicators*, 85.

49. For the views of William J. Bennett, former Secretary of Education, on this

matter, consult his book *The De-Valuing of America: The Fight for Our Children and Our Culture* (New York: Simon & Schuster, 1994).

50. Toffler, *Power Shift*, 368.

51. Skinner, *Beyond Freedom and Dignity*, 200.

52. C. S. Lewis, *The Abolition of Man* (New York: Macmillan, 1947), 73.

53. Skinner, *Science and Human Behavior*, 443.

54. Aldous Huxley, *Collected Essays* (New York: Harper & Row, 1958), 344.

Chapter 13: "Everything Is Relative"

1. *The American Heritage Dictionary of the English Language* (1975).

2. J. P. Moreland, *Scaling the Secular City* (Grand Rapids, Mich.: Baker, 1987), 242.

3. Ibid., 244.

4. Michael Inwood, *Heidegger* (Oxford: Oxford University Press, 1997), 88.

5. Phillip E. Johnson, *Reason in the Balance* (Downers Grove, Ill.: InterVarsity, 1995), 119, 118.

6. Timothy Leary, *Harvard Letters*, http://www.garage.co.jp/~leary/archives/text/Letters/ Harvard/TableofContents.html.

7. Ram Dass, "*Brave New World* or *Island*: The World Must Decide," http://www.island.org/ ISLANDVIEWS/VIEWS4/bnwisland.html.

8. Sybille Bedford, *Aldous Huxley: A Biography* (New York: Knopf/Harper & Row, 1974), 155.

9. Aldous Huxley, *Collected Essays* (New York: Harper & Row, 1958), 71, 82-86.

10. Ibid., 377-378, 380, 388, 398.

11. Ibid., 360, 353, 357.

12. Aldous Huxley, *The Perennial Philosophy* (New York: Harper & Row, 1945), vii.

13. Huxley, *Collected Essays*, 361.

14. Huxley, *The Perennial Philosophy*, 194, 128, 51, 54, 242, 376, 239, 207, 49.

15. Ibid., 200.

16. Aldous Huxley, *The Doors of Perception and Heaven and Hell* (New York: Perennial Library, Harper & Row, 1990), 13. The title *The Doors of Perception* is taken from a quotation by William Blake, the visionary poet of the eighteenth century: "If the doors of perception were cleansed every thing would appear to man as it is, infinite."

17. Ibid., 36, 33, 45, 70-72, 73, 54-55, 79.

18. Huxley, *Collected Essays*, 343-345.

19. Aldous Huxley, *The Island* (New York: Harper & Row, 1962), 162-163, 102, 277, 160, 197, 41, 200.

20. Huxley, *Collected Essays*, 376.

21. "Partnership for a Drug-Free America Reports on Teens' and Parents' Attitudes About Drugs," *New Briefs*, http://www.ndsn.org/APRIL96/PDFA.html. April 1996.

22. Francis Schaeffer, *Escape from Reason*, *The Francis Schaeffer Trilogy* (Wheaton, Ill.: Crossway Books, 1990), 242.

23. Ibid., 242.

24. Ibid., 23.

25. Alvin Toffler, *Powershift* (New York: Bantam, 1990), 368.

26. "Aldous Huxley," *The Encyclopedia American International Edition*, Vol. 14 (Danbury, Conn.: Grolier, 1991), 622.

Chapter 14: "All We Need Is Love"

1. George Barna, *The Index of Leading Spiritual Indicators* (Dallas: Word, 1996), 130.

2. Henry C. Thiessen, *Introduction to the New Testament*, rpt. 1989 (Grand Rapids, Mich.: Eerdmans, 1943), xvi-xix, 119. See also J. Barton Payne, "Higher Criticism and Biblical Inerrancy," *Inerrancy*, ed. Norman L. Geisler (Grand Rapids, Mich.: Zondervan, 1980), 85-113.

3. Harvey Cox, *Many Mansions: A Christian's Encounter with Other Faiths* (Boston: Beacon Press, 1988), 52, 18, 212.

4. Ibid., 14.

5. Hans Küng, *Theology for the Third Millennium: An Ecumenical View*, trans. Peter Heinegg (New York: Doubleday, 1988), 243-244, 236, 232.

6. Huston Smith, *Beyond the Post-Modern Mind* (Wheaton, Ill.: Quest Books, 1989), 51, 242.

7. Mortimer J. Adler, *Truth in Religion: The Plurality of Religions and the Unity of Truth* (New York: Macmillan, 1990), 81.

8. Cox, *Many Mansions*, 67.

9. Ibid., 16.

10. Küng, *Theology for the Third Millennium*, 181, 204.

11. Ibid., 176.

12. Smith, *Beyond the Post-Modern Mind*, 50-51.

13. Gregory A. Boyd, *Jesus Under Siege* (Wheaton, Ill.: Victor Books, 1995), 9-18.

14. Marcus Borg, *Jesus in Contemporary Scholarship* (Valley Forge, Penn.: Trinity Press, 1994), 162.

15. As cited in Michael J. Watkins and J. P. Moreland, "Introduction: The Furor Surrounding Jesus," in *Jesus Under Fire: Modern Scholarship Reinvents the Historical Jesus*, eds. Watkins and Moreland (Grand Rapids, Mich.: Zondervan, 1995), 2.

16. Robert W. Funk, Roy W. Hoover, and The Jesus Seminar, *The Five Gospels: What Did Jesus Really Say?* (New York: Macmillan, 1993), 5.

17. Ibid., 32-33.

18. Ibid., 10, 15-19, 549-553.

19. Ibid., 32-33.

20. David Van Biema, "The Gospel Truth?" *Time*, 8 April 1996, 3.

21. R. Watson, "A Lesser Child of God," *Newsweek*, April 4, 1994, 53.

22. As cited in Luke Timothy Johnson, *The Real Jesus: The Misguided Quest for the Historical Jesus and the Truth of the Traditional Gospels* (San Francisco: HarperCollins, 1996), 40.

23. Funk, Hoover, and The Jesus Seminar, *The Five Gospels*, 2.

24. Ibid., 41.

25. Matthew Fox, *The Coming of the Cosmic Christ: The Healing of Mother Earth*

and the Birth of a Global Renaissance (San Francisco: HarperSanFrancisco, 1988), 79, 145, 154, 230-231, 235.

26. Smith, *Beyond the Post-Modern Mind*, 64, 191, 261.

27. Fox, *The Coming of the Cosmic Christ*, 80.

28. Ibid., 65.

29. The World Council of Churches, *Towards a Common Understanding and Vision of the World Council of Churches: A Policy Statement*, http://www.wcc-coe.org/cuv/index.html, September 1997, 3-13. The WCC's homepage is http:www.wcc-coe.org/

30. See the excellent book by Peter Jones, *The Gnostic Empire Strikes Back* (Phillipsburg, N.J.: Presbyterian and Reformed 1992).

31. Tal Brooke, *When the World Will Be as One: The Coming New World Order* (Eugene, Ore.: Harvest House, 1989), 206.

32. As cited in ibid., 75.

33. GaiaMind, http://www.gaiamind.com/printout.html, 1-3.

34. Fox, *The Coming of the Cosmic Christ*, 235-236.

35. Peter Jones, "Apostasy in America: An Overview of Warning Signs in Our Time," *SCP Journal*, 20:3-4, 1996, "Jesus and the Den of Thieves," Part I, 14-23.

36. George Barna, *The Index of Leading Spiritual Indicators*, 18, 23, 75.

37. Huston Smith, *Beyond the Post-Modern Mind*, 262.

38. See Joseph Campbell, *The Inner Reaches of Outer Space: Metaphor as Myth and as Religion* (New York: HarperCollins, 1988).

39. Aldous Huxley, *Collected Essays* (New York: Harper & Row, 1958), 380.

40. "United Church Leader's View on Jesus," *The Toronto Star*, November 15, 1997, A2.

41. World Council of Churches, "Towards a Common Understanding . . . ," 14.

42. "French Diplomat Urges Protestants to Support European Unity," *Ecumenical News International*, News Highlights, http://www.wcc-coe.org/eni/latest.html,16 March 1998.

43. Mortimer J. Adler, *Truth in Religion*, 141-142, 156.

Chapter 15: A Defense of Christian Absolutism

1. Gavin Reid, "The Spiritual Dimension," *Exploring the Christian Faith: A Contemporary Handbook of What Christians Believe and Why*, ed. Robin Keeley (Nashville: Thomas Nelson, 1996), 22.

2. Francis Schaeffer, *He Is There and He Is Not Silent*, from *Francis Schaeffer Trilogy* (Wheaton, Ill.: Crossway Books, 1990), 306-307.

3. Ibid., 343-347.

4. Charles Williams, *Descent of the Dove: A Short History of the Holy Spirit in the Church*, rpt. 1980 (Grand Rapids, Mich.: Eerdmans, 1930), 1.

5. J. P. Moreland, *Scaling the Secular City: A Defense of Christianity* (Grand Rapids, Mich.: Baker, 1987), 13.

6. Neil Postman, *Technopoly: The Surrender of Culture to Technology* (New York: Vintage, 1993), 184-185.

7. Francis Schaeffer, *How Should We Then Live?* (Wheaton, Ill.: Crossway Books, 1976), 254.

8. Josiah Royce, "The Problem of Christianity," *The Philosophy of Josiah Royce*, ed. John K. Roth (New York: Thomas Y. Crowell Co., 1971), 361-362.

9. Gene Edward Veith, Jr., *Postmodern Times: A Christian Guide to Contemporary Thought and Culture* (Wheaton, Ill.: Crossway Books, 1994), 193.

10. As cited in Francis Schaeffer, *The Great Evangelical Disaster* (Wheaton, Ill.: Crossway Books, 1984), 50-51.

11. Craig A. Evans, "What Did Jesus Do?" in *Jesus Under Fire: Modern Scholarship Reinvents the Historical Jesus*, eds. Michael J. Wilkins and J. P. Moreland (Grand Rapids, Mich.: Zondervan, 1995), 105-106.

12. Henry Bettenson, *Documents of the Christian Church* (London: Oxford University Press, 1967), 1-4.

13. C. S. Lewis, "Modern Theology and Biblical Criticism," *The Seeing Eye and Other Selected Essays from Christian Reflections*, ed. Walter Hooper (New York: Ballantine, 1967), 203-223.

14. Josh McDowell, *More Than a Carpenter* (Wheaton, Ill.: Tyndale, 1977), 42-43.

15. Craig L. Blomberg, "Where Do We Start Studying Jesus?" in *Jesus Under Fire*, eds. Wilkins and Moreland, 41.

16. Josh McDowell, *Evidence That Demands a Verdict: Historical Evidences for the Christian Faith* (San Bernardino, Calif:: Campus Crusade for Christ, 1972), 72-76.

17. J. P. Moreland, *Scaling the Secular City*, 136.

18. Josh McDowell, *More Than a Carpenter*, 48; and Henry C. Thiessen, *Introduction to the New Testament* (Grand Rapids, Mich.: Eerdmans, 1943), 31-77.

19. Gleason L. Archer, "The Witness of the Bible to Its Own Inerrancy," *The Foundation of Biblical Authority*, ed. James Montgomery Boice (Grand Rapids, Mich.: Zondervan, 1978), 86.

20. Norman L. Geisler and William E. Nix, *A General Introduction to the Bible* (Chicago: Moody Press, 1968), 365.

21. Harold Lindsell, *The Battle for the Bible* (Grand Rapids, Mich.: Zondervan, 1976), 35.

22. See John W. Wenham, "Christ's View of Scripture," *Inerrancy*, ed. Norman L. Geisler (Grand Rapids, Mich.: Zondervan, 1980), 3-36; and Archer, "The Witness of the Bible to Its Own Inerrancy," *The Foundation of Biblical Authority*, ed. Boice, 85-99.

23. As cited in Norman L. Geisler, "Philosophical Presuppositions of Biblical Errancy," *Inerrancy*, 309.

24. George C. Fuller and Samuel T. Logan, "Bible Authority: When Christians Do Not Agree," *Inerrancy and Hermeneutic: A Tradition, A Challenge, A Debate*, ed. Harvie M. Conn (Grand Rapids, Mich.: Baker, 1988), 238-239, 240.

25. E. D. Hirsch, Jr., *Validity in Interpretation* (New Haven, Conn.: Yale University Press, 1967), 5.

26. Walter C. Kaiser, Jr., "Legitimate Hermeneutics," in Geisler, *Inerrancy*, 118.

27. Henry A. Virkler, *Hermeneutics: Principles and Processes of Biblical Interpretation* (Grand Rapids, Mich.: Baker, 1981), 76-77.

28. C. S. Lewis, *Mere Christianity* (New York: Macmillan, 1943), 63.

29. Albert Einstein, *Essays in Science* (New York: Philosophical Library, 1934), 11.

30. Francis Schaeffer, *He Is There and He Is Not Silent*, from *Francis Schaeffer Trilogy*, 325.

31. Ibid., 338.

32. Thomas à Kempis, *The Imitation of Christ,* trans. with an introduction by Leo Shirley-Price (New York: Penguin, 1977), 27.

33. R. V. G. Tasker, *The Gospel According to John: An Introduction and Commentary* (Grand Rapids, Mich.: Eerdmans, 1994), 191.

34. Royce, *The Philosophy of Josiah Royce*, 388.

35. Moreland, *Scaling the Secular City*, 292.

36. C. S. Lewis, "What Are We to Make of Jesus Christ?" in *God in the Dock: Essays on Theology and Ethics*, ed. Walter Hooper (Grand Rapids, Mich.: Eerdmans, 1970), 157-158.

37. Josh McDowell, *More Than a Carpenter*, 27-28.

38. C. S. Lewis, "What Are We to Make of Jesus Christ?" in *God in the Dock*, 158.

39. Lewis, *Mere Christianity*, 62.

INDEX

Abolition of Man, The (Lewis), 13, 226
Abortion, 21, 94, 118
Absolutes, 19, 31, 41, 141, 229, 230, 233, 288
Absolutism, 13, 267 (Chapter 15 *passim*)
Adler, Mortimer, 14, 31, 49, 93, 254, 265
Agassiz, Louis, 105
Agnostics, 81, 155, 176, 186, 187, 189
Anaximander, 103
And That's the Way It Isn't, 187
Angst, 197, 199, 200, 204, 206, 208, 210
Anselm, 51, 54
Aquarian Gospel of Jesus Christ, The (Dowling), 189, 249
Aquinas, Thomas, 37, 46, 54, 180
Archer, Gleason, 277
Aristotle, 38, 49, 55, 135
Asimov, Isaac, 210, 213, 216, 217, 218
Astonishing Hypothesis, The (Crick), 217
Atheism, atheists, 80, 81, 140, 141, 155, 174, 175, 176, 177, 187, 191, 196, 202, 217, 218, 292
Augustine, 13, 37, 46, 69, 81, 278, 280
Autonomous Technology (Winner), 219

Baby boomers, 128
Bacon, Francis, 26, 44, 45, 58
Bad faith, 208
Barna, George, 249, 262
Barrett, William, 37
Barth, Karl, 46
Barthes, R., 289
Baudelaire, 117
Bauer, Bruno, 123, 250
Baur, F. C., 250, 289
Beatles, the, 63, 150, 169, 240
Beats, the, 198
Behaviorism, behaviorists, 211 (Chapter 12 *passim*), 292
Behe, Michael J., 105
Being and Nothingness (Sartre), 195, 198
Being and Time (Heidegger), 195
Bennett, William J., 188
Bentham, Jeremy, 54, 59, 85, 86, 88, 89, 90, 91, 113, 114
Bergson, H., 289, 292
Berkeley, 54, 55, 58

Beyond Freedom and Dignity (Skinner), 215
Beyond Good and Evil (Nietzsche), 145
Beyond the Post-Modern Mind (H. Smith), 254
Bible, the, Scripture, 51, 153, 270, 278, 279, 280, 281, 286
Blavatsky, Madame, 189
Blind Watchmaker, The (Dawkins), 105
Bloom, Allan, 23, 117, 136, 138, 140, 147, 154, 160, 169, 188
Book of Mormon, 282
Borg, Marcus, 256, 257
Bourgeoisie, the 124, 125, 126, 127, 128, 230
Brave New World (Huxley), 231, 232
Brothers Karamazov (Dostoyevsky), 196
Brooke, Tal, 260, 264
Brown, Harold O. J., 115, 116, 133, 149, 152
Buckley, William, 105
Buddha, 182, 191, 282
Buddhism, 141, 190, 244, 269, 281
Bultmann, Rudolf, 46, 196, 250, 263
Bunick, Nick, 190, 242
Byron, 22, 70, 78, 289

Calvin, John, 38, 46
Campbell, Joseph, 263, 289
Camus, Albert, 195, 196, 201, 202, 204, 289
Capital (Marx), 123, 124, 125, 128
Castenada, Carlos, 148, 242
Categorical imperative, 86, 87
Chardin Teilhard de, 46
Chesterton, G.K., 31
Chomsky, Noam, 117
Chopra, Deepak, 240, 242, 249
Christianity, Christian worldview, 14, 28, 31, 51, 80, 126, 136, 141, 154, 167, 174, 226, 239, 244, 262, 266, 268, 269, 271, 272, 273, 274, 275, 283, 284, 286, 287, 288
Civilization, 72, 74, 164, 165
Civilization and Its Discontents (Freud), 162, 163, 164, 166, 172
Closing of the American Mind, The (Bloom), 23, 136
Collected Essays (A. Huxley), 232
Colson, Chuck, 153, 222
Coming of the Cosmic Christ, The (Fox), 257

Communism, 121 (Chapter 7 *passim*), 176
Comte, A., 289
Condemned of Altona, The (Sartre), 208
Confessions (Rousseau), 69, 77
Consciousness-raising, 122, 127, 133
Constitution, U.S., 47, 48, 116
Cooper, David E., 196, 197, 198, 204
Copleston, F. C., 181, 186
Cox, Harvey, 251, 252, 253, 254, 255, 265, 289
Crick, Francis, 104, 210, 212, 213, 217, 218, 219, 224, 230, 289
Crime, 21, 222, 223
Cronkite, Walter, 187
Crossan, J. Dominic, 256, 257
Cult of personality, 76, 77, 78, 79
Culture designers, 50, 215, 216, 224, 226, 227, 257, 260, 265
Cuvier, 45
Cynicism, 23, 50, 154, 222

Daly, Mary, 261
Darwin, Charles, 13, 22, 45, 61, 100, 103 (Chapter 6 *passim*), 125, 146, 164, 165, 173, 183, 210, 212, 230, 231, 289
Darwin, Erasmus, 103
Darwinism, 90, 103 (Chapter 6 *passim*), 292
Dasein, 197, 198, 199, 205, 206, 208
Dawkins, Richard, 104, 210, 211, 212, 213, 217, 218, 223, 224, 230, 289
Death-instinct, 161, 172
Death of Literature, The (Kernan), 23
de Beauvoir, Simone, 195, 197, 198, 204
Decline of the West, The (Spengler), 230
Deism, Deists, 38, 292
Democritus, 103
Denton, Michael, 106, 112
Derrida, Jacques, 153, 196, 230, 289
Descent of Man, The (Darwin), 104, 105, 110, 111, 113, 114
Despair, 202, 203, 204
Determinism, determinists, 38, 43, 89, 90, 162, 173, 210, 212, 213, 215, 216, 217, 219, 220, 221, 223, 224, 226, 227, 273
Dewey, John, 13, 86, 223, 224, 289
d'Holbach, 26, 36, 289
Dialectic, 123, 124, 126, 135, 136
Dialogues Concerning Natural Religion (Hume), 64
Diderot, 36, 53, 54, 69, 289

Dirty Hands (Sartre), 208
Discourse on the Origin and Basis of Inequality Among Men (Rousseau), 71, 72, 74, 75
Dobson, James, 153
Doll's House, A (Ibsen), 24
Doors, the, 232
Doors of Perception, The (A. Huxley), 22, 232, 237
Dostoevsky, Fyodor, 196, 201
Dowling, Levi, 189, 249
Drugs, 20, 22, 147, 240, 241
D'Souza, Dinesh, 23, 188
Durant, Will, 51, 113, 140, 146, 176
Durants (Will and Ariel), 54, 55, 56, 61, 81, 126

Eckhart, Meister, 236
Edwards, Jonathan, 81
Ego, 159, 163, 164, 172
Ego and the Id, The (Freud), 163, 168
Einstein, Albert, 159, 161, 174, 176, 280
Eldridge, Niles, 110
Electric Kool-Aid Acid Test, The (Wolfe), 240
Elitists, 97, 98, 99, 139, 229, 289
Ellul, Jacques, 220
Embraced by the Darkness (Scott), 243
Emerson, Ralph Waldo, 13, 24, 70, 79, 80, 234, 289
Émile (Rousseau), 9, 72, 75, 81, 213
Encyclopedia of Pacifism, The (Huxley, editor), 246
Empiricism, empiricists, 43, 55, 58, 67, 87, 292
Engels, Friedrich, 125, 127, 289
Enlightenment, the, 26, 53, 54, 76, 267, 278
Enquiry Concerning Human Understanding, An (Hume), 53, 55, 56, 57, 58, 60, 61, 64
Epicurus, 90, 93
Epistemology, 59
Erasmus, 26
Escape from Reason (Schaeffer), 242
Essence, 44, 101, 122, 197, 288
Ethics, 178, 186, 199, 201
Eugenics, 114
Evolution, 19, 20, 22, 46, 61, 62, 103 (Chapter 6 *passim*), 122, 125, 164, 165, 214, 215, 216, 217, 223, 224, 259, 287, 289
Existence, 44, 101, 122, 197, 198, 288

Existentialism, existentialists, 44, 191, 195 (Chapter 11 *passim*), 214, 250, 289, 292
Existentialism (Sartre), 195

Feminism, feminists, 71, 97, 98, 114, 131, 132, 134, 153, 260, 292
Feuerbach, 123
Fish, Stanley, 220
Five Gospels, The (The Jesus Seminar), 256
Flaubert, 117
Flies, The (Sartre), 195
Forgotten Truth (Smith), 253
Foucault, M., 289
Four Dissertations (Hume), 53
Fox, Matthew, 257, 258, 259, 261, 289
Frankl, Viktor, 208
Free will, 11, 38, 43, 44, 56, 210, 213, 217, 218, 219, 220, 221, 226, 288
Freud, Sigmund, 13, 39, 105, 116, 152, 153, 155, 159 (Chapter 9 *passim*), 178, 180, 183, 185, 212, 227, 230, 289
Funk, Robert W., 256
Future of an Illusion (Freud), 166, 172

Gaia, Gaia Mind Project, 260, 261
Galileo, 45, 103
Gandhi, M., 289
Gates, Louis Henry, 188
Gay Science (Nietzsche), 140
Gay, John, 86, 88
Gibbon, 54
Ginsberg, Allen, 232
God Who Is There, The (Schaeffer), 135, 242
Goethe, J. W., 289
Gospel, the, 28, 31, 270, 281
Gould, Stephen Jay, 110
Great Christian Doctrine of Original Sin Defended, The (Edwards), 81
Greatest-happiness principle, 88, 89, 90, 93, 96, 113, 157, 253, 289
Grimm, 69
Ground of being, 231, 236, 242, 256, 262, 267
Groupthink, 20, 94

Haeckel, Ernst, 104, 289
Happiness, 85, 86, 87, 90, 93, 94, 95, 98, 162, 177, 183, 184, 185, 186, 202, 210, 227, 267, 288
Has Man a Future? (Russell), 176
Hayward, Alan, 105

Hedonism, hedonists, 24, 59, 66, 93, 94, 95, 97, 115, 240, 244
Hegel Georg, 123, 125, 289
Heidegger, Martin, 195, 196, 197, 198, 199, 200, 202, 205, 206, 208, 289
Heisenberg, Werner, 62
Hell's Angels, 240
Helvetius, 36, 88
Hendrix, Jimi, 63
Hermeneutics, 279
Higher criticism, higher critics, 123, 250, 289
Hinduism, 190, 244, 254, 262, 269, 281
Hippies, 66, 240
Hirsch, E. D., Jr., 279
History of Western Philosophy (Russell), 175
Hitler Adolf, 22, 83, 137, 138
Hobbes, Thomas, 13, 26, 35 (Chapter 2 *passim*), 54, 55, 58, 59, 60, 63, 67, 70, 71, 72, 86, 90, 100, 115, 122, 146, 164, 178, 183, 210, 212, 213, 221, 230, 245, 246, 289
Homosexuality, homosexuals, 18, 25, 94, 116, 213
Hume, David, 24, 26, 49, 52, 53 (Chapter 3 *passim*), 69, 70, 73, 75, 86, 87, 88, 103, 113, 168, 181, 183, 210, 230, 289
Huxley, Aldous, 22, 104, 227, 229 (Chapter 13 *passim*), 253, 257, 262, 263, 289
Huxley, Julian, 104, 289
Huxley, Thomas H., 104, 109, 113, 152, 231, 289

Ibsen, Henrik, 24
Id, 147, 159, 163, 164
Illiberal Education, An (D'Souza), 23, 188
Inwood, Michael, 198, 202
Interpretation of Dreams, The (Freud), 159
Introduction to Mathematical Philosophy (Russell), 175
Intuition, 79, 80, 100, 193, 262, 281, 282
Island, The (A. Huxley), 22, 232, 237, 238

Jagger, Mick, 147, 150
James, William, 86, 289
Jaspers, Karl, 196
Jefferson, Thomas, 47, 48

Jefferson Airplane, 63
Jesus Seminar, The, 255, 256, 257, 264, 265, 276, 289
Jewish Antiquities (Josephus), 275
Johnson, Phillip E., 65, 67, 105, 116, 153, 218, 219, 231
Jones, Peter, 261
Josephus, 275
Judaism, 140
Judeo-Christian faith and thought, 18, 131, 135, 136, 226, 267
Jung, Carl, Jungian thought, 159, 160, 243, 289

Kaiser, Walter C., 279
Kant, Immanuel, 54, 61, 86, 87, 289
Kaufmann, Walter, 196
Kernan, Alan, 23
Kerouac, Jack, 232
Kesey, Ken, 240
Kierkegaard, Soren, 49, 196
Kiernan, Alvin, 188
Kinsey, Alfred C., 117, 118, 119
Kuhn, Thomas, 62, 251, 289
Küng, Hans, 252, 253, 254, 255, 265, 289

Lady Chatterley's Lover (Lawrence), 117
Lamarck, Jean-Baptist, 103, 289
Lasch, Christopher, 99, 134, 151, 152, 170
Law, William, 234
Lawrence, D. H., 117, 159, 231
Leary, Timothy, 227, 232, 237, 240, 241
Legal positivism, 116
Leibniz, Gottfried Wilhelm von, 235, 289
Lennon, John, 150, 249
Lenz, Frederick, 148, 242
Lesbianism, lesbians, 67, 98
Leviathan (Hobbes), 26, 35, 37, 43, 46, 52, 213
Levi-Strauss, C., 289
Lewis, C. S., 13, 31, 62, 167, 185, 186, 226, 276, 279, 284, 287
Liberalism, liberals, 67, 71, 93, 153, 186, 187, 188, 189, 218
Liberty, freedom, 11, 31, 40, 52, 56, 91, 92
Linnaeus, 45
Locke, John, 26, 44, 47, 49, 54, 55, 58, 67, 87
Logical analysis, 177, 178, 179

LSD, 22, 63, 227, 232, 241
Lucretius, 180
Luther, Martin, 38, 46, 275
Lyell, 45

McDowell, Josh, 21, 284
Machiavelli, 26
McLuhan, Marshall, 220
Macroevolution, 105, 106
Malthus, Thomas, 103, 113, 146
Manifesto of the Communist Party (Marx and Engels), 123, 125, 126
Man's Search for Meaning (Frankl), 208
Marcel, Gabriel, 195, 196
Marcuse, Herbert, 121, 128, 159
Marijuana, 21, 95, 241
Marx, Karl, Marxism, 105, 119, 121 (Chapter 7 *passim*), 143, 146, 153, 164, 172, 183, 185, 201, 204, 212, 230, 289, 292
Maslow, Abraham, 24, 196, 232, 289
Materialism, materialists, 24, 26, 37, 38, 39, 43, 44, 45, 46, 48, 50, 122, 123, 126, 131, 166, 173
May, Rollo, 196
Meaninglessness, 205, 208, 210
Media, the, 98, 129, 187, 188, 219
Medium Is the Message, The (McLuhan), 220
Media Elite, The (Lichter and Rothman), 187
Mendel, G., 289
Mental illness, 163, 170, 209
Mescaline, 63, 227, 232, 237, 238
Merton, Thomas, 254, 289
Microevolution, 106
Mill, James, 59, 85
Mill, John Stuart, 22, 24, 59, 67, 85, 86, 87, 90, 91, 92, 93, 95, 97, 99, 100, 113, 181, 183, 210, 213, 289
Miracles, 31, 64, 73, 276, 285
Modernism, 26, 49
Mollenkott, Virginia, 261
Montesquieu, 54
Morality, 25, 50, 51, 55, 59, 60, 66, 93, 181, 184, 202, 230, 235, 239
Moreland, J. P., 62, 272
Movies, 129, 130, 131, 169, 185, 205, 245
Multiculturalism, 131, 133, 134, 153, 173, 273, 292
Music, 131, 159
Mysticism, 80, 233, 242, 253, 258, 259, 261
Myth of Sisyphus (Camus), 204

Naturalism, naturalists, 64, 65, 101,
    108, 161, 217, 219, 268, 273, 285
Natural law, 37, 115, 270
Natural reason, 46, 47, 51
Natural religion, 73, 80, 268
Natural selection, 103, 105, 106, 107,
    108, 109, 112, 218
New Age, the, New Agers, 19, 20, 24,
    25, 80, 190, 247, 249, 250, 251, 260,
    265, 289
New Genesis (Muller), 260
*New Introductory Lectures on Psycho-
    Analysis* (Freud), 163, 166
Newton, Sir Isaac, 45, 103
Niebuhr, Reinhold, 250
Nietzsche, Friedrich Wilhelm, 22, 114,
    136, 137 (Chapter 8 *passim*), 159,
    172, 183, 185, 196, 207, 230, 289
Nihilism, 201
No Exit (Sartre), 195
Noble savage, the, 22, 70, 74, 75
Nominalism, nominalists, 43
Not in Our Genes, 218
Novum Organum (Bacon), 44

Oedipus complex, 160, 163, 164
On Liberty (J. S. Mill), 87, 91, 92, 95,
    97, 100
On Non-Christian Religions, 259
On the Genealogy of Morals
    (Nietzsche), 137, 141
On Writing Well (Zinsser), 77
Oprah, 24
*Origin and Development of Psycho-
    Analysis, The* (Freud), 162, 164
Origin of Species, The (Darwin), 100,
    103, 104, 105, 106, 108, 109, 110,
    111, 117
Original sin, 76, 81, 82
Otto, Rudolf, 283
Owen, Richard, 105

Pacifism, pacifists, 175, 187, 246
Packer, J.I., 49
Pain, 59, 61, 88, 89, 90, 93, 94, 95, 288
Paine, Thomas, 289
Paley, William, 54
Paradigms, paradigm shifts, 251, 255,
    257, 258, 262
Pascal, Blaise, 26, 202
Passion, 38, 59, 64, 65, 66, 67, 186,
    267, 282, 288
Path of Love, The (Chopra), 249
Pavlov, Ivan, 210, 214
Pearls, F., 289

Pensées (Pascal), 202
Perennial Philosophy, The (A. Huxley),
    232, 235, 241, 257
Philosophes, 36, 53, 64, 69, 88, 136,
    152, 289
Phipps, Bill, 263
Plato, 9, 10, 38
Please Explain (Asimov), 216
Pleasure, 39, 40, 50, 59, 60, 61, 66, 87,
    88, 89, 90, 93, 94, 95, 96, 97, 99,
    116, 162, 210, 267, 288
Pleasure-principle, 162
Pleasures of Philosophy, The (Durant),
    113
Pliny the Younger, 275
Pluralism, 18, 26, 133, 134, 173, 223,
    269, 273, 274, 292
Political correctness, 23
Pornography, 19, 150, 151
Positivism (logical), positivists, 44, 122,
    292
Postman, Neil, 152, 205, 219, 272
Postmodernism, postmodernists, 66,
    172, 196, 229, 247, 251, 257, 268,
    269, 292
Powershift (Toffler), 113
Pragmatism, 86, 223, 224, 272, 292
Premarital sex, 95, 96, 174, 184
Presley, Elvis, 150
Priestley, Joseph, 86, 88
Principia Mathematica (Russell and
    Whitehead), 175
Progress, 26, 47, 49, 50, 105, 122, 155,
    177, 182, 190, 263, 285, 287
Provincial Letters, The (Pascal), 26
Psychoanalysis, 155, 163, 168, 170, 172
Punctuated equilibrium, 110

Ram Dass, 232, 240, 289
Ramacharaka, Yogi, 189
Rationalism, scientific rationalism, 24,
    37, 44, 45, 177, 178, 179, 180, 181,
    190, 250, 268
Ratzsch, Del, 105
Reality, 10, 62, 63, 66, 67, 203, 204,
    205, 224, 234, 254
Reason in the Balance (Johnson), 153,
    218
Rebellion, 49, 50, 78, 201
Reductionism, 172, 281
Relationships, 58, 96, 203, 280, 282,
    283
Relativism, relativists, 13, 18, 19, 24,
    26, 33, 40, 41, 42, 46, 105, 128, 134,
    143, 145, 152, 153, 173, 193, 210,

220, 224, 226, 227, 229 (Chapter 13
  passim), 247, 250, 251, 259, 267,
  268, 269, 273, 274, 285, 287, 288,
  289, 292
Renaissance, the, 26, 55
Renan, Ernest, 189, 250, 289
Republic (Plato), 9
Revelation, 33, 37, 51, 55, 80, 100,
  262, 269, 270, 281, 289
*Revolt of the Elite and the Betrayal of
  Democracy, The* (Lasch), 99, 170
Rieff, Philip, 170
Right from Wrong (McDowell and
  Hostetler), 21
Robespierre, 83
Robinson, James M., 261
Rogers, Carl, 289
Romanes, G. F., 289
Romanticism, Romantics, 13, 24, 26,
  52, 61, 68, 70, 76, 77, 78, 80, 90,
  136, 168, 214, 289
Rorty, Richard, 196, 230, 231, 244, 289
Roseanne, 24, 50, 98
Rousseau, Jean-Jacques, 9, 13, 22, 24,
  54, 61, 69 (Chapter 4 *passim*), 130,
  138, 164, 165, 168, 183, 185, 206,
  210, 213, 214, 221, 230, 262, 289
Royce, Josiah, 274, 283
Russell, Bertrand, 13, 35, 39, 43, 54,
  57, 58, 67, 73, 80, 81, 83, 85, 89, 93,
  103, 113, 114, 124, 140, 144, 152,
  174, 175 (Chapter 10 *passim*), 206,
  210, 213, 214, 223, 227, 230, 246,
  289
Russell-Einstein Manifesto, 176, 246

Sagan, Carl, 104
Sapir-Whorf theory of linguistics, 220
Sartre, Jean-Paul, 13, 24, 191, 195
  (Chapter 11 *passim*), 227, 230, 289
Savoyard Vicar, the, 72, 73, 75, 76, 79,
  80, 81
Schaeffer, Francis, 135, 136, 154, 207,
  242, 268, 274
Schleiermacher, Friedrich, 250
Scholasticism, 37
Schopenhauer, 146
Science and Human Behavior (Skinner),
  215, 216
Scientism, 190, 191
Scopes Trial, 104
Second Coming of Christ, the, 266, 287
Secularism, secularists, 47, 48, 65, 190,
  220, 227, 288
Selfish Gene, The (Dawkins), 105, 211

Self-preservation, 39, 40, 50, 71
Self-Reliance (Emerson), 80
Semler, J. S., 250
Sensate Culture, The (Brown), 133
Sense experiences or impressions, 37,
  38, 44, 45, 46, 47, 56, 59
Separation of church and state, 47
Sexual Behavior in the Human Male
  (Kinsey), 117
Sexual liberation, 185, 187
Sexual revolution, 174, 184, 185, 292
Shelley, 78
Singer, Peter, 118
Skepticism, 14, 47, 52, 54, 57, 58, 61,
  62, 63, 73, 179, 186
Skinner, B. F., 210, 211 (Chapter 12
  passim), 230, 289
Smith, Adam, 54, 67
Smith, Huston, 253, 254, 255, 256,
  257, 258, 262, 265, 289
Smith, Joseph, 282
Snowboarding to Nirvana (Lenz), 148
Social contract, 22, 70, 100
*Social Contract or Principles of Political
  Right, The* (Rousseau), 75
Social Darwinism, 112, 114, 115
Social engineers, 122, 129, 134, 220,
  223, 225, 239
Socialism, 18, 121, 126, 127, 203, 260
Social Shaping of Technology, The
  (MacKenzie and Wajcman), 219
Socrates, 9, 168, 170, 182
Solipsism, solipsists, 66, 199
Sorokin, Pitrim, 149, 152
Speciesism, 118
Spencer, Herbert, 104, 112, 146, 289
Spengler, Oswald, 230, 289
Spinoza, 26
Stern, Howard, 50
Stranger, The (Camus), 195
Strauss, David, 123, 189, 250, 289
Subjectivism, subjectivists, 24, 26, 54,
  62, 64, 65, 67, 100, 168, 181, 186,
  190, 191, 199, 201, 210, 226, 230,
  232, 233, 235, 243, 245, 250, 255,
  273, 285
Summa Theologica (Aquinas), 180
Superego, 159, 163, 164, 165, 171, 172
Supermen, the Superman, 22, 136, 139,
  141, 143, 144, 145, 230
Survival of the fittest, 103, 107, 109,
  112, 113
Sympathy, 60, 61, 114

Tacitus, 275

Technology, 22, 25, 29, 205, 219, 220,
    272
Technopoly (Postman), 205, 219
Teens, 21, 209, 241
Ten Philosophical Mistakes (Adler), 14,
    49, 93
Theater of the Absurd, 204
Thomas à Kempis, 282
Thoreau, 13, 78, 80
Thorndike, Edward, 214
Thus Spoke Zarathustra (Nietzsche), 22,
    140, 141, 151
Tillich, Paul, 196, 250, 251, 254
Time Machine, The (Wells), 265
Toffler, Alvin, 113, 226, 243, 244
*Tomorrow and Tomorrow and
    Tomorrow* (A. Huxley), 233
Toynbee, Arnold, 117
Tradition, 33, 37, 46, 49, 50, 55, 74,
    86, 100, 115, 224, 227, 239, 283,
    289
Treatise of Human Nature, A (Hume),
    53, 55, 57, 58, 59, 64
Truth, 31, 41, 46, 51, 55, 58, 59, 79,
    80, 202, 224, 231, 233, 236, 254,
    262
TV, 67, 98, 129, 130, 131, 185, 245,
    287
Tyndall, J., 289

Übermenschen, 136, 152
Uncertainty principle, 62
Unconscious, the, 147, 159, 161, 162,
    166, 167, 288
Uncovering the Right on Campus, 188
United Nations, 260, 264
Universalism, 73, 244, 255, 257, 259,
    266, 268
Utilitarianism, utilitarians, 59, 60, 83,
    85 (Chapter 5 *passim*), 115, 136,
    186, 253, 272, 289, 292
Utilitarianism (Mill), 92, 93, 97

Values, 18, 19, 29, 99, 129, 197, 200,
    202, 226, 229, 230, 267, 273, 274
Values clarification, 136, 225
Values Clarification (Simon and Raths),
    225
Veith, Gene Edward, 133, 153, 275
Voltaire, 26, 36, 53, 54, 69, 289

Watson, James D., 104, 212
Watson, J. B., 214
Watts, Alan, 232
Weber, Max, 230, 289

Wellhausen, Julius, 250
Wells, H. G., 265
Wesley, John, 36
Western culture or civilization, 25, 44,
    55, 61, 127, 134, 183, 189, 211, 231,
    251, 269, 271, 284, 286
When the World Will Be as One
    (Brooke), 264
Whitehead, A. N., 175, 289
Why America Doesn't Work (Colson),
    222
Why I Am Not a Christian (Russell),
    176, 180, 181
Wilberforce, 104, 152
Williams, Charles, 271
Will-to-power, 147, 148, 149, 151, 152,
    206
Winner, Langdon, 219
Wittgenstein, Ludwig, 230, 289
Wokler, Robert, 79
Wolfe, Tom, 240
Woodstock, 21
World Council of Churches (WCC),
    251, 259, 260, 261, 264, 265, 289
World's Religions, The (Smith), 253
Worldviews, 21, 48

Zarathustra, 140, 141, 142, 143, 144,
    145
Zinsser, William, 76, 77
Zola, 116